The Theory
and Practice
of History

Leopold von Ranke

THE EUROPEAN HISTORIOGRAPHY SERIES
F. J. Levy, General Editor

The Theory and Practice of History

Leopold von Ranke

Edited with an Introduction by
Georg G. Iggers and Konrad von Moltke

New Translations by
Wilma A. Iggers and Konrad von Moltke

THE BOBBS-MERRILL COMPANY, INC.
INDIANAPOLIS · NEW YORK

Copyright © 1973 by The Bobbs-Merrill Company, Inc.
Printed in the United States of America
Library of Congress Catalog Card Number 79–167691
ISBN 0-672-51673-X
ISBN 0-672-60920-7 (pbk)
First Printing

Contents

Editor's Foreword

Historians, at their best, are problem-solvers. Sometimes the problems appear simple: "What happened?" At other times, they may be much more difficult: "Why did it happen this way and not another? Why did it happen this year and not earlier or later?" Or, at the highest level of abstraction, a historian may ask: "Is there a pattern in human events? Are there laws of history?" Sometimes a historian's answers to problems are accepted by all, or almost all of his successors. More commonly, later generations, while rejecting their predecessors' answers to specific questions, nonetheless adopt (or adapt) the method used to seek out such answers.

The student of historiography, therefore, is interested primarily in the methods previous historians have used to attain their results. To conduct his own investigation, he needs to remember that any historian is influenced by his predecessors as well as by his contemporaries; that is, there is a tradition of historical writing to which historians are heir while, at the same time, the intellectual life of their own day plays its part in forming their outlook. Gibbon was the product of seventeenth-century erudition as well as of eighteenth-century rationalism. In one sense, the study of historiography is part of the more general study of intellectual history; in another, it is the study of a tradition of hisorical writing which, while not independent of more general currents of ideas, may nonetheless be isolated for detailed examination.

Thus, the study of historiography serves to remind us to accept our predecessors only after due criticism. We must ask: "Why was that problem investigated? Why was that method chosen?" before we decide if the results are correct or incorrect, stimulating or barren. Similarly, the study of historiography reminds us (as historians) that we are part of the subject we profess, just as our predecessors have always been. There is no way for a western historian to escape from the tradition of European historiography. Finally, if there is a distinctly historical mode of thought—as I am convinced there is—then it can do us only good to examine how that mode grew and developed, how it may be used and misused.

"Historical thinking is more than historical knowledge." Lord Acton's dictum might serve as our motto. The European Historiography Series has been designed to make texts available for those whose primary interest is in historical thought. The purpose of each volume is to present a historian in as much detail as is necessary to understand how he undertakes to solve historical problems. Where they exist, the historian's own pronouncements concerning his historical method will be printed; but practice will always be tested against theory, and narrative will not be ignored. Where possible, texts will be printed in their entirety; where a text proves too long, it will be abbreviated in such a way as to present to the reader the most accurate possible portrait of the historian.

The picture of Ranke that comes most readily to mind is that of the master, seated in his seminar room, surrounded by disciples. Ranke is usually thought of as the father of the seminar as a means of instruction and thus, by extension, of graduate education in the discipline of history. Nor is this, by itself, incorrect. It is the detailed touches added to the portrait which make it false. Inevitably, Ranke's method was carried to extremes: one thinks of Herbert Baxter Adams, around the turn of the century, designing and redesigning the "perfect" seminar-room, as if the physical embodiment of the idea were sufficient; one thinks of generations of graduate students who were told that "wie es eigentlich gewessen" meant that one gathered facts without any interpretation, as if that were either possible or desirable.

Ranke's reputation (especially outside Germany) was, to a large extent, the victim of some of the most basic of nineteenth-century ideas. In an age of burgeoning science, men felt that history, too, could be made scientific, and they fathered that belief on Ranke. Lord Acton himself said of Ranke that "We meet him at every step, and he has done more for us than any other man." Yet despite that fulsome praise, Acton distrusted Ranke, and felt that Ranke "never impresses with overwhelming mental power." For many of Acton's contemporaries, that was precisely Ranke's importance: he showed how everyone could contribute to historical knowledge, regardless of how great a supply of genius they might have. By the end of the nineteenth century, the profession of history was thought of as supplying bricks of unemotional fact for an edifice of historical truth that would be built when enough of the requisite material accumulated. A good historian contributed many bricks, a bad one brought in only a few. And this idea, too, was fathered on Ranke.

As Professors Iggers and von Moltke show, all of this bears hardly a tangential relation to what Ranke really believed and practiced. But even the more recent debate over Ranke's views soon leaves Ranke behind. In a classic essay on "Ranke and Burckhardt," written soon after the end of the Second World War, Friedrich Meinecke, a leading German historian of the Ranke school, revived a criticism first made by Lord Acton, that Ranke's value-neutral history writing tended to enshrine the winners of the world's struggles, with the result that neutrality could come close to being immorality. Might makes right. Yet there is misrepresentation in this view of Ranke as well, and Professors Iggers and von Moltke point out what it is. Ranke, more than most historians, has been seen out of context, anachronistically. It is the virtue of this book that the great historian is seen once more in his own proper place.

F. J. Levy

Preface

American historians have generally regarded Ranke as the father of the critical method in history. This distinction, however, he must share with others. The criteria of historical criticism were already well developed before him. Ranke's contribution consisted in masterfully integrating the critical use of documents with narrative history. But more important Ranke in his great histories provided a pattern of historical writing which dominated historical scholarship well into the twentieth century. In the place of the broad cultural perspective of the Enlightenment historians who were willing to rely heavily on literary sources, Ranke introduced a history which centered on political—and in Ranke's own case also religious—affairs as they could be reconstructed from official documents of state.

Ranke should still be read not only as one of the master historians of the nineteenth century but also as one of the relatively few historians of that century who thought seriously about the theoretical bases of their historical practice. In the nineteenth century historians throughout the world adopted the Rankean model of scholarship as history became a professional discipline. But outside of Germany disciples and critics of Ranke alike generally ignored the fact that Ranke's historiography rested on certain assumptions regarding the nature of history and politics which had deep roots in German idealistic philosophy. This often led to a soulless fact-oriented positivism which Ranke rejected but with which he was often wrongly identified. A reexamination of the premises of Ranke's historiography is called for at a time when historical science in much of the world is seriously questioning its classical heritage. It remains to be seen what elements of Ranke's conception of historical science, conceived in a pre-industrial, pre-democratic age, remain valid for modern historians. In important ways the German idealistic conception of the *Geisteswissenschaften*[1] to which Ranke contributed has in recent years modified social science concepts in Western Europe and America at a time when the positivistic heritage of the nineteenth century appeared overly restrictive and mechanistic. In turn American and French social science concepts in the years since World War II have led historians in the West, including Germany, to reexamine critically traditional historiographical approaches inadequately suited to deal with the impersonal collective processes operating in modern technological mass societies.

The selections in this volume seek to make clear Ranke's basic theoretical concerns and the impact of these concerns on his historical practice. We have chosen two of his best essays, "The Great Powers" and "A Dialogue on Politics," in which he most succinctly outlines his conception of history and politics, a number of shorter fragments on the nature of history, and several of the prefaces to his major works in which he reflects on his methodological procedures and discusses what he considers to be historically significant. We have preceded Ranke's theoretical statements with Wilhelm von Humboldt's essay, "On the Historian's Task," perhaps the best formulation of the German idealistic conception of history. The major part of the book consists of an abridged edition of the *History of the Popes*, the work of Ranke most widely read

[1] For a discussion of the term *Geisteswissenschaften,* see the Introduction.

in the English-speaking world in the nineteenth century which has not until now been available to students in an inexpensive edition. Where good translations existed, we have used them. We acknowledge the permission of *History and Theory* and the Wesleyan University Press for the use of Humboldt's "On the Historian's Task" and permission by Professor and Mrs. Theodore Von Laue and the Princeton University Press for the use of their translations of "A Dialogue on Politics" and "The Great Powers." Several theoretical essays have been translated for the first time by Wilma A. Iggers. Nineteenth-century versions of other essays and prefaces were jointly revised and corrected by the editors. Konrad von Moltke has revised and abridged the 1901 Fowler translation of the *History of the Popes* and translated the last two sections which were not previously available in English. Georg G. Iggers wrote the major part of the Introduction and edited the theoretical essays.

We are grateful to several German scholars, particularly conversant with Ranke or nineteenth-century German historiography, who read through the draft version of the Introduction and made suggestions for revisions. These include Professor Rudolf Vierhaus of the Ruhr University in Bochum; Professor Eberhard Kessel of the University of Mainz; Dr. Dieter Groh of the University of Heidelberg; Dr. Günter Birtsch of the Max-Planck-Institut für Geschichte in Göttingen; Dr. Hans Schleier of the Leipzig office of the Deutsche Akademie der Wissenschaften zu Berlin; Professor Ernst Schulin of the Technische Hochschule in Berlin; and Professor Walther Peter Fuchs of the University of Erlangen. Professor Eberhard Kessel and the *Historische Zeitschrift* were gracious enough to permit us to use Professor Kessel's version of the two fragments "On the Character of Historical Science" and "The Pitfalls of a Philosophy of History" as the basis of our translation; Professor Walther Peter Fuchs provided us with his as yet unpublished reading of these two manuscripts. We are very thankful to our colleague, Professor John T. Horton, of the State University of New York at Buffalo and Dr. Bernard Knieger of Haifa University in Israel for reading carefully through our new translations and making suggestions for stylistic revision. We are also grateful to Professor F. J. Levy of the University of Washington, the editor of the series, for his many valuable suggestions.

GEORG G. IGGERS AND KONRAD VON MOLTKE

Buffalo, New York

Introduction

Probably no historian in the nineteenth century has had an influence on the development of historical scholarship equal to that of Leopold von Ranke. Ranke has been called the "father of historical science."[1] And indeed Ranke's critical use of documents became the model for historical research and writing in the nineteenth century, first in Germany and then generally throughout the world, as history increasingly became a professional, university-centered discipline. Ranke was extensively and repeatedly translated into English. Five separate translations of the *History of the Popes* appeared in the last century. The newly formed American Historical Association in 1885 elected Ranke, whom George Bancroft at this occasion called "the greatest living historian," as its first honorary member. Nevertheless since the First World War, Ranke has been largely ignored outside of Germany. This lack of interest is related to the identification of Ranke with

[1] Herbert B. Adams, "New Methods of Study in History," *Johns Hopkins University Studies in History and Political Science*, II (1884), 65.

modes of historical writing that appeared outdated in later time.

Despite the reverence in which the new historical profession held Ranke, he was little understood in America or in Great Britain.[2] Indeed the reverence rested in part on misunderstanding. He was viewed as the prototype of the technically trained historian and as a great representative of the positivistic scientific tradition of the nineteenth century, a contemporary of Lyell, Wallace, Darwin, and Renan, who "turned the lecture room into a laboratory, using documents instead of 'bushels of clams.' "[3] The core of Ranke's method was seen to lie in his determination "to hold strictly to the facts of history,"[4] "his formulation of the principles of internal criticism and his insistence upon entire objectivity in the treatment of the past,"[5] his avoidance of questions of theory which he rightly left to the poets, philosophers, and theologians,[6] and his stress on technical training at the cost of literary brilliance.[7] Ranke let the facts speak for themselves; and since history was past politics, these facts were contained primarily in the documents of state. The method of Ranke, it was believed, pointed above all to detailed monographic studies. But such

[2] On the interpretations of Ranke in America, see Georg G. Iggers, "The Image of Ranke in American and German Historical Thought," *History and Theory*, II (1962), 17–40.

[3] Walter P. Webb, "The Historical Seminar: Its Outer Shell and Its Inner Spirit," *Mississippi Valley Historical Review*, XLII (1955–1956), 11.

[4] Herbert B. Adams, "Leopold von Ranke," *Johns Hopkins Studies . . .* , III (1888), 104–105: "Ranke, on the other hand, determined to hold strictly to the facts of history, to preach no sermon, to point no moral, to adorn no tale, but to tell the simple historic truth. His sole ambition was to narrate things as they really were, *wie es eigentlich gewesen.*"

[5] H. E. Barnes, "History: Its Rise and Development," in *Encyclopedia Americana* (New York, 1932), XIV, 245.

[6] George B. Adams, "History and the Philosophy of History," *American Historical Review*, XIV (1908–1909), 223.

[7] Ephraim Emerton, "The Practice Method in Higher Historical Instruction," in *Methods of Teaching History* (Boston, 1885), p. 42.

an approach appeared increasingly irrelevant to historians who operated, in a period of rapid industrialization and democratization, with a concept of science more in line with the revision of scientific thought in the twentieth century. By the turn of the century, important historians such as Frederick Turner, James Harvey Robinson, and Charles Beard in the United States, Henri Berr in France, and Karl Lamprecht in Germany, rejected the classical academic history which they identified with Ranke and sought to go beyond a fact-oriented political history to the analysis of underlying social and economic forces. "History is all the remains that have come down to us" not just documents, Turner wrote in criticism of Ranke.[8] F. J. Teggart agreed at the time with Karl Lamprecht that Ranke represented an earlier stage in the development of science which was concerned with the accumulation of facts rather than with induction and which "by intellectual predilection no less than in point of date, antecedes the period of Darwinian biology."[9]

The result was a profound indifference to Ranke in the English-speaking countries and France which in the nineteenth century had taken him so seriously. From 1910 until the 1960s no new edition of any of Ranke's major works appeared in English or French.[10] Only in Germany was Ranke still taken seriously, and this for two very different reasons. The political and social climate remained more congenial to Ranke's historiography, such as it was then understood to be, at least until the catastrophe of National Socialism and the reexamination of historiographical traditions after 1945. The incomplete democratization of the country favored a historiography which stressed the actions of states-

---

[8] "The Significance of History," in *The Early Writings of Frederick Jackson Turner* (Madison, 1938), p. 54; for Turner on Ranke, see *ibid.*, p. 51.

[9] "The Circumstances or the Substance of History," *American Historical Review*, XV (1909–1910), 709.

[10] Recent years have seen reprint editions in the United States of several nineteenth- and early twentieth-century editions of Ranke's works.

men to the neglect of the history of the masses. Moreover, Ranke's methodology and his idealistic theoretical presuppositions fitted well into a tradition of historical and cultural sciences dominant in Germany. German scholars in the twentieth century attempted self-consciously to differentiate their methods, their conception of society, and their political values from the supposedly positivistic, natural science oriented approach of the social sciences in the Western countries which they identified with the ideology of democracy. They viewed Ranke as one of the main contributors to a peculiarly German outlook in the cultural sciences suited to a uniquely German form of political and social conservatism. Friedrich Meinecke considered this tradition of thought, which was named "historicism" (*Historismus*), to be Germany's greatest contribution to Western thought since the Reformation and the "highest stage of understanding of things human attained by man."[11] German thought alone had freed itself from the rigidity of a natural law outlook which supposedly still dominated Western social

[11] On the continuity of German historiographical and social science traditions, see Georg G. Iggers, *The German Conception of History* (Middletown, Conn., 1968). We are hesitant to use the English term, "historicism," as a translation for *Historismus*. The term "historicism" in English has acquired a large number of meanings which the term *Historismus* did not possess. The term *Historismus* refers primarily to the historical faith of the German classical tradition of historiography. The term "historicism" came into English in the 1930s apparently as a translation of Croce's term, *storicismo*. Since then it has acquired connotations of radical historical relativism. Karl Popper in *The Poverty of Historicism* used it to denote a form of historical determinism. We would have preferred to use the term "historism," now out of use, which was current in English until the 1900s and which more closely translated the German term, *Historismus*. For a discussion of the meaning of the term "historicism," see Dwight E. Lee and Robert N. Beck, "The Meaning of 'Historicism,' " *American Historical Review*, LIX (1953–1954), 568–577; for the meaning of the terms "historism," "historicism," and "*Historismus*," see Georg G. Iggers, *The German Conception of History* (Middletown, Conn., 1968), pp. 287–290.

science thought and thus attained an understanding of the fullness and diversity of man's historical experience. The attempt by
Karl Lamprecht at the turn of the century to repudiate Ranke had
little influence. Indeed, the twentieth century saw increased interest in Ranke. Only after 1945 did a searching criticism of
Ranke's historiographical ideas set in.

The purpose of the present volume is in part to correct the
image of Ranke as a narrow and fact-oriented historian hostile
to theory and to present elements of his writings which are of
continuing relevance, not only as historically significant examples
of nineteenth-century historiography but also as good historical
writing in their own right and as important contributions to historical and social theory. Far from being hostile to theory, Ranke
was guided more than most historians by conscious theoretical
assumptions. Indeed, his main contribution to German historical
science was not the critical method in the treatment of historical
documents, which very much predated Ranke's writings, but his
formulation and translation into practice of a conception of history which affected the main currents of historical writing in Germany and to a lesser extent elsewhere well into the twentieth century. Ranke's emphasis on the application of the critical method
must be understood within the framework of his idealistic notions of history. These notions, largely ignored in the United
States where the early generation of professional historians created an image of an essentially positivistic Ranke, were deeply
influential in Germany into the twentieth century. Indeed Ranke's
oft quoted dictum, *"wie es eigentlich gewesen,"* has generally been
misunderstood in this country as asking the historian to be satisfied with a purely factual recreation of the past. Ranke's writings make it clear that he did not mean this. In fact the word
"eigentlich" which is the key to the phrase just quoted has been
poorly translated into English. In the nineteenth century this word
was ambiguous in a way in which it no longer is. It certainly had
the modern meaning of "actually" already, but it also meant
"characteristic, essential," and the latter is the form in which
Ranke most frequently uses this term. This gives the phrase an

entirely different meaning, and one much more in keeping with Ranke's philosophical ideas. It is not factuality, but the emphasis on the essential that makes an account historical.

Ranke belonged to the tradition of nineteenth-century German thinkers who stressed that the historical and cultural sciences dealing with values, intentions, and volitions were fundamentally different from the natural sciences and required unique methods aiming at concrete understanding (*Verstehen*) of historical phenomena rather than abstract causal explanation. This tradition viewed history as the realm of spirit and ideas, not in the sense of Hegel's absolute ideas but as the concrete intentions and thoughts of concrete individuals and institutions existing in time. Every abstraction detracted from the living reality of history. And although the historian could not dispense with generalizations, these must be generalizations rooted in the historical subject matter. Again the originality of Ranke's thought should not be overstressed. Ranke did not originate the *Verstehen* approach which was reflected in broad currents of German idealistic thought in theology, philology, philosophy, and jurisprudence and which found its most systematic formulations late in the nineteenth and early in the twentieth century in the writings of Wilhelm Dilthey and Max Weber.[12] The historicism of this approach, which stressed that every society must be seen as a complex of values but that these values must be *understood* in their own terms rather than by reference to standards external to the society, was to be integrated into a good deal of sociological and anthropological thought in France and the English-speaking countries in the twentieth century.

Parts II, III, and IV of this volume consist of certain of the more important theoretical statements of Ranke. Part V presents an extensive selection from Ranke's *History of the Popes* as an example of Ranke's narrative history at its best. To be sure,

---

[12] For a discussion of the *Verstehen* tradition in German *Geisteswissenschaften*, see Joachim Wach, *Das Verstehen* (Tübingen, 1926–1933), 3 vols., and Hans-Georg Gadamer, *Wahrheit und Methode* (Tübingen, 1960).

Ranke's style, his biases, and his interests are less familiar to us than those of Jacob Burckhardt or Alexis de Tocqueville. The historians most widely read in their own time, Ranke, Michelet, and Macaulay, were men relatively at peace with the dominant political trends in their countries and satisfied to live in the nineteenth century. They have perhaps less to tell us today than Burckhardt and Tocqueville who searched more deeply for the forces operating beneath the surface of politics and who were more keenly aware of the destructive tendencies of their age. Nevertheless, Ranke remains important as one of the great narrative historians of the nineteenth century who continues to read well today, a master of historical prose who combines technical skill with a universality of scope and interest seldom found again in later professional historical writing.

Life

Despite his desire to stand above parties, his striving for objectivity, Ranke cannot be understood apart from the intellectual and political climate of his time. Born in 1795, Leopold Ranke— the von was added in 1863 when he was raised to the nobility—reflects currents of early nineteenth-century thought, the romantic interest in the past, the organic conception of society, the distrust of the French Enlightenment and of the political ideology of the Revolution, but he also retains an element of eighteenth-century cosmopolitanism which preserves him from the one-sided nationalism of many of his contemporaries. We may perhaps distinguish four major influences on Ranke's intellectual formation: (1) the Lutheran religious background in which he grew up; (2) the classical humanistic education he received as a youth; (3) the German idealistic philosophy, which dominated the intellectual atmosphere; and (4) the politics of the Restoration.

Ranke was born in Thuringia, in the small town of Wiehe, at the time a part of the Electorate of Saxony. He was thus not a Prussian by birth. Wiehe and the region in which it lay, the "Goldene Aue," were annexed by Prussia only in 1815 at the

Congress of Vienna. Ranke did not possess the deep emotional commitment to Prussia of later German historians. He was relatively little affected by the enthusiasm of the Prussian Wars of Liberation. The decisive political experience for him was not the French Revolution or the Napoleonic Wars but the post-1815 Restoration. His childhood in Saxony undoubtedly contributed to his conception of a federal Germany within a European framework of powers. Ranke maintained a deep sympathy for Austria and her role in a European order such as that attempted in 1815 in the Holy Alliance.

Since the early seventeenth century all the Rankes had been Lutheran ministers in Thuringia except Ranke's father, a lawyer, who regretted not having followed the profession of his fathers. The Lutheran religiosity of the home was reinforced in the two Latin schools Ranke attended, at nearby Donndorf and at the famous school of Schulpforta, maintained by the Saxon princes, at which Lessing and Klopstock had studied. In 1814 Ranke went to the University of Leipzig with the intention of studying theology and philology. His first major scholarly work was an uncompleted study of Luther. What dissuaded him from completing his theological studies was the rationalistic atmosphere which still permeated the theological faculties, a rationalism which he described later as "unsatisfactory, shallow and flat" in its attempt to "combine opposing principles, the unconditionally valid which has been proclaimed and recognized as the word of God and the reasoning of the moment." "I believed unconditionally," he wrote.[13] Convinced that "God dwells, lives, and is recognizable in all history,"[14] he nevertheless was free of a narrow fundamentalism which saw the intervention of God in natural processes. His religious belief has been repeatedly described as panentheism which, in contrast to pantheism, recognized the separateness of all human

[13] See his autobiographical "Dictat vom October 1863," in Leopold von Ranke's *Sämmtliche Werke* (to be hence cited as SW) (Leipzig, 1873–1890), LIII/LIV, 29.

[14] Letter to Heinrich Ranke, Frankfurt a. O., Ende März 1820, in SW, LIII/LIV, 89.

existence from God, yet sees the reflection of God in all existence.
The historian's task resembled that of the priest; he was to decipher the "holy hieroglyph" contained in history.[15]

Studies of Ranke have generally stressed his Lutheran religiosity.[16] It is questionable, however, whether his panentheism
was really in harmony with Lutheran teaching. For Luther, as for
Saint Paul, the "world into which God sent his Word was thoroughly debased and alienated." There was basically no room for
evil in Ranke's world. History manifested the unfolding of moral
energies, of ideas embodied in concrete individualities and institutions. This was an idea derived from German Idealistic thought,
from Fichte, Schelling, and Goethe—whom Ranke read extensively at this period—which had little in common with the pessimism of Luther or Saint Paul.[17]

Ranke had almost no formal training as a historian. At Donndorf and Schulpforta, Ranke received a classical humanistic education. At Leipzig he studied classical philology. He attended a
mandatory course in history at Leipzig but disdained the historical works he encountered which he considered "a mass of un-
digested notes, indeed of facts not understood."[18] Nevertheless
he received at Leipzig the foundations of his training as a historian. The one German historical work which made a positive impression on him was Niebuhr's *Roman History*. The other historian who deeply influenced him was Thucydides on whom he
wrote his dissertation. More important, he was introduced by his

[15] *Ibid.*, p. 90.

[16] See, e.g., Carl Hinrichs, *Ranke und die Geschichtstheologie der
Goethezeit* (Göttingen, 1954).

[17] Hans Liebeschütz in "Ranke," a pamphlet of the Historical Association (London, 1954), p. 5, also points at Ranke's inability to grasp
the role of evil in Luther's theology. This point has generally been overlooked in the German literature which has stressed Ranke's Lutheran
religiosity. Ilse Mayer-Kulenkampff in "Rankes Lutherverhältnis. Dar-
gestellt von dem Lutherfragment von 1817," *Historische Zeitschrift*,
CLXXII (1951), 65–99, stressed the extent to which Ranke misinter-
preted Luther from the standpoint of German Idealism.

[18] "Dictat vom October 1863," in SW, LIII/LIV, 28.

teacher Gottfried Hermann to the critical methods of classical
philology, which as we shall see were to play an important role
in his development of a critical method for history.[19]

Ranke's active interest in modern history dated from his days
at the *Gymnasium* in Frankfurt on the Oder, a Prussian city east
of Berlin, at which he taught classics and history. Here he devoted
himself first to ancient and medieval history, reading the ancient
historians extensively in preparation for his teaching. Using the
rich collection of medieval and early modern sources contained
in the *Gymnasium* library, he began a critical study of these documents. He was struck by the contradictions and inconsistencies in
the works of Guicciardini and Giovio. The result was a critical
study of the histories of the period, published as an appendix to
Ranke's own synthesis of the period, *Histories of the Latin and
Germanic Nations (1494 to 1514)*, in 1824. Guicciardini, whose
Historia d'Italia had served as the basis of most succeeding modern histories, had relied heavily on secondary sources and em-
bellished and fabricated facts. Ranke in the preface promised to
use "memoirs, diaries, letters, reports from embassies and original
narratives of eye witnesses; other writings . . . only when they
seemed either to have been immediately derived from the former,
or to equal them through some kind of original information." The
"strict presentation of the facts, no matter how conditional and
unattractive they might be," he asserted, "is undoubtedly the su-

[19] For a discussion of historical method before Ranke, see J. P.
Thompson, *A History of Historical Writing* (New York, 1942), particularly II, 3–146; George P. Gooch, *History and Historians in the Nineteenth Century* (London, 1913), chap. I; Harry Elmer Barnes, *A History
of Historical Writing* (New York, 1963), particularly pp. 239–245; Andreas Kraus, *Vernunft und Geschichte* (Freiburg i.B., 1963); and Herbert Butterfield, *Man on His Past* (Boston, 1966), particularly chap. II.
The methods Ranke applied to the study of documents of modern history were basically, of course, similar to those applied by the great
classical philologists of the late eighteenth and early nineteenth centuries, Friedrich August Wolf, August Böckh, and Gottfried Hermann
to the monuments of classical literature and by Barthold Georg Niebuhr
to Roman antiquities.

preme law." But the presentation of the isolated event, he continued, was not the purpose of the historical work; it rather sought "the development of unity and the progress of events." The theme of the book was the emergence of the modern state system and the balance of power. The book was to pave the way for a more comprehensive historical view of the great schism brought about by the Reformation. Ranke proceeded from the assumptions of the interrelatedness of the "Latin and Germanic nations" of Europe, to "show to what extent these nations have developed in unity and kindred movement." In actual practice, Ranke was unable to maintain the broad sweep of narrative. The story is interrupted by a mass of details on diplomatic negotiations, political decisions, and military events. Ranke himself admitted that the book contained only "histories, not history" (p. 136).[20] Theodore Von Laue was justified when he observed "the use of the plural in the title was indicative of the uncorrelated multitude of events and developments, mostly matters of war and foreign policy, in which the book abounded. It resembled a wild garden before the gardener brought order, clarity and form into its profuse growth."[21]

The book nevertheless brought Ranke a call to the University of Berlin. The University of Berlin had been founded in 1810 largely upon the initiative of Wilhelm von Humboldt, then head of the section for education in the Prussian ministry of the interior, as a new type of institution of higher learning in which teaching would be closely related to research. This became the model of the nineteenth-century German university. In 1825 Berlin was the most challenging of the German universities. Georg Wilhelm Friedrich Hegel held the chair of philosophy, Friedrich Daniel Schleiermacher taught theology, Friedrich Karl von Savigny and Karl Friedrich Eichhorn law. Two major orientations in the cultural sciences, represented by Hegelianism and the Historical School, were present there. Both orientations believed that all cultural manifestations must be understood in terms of their historical gen-

[20] Page references in parentheses refer to this edition
[21] *Leopold Ranke. The Formative Years* (Princeton, 1950), p. 109.

esis. But while Hegel saw history as a unitary, all embracing process leading toward greater rationality, Savigny and Eichhorn, the founders of the Historical School of Jurisprudence, stressed the variety of expression within history. In the late eighteenth century Herder had already argued that mankind fulfills itself not in a unilinear progressive development but in the flowering of unique national cultures, each fundamentally different and each developing its own genius in terms of its inherent principles of growth. Each culture was the expression of the will of God in a unique historical form. This position, which enjoins the study of all civilizations in terms of their own standards of value and refuses to apply any universally valid human norms in the assessment of a historical situation, has been called historicism (*Historismus*). In this spirit, for example, Savigny and Eichhorn opposed the codification of the law. Law, they maintained, grows organically with a culture; legal norms manifest themselves only in concrete historical contexts in the evolution of the spirit of a people. The task of the jurist is to understand the law as it developed historically not to reduce it to abstract rational formulations. Ranke's own position was akin to that of the Historical School.

The call to Berlin gave Ranke an opportunity to play a central role in the training of historians. Most of the great German historians of the nineteenth century, among them Heinrich von Sybel, Wilhelm von Giesebrecht, Georg Waitz, and the Swiss Jacob Burckhardt, passed through Ranke's seminar in which he applied the critical method to historical writing. These students in turn trained a generation of scholars who dominated German university chairs of history well into the twentieth century. Ranke thus became in fact the father of modern historical science in Germany. Critical historical research, however, preceded Ranke. Already in *De re diplomatica* (1681), the French historian Jean Mabillon had developed rules and criteria for judging sources and determining their authenticity. There had developed in the eighteenth century at the University of Göttingen a school of historians, including Johann Christoph Gatterer, August Ludwig Schlözer, Arnold Hermann Heeren, and Johann von Müller, who combined the critical method of *érudits* like Mabillon with the concern of the philosophic historians of the eighteenth century, such as Voltaire and Gibbon, who sought to write universal history without bothering particularly about the critical evaluation of their sources.[22] Niebuhr and Ranke refined the concern with critical method; Ranke in the process narrowed the universality of outlook of the Göttingen historians. What Ranke brought to history was less a new method—this had been developed to a great extent by the Göttingen school—than a greater emphasis on the professional and technical character of history and a conception of history which we shall discuss later in this Introduction. His contemporaries, Friedrich Christoph Schlosser, Karl von Rotteck, and Georg Gottfried Gervinus, appeared to him as moralists and political publicists rather than as technical historians who wrote history on the basis of a critical examination of the sources.

The *Histories of the Latin and Germanic Nations* had been based on a critical examination of published works. In Berlin Ranke discovered copies of Venetian diplomatic documents from the sixteenth and seventeenth centuries which he utilized in his second book, *Princes and Peoples of Southern Europe. The Ottomans and the Spanish Monarchy*. Published in 1827, the book was a broad survey of three centuries of history in which Ranke devoted considerably more space to the discussion of administration, trade, and finance than in his earlier work. In the same year Ranke set out on a four-year journey to peruse source materials in the Austrian and Italian archives, particularly the Venetian *Relazioni* (the reports of Venetian ambassadors sent from the various courts of Europe over three centuries), which threw light not only on Venetian diplomatic relations but on the internal political history of the various European states. From the fall of 1827 to the fall of 1828, he worked in Vienna where he developed a friendship with Friedrich Gentz, the Catholic conservative political theorist, publicist, and advisor to Prince Metternich, who arranged for him to receive permission to use the Venetian papers in

---

[22] Cf. Butterfield, *Man on His Past*; Gordon Craig, "Johannes von Müller: The Historian in Search of a Hero," *American Historical Review*, LXXIV (1968–1969), 1487–1502.

the Vienna archives. A by-product of his stay in Vienna was the *History of Servia and the Servian Revolution*, written in part with material made available to him by Serbian patriots with whom he came in close contact. In October 1828 he arrived in Italy where he became the first historian to work thoroughly through the *Relazioni* in Venice; he also used archives in Rome and Florence. The Vatican archives remained closed to him but he was able to use important private archives in Rome. The Viennese and Italian researches provided the basis for his *History of the Popes* which appeared between 1834 and 1836.

Upon his return to Berlin in 1831, Ranke became for the first and only time closely involved in politics. This involvement would be of little interest to us except that it resulted in a crystallization of Ranke's political views and his conception of society and history which was reflected in his historical writings. In his student days, Ranke had been aloof from the *Burschenschaften*, the nationalistic student movement. In his autobiography he describes the interest but lack of involvement with which he followed Turnvater Jahn's visit to Frankfurt on the Oder. After Ranke's arrival in Berlin in 1825, the reactionary First Director of the Section for Public Instruction, Heinrich von Kamptz, was his sponsor. However, his closest friends were the liberal Varnhagen von Ense and his brilliant wife Rachel whose salon was a gathering place for liberal intellectuals. He was on good terms with the liberal Alexander von Humboldt and with Friedrich Carl von Savigny and Friedrich Schleiermacher. The intermediate political position of the latter two resembled that occupied by Ranke in the 1830s. His sympathies for the existing European order had made possible congenial conversations during his weekly evening visits to Friedrich Gentz in Vienna during his stay there in 1827 and 1828. The 1830 Revolution seems to have deeply disturbed him. He believed the European order to be threatened by a renewal of revolutionary activity. On his return to Berlin in 1831 he agreed to edit a political journal, the *Historisch-Politische Zeitschrift*, sponsored by the Prussian government, an undertaking which was to alienate him from his liberal friends, the Varnhagen von Enses and Alexander von Humboldt. He did not consider his position in the journal to be a reactionary one. In his autobiography, he wrote "The direction I decided to follow was neither revolutionary nor reactionary. I was so bold as to undertake to defend a third direction midway between the two points of view that confronted each other in every public and private discussion. This new orientation, which adhered to a *status quo* which rests on the past, aimed at opening up a future in which one would be able to do justice to new ideas, too, as long as they contained truth."[23] And in effect the journal was founded to counter the *Berliner Politisches Wochenblatt*, established in late 1831 by the highly conservative Friedrich von Raumer and Ranke's acquaintances Joseph von Radowitz and the brothers Ernst Ludwig and Leopold von Gerlach to propagate the feudal, corporative doctrines of the late Karl Ludwig von Haller. To be sure, like Hegel, Ranke was not an admirer of an old regime which provided social and political functions to a privileged Junker aristocracy, but instead he supported the bureaucratic, centralized Prussian monarchy as reformed in the period after 1806. The Prussian state, for Ranke as for Hegel, stood for progress, but progress based organically on the foundations of the past.

In practice, Ranke's articles contained much more criticism of the liberals than of the right. He argued against the transferability of foreign political ideas and institutions, specifically those of the French Revolution, to Germany. The French Revolution itself had shown the ill effects of grafting foreign, British, and especially North American political ideas onto traditional institutions. The danger of the French Revolution rested less in the military extension of France than in the threat presented by its ideas. Every state, Ranke held, is unique and must develop according to its own inner principles. Radical change marks a break with organic development. Ranke opposed a constitution for Prussia and argued against a Prussian parliament representing the estates (*Ständeversammlung*) which moderate liberals like the Baron von Stein and Wilhelm von Humboldt had advocated. Ranke nowhere

---

[23] Autobiographical "Dictat vom November 1885," in SW, LIII/LIV, 48.

acknowledged the rights of the individuals against the state which Humboldt and Haller had defended from opposing political positions. Ranke's position was essentially conservative; he defended neither the reactionary conception of traditional "liberties" (*Libertäten*) nor the liberal one of the rights of the individual. The journal turned out to be a failure and was suspended in 1836. Nevertheless, it was to contain several of Ranke's most important theoretical statements, including the two essays "The Great Powers" and "A Dialogue on Politics" which we have reprinted in this collection.

The remainder of Ranke's life was uneventful, closely related to his work. In late 1833 Ranke had been elevated to a full professorship (*Ordinariat*) at the University of Berlin where he remained for the rest of his life, missing only four semesters in four decades on study tours to archives, mostly to France and Great Britain. Ranke only once seriously considered an offer to move from Berlin, when in 1853 his admirer and former student King Maximilian II of Bavaria urged him to accept a call to the University of Munich. In Berlin Ranke led a relatively solitary life. He followed a rigid daily schedule of work, interrupted by a walk in the Tiergarten, his favorite spot for repose and reflection. In his bachelor days in the 1830s and early 1840s, he was a welcome guest in Berlin's cultured social circle, although no longer in the circle of liberal intellectuals which he had frequented before his trip to Italy. Ranke was on the whole isolated from his colleagues at the university. He was on good terms with Savigny and Eichhorn and had formed a close friendship with the philosopher Heinrich Ritter. Ritter, however, left Berlin in 1833. Among historians, a lifelong correspondence connected him with Gustav Adolf Harald Stenzel, who had been a fellow student in Leipzig. It was Stenzel who at Leipzig had first introduced Ranke to the critical study of medieval documents. The person closest to him, however, was his younger brother Heinrich, who had joined him at the *Gymnasium* in Frankfurt on the Oder and with whom more than with his other brothers he was able to exchange ideas. In later years he developed a certain affinity with his brother Ferdinand. Shortly before his forty-ninth birthday, he married Clara Graves, twelve years his junior, the daughter of a Protestant barrister from Ireland. The marriage was hardly a romantic one. As he wrote to his brother Heinrich, it was a step which he took after considerable deliberation because he was "frightened by the character of several old bachelors whose acquaintance (he) had made shortly before."[24] Nevertheless, it seems to have been a good marriage and judging by the letters Ranke has left, a warm human although probably not an intellectually stimulating relationship. The year 1871 turned out to be a particularly tragic point in Ranke's life. His wife died shortly after the youngest of Ranke's children had married and left home; Ranke retired from his lectures under not entirely happy circumstances; and his eyesight rapidly faded. The remaining fifteen years of Ranke's life were nevertheless years of intense activity. With the help of readers and secretaries he continued his research and writing and in the final years of his life turned to his lifelong hope of writing a universal history.

Ranke's existence consisted mostly of research, writing, and teaching. Various students, both friendly and hostile, have left accounts of his lectures. They generally agree that he was an ineffective lecturer. "That was no lecture, but a mumbled, whispered, groaned monologue, delivered with arbitrary interruptions, of which we understood only individual words. Only the mimicry of the old gentlemen was interesting," wrote an annoyed auditor about his visit to a Ranke lecture in 1857.[25] But even his disciple and admirer Wilhelm von Giesebrecht paints a not very dissimilar picture of a lecture course in 1837. Actually Ranke appears to

[24] To Heinrich Ranke, Berlin, November 4, 1843, in Leopold von Ranke, *Das Briefwerk*, ed. Walther Peter Fuchs (Hamburg, 1949), p. 321.

[25] Gunter Berg, *Leopold von Ranke als akademischer Lehrer. Studien zu seinen Vorlesungen und seinem Geschichtsdenken* (Göttingen, 1968), p. 60. For a description of Ranke's lectures by his students, see also George P. Gooch, *History and Historians in the Nineteenth Century* (Boston, 1959), pp. 106–107. On Ranke's tenure at the University of Berlin, see also Max Lenz, *Geschichte der Königlichen Friedrich-Wilhelms-Universität zu Berlin* (Halle, 1910–1918), II, i, 264–281, 503–505; II, ii, 152–153.

have put great care into the preparation of his lectures. Extensive lecture notes still exist. These notes he would regularly revise. He spoke freely, however, following notes loosely rather than reading a prepared manuscript. Ranke conscientiously gave his lectures. He declined to cancel them even to attend his father's funeral. The topics of his lectures reflected Ranke's broad historical interests.[26] He repeatedly lectured on universal history. He gave sequences of lecture courses not only on German history since the Middle Ages but also on general European history. Frequently he lectured about the most recent past, occasionally on the Romans, at times (after his research led him in that direction) on English history. During most of his career attendance at his lectures was not good considering his renown as a historian. Only three students enrolled for his lectures on Universal History in the summer of 1833, two years after he had returned from Italy. For a short time, his popularity increased. In the winter semester 1841–1842, 153 auditors, almost 35 percent of the students in the Philosophical Faculty, attended his lectures. After 1848, interest in his lectures rapidly declined. He seemed out of step with the intellectual and political climate among the students. By 1860 he had only 20 auditors left. In the summer semester of 1871 Ranke canceled his course, the last one he intended to hold and which he had once more prepared with especial care, for lack of enrollment after the first meeting.[27] Ironically soon after Ranke's retirement the ultranationalistic and demagogic historian, Heinrich von Treitschke was called to the University of Berlin. The faculty justified its appointment with the explanation that it sought "to do justice also to those circles of students who seek instruction in history for other purposes than to dedicate themselves exclusively to the study of history and historical research."[28]

[26] For a list of lecture courses given by Ranke from 1825 to 1871, see Gunter Berg, *Leopold von Ranke*, pp. 243–245; for a lengthy, although partial, list of auditors, see *ibid.*, pp. 222–242; the list of lecture courses is also found in Ernst Schulin, *Die weltgeschichtliche Erfassung des Orients bei Hegel und Ranke* (Göttingen, 1958), pp. 306–308.

[27] Gunter Berg, *Leopold von Ranke*, pp. 56–58.

[28] *Ibid.*, pp. 50–51.

Ranke's effective influence on the development of the historical profession was through his seminars.[29] Already during his first semester at the University of Berlin, he announced that he would hold exercises (*Übungen*) in his home in order to become well acquainted with and guide those students who devoted themselves seriously to history. After his return from Italy, these became a regular institution. Two types of questions were to be raised in these sessions: those relating to theory and philosophy of history and those dealing with the critical treatment of sources. The latter predominated, but Ranke never neglected to raise basic theoretical questions of historical science. The seminar was a working community. The number of participants was restricted. Generally five to ten students participated, sometimes as few as three, only once as many as eighteen. Students would critically discuss each other's papers or they would together discuss an author or a group of authors. It was considered a special honor when Ranke himself assumed the criticism of a paper. The main emphasis was on critical method. He permitted the students considerable freedom in the selection of topics. He does not seem to have made their choice dependent on his own research interests. Most of the papers chose medieval themes. Beginning in 1837, his students began to publish the *Annals of the German Empire under the House of Saxony*. "These little volumes," George P. Gooch judged, "inaugurated the critical study of the Middle Ages."[30] Ranke remained in close touch with the participants of the seminars over the years. It was essentially in the seminars that the "Rankean School" of historiography was born.

Ranke permitted relatively few public activities to interfere with his rigid schedule of scholarship and writing. He was largely inactive in university affairs. He frequently missed meetings of the faculty. He was never elected *Rektor* of the university as might have been expected in terms of his eminence and the small number

[29] Cf. *ibid.*, pp. 51–56; cf. Edward G. Bourne, "Ranke and the Beginning of the Seminary Method," in *Essays in Historical Criticisms* (New York, 1901), pp. 265–274.

[30] George P. Gooch, *History and Historians*, p. 108.

of full professors at the university eligible for the position. As a matter of fact several of his colleagues occupied this position more than once. Only once did he serve as dean of the faculty. Only purely routine business was transacted during his term of office. In 1841 the new King of Prussia, Friedrich Wilhelm IV, who had been an admirer of Ranke for many years and had had a personal acquaintance with him since he visited Ranke in Venice in 1828, appointed him official historiographer of the Prussian state. This, however, was a scholarly rather than a public position which resulted in the multivolume history of Prussia. In the years after 1848 Friedrich Wilhelm called on Ranke as an adviser and in 1854 appointed him to the newly reconstituted Council of State. Ranke's political influence, however, was negligible. Ranke saw Friedrich Wilhelm regularly in the 1850s. Most of the meetings, however, seem to have been devoted to historical interests. Ranke read to the king from his manuscript on the history of France. It is not unlikely, of course, that the king also discussed political matters with him. His other royal admirer, Maximilian II of Bavaria, unsuccessful in drawing Ranke to Munich permanently, did succeed in persuading Ranke to accept the chairmanship of the newly formed Historical Commission of the Bavarian Academy of Sciences. Despite its Bavarian title and the financial support it received from the Bavarian state, the Historical Commission formed a central institution for the scholarly study of German history throughout the German-speaking world. Heinrich von Sybel, Ranke's former student, was its secretary. Ranke virtually chose the first members, and the Commission brought together the leading German-speaking historians. It published major series of sources and monographs such as the *Annals of the Medieval Empire* and the *Acts of the Imperial Diet* as well as the comprehensive German biographical dictionary, the *Allgemeine Deutsche Biographie*. In 1859 with the support of the Commission, Heinrich Sybel began to publish the *Historische Zeitschrift*, the central journal of the German historical profession ever since. Ranke, however, did not play a significant role in the enterprise.

After the suspension of the *Historisch-Politische Zeitschrift* in 1836, Ranke ceased to take a public political stand. He remained deeply afraid of social revolution. The "Political Memoranda" which he wrote for King Friedrich Wilhelm IV of Prussia on the revolutionary events between 1848 and 1851 show how inflexible his political opinions had remained in the face of political changes. The revolutions in Vienna and Berlin, he believed, were directed and partly financed from France. He opposed the Prussian electoral law of 1848 which granted universal suffrage and thus paved the way for a republic and the rule by artisans and journeymen who had no notion about the use of political power.[31] He advised Friedrich Wilhelm to dissolve the assembly, restrict the suffrage, and issue a constitution which would leave ultimate political control in royal hands. The Prussian army alone had prevented the revolution from succeeding. King and army were for him the only stable forces in Germany. Control of the army needed to be kept out of the hands of the parliament. Ranke remained lukewarm about the nationalistic movement which he identified with the movement for democratization. He had preferred to see the preservation of a German Confederation based on an Austrian-Prussian dualism which would preserve the diversity of the German states. But after the failure of the attempt at German unification in 1848–1849 and the Prussian humiliation at Olmütz, he began to favor a policy which would establish Prussian dominance in a North German union still affiliated with a German Confederation leaving Austria to maintain a similar position in the south. Ranke followed with misgivings the course of Bismarck's policy which led to the Austro-Prussian war of 1866. He later defended the war as having been necessary to lay the foundations of a strong German state which would meet the threat of France to Germany. He welcomed the campaign against Napoleon III, considered the defeat of France a victory of the conservative over the revolutionary principle, but greeted with mixed feelings the creation of the German Empire in 1871. He was alarmed by the concessions which Bismarck made to the liberals in the years between 1871 and 1878, the introduction of universal suffrage in the elections to the Reichstag which enabled the Social Demo-

---

[31] SW, XLIX/L, 588.

crats to appear on the political scene, and the legislation of the *Kulturkampf* which threatened the religious basis upon which a stable society rested. Bismarck's break with the liberals in 1878 reassured him. Despite his fears of social revolution, Ranke did not share the pessimism of Burckhardt regarding the future of European civilization. The course of the nineteenth century had shown that conservative, restorative forces were able to maintain themselves against the forces of revolution. "European humanity," he remarked confidently in 1881, "still rests on its old foundations."[32]

Works

Indeed Ranke's understanding of the forces operating in the modern world differed profoundly from that of such contemporaries as Alexis de Tocqueville and Jacob Burckhardt. Almost all of Ranke's histories dealt with the question of the emergence of a modern world, primarily in the sixteenth and seventeenth centuries, to an extent in the eighteenth and early nineteenth centuries. The forces at work in the modern world were, however, not those which led to greater rationalization, the secularization of religious values, the leveling of social differences. The modern world, as Ranke saw it in his writings from the *Histories of the Latin and Germanic Nations* to his *History of England*, was monarchical and Christian. The developments which led to the rise of modern society were political and religious; the two could not be isolated. In the realm of politics, the key event was the emergence of the modern state system. The modern state was a monarchy—bureaucratic but also constitutional—restricting but by no means eliminating the role of the aristocracy and providing a place for the middle classes. Nationality was a mark of the modern age but the interrelatedness of the European world was maintained through the balance of power. Confident in the stability of the European order, Ranke did not recognize the revolutionary potentialities in-

[32] "Tagebuchblätter," SW, LIII/LIV, 640.

herent in modern war. The modern world as seen by Ranke was also profoundly religious. Modernization was indeed marked by secularization of political life, but this secularization of political life corresponded to Christian notions which freed the spiritual from the material involvements which had corrupted the medieval church. One of the origins of the modern world was the Reformation which marked the renewal, not the denial, of religion. "It is one of the greatest coincidences of world history," Ranke writes, "that at the very moment in which the system of Latin and German peoples adhering to the Latin church was presented with the prospect of acquiring a predominant development on the other continent there simultaneously arose a religious development which aimed at restoring the purity of Revelation."[33]

Ranke's original intention had been to write a comprehensive history of the modern European world.[34] The *Histories of the Latin and Germanic Nations* was to be followed by a second volume bringing the history of Europe up to 1535. All history, Ranke concluded, must be universal history, universal history for him being essentially identical with the history of the Latin and Germanic nations. Ranke became increasingly aware of the limitation of his first book which rested exclusively on printed authorities. The second volume was never completed. Instead, on the basis of his archival work, Ranke turned first to the history of the papacy, then to that of the Reformation, and then to that of the major European states, Prussia, France, and England, to return to universal history only in his old age. National history replaced world history. The history of the Reformation, entitled *German History in the Era of the Reformation*, already centered on German rather than general European development. What interested him, nevertheless, as he wrote in the preface to his French his-

[33] *Deutsche Geschichte im Zeitalter der Reformation*, Ranke-Ausgabe der Deutschen Akademie—(München, 1925–1926), I, 176.

[34] In a letter to his brother Heinrich from Rome in April 1830 he describes as his life task a "history of the most important moments of modern times" which would be universal in scope, embracing cultural as well as political history. SW, LIII/LIV, 233–234.

tory, was the world-historical, not merely the national significance of the history of the various nations (p. 148). Nevertheless, Ranke's turn away from the universal approach of his early writing was indicative of the growing national orientation of historiography generally in Europe after 1830.

Taken together, Ranke's histories present a monumental analysis of the growth of modern Europe. The history of the popes interested Ranke less for its own sake, for the papacy "no longer exercises any essential influence," but as "a portion of general history, of the overall development of the world" (p. 145). "We are forced irresistibly," Ranke comments, "to the conviction that all the purposes and efforts of humanity are subjected to the silent and often imperceptible, but invincible and ceaseless march of events." If the Church had once fulfilled the purpose of molding the Germanic and Latin peoples of Europe into a common Christian civilization, and the existence of the papal authority was demanded by the earlier phases of the world's progress, this power was now challenged by the new forces of nationality and of the modern monarchies in a period when "the ecclesiastical power was no longer as necessary as before to the well being of nations" (p. 185).

The German History in the Era of the Reformation is the most personal of Ranke's works in that it clearly reveals his German Protestant background while still achieving a remarkably balanced account of the events it portrays. Of all his works this is the one which still most merits reading for its factual account and its interpretations alone rather than for purely historiographical interests. In this work, Ranke sees the Protestant Reformation not merely as a religious, but also as a political phenomenon—the struggle of the German princes against the control of both the emperors and the popes. The result of the conflict is the purification of Christian religion and the awakening of the German nationality. Unlike Hegel, Ranke does not see the logic of history as the sole force of history; great individuals play a decisive role in the *History of the Popes* and in all his later histories. "It was not, as we see, the quiet course of events alone or the noiseless progressive development of political and legal relations which established princely power, but mainly clever politics, successful wars, and the force of powerful personalities."[35]

The books on the popes and the Reformation were followed by three major state histories concentrating on the rise of the Great Powers—Prussia, France, and England—each seeking to deal with a period in which the national history of each country "through the importance of the events whose occurrence it details, and the extent of their operation, acquired in itself a world historical character" (p. 148). The *Nine Books of Prussian History*, later expanded into *Twelve Books of Prussian History*, is in a sense a continuation of the work on the Reformation as a study of the major Protestant German state. It follows the history of the Hohenzollern family from the fifteenth century on but focuses on the eighteenth century and particularly on the reign of Fredrick the Great during which Prussia emerged as a major power. Ranke's study is free of the attempt to read a German national mission into Prussian history or to portray Austria as the main antagonist of German unity which marked Droysen's work. Rather, Prussia emerged as a major force in the eighteenth century to fill the power vacuum in northern Germany and equilibrate the European balance of power. *The Civil Wars and Monarchy in France* dealt with consolidation of monarchical power in France which contended not only with the internal opposition of the nobility but also with the power of the Spanish Habsburgs. Again the story is told in terms of politico-religious conflicts and these conflicts are seen not only as clashes of doctrines or struggles for power but also in relation to the international balance of power. The latter, especially the threat of the Habsburgs, forced the French state to place political over confessional considerations. Similar forces are at work in Ranke's *History of England Principally in the Seventeenth Century* in which the religious conflict is inseparably related to the constitutional struggle and the Revolution of 1688 is seen not merely as a victory for constitutionalism and Protestantism within England but as a check against the hegemonial ambitions of France. Ranke portrays the direct involve-

[35] *Deutsche Geschichte,* I, 44.

ment of German Protestant states and especially of Holland in the events of 1688, as motivated not merely by religious convictions but by cold reason of state.

Several monographic studies followed these major works in the 1870s, continuing Ranke's histories of the Reformation and of Prussia and dealing for the first time extensively with the era of the French Revolution.[36] More important, however, Ranke finally undertook in 1880 to write a universal history which was to stress the continuity of a civilization which would endure. He was 85. In 1830 he had written of his desire to write a broad cultural history which would be "no longer national, but wholly universal."[37] To an extent this is what he now did, although the history of thought, literature, and religion continued to be embedded within the framework of the political struggle for existence. As he wrote in the preface to the *Universal History:* "But historical development does not alone rest on the tendency toward civilization. It arises also from impulses of a very different kind, especially from the rivalry of nations engaged in conflict with each other for the possession of the soil or for political supremacy. It is in and through this conflict, which always also affects the domains of culture, that the great powers of history are formed. In their unceasing struggle for dominion the peculiar characteristics of each nation are modified by universal tendencies, but at the same time resist and react upon them" (pp. 162–163). His history turned out not to be universal in the sense he had prescribed, embracing "the events of all times and nations" (p. 161), but was a history of the West. His task was to show the development since Antiquity of a heritage upon which modern civilization firmly rested. At the time of his death, he had traced the story from the ancient Near Eastern civilizations to the death of Otto the Great. His students, using his notes continued the history into the beginning of modern times and completed the work by publishing the

[36] Ranke had gone to Paris in the 1840s to work on the history of the French Revolution but postponed his work after discovering important papers in Paris relating to the history of Prussia.

[37] See note 34.

lectures "On the Epochs of Modern History" which Ranke delivered to King Maximilian II of Bavaria in 1854.

Theory

Ranke was foremost a practicing historian, not a theorist. Nevertheless Ranke was very conscious of the theoretical assumptions upon which his historical work rested. He sought to give these assumptions written expression at various times, in his great essays in the *Historisch-Politische Zeitschrift* of the 1830s, in the theoretical discussions (some of which survive in his unpublished lecture notes) with which Ranke introduced many of his general lecture courses, and in random remarks scattered through Ranke's histories, letters, and diaries. There is a remarkable continuity in his comments on the nature of history from the fragment of his Luther manuscript, written at the age of 21 in the winter of 1816–1817, to his lectures in the 1860s.

Ranke belonged to a broad current of German idealistic philosophy which permeated and dominated the social and cultural sciences in Germany throughout the nineteenth and well into the twentieth century. Ranke was nevertheless the first important historian to explore the significance of this orientation for historical practice. This tradition, as we remarked earlier, has been called historicism (*Historismus*). At the core of the historicist orientation was the insistence that man can be understood only in terms of his history, that the sciences dealing with man's cultural creativity are historical sciences and that the methods of the historical sciences are fundamentally different from those of the natural sciences or of traditional philosophy. The subject matter of history is living individualities, persons, institutions, cultures. But these individualities cannot be understood in terms of causal explanation. A sharp distinction exists between the inorganic, the organic, and the human historical world. The former two can be explained in terms of general laws. But there is an element of meaning, uniqueness, originality in every individual which defies rational deduction. The approach to the understanding of human facts must thus be fundamentally different from that of philosophy or natural science seeking abstractions and generalizations. "First of all, philosophy always reminds us of the claim of the supreme idea. History, on the other hand, reminds us of the conditions of existence," writes Ranke. Philosophy, as also natural science, is always concerned with the general, with seeing the particular and considers "every particular only as a part of the whole," as part of a total process (p. 37); history is always concerned with the particular, the individual. Its task is not explanation of general relationships but understanding of the uniqueness of a situation, an individuality, an institution, a culture. This leads to an idealistic conception of history. For the subject matter of history is ultimately human spirit, the unique element of personality which gives individuals in history their character.

For Ranke this emphasis on the understanding of the uniqueness of historical characters and situation leads to a rejection of speculation. To understand the unique individuality which appears in history demands a reconstruction of the past *"wie es eigentlich gewesen,"* which begins with a strict dedication to the relevant facts. Therefore the insistence on strict critical method. But the factual establishment of events does not yet constitute history. The historian is not a passive observer who merely records the events of the past but, rather like the poet, he actively recreates a situation. Unlike the poet, however, he is required to rely on empirical observation and is bound by the reality of his subject matter. To grasp the reality which confronts him, he must penetrate the external events which present themselves to his empirical observation and comprehend the "causal nexus," the greater *Zusammenhang* within history. This demand on the historian presupposes certain theoretical assumptions. It assumes that every individual, institution, or culture constitutes a meaningful unity, a *geistige Einheit,* which is capable of comprehension. To be sure the spiritual content of a historical individuality is not immediately evident. Nevertheless it permeates all expressions of the individual, the culture, or the nation. While the external facts the historian observes do not in themselves reveal this basic character, they reflect this character, and it is only through immersion in the external manifestations of the individuality that the historian can approach its basic spiritual content. Every cultural object or event, unlike a natural object or event, expresses an act of human thought or spirit. If we are dealing with a people, "we are not interested only in the individual moments of its living expressions. Rather from the totality of its development, its deeds, its institutions, and its literature, the idea speaks to us so that we simply cannot deny our attention" (pp. 43–44).

It would seem that the task of the historian is fundamentally different from that of the philosopher insofar as the latter seeks eternal truths while the historian is concerned with ephemeral phenomena, persons who die and institutions that sooner or later dissolve. History is flux. This position would deny that history has any meaning in a transcendent sense. Whatever meaning it has is limited to the subjective consciousness of mortal historians, the products of always changing historical situations. This, however, Ranke and the whole German idealistic tradition in the historical and cultural sciences deny. Instead they insist that history is an objective process which can be studied scientifically and that, in fact, history is the guide, indeed the only guide, to philosophic truth.

Basically, Ranke assumes that the aims of mature philosophy and of history are not entirely dissimilar even if their methods are fundamentally different. The historian, like the philosopher, seeks ideas of eternal validity. Already in the Luther fragments of 1816–1817, Ranke wrote: "Since history is an empirical science, it only too often happens to her that she splits herself into specialized areas and is far removed from doing what she is generally praised for, namely educating men. Only he who weds the empirical element with the idea can truly attract the spirit."[38] The kind of ideas which the historian seeks are, however, basically different from those of the philosopher. The idea of the philosopher, for example that of Hegel, is a lifeless abstraction; the idea the historian searches for is concrete, alive, and temporal. "While the

[38] "Das Luther-Fragment von 1817," in *Deutsche Geschichte,* VI, 233.

philosopher, viewing history from his vantage point, seeks infinity merely in progression, development, and totality, history recognizes something infinite in every existence" (p. 38). This "recognition" does, nevertheless, involve a philosophic and religious assumption as speculative in nature as those upon which the Hegelian philosophy rests. History, Ranke continues, recognizes, "in every being, something eternal, coming from God; and this is its vital principle." This recognition is beyond proof. "It is not necessary for us to prove at length that the eternal dwells in the individual. This is the religious foundation on which our efforts rest. We believe that there is nothing without God, and nothing lives except through God" (p. 38).

Ranke's conception of history, thus, involves not merely a method but a firm religious faith and a highly speculative philosophy shared by much of the German idealistic tradition in the *Geisteswissenschaften* in the nineteenth century. This philosophy, as it applies to historical study, has probably received its most concise definition in Wilhelm von Humboldt's essay "On the Historian's Task" which we have reprinted in this volume for this reason. But the basic ideas of Humboldt are all contained in less systematic form in Ranke's writings.

Central to Humboldt's and Ranke's conception of history is their "doctrine of ideas" (*Ideenlehre*). "An event," Humboldt writes, "is only partially visible in the world of the senses; the rest has to be added by intuition, inference, and guesswork. The manifestations of an event are scattered, disjointed, isolated; what it is that gives unity to this patchwork, puts the isolated fragments into its proper perspective, and gives shape to the whole, remains removed from direct observation. . . . The truth of any event is predicated on the addition—mentioned above—of that invisible part of every fact, and it is this part, therefore, which the historian has to add" (pp. 5–6). The historian must "separate the necessary from the accidental, uncover its inner structure, and make visible the truly activating forces" (p. 10). For Humboldt as for Ranke, the historian first of all proceeds through "the exact, impartial, critical investigation of events" (p. 7). But after the historian has considered all the forces acting on an event, "there still remains an even more powerfully active principle which, though not directly visible, imparts to these forces themselves their impetus and direction: that is, ideas which by their very nature lie outside the compass of the finite, and yet pervade and dominate every part of world history" (p. 19).

"All life," Ranke writes, "carries its ideal in itself" (p. 128). "The idea that inspires and dominates the whole, the prevailing tendency of the minds, and conditions in general, these are what determine the formation and the character of every institution" (p. 110). These ideas, although eternal, are not universal. They are not abstract ideas in the sense of traditional philosophy but concrete ideas manifested in time. "An idea," Humboldt writes, "can only appear in conjunction with nature" (p. 20). The theory of ideas in Humboldt and Ranke is inseparably related to their conception of individuality. "Every human individuality," Humboldt writes, "is an idea rooted in actuality" (p. 21). The same, he writes, is true of the individuality of nations. Similarly Ranke sees in every state the manifestation of an individualized idea (p. 123). The idea is not a static principle; it is essentially the vital energy, the principle inherent in the individual which governs its growth. "The innermost urge of spiritual life," Ranke writes, "is movement toward its idea, toward greater perfection. This urge is innate in it, implanted in it at its origin" (p. 128).

This theory of ideas has been called Neo-Platonic.[39] It assumes a universe less closely akin to the mechanistic cosmos of Newton than to the view of Leibniz, which conceives the world in terms of self-contained monads, each governed by an inner principle of development yet in harmony in their growth with the will of God. Newton's universe can be reduced to mathematical terms; in the world of Ranke and Humboldt quality defies reduction to quantity. The ideas have their origin in the will of

[39] Cf. Carl Hinrichs, *Ranke und die Geschichtstheologie der Goethezeit*; Friedrich Meinecke, *Die Entstehung des Historismus*, vol. III of *Werke*.

God.[40] The conception of individuals as the expression of an idea inherent within them limits the applicability of the principle of causation to the historical scene. For the idea itself can never be subjected to the laws governing nature. It is governed by a law of its own. The uniqueness of individuality guarantees a residue of spontaneity and freedom in history which defies all determinism. Regularity and growth can be understood only in terms of the unique principles inherent in the individualities that compose history. The "idea," Humboldt writes, "manifests itself . . . as a creation of energies which cannot be deduced in all their scope and majesty from attendant circumstances" (p. 19). The origin of individuality remains a mystery. Although we can point at antecedent traditions, the "eruption" of a uniquely Egyptian form of art or "the sudden development" of Hellenic individualism or of a Hellenic style in art or literature defies all causal explanation (p. 20). The element of individuality, and of spontaneity and freedom connected with individuality, makes impossible any philosophy of history which reduces history to a scheme.

The implications of the theory of ideas for the study of history is that every historical individuality must be studied for its own sake. Any attempt to apply schemes or abstract concepts to living individuals is a violation of historical reality, as is the at-

---

[40] Ernst Troeltsch sought to trace the German idealistic conception of the state as an expression of the will of God to Luther. Relying on Paul's admonition that "there is no power but of God; the powers that be are ordained of God" (Romans 13:1), Luther, Troeltsch argued, basically transformed the traditional Christian conception of natural law which posited a universally valid moral absolute by which the actions of states could be judged. The historically existing authorities themselves, Luther reasoned according to Troeltsch, were the concrete and individualized manifestations of natural law and were to be judged in terms of their own inherent principles rather than by external criteria. See Ernst Troeltsch, *Soziallehren der christlichen Kirchen und Gruppen* in *Gesammelte Schriften*, I (Tübingen, 1919), especially 560–571. Translated by Olive Wyon as *The Social Doctrines of the Christian Churches* (London, 1932), 2 vols.

tempt to formulate generalized explanations of social behavior. The historian must let the things speak for themselves.

Historical knowledge is possible because both the historian and his subject are part of the process of history and both have their basis in God's will. "All understanding," writes Humboldt, "presupposes in the person who understands, as a condition of its possibility, an analogue of that which will actually be understood later: an original, antecedent congruity between subject and object." For "when two beings are completely separated by a chasm, there is no bridge of communication between them; and in order to understand each other, they must, in some other sense, have already understood each other" (pp. 15–16). The first step is, as we have already seen, "the exact, impartial, critical investigation of events" (p. 7), or in Ranke's words the "thorough investigation of the particular." But Ranke then warns that one should not associate the expression, "the bare truth," with the "silly notion" that the truth consists in mechanically "copying" the original. "I have never had this idea," he continues. "In my criticism of historians I merely sought where originality, the historian's own perspective (*Anschauung*) and the fullness of life were to be found. And I did not want to be lied to. That is all."[41] Historical research must go further for Humboldt toward "the connecting of the events explored and the intuitive understanding of them which could not be reached by the first means." The latter requires the "fusion of the inquiring intellect and the object of inquiry" (p. 8). Ranke reminds us that history is concerned not merely with the collection of facts but with understanding these facts.[42] But this understanding proceeds only from the intuitive contemplation (*Anschauung*) of the historical subject matter. Such contemplation for Ranke requires that the historian consciously avoid projecting his subjectivity into the subject of inquiry. "The ideal of historical culture would consist in enabling

[41] "Erwiderung auf Heinrich Leo's Angriff," in SW, LIII/LIV, 663.
[42] "Über die Verwandtschaft und den Unterschied der Historie und der Politik," in SW, XXIV, 284.

the subject to make himself the pure organ of the object."[43] But the process of cognition is not exhausted by empirical observation, nor is it deductive, for abstract concepts cannot grasp historical reality. It is rather an intuitive one, in which the active intellect grasps the essence of its subject matter. In contemplating the particular (*Betrachtung des Einzelnen*), the way opens itself to the historian to the recognition of the "course which . . . the world in general has taken" (p. 31), a course which both Humboldt and Ranke agree can never be fully known but only divined (*ahnen*).

Involved in the theory of individuality is a highly optimistic philosophy of value. As we already suggested, there lurks behind Ranke's avowed Lutheran religiosity an outlook basically incompatible with orthodox Protestant belief. Because every individuality is the manifestation of an idea that has its origin in God, there is no room for evil. The ethical task of every historical individual for Ranke, and also for Humboldt, is the full development of the self. An individual must be judged in terms of the ideals inherent in it. There are no universal values. All values assume a concrete historical form, as the specific values of historical individualities. Not philosophy but history is the true guide to value. The values embodied in historical societies are not temporal, fleeting attitudes; they are timeless ideas, but they have no universal validity. They relate only to concrete historical individuals or institutions. In this sense, Ranke's call for impartiality (*Unparteilichkeit*) must be understood. We must, "view every existence as permeated with original life." Where there is a conflict of values, "both parties must be viewed on their own ground, in their own environment, so to speak, in their own . . . inner state. . . . It is not up to us to judge about error and truth as such," Ranke continues. "We merely observe one figure (*Gestalt*) arising side by side with another figure; life, side by side with life; effect, side by side with countereffect" (p. 42). The ability to portray the forces of history without interjecting one's own set of values is the core of objectivity. The historian himself will have value posi-

---

[43] Letter to King Maximilian II, von Bayern, Berlin, 26 November 1859, in SW, LIII/LIV, 404–405; cf. SW, XXV, ix.

tions. History centers around values. Yet Ranke, like Weber, calls for a value-free understanding of these values. "It would be impossible not to have one's own opinion in the midst of all the struggles of power and of ideas which bear within them decisions of the greatest magnitude. Even so, the essence of impartiality can be preserved. For this consists merely in recognizing the positions occupied by the acting forces and in respecting the unique relationships which characterize each of them. One observes how these forces appear in their distinctive identity, confront and struggle with one another; the events and the fates which dominate the world take place in this opposition. Objectivity is also always impartiality."[44]

Such a conception, which stresses the ethical autonomy of every individual and every culture, should logically exclude the idea that there is progress in history. For every stage of history must be judged as an end in itself, not as a step in a progression to a higher state. "Every epoch is immediate to God," Ranke observes, "and its worth is not at all based on what derives from it but rests in its own existence, in its own self" (p. 53). Similarly Humboldt considers it a mistake "that one seeks the fulfillment of the human race in the attainment of a general, abstractly conceived perfection rather than in the development of a wealth of great individual forms."[45] Mankind as a whole, he remarks, exists only "in the never attainable totality of all individualities which in the course of time become real."[46] Nevertheless Ranke is not fully consistent. In his histories he steadfastly assumes the superiority of the Christian religion and of Protestantism, and is convinced of the essential soundness of the civilization of the nineteenth century. Confident about the future of modern civilization, Ranke writes to King Maximilian II of Bavaria in 1859, "Until now cultural (*geistige*) development in the

[44] *Die deutschen Mächte und der Fürstenbund. Deutsche Geschichte von 1780 bis 1790*, "Vorwort," in SW, XXXI/XXXII, vii–viii.
[45] Wilhelm von Humboldt, "Die bewegenden Kräfte der Weltgeschichte," in *Werke in fünf Bänden* (Darmstadt, 1960–   ), I, 578.
[46] *Ibid.*, I, 575.

Western nations has ever progressed and is still progressing—in spite of the greatest obstacles and adverse interventions. Why should this not continue? For the goal has not yet been reached by far and the cultural (*geistige*) road is perhaps infinite."[47] Similarly the thread of progress runs through the *Universal History* which seeks to show how "in the course of centuries the human race has won for itself a sort of heirloom in the material and social progress which it has made, but still more in its religious development" (pp. 163–164).

Ranke's political philosophy is spelled out in its most systematic form in the essay, "A Dialogue on Politics," reproduced in this volume, but finds theoretical formulation in many of the essays in the *Historisch-Politische Zeitschrift* and serves as a foundation of his historical writings. His political theory is an application of his theory of ideas and the doctrine of individuality. The state, he argues, is not a conglomeration of individuals bound by a social contract nor is it a mere concentration of power. Rather every state rests on a "spiritual basis" (*geistige Grundlage*) (p. 31). The "states are individuals," and as such they are manifestations of an individualized, eternal idea in history. All states "are motivated by special tendencies of their own" and "these tendencies are of a spiritual nature" (p. 118). A state's fundamental idea directs its development and "penetrates and dominates its entire environment" (p. 119). This idea is of divine origin. "Instead of the passing conglomerations which the contractual theory of the state creates like cloud formations," Ranke perceives "spiritual substances, original creations of the human mind—I might say, thoughts of God" (p. 119). Each state is unique, different in its idea, its spirit, its development and needs, from all others. Similarities between states are purely formal— for example, all states have some form of constitution—but these formal similarities do not touch the essence of the state. "There is an element which makes a state not a subdivision of general categories, but a living thing, an individual, a unique self" (p. 112). The uniqueness of the state makes it impossible to transfer the political institutions to another state—for example French or En-

[47] See note 43.

glish parliamentarism to Prussia—without fundamentally changing the content and nature of these institutions. "Identical institutions, of the same purpose, resting on common historical
foundations, still assume, as we saw, the most divergent forms
in different countries" (pp. 110–111).

Ranke's position involves a radical rejection of the theory
of natural law. The state must not be judged by any external criteria. It is a law unto itself which must be understood in terms of
its inherent principle of growth. The individuals have no claim to
the state. "It would be ridiculous to explain (the states) as ever
so many police departments for the benefit of those individuals
who, let us say, have made a contract for the protection of private
property" (p. 118). Rather the individual can fulfill himself only
within the state. "There is no purely private existence for him.
He would not be himself, did he not belong to this particular state
as his spiritual fatherland" (p. 123). The state, however, must be
guided in its actions by its best interests and these interests Ranke
interprets primarily in terms of foreign affairs. "The position of
a state in the world depends on the degree of independence it
has attained" (pp. 117–118). The cultural creativity of a state depends on its power. The great age of French literature corresponded to that of French power. Frederick II set much of the
foundation of Germany's cultural revival. "A nation must feel
independent in order to develop freely, and never has a literature
flourished save when a climax of history prepared the way for it"
(p. 88). It is necessary therefore for the state "to organize all its
internal resources for the purpose of self-preservation" (p. 118),
to subordinate considerations of domestic politics to the demands
of foreign policy. The area of international relations is viewed,
however, as a battlefield in which every state must fight for its
independence and its rights. The central concern of the state must
be power on the international scene.

This emphasis on power for Ranke is, however, linked with
his conviction that power is never brute force but rather an expression of spiritual energy. "For it would be infinitely wrong to
seek in the struggles of historical powers only the work of brute
force, and thus to grasp only the transitory in its external manifestation: no state has ever existed without a spiritual (*geistige*)

basis and a spiritual content. In power itself a spiritual essence manifests itself. An original genius, which has its own life. . . . It is the task of history to observe this life, which cannot be characterized through only one idea or one word" (pp. 31–32). War for Ranke, as for Hegel, is therefore not a misfortune but a testing of ethical forces. "You will be able to name few significant wars," Ranke confidently asserts, "for which it could not be proved that genuine moral energy achieved the final victory" (p. 117). There is no real danger of war destroying the foundations of civilizations. Ranke recognized that the French Revolution brought about an intensification in the nature of warfare and that "now the nations, armed as they are, fight almost man for man, with all their might" (p. 104). Nevertheless, he is convinced, as he suggests in the essay on "The Great Powers," that "world history does not present such a chaotic tumult, warring, and planless succession of states and peoples as appear at first sight" (p. 100). There is a balance of power at work in the relations of states and although "world agitations now and again destroy this system of law and order, . . . after they have subsided, it is reconstituted" (p. 71).

The protestations with which Ranke and much of the tradition of German historicism greeted the Hegelian philosophy of history make us overlook the close affinities that existed between the two orientations. Both saw history as a meaningful and essentially benevolent process in which spiritual forces assumed concrete reality in social and political institutions. Ranke and Hegel's view of the state were particularly close. Both insisted that the state was the manifestation of an "ethical idea," that in Hegel's words "each nation as an existing individuality is guided by its particular principles,"[48] and that the state was subject to no external moral principles nor consideration of human rights in the pursuit of its political interests, particularly in the area of international relations. Power possessed a spiritual basis and war had an ethical element. For the victor in war represented the higher moral energies and thus world history, for Ranke as for Hegel, became in a sense the world court of justice.

[48] Hegel, *Selections*, ed. Jacob Loewenberg, p. 468; state as ethical idea, p. 443.

The Implications Of Theory For Historical Practice

In the section following this one, we shall examine the extent to which Ranke's stated theoretical views actually underlay his historical practice in the particular work, *The History of the Popes*. We shall also consider here briefly some of the main implications of Ranke's theoretical concepts for his historiography generally, implications which were not free of certain ambiguities and contradictions.

1.   We have already discussed the place of critical method in Ranke's theory of historical knowledge, the factual reconstruction of the events of the past. Nevertheless, as Ranke stressed, historical science must go beyond the facts and "rise in its own way from the investigation and contemplation of the particular to a general view of events and to the recognition of their objectively existing relatedness" (p. 30). "The particular bears the general within it," Ranke observes. "Out of the variety of individual perceptions a vision of their unity involuntarily arises" (p. 66). Such knowledge proceeds from the recognition of the inner structure of an event to the perception of the tendencies and leading ideas which give an age or a nation their character and finally to the attempt to penetrate the secret of world history itself. The latter to be sure is never fully accessible to man. "God alone knows world history. We recognize the contradictions—the harmonies . . . we can only divine (*ahnen*)" (p. 44). Yet in going beyond the facts, the historian leaves the ground of critical empirical knowledge and since Ranke rejected both deductive and inductive reasoning as incapable of comprehending the individualities which compose history, he is forced to turn to intuitive apprehension, in Ranke's words, "divination" (*Ahnung*). But such divination defies rational or empirical proof and thus violates the very principles of criticism which Ranke demands for historical study.

2.   It is not clear, therefore, where the borderline lies for Ranke between objective knowledge and subjectivity. The factual

reconstruction of events, as we just pointed out, did not yet constitute objective history. The historian must proceed from the particular to the general, to the perception of the objective tendencies operating in history. But Ranke insists that these cannot be grasped conceptually. The "creative forces" in history, Ranke explains, "cannot be defined or put in abstract terms, but one can behold them and observe them. One can develop a sympathy for their existence" (p. 100). For Ranke all abstraction violates the unique individuality of historical personalities and institutions. The general truths contained within the particular too are unique and cannot be reduced to concepts. The general is thus to be grasped through intuitive contemplation (*Anschauung*) or divination (*Ahnung*). Intuitive contemplation (*Anschauung*) for Ranke means an act, or better a state, by which the historian permits the concrete reality to confront him. He does not project his preconceived ideas into this reality; nor does he seek to analyze it. Rather he tries to receive it as it is. From this contemplation (*Anschauung*) insight into the inner connectedness of historical forces may result. But his insight does not take the form of precise, communicable knowledge. It is rather an inkling (*Ahnung*) on the part of the historian, something he suspects (*ahnen*), intuitively gathers. There are no rational criteria by which the objectivity of such historical knowledge can be judged other than a subjective sense of certainty on the part of the historian.

It is questionable, however, whether scientific or scholarly knowledge is possible without the use of concepts. Without translation into communicable conceptual terms, knowledge would remain a subjective matter. This question was to be raised later by men rooted deeply in the German historical tradition, such as Wilhelm Dilthey and Max Weber, who insisted that understanding in history, no less than in natural science, required the reduction of the plenitude of raw data into concepts. Such concepts, they recognized, must permit the historian to take into account the uniqueness of the meaning-filled and value-related phenomena of the cultural scene. The cultural sciences (*Geisteswissenschaften*) no less than the natural sciences, Dilthey and Weber insisted, required a logic and a methodology of their own. For Ranke rational method did not extend beyond the critical examination of evidence. The links between the facts, the general within the particular, revealed themselves translogically. Ranke's position ruled out not only the possibility of speculative philosophy of history but of any social science as well, of any attempts at the formulation of systematic theories for the explanation of historical events, whether of theories seeking to explain a limited set of phenomena or of explanations of broad scope. The uniqueness of historical personalities and institutions made impossible any attempt to establish uniformities or set up hypothetical models of behavior and made meaningless any effort at comparative history. Max Weber later was to challenge effectively the assumption that a conception of history which stressed the uniqueness and spontaneity of the agents of history necessarily had to assume the total unpredictability of historical events.

3. Ranke's position implies that history must strive to become world history not because human history is a unified process, but because all human societies are of equal dignity and hence of equal interest to the historian. There is a conflict, however, between Ranke's insistence that the individual must be studied for its own sake and his desire not to "devote much space to less significant events" but "to pay the greater attention to those of world-historical importance" (p. 150) and to "direct his attention to those epochs which have had the most effectual influence on the development of mankind" (p. 152). For the latter implies that mankind has a continuous development in which not all events and all epochs are of equal interest and value. In Ranke's concern with the world historical aspects of the history of the nations and institutions he studies, there is an affinity to Hegel's conception of world historical significance. In fact, Ranke does not write universal but Western history, and except in his final work, modern European history. And although he seeks to maintain a European perspective, for the most part he writes national history. For Ranke as for Hegel, Europe is not merely one culture among others but is identical with civilization in the modern world. In Asia by contrast, Ranke agrees with Hegel; cultural development stopped (p. 56). The histories of the non-European

peoples, including those of India and China, he argues, are of little interest to the historian and belong more properly to the province of natural history (p. 46). This, however, implies that all epochs and nations are not equally immediate to God and that there are higher and lower stages of civilization.

4. Ranke's joy in historical reality, in all aspects of the individualities, nations, and cultures which make up history, should have led him to a broad social and cultural approach to history. Indeed Ranke in 1830 wrote from Rome to his brother, Heinrich, of his desire to compose a history which would take into account the history of art and literature, an approach which reminds one of Ranke's student, Jacob Burckhardt.[49] In his notebook, Ranke jotted down in the 1830s the idea that "it should be possible to write a history of the world or of the European nations which would present the progressive development of its population numbers and their predominant activities," which would take into account the history of religion as a fundamental characteristic of the sixteenth and the "tremendous development of industry" in the nineteenth century.[50] In actuality, Ranke wrote little cultural or social history, and largely ignored economic factors. Ranke made no use of the statistical material which, as Rudolf Vierhaus has pointed out, was already available in his time. As Vierhaus suggests, this was in part because Ranke oriented his historiography on the literary model of the productive artist, despite his insistence on scholarliness. This model demanded narrative history, rather than the analysis of the natural scientist.[51] The central role which Ranke gave to state and church in society determined his emphasis on the interaction of politics and religion and his stress on foreign affairs. Similarly Ranke placed heavy emphasis on the great individuals. Yet the doctrine of individuality is in a sense in conflict with Ranke's focus on the world historical

[49] Letter to Heinrich Ranke, Rome, Anfang April 1830, in SW, LIII/LIV, 234.

[50] Leopold von Ranke, *Aus Werk und Nachlass*, vol. I, *Tagebücher*, ed. Walther Peter Fuchs (München, 1964), p. 239.

[51] Rudolf Vierhaus, *Ranke und die soziale Welt* (Münster, 1957), p. 130.

individuals. Here again Ranke approaches Hegel. For carried to its logical conclusion, the doctrine of individuality would not permit the writing of history because this process requires selection, a selection which is possible only if there are distinctions between significant and insignificant events and if all individuals and epochs are not equally immediate to God.[52]

5. This recognition of points of significance in history leads Ranke to seek to identify forces in history which transcend individuals and to an extent provide historical events with unity and direction. The task of the historian is to identify the "leading ideas," the "dominant tendencies in every century." Careful to avoid the attempt of the Hegelian school to reduce these ideas to rational concepts, Ranke writes that "these tendencies can only be described, but in the last analysis they cannot be subsumed under one concept" (p. 55). All of Ranke's histories in a sense are attempts to trace these great tendencies—the emergence of the modern state system, the emancipation of the political from the religious sphere, the balance of power—in the modern world. The essay on "The Great Powers" is a compact example of an attempt to portray these "leading ideas," as is the *History of the Popes*. In contrast to Hegel, however, Ranke denies that these tendencies lead to an end. The "secret of world history" rather lies in the manifold expressions, the conflict, interaction, and succession of these forces.

The "History Of The Popes" As An Example
Of Ranke's Historiography

A study of the history of the papacy was a natural part of Ranke's development of a universal history out of the national histories of the European nations. As he stated again and again in his Prefaces, his interest in the history of nations not his own was based on their importance for all of European history. The papacy, while not a nation, in Ranke's eyes exerted an influence on Euro-

---

[52] On Ranke's conception of objective forces and the objective spirit in history, see Gunter Berg, *Leopold von Ranke*, pp. 205–206.

pean history which made it a force comparable to that of the nation states. Moreover, the peculiar role of religion as a political
force in history was a question of lasting interest to Ranke who
saw in this one of the direct expressions of the transcendental in
the world. Thus everything tended to lead him to a study of the
papacy, not for its own sake, but as an expression of the religious
idea and as an important force on the European scene.

This approach at once determined the form of Ranke's study
and the nature of the sources he used. One of the most remarkable facts about Ranke's *History of the Popes* is its compass. It
includes not only the immediate sphere of the popes' political influence in Italy, nor merely their impact as spiritual head of the
Catholic Church, but also the course of Catholic religion and the
impact of the religious idea as expressed in Catholicism. Nowhere
is this more evident than in his treatment of the life of Sixtus V.
The biography, which begins in the middle of Book IV, is interrupted by a long disquisition on the "Idea of Modern Catholicism." Thus it forms the center of the book and the section on
modern Catholicism clearly expresses what Ranke sees as the impact of the papacy on European history in the sixteenth and
seventeenth centuries.

Because Ranke is not interested in the papacy for its own
sake, he has no hesitation in relying heavily on outside sources
which reflect more of the impact of its actions than the context
of the actions themselves. The most remarkable fact about his
source material is the lack of Roman material, except for secondary sources such as memoirs and collections of documents. The
Vatican archives were of course not available for serious study
before 1881. Nevertheless, one might have expected Ranke to
make an effort to obtain more specifically papal sources while
he was there.[53] In the light of his purpose, one readily understands
that he felt German, French, and Venetian sources would serve
him as well as Roman ones might have.

The *History of the Popes* posed some remarkable problems

---

[53] On Ranke's use of Roman archives, see the Preface to the *History of the Popes*, below, pp. 142–144.

for Ranke, accustomed as he was to thinking of history in a political and a national context. In all his other major works, the course of national political history, essentially independent of individuals, defined the structure of Ranke's writing—the history of the popes offered no such framework as the Papal States were manifestly not a nation and the papal influence was subject to great change with the changes of the popes. This led him to adopt a biographical framework. The structure of the *History of the Popes* is based on the biographies of the individual popes. In this respect it is unrepresentative of Ranke's work. The biographical element is, however, no more than a framework: the overall impression remains one of political history because Ranke always managed to expand his biographies to encompass what really interested him, namely the development and impact of the institution of the papacy on modern Europe.

The *History of the Popes* offers a good example of Ranke's pragmatic approach to the writing of history. Paradoxically, this becomes most visible in the passages in which he introduces considerations of a general or philosophical nature. In many instances these passages are visibly superimposed on the course of the narrative—Ranke first created a framework of facts which he then enriched with general observations. This approach has two consequences. First, Ranke does not employ a predetermined framework. Instead he seeks to reveal the actual forces at work in history by a narrative presentation of the flow of events. Second, through his empirical approach to the actual writing of history, Ranke achieves a remarkable degree of impartiality. This approach to his subject matter is the essence of Ranke's objectivity—he establishes his facts before interpreting them. As will be seen later, Ranke is at the same time acutely aware that the selection of his facts is an important step, probably even the vital one, in the work of a historian. In this regard the underlying principle is not that of factual objectivity but that of portrayal of the essential.

Even a cursory reading of the *History of the Popes* will reveal a number of underlying principles of Ranke's narrative. The most important is the dramatic. The desire to enliven his account (in the interests of better portrayal) has led him to emphasize unduly the fluctuations in the fortunes of Catholics and Protestants in the sixteenth and seventeenth centuries. Again and again one is "supreme" while the other faces a "hopeless" situation—only to have fortunes reversed in the next chapter. We would consider this emphasis of the fluctuations an overemphasis; Ranke implies that the extremes of the fluctuation reflect the essential rather than the superficial course of events. This identifies a second narrative principle: the constant conflict between the superficial and the essential, between the particular and the general. Again conflict is here used as a dramatic device intended to make the narrative—the portrayal of the essential—more clear. Occasionally the dramatic narrative becomes melodramatic. Repeatedly Ranke introduces statements which serve only to maintain the flow of the narrative. These rhetorical bridges can be observed at the end of every section, a short sentence or paragraph designed to close the preceding section and to introduce the next. Often such purely contextual sentences may be found within sections, or even from paragraph to paragraph, without being essential to the factual account. They are essential to the portrayal, because they always reflect the deeper unity of the whole topic.[54]

The result of all this is an intricate web of narrative by the aid of which Ranke portrays the history of the popes. Ranke's whole approach to writing history derives its interest from the conflict between what is essential and what is factual. Only thus can one understand the anecdotal character of much that he includes, while disregarding items important to anything like a complete factual account. The anecdotes, and there are many, are introduced because they are considered characteristic; the factual material is excluded because it is not considered essential. In this form, rather than in any conceptual framework, the basic idealism of Ranke's philosophy manifests itself. The repeated allusions to the "idea" of the papacy and of the state do not influence the interpretation of the papacy or the state. They do, however, provide the basis for his conviction that an anecdote or an episode

[54] See the treatment of Pope Sixtus V, below, pp. 281, 356.

can reveal the essence of an event better than any factual account, because the anecdote will reveal the entire idea in one flash of light, whereas an integral account would tend to diffuse the idea into the uniform gray of its manifestation.

The result of this technique in writing history is a highly structured account of the history of the popes. Quite revealing is the existence of three independent conclusions to the book: at the end of Book VIII, at the end of the section on the Restoration, and at the conclusion of the chapter dealing with the Vatican Council. It is noticeable that Ranke could not, even in the 1830s, conceive of the Restoration as a final act—the conclusion he offers is inconclusive. However, the first and the last conclusions are real to him; he sees them as corresponding to the actual course of history. The balance which was achieved between the two major Christian confessions in the middle of the seventeenth century ended what he considered the era of religion—the period during which the religious impulses were the leading idea of the time. The close of the Vatican Council symbolized the ascendancy of the secular, the leading idea of the period following the one he covers in the main part of the *History of the Popes*. By this Ranke did not mean to imply that modern European institutions lacked religious foundations. He felt that a Protestant conception of the state, which recognized the autonomy of the political sphere, had become dominant. Thus the final demise of the Papal States was a fitting conclusion to his *History of the Popes*.

Ranke's Impact On Later Historical Thought And Practice

Ranke's influence on German historiography cannot be underestimated. To a large extent the impact of Ranke is still felt in German historical science today. For this reason, the reexamination by German historians since World War II of their national tradition of historiography in the light of the political catastrophe of the years 1933 to 1945 has involved an extensive reexamination of Ranke's basic presuppositions.

Ranke's two major contributions to the national tradition of academic history in Germany were his adaptation of critical method to historical study and his conception of the state. The former was integrated into historical practice not only in Germany but throughout the world as historical scholarship became increasingly a university-centered profession. The latter, the conception of the state as an institution guided by no ethics other than that of its own interests of growth, the emphasis on the power position of the state in international affairs, and the subordination of domestic to foreign policy, remained intact in Germany into the twentieth century and was seriously challenged only in the years after 1945. To be sure, Ranke's historical writing was viewed very critically by many of his students, not on methodological but on political grounds. This rejection was particularly pronounced among the historians of the so-called Prussian school who viewed historical scholarship as an instrument of German unification. Ranke's student, Heinrich von Sybel, regretted Ranke's "lack of warmth" and overly great concern with technical considerations.[55]

Ranke was politically out of step with the historians of the Prussian school. He recognized the "rejuvenation of the national spirit in the whole compass of European peoples and states" (p. 98) but saw this new nationalism as a force which would strengthen the existing powers and support the balance of power. The historians of the Prussian school rejected Ranke's concept of the European system of great powers which they believed maintained the conservative status quo. Foreign policy, Droysen insisted, must be determined by national interest and conducted openly in the presence of public opinion rather than by secret diplomacy.[56] Prussia must cease to be European and become German. Her primary aim must be the unification of Germany and the pursuit of German national interests, not the balance of power.

[55] Translated as "Ranke and Burckhardt," in *German History. Some New German Views,* ed. Hans Kohn (London, 1954), pp. 142–156.
[56] Cf. Wolfgang Hoch, *Liberales Denken im Zeitalter der Paulskirche, Droysen und die Frankfurter Mitte* (Münster, 1957), p. 123.

Nationalism for the Prussian school was linked, at least until 1866, to a liberalism for which Ranke had little sympathy, a liberalism, however, which always subordinated domestic political aims to the demands of the reason of state and, indeed, saw in political reform an instrument for strengthening the national state rather than an end in itself. Rejecting Ranke's conception of balance, the Prussian historians nevertheless maintained the basic essence of his conception of the state as an autonomous end. The more conservative atmosphere of the German Empire brought with it a new appreciation for Ranke's "objectivity," his conception of the state as standing above parties. The "Neo-Rankeans," a generation of historians at the turn of the century advocating German imperial expansion, sought to project Ranke's conception of the balance of power from a European to a world scene.[57]

By the turn of the century, the Rankean tradition of political history based on the critical analysis of documents, which by then dominated historical scholarship not only in Germany but throughout the world, was seriously challenged by the "New Historians," J. H. Robinson, Frederick Turner, and Charles Beard in the United States, by Henri Berr in France, and by Karl Lamprecht in Germany. The Rankean conception of "scientific history," these men held, was inadequate for the understanding of the social, economic, and cultural transformation of the modern world. In the United States and France, this revolt led to an increasing concern to link history with the social sciences.

In Germany the attempt by Karl Lamprecht to carry hypothesis and generalization into history led to a bitter controversy, the famous *Methodenstreit*. The historical profession saw in Lamprecht a threat not only to German historiographical but also political traditions. The failure of Germany to achieve parliamentary government in the nineteenth century was reflected in the opposition of the basically conservative and nationally oriented

[57] On the Neo-Rankeans see Ludwig Dehio's essay in *Germany and World Politics in the Twentieth Century*; also Hans-Heinz Krill, *Die Rankerenaissance* (Berlin, 1962).

German academic establishment to Lamprecht's approach. These men saw in the German idealistic tradition, with its emphasis on the particular, its reverence for the state, and its concern with the role of individual statesmen in historical change, the ideological foundation for the political and social order which had emerged in Germany with Bismarck's defeat of the Prussian liberals and his unification of Germany under the auspices of a semi-autocratic Prussian monarchy. The defeat of Germany in World War I and the effects of the Treaty of Versailles solidified the hold of the Rankean idealistic tradition over German historians. The 1920s saw a steady increase in the interest in social history in France, Belgium, and the United States, but also saw the decline of the struggling German tradition of social history. As German historians passionately disputed the thesis of German war guilt contained in the Treaty of Versailles, they increasingly viewed all social history as subversive of German national political and intellectual traditions. This rejection included even the relatively conservative, state-oriented type of social history best represented before World War I by Gustav Schmoller.

Only after 1945 was there a serious reexamination of the Rankean tradition of historiography in Germany. Meinecke, then the dean of German historians, in his now famous lecture on "Ranke and Burckhardt" in 1948 suggested that Burckhardt with his deep pessimism regarding men, material civilization, power, and the masses had understood the modern world more correctly than Ranke. Meinecke now recognized that Ranke's idealistic notion of the state as an ethical individual was no longer tenable. It was questionable, however, whether Meinecke was right when he predicted that Burckhardt in the mid-twentieth century "would still have greater importance than Ranke for us and for later historians."[58] Burckhardt concerned himself with the cultural life of elites. Idealistic in philosophic outlook, Burckhardt showed little concern for the relation of culture to the wider context of society, including its material foundations. A new generation of historians, including men like Theodor Schieder, Werner Conze, and Otto

[58] Cf. "Über den Stand der neueren deutschen Geschichtsschreibung," in *Kleine historische Schriften,* I (München, 1863), 349.

Brunner, increasingly called for a historiography which while keeping alive what is valid in the idealistic tradition—the recognition of the role of individual creativity and of ideas—would take into account the fundamental rupture in the very structure of history which emerged with the technological mass society. Greater concern was given to the analysis of social structure. The concepts and methods of political science for the first time occupied an important role in the analysis of modern political processes in a work such as K. D. Bracher's *Auflösung der Weimarer Republik.* Marxism played a relatively insignificant role in German historical scholarship outside of East Germany. Nevertheless, the great controversy aroused by Fritz Fischer's work, *Deutschlands Griff nach der Weltmacht,* published in 1961—a shortened English version, *Germany's Aims in the First World War,* appeared in 1967—involved not only the reassessment of German political traditions but of historiographical practices.

West German historiography thus moved slowly in directions in which historical scholarship in France, the United States, and to a lesser extent in Great Britain and Italy had been moving since the turn of the century.[59] Social science-oriented historians in the United States and particularly in France centered around the journal, *Annales,* founded in 1929 by Lucien Febvre and Marc Bloch. They had increasingly parted ways with the Rankean conception of historiography, seeking to study politics within the broader framework of the economy, the society, and the culture. The new historiography rejected the German idealistic distinction between the "idiographic" methods of history and the cultural sciences concerned with the "understanding" of unique phenomena and the "nomothetic" methods of the natural sciences seeking causal explanations.[60] History, the new historians insisted,

[59] Cf. Georg G. Iggers, "The Decline of the Classical National Tradition of German Historiography," in *History and Theory,* VI (1967), 382–412.

[60] The terms "nomothetic" and "idiographic" were coined by the philosopher Wilhelm Windelband in his famous inaugural address as rector of the University of Strassburg in 1894 on "History and Natural Science."

is a social science seeking generalizations regarding social behavior and development. According to the *Annales* historians, who attracted considerable attention in Germany after 1945, history is ultimately more concerned with analyzing the enduring "structures" of a society than with the narration of unique events which in a sense represent phenomena on the surface of a society. In the study of the structural basis of a society, the historian dealt with impersonal social forces susceptible to generalizations, comparisons, and often quantification. Historical methods and concepts thus became increasingly integrated with those of economics, sociology, geography, psychology, and most recently, especially in France, with anthropology.

The social sciences reentered West German historiography largely by way of the sociology of Max Weber. Weber had written in the early part of the century, but his influence made itself fully felt in Germany only after 1945. In a sense, Weber succeeded in combining the best in the German idealistic tradition—the recognition of historical individuality which was lacking in much of Western sociology and sociologically oriented history—with a recognition of the role of general concepts in social science and history. As H. Stuart Hughes observed, Weber "introduce(d) conceptual rigor into a tradition where either intuition or a naive concern for the 'facts' had hitherto ruled unchallenged."[61] Fully acknowledging the residues of irrationality in human behavior, Weber nevertheless recognized that such behavior is never without a degree of structure and regularity. Unpredictability, he observed, is the privilege of the insane. These elements of recurrence and structure permitted the formulation of generalizations of limited scope, which took into full account the uniqueness of every historical situation, but which made possible nevertheless the comparability of persons, social systems, and cultures. Thus for Weber, as for Western social science-oriented historians, history had both a narrative and an analytical function. Deeply influenced by Weber in the 1920s, Otto Hintze sought to bridge the gap

[61] H. Stuart Hughes, *Consciousness and Society* (New York, 1958), pp. 302–303.

between Ranke's event-oriented political history and Weber's analysis of social institutions. However, only after 1945 was the hold of the German idealistic tradition sufficiently weakened to permit the introduction of sociological and political science concepts and methods into German historiography.

Conclusion

In a number of important ways, Ranke's concepts of history need reexamination.

1.   Although Ranke called on the historian to show a "universal interest," which expresses itself in concern with social institutions, scientific progress, art, politics, and their interrelation, and complained that "most of history thus far has dealt with war and peace" (p. 40), in practice he restricted the compass of what he considered historically significant to the spheres of politics and religion.

2.   Despite his conviction that politics must deal with the concrete and the historical, Ranke's conception of the state was essentially abstract and historical. Ranke saw the state as an integrated individuality, not as itself a balance of conflicting forces and interests. He had little understanding for the political conflicts and the clashes of interests which take place in the state. Ranke's conception of the state as a metaphysical reality was essentially incompatible with an empirical study of political forces and functions.

3.   Related to Ranke's narrow conception of the state was a narrow conception of what constituted historical evidence. The reliance on written, and particularly political, documents introduced a methodological bias in the writing of history.[62] It placed primary emphasis on the conscious acts of political personalities. It

[62] Cf. Ranke's remark: "We can only clearly recognize again that part of life which has been preserved in writing," quoted by Alfred Dove, "Leopold von Ranke," in *Allgemeine Deutsche Biographie*, XXVII (Leipzig, 1888), 248.

tended to ignore the role of impersonal forces below the conscious level, not only of economic and sociological factors but also of myths and *Weltanschauung*.

4.   Thus despite his desire to make history into a scientific discipline, Ranke imposed an extremely narrow conception of science on historical scholarship. By identifying scientific method in history with the critical examination of documents, Ranke asked the historian to take the political and intellectual phenomena he observed at their face value rather than to inquire into the broader context and dynamic relationships of which they formed a part. In fact, Ranke held a relatively simple theory of knowledge. He assumed that the past spoke directly to the historian who would honestly listen to it. Social analysis was unnecessary in historical science. It distorted historical reality. Through direct contemplation of historical reality, immersion in the facts, the great coherences of history would reveal themselves to the historian. This optimism is no longer credible to contemporary historians or social scientists who believe that the investigator must approach his subject matter with questions and hypotheses. In a sense, far from placing history on scientific foundations, Ranke in fact excluded the study of the past from scientific analysis and reserved an important place for intuition and subjectivism in the interpretation of historical processes.

5.   But finally and most important, Ranke's philosophy of value, teaching that every individual and state must be understood in terms of its own standards and that "every epoch is immediate to God" (p. 53), is no longer credible to many historians after the political catastrophes of the twentieth century. On the surface, Ranke's insistence on the value neutrality or "impartiality" (*Unparteilichkeit*) of the historian has a certain kinship with later value positivism. Like the latter, Ranke believed that the historian and the social scientist must refrain from judging the values that manifest themselves in societies but must accept these values in their historical context; he believed that all societies and all value systems they embody are of equal dignity. In the realm of politics this means that the historian must not judge the actions of states

in terms of external moral or political standards but must understand them in terms of the vital interests of each state.

German historians have stressed the realism of this position and contrasted it with the supposed inability of Western historians and social scientists whom they considered not yet fully emancipated from natural law traditions to understand the realities of power. On closer view, Ranke's realism proves to be of questionable quality. We can follow Ranke completely when he asks the historian not to read the values of the present into the past but to understand the past in its own terms. It does not follow from this, however, as Ranke suggests, that the values and policies of existing states are not subject to critical analysis in the light of reason or human value.

There was nothing realistic about Ranke's assumption that institutions which had developed historically represented a higher form of reality or that the acts of states in pursuit of their great historic power-political interests reflected a higher form of morality, even if these acts seemed to be in conflict with traditional standards of morality. Ranke's value positivism rested on a boundless optimism regarding the course of history. Much more optimistic than the advocates of the idea of progress who projected the attainment of a rational political and social order into the future, Ranke and many of the German historians in the national tradition were convinced that such an order had already been achieved in the great historical institutions of the past and of the present. This optimism introduced an element of bias into Ranke's historiography in favor of the established political order. Ranke to be sure remained sublimely unaware of the role which his conservative attitudes played in his construction of the past. What Ranke considered to be the objective forces operating in history was to an extent the projection of his own value views into history. This bias led him to place the power interests of the established political order over the welfare, rights, and interests of its citizens. It led him to an uncritical reverence for political power. The events of the twentieth century in a most cruel way were to disprove the soundness of Ranke's optimism.

In the post-World War II years, German historians have sensed the danger inherent in Ranke's position.[63] They have ascribed the willingness with which German historians in the Rankean tradition accepted the aberrations of German politics to their failure to judge the state in terms of humane values. It is possible for the historian to be strictly committed to the reconstruction of the past in its individuality *"wie es eigentlich gewesen"* and yet be ethically critical. Although ethical norms are doubtless largely culture conditioned, it is by no means as certain as Ranke makes it appear that ethical and political norms are devoid of any rational basis which would extend their applicability beyond a given society. The historian cannot presume to establish universally valid moral norms for mankind. We share sufficiently in a common humanity, however, to recognize the violations of human dignity and human personality. Objectivity requires the historian to view the state free of all idealization, as it is in its empirical reality not as the historical manifestation of a metaphysical idea. The historian must seek for standards of values not in the ethically uncritical study of historical processes but in his own conscience, perhaps in the humanity he shares with his fellowman. As many contemporary German historians have realized, a democratically oriented historiography requires a conscious commitment to the worth and dignity of the individual as a standard by which political institutions and political acts are to be judged. The historian's awareness of his bias and his value commitments may be an important element in assuring his greater objectivity and enabling him to reconstruct and understand, but not necessarily to condone, the past in its own terms.

Nevertheless Ranke's contribution to historical science cannot be minimized. Ranke continues to be of interest to us as an im-

---

[63] Even conservative German historians attached to the German classical tradition of historiography after 1945 recognized Ranke's failure to understand the dangers inherent in political power. See, e.g., Meinecke's above mentioned lecture on "Ranke and Burckhardt" and Gerhardt Ritter, *Vom sittlichen Problem der Macht*, 2nd ed. (Bern, 1961), pp. 101–102.

portant contributor to a tradition of historical and social science which sought to develop a methodology and a theory of knowledge suited to the nature of history and society. He not only contributed to putting history on a more scholarly footing by his insistence on the critical examination of documents but more so than his predecessors succeeded in going from the critical analysis of texts to historical synthesis. He contributed to the formation of a historical sense which sought to recapture the past as it essentially occurred freed of the preoccupations which older philosophic historians had brought to their subject matter. He pointed at the elements of uniqueness, spontaneity, and intention in human affairs which defy reduction to abstract formulations, even if he may have overly limited the role which concepts and generalizations play in the understanding of human affairs. And not least of all, as we shall see in the following selections from the *History of the Popes*, Ranke deserves to be read as one of the greatest writers of historical prose.

Bibliographical Note

There are two works which when used together provide an almost complete bibliography of Ranke's writings and of the literature on Ranke. They are H. F. Helmolt, *Ranke-Bibliographie* (Leipzig, 1910) and Günter Johann Henz, *Leopold Ranke, Leben, Denken, Wort 1795–1814* (Köln, 1968), which on pages 230 to 259 brings the Helmolt bibliography up to date.[1] Less exhaustive but more easily available in American libraries is the 10th edition of the Dahlmann-Waitz, *Quellenkunde der deutschen Geschichte* (Stuttgart, 1965–   ) which in Abschnitt 7, entries 775 to 906, includes an extensive listing of Ranke editions and secondary literature. A valuable "Bibliographical Essay" is contained in Theodore H. Von Laue, *Leopold Ranke: The Formative Years* (Princeton, 1950), pp.

[1] There are some omissions, however, in the Henz bibliography, including any mention of the recent Soviet literature on Ranke. See *Istoriografia novogo vremeni stran evropi i ameriki* (Moscow, 1967), p. 647; and N. I. Smolenskiy, "L. Ranke i F. Meinecke," in *Metodologicheskie i istoriograficheskie voprosy istoricheskoy nauki*, Vypusk 5 (Tomsk, 1967), pp. 149–194.

219–227. Georg G. Iggers, "The Image of Ranke in American and German Historical Thought," *History and Theory*, II (1962), 17–40, contains a critical discussion of much of the German and American literature on Ranke.[2]

Ranke's works were published in the fifty-four volumes of the *Sämmtliche Werke* (Leipzig, 1873–1890). This edition of Ranke's collective works was begun by Ranke and completed after his death by his student, Alfred Dove. All of Ranke's major works except the *Universal History* and many of his important essays, including those which originally appeared in the *Historisch-Politische Zeitschrift*, are contained in the edition. Ranke, however, revised his earlier works for the collected edition so that a student of Ranke's historical thought will also have to look at the original works. The final volume of the edition, LIII/LIV, edited after Ranke's death by Alfred Dove, contains a large collection of letters, diary notes, and three autobiographical sketches dictated by Ranke in his old age. The *Weltgeschichte (Universal History)* was published separately in nine volumes, Leipzig, 1881–1888. Part II of volume IX, edited by Alfred Dove, contains *On the Epochs of Modern History*, the previously unpublished lectures delivered by Ranke in 1854 before King Maximilian II of Bavaria. The *Deutsche Akademie* in the 1920s began the publication of a critical edition of Ranke's collected works. This edition was never completed; only the *German History in the Age of the Reformation*, ed. P. Joachimsen (München, 1925–1926), 6 vols., and *Twelve Books of Prussian History*, ed. G. Küntzel (München, 1930), 3 vols., appeared. There have been several collections of Ranke's major works, including a twenty-five-volume edition, *Historische Meisterwerke*, selected and edited by A. Meyer and

---

[2] An extremely interesting and useful bibliographical work is the doctoral dissertation of Rainald Stromeyer, "Ranke und sein Werk im Spiegel der Kritik," submitted to the University of Heidelberg in 1950. Unfortunately this dissertation exists only in typescript. A copy is available in the Library of Congress. On Ranke literature of the 1950s, see the very useful essay by Walther Peter Fuchs, "Neuere Ranke-Forschungen," *Das Historisch-Politische Buch*, VIII (1960), 1–4.

H. Michael (Hamburg, 1928–1931) and a twelve-volume edition, *Hauptwerke*, ed. W. Andreas (Wiesbaden, 1957). For a list of major individual works by Ranke and of English translations, see the end of this bibliographical note.

Some of Ranke's correspondence was published in volume LIII/LIV of the *Sämmtliche Werke*, as we mentioned above. Additional letters are contained in Leopold von Ranke, *Das Briefwerk*, ed. Walther Peter Fuchs (Hamburg, 1949) and *Neue Briefe*, ed. Bernhard Hoeft and Hans Herzfeld (Hamburg, 1949). An edition of Ranke's literary estate, *Aus Werk und Nachlass*, is being edited by Walther Peter Fuchs and Theodor Schieder. The first volume, *Tagebücher* (München, 1964), edited by Walther Peter Fuchs, consists of diary and notebook entries arranged by subject matter rather than chronologically. A second volume which will contain a critical edition of *On the Epochs of Modern History* and a third volume containing young Ranke's writings until 1824 are in preparation.

As yet there is no adequate biography of Ranke. His autobiographical sketches mentioned above are fragmentary and at points unreliable. Three essays written by students of Ranke at the time of his death are very useful: Alfred Dove's biographical essay in the *Allgemeine Deutsche Biographie*, XXVII (Leipzig, 1888), 242–269; Heinrich von Sybel's obituary speech, "Gedächtnisrede auf Leopold von Ranke," in *Historische Zeitschrift*, LVI (1886), 463–481, also in *Vorträge und Abhandlungen* (München, 1897), pp. 290–307; and Wilhelm Giesebrecht's "Gedächtnisrede auf Leopold von Ranke" (München, 1887). Other contributions to Ranke's biography include Eugen Guglia, *Leopold von Rankes Leben und Werk* (Leipzig, 1893); H. F. Helmolt, *Leopold von Rankes Leben und Wirken* (Leipzig, 1921); Hermann Oncken, "Leopold von Ranke," in *Die grossen Deutschen*, III (Berlin, 1936), 203–221; Carl Hinrichs, "Leopold von Ranke," *Die grossen Deutschen*, 2nd ed. (Berlin, 1956), pp. 293–312; and a brief pamphlet published by the Historical Association, Hans Liebeschütz, *Ranke* (London, 1954). On Ranke's youth, Hermann Oncken, *Aus Rankes Frühzeit* (Gotha, 1922) and the above cited Günter Johann Henz, *Leopold Ranke, Leben, Denken, Wert 1795–*

1814, should be mentioned. There are a large number of analyses of Ranke's work and thought. There are, of course, chapters on Ranke in all major histories of historiography or of German historiography, including Eduard Fueter, *Geschichte der neueren Historiographie* (München, 1912), pp. 472–492; George P. Gooch, *History and Historians in the Nineteenth Century* (London, 1913), chap. VI, "Ranke," pp. 72–97 and chap. VII, "Ranke's Critics and Pupils," pp. 98–121; James Westfall Thompson, *A History of Historical Writing,* II (New York, 1942), chap. XLI, "The University of Berlin: Niebuhr and Ranke," pp. 149–186 and chap. XLII, "The Ranke School," pp. 187–204; Heinrich Ritter von Srbik, *Geist und Geschichte vom Deutschen Humanismus bis zur Gegenwart,* I (Salzburg, 1950), 239–292; Friedrich Engel-Jánosi, *The Growth of German Historicism* (Baltimore, 1944), pp. 51–62; Gerhard Schilfert, "Leopold von Ranke," in *Die deutsche Geschichtwissenschaft vom Beginn des 19 Jahrhunderts bis zur Reichseinigung von oben,* ed. Joachim Streisand (Berlin, 1963), pp. 241–270; and Georg G. Iggers, *The German Conception of History* (Middletown, Conn., 1968), pp. 63–89. In all three of his major works, *Weltbürgertum und Nationalstaat*—first published in 1907—(München, 1962), pp. 244–277; *Die Idee der Staatsraison* —first published in 1924—(München, 1957), pp. 442–459; and especially *Die Entstehung des Historismus*—first published in 1936—(München, 1959), pp. 585–602, Meinecke deals extensively with Ranke. In the last mentioned book, he regards Ranke and Goethe as the two high points of historicist thought. A much more critical view of Ranke's emphasis on political history and his optimism regarding power is contained in Meinecke's famous lecture, "Ranke and Burckhardt," held in East Berlin in 1948 and translated in Hans Kohn, ed., *German History. Some New German Views* (Boston, 1954), pp. 142–156. The best analysis, certainly in English, of Ranke's conception of history is Theodore H. Von Laue, *Leopold Ranke, the Formative Years* (Princeton, 1950). Important works dealing with aspects of Ranke's thought are Otto Diether, *Leopold von Ranke als Politiker* (Leipzig, 1911), one of the few German works critical of Ranke; Gerhard Masur, *Rankes Begriff der Weltgeschichte,* in *Historische Zeitschrift,* Beiheft 6 (1926);

Ernst Simon, *Ranke und Hegel,* in *Historische Zeitschrift,* Beiheft 15 (1928); Ernst Schulin, *Die weltgeschichtliche Erfassung des Orients bei Hegel und Ranke* (Göttingen, 1958); Carl Hinrichs, *Ranke und die Geschichtstheologie der Goethezeit* (Göttingen, 1954); on Ranke's political views, Wilhelm Mommsen, *Stein, Ranke, Bismarck* (München, 1954); on his conception of society, Rudolf Vierhaus, *Ranke und die soziale Welt* (Münster, 1957).

A Chronological Table Of Ranke's Main Writings

1817 "Luther Fragment"[3]
1824 *Histories of the Latin and Germanic Nations In Criticism of Modern Historians. A Supplement*
1827 *Princes and Nations of Southern Europe,* vol. I
1829 *The Servian Revolution*
1832–36 Editor, *Historisch-Politische Zeitschrift*
1834 *Princes and Nations of Southern Europe,* vol. II
History of the Popes, vol. I
1836 *Princes and Nations of Southern Europe,* vols. III and IV
History of the Popes, vols. II and III
1837 *On the History of Italian Poetry*
1839–47 *German History in the Era of the Reformation*
1844 *On the Outbreak of the Seven Year War*
1846 *On the Assembly of the French Notables in 1787*
1847–48 *Nine Books of Prussian History*
1852–61 *History of France, Principally in the 16th and 17th Centuries*
1859–66 *History of England, Principally in the 16th and 17th Centuries*
1854 "On the Epochs of Modern History," lectures delivered before King Maximilian II of Bavaria
1867 *Collected Works,* vol. I
1868 *On German History, From the Religious Peace to the Thirty Year War*
1869 *History of Wallenstein*

---

[3] "Das Luther-Fragment von 1817," ed. Elisabeth Schweitzer in Leopold von Ranke, *Deutsche Geschichte im Zeitalter der Reformation*—Gesamtausgabe der Deutschen Akademie—(München, 1925–1926), VI, 311–399.

1871–72   *The German Powers and the League of the German Princes*
1874   *The Genesis of the Prussian State*
1875   *The Origin and Beginning of the Revolutionary Wars*
       *On the History of Austria and Prussia from the Treaty of Aix-
       la-Chapelle to that of Hubertusburg*
1877   *Historical-Biographical Studies*
1878   *Frederick the Great*
       Frederick William IV
1878–79   *Twelve Books of Prussian History*
1879–81   *Hardenberg and the History of the Prussian State*
1880–88   *Universal History*, vols. I-IX.

Ranke's Works In English Translation

History of the Latin and Teutonic Nations, 1494-1514, trans. P. A.
    Ashworth (London, 1887), later revised edition. Translation does
    not contain the critical appendix, "In Criticism of Modern His-
    torians."
*History of Servia and the Servian Revolution. With an Account of the
    Insurrection in Bosnia*, trans. Mrs. A. Kerr (London, 1847), later
    edition.
History of Ottoman and Spanish Empires, trans. Walter K. Kelly (Lon-
    don, 1843), later edition.
*History of the Popes, Their Church and State, and Especially of Their
    Conflicts with Protestantism in the Sixteenth and Seventeenth
    Centuries*, trans. E. Foster, 3 vols. (London, 1853–1856), later re-
    vised editions.
————, trans. S. Austin, 3 vols. (London, 1866).
————, trans. Walter K. Kelly (London, 1843), later editions.
————, trans. D. D. Scott, 2 vols. (London, 1851).
————, trans. E. Fowler (London, 1901), reprinted 1966.
History of Reformation in Germany, trans. S. Austin, 3 vols. (London,
    1845–1847), later editions, reprinted 1966.
History of the Prussian Monarchy from its Rise to the Present Time,
    trans. Franz C. F. Demmler, vol. I (London, 1847).
*Memoirs of the House of Brandenburg and History of Prussia, During
    the Seventeenth and Eighteenth Centuries*, trans. Sir A. and Lady
    Duff-Gordon, 3 vols. (London, 1819).

History of Civil Wars and Monarchy in France, trans. M. A. Garney, 2 vols. (London, 1852).

Ferdinand First and Maximilian Second of Austria, trans. Lady Duff-Gordon (London, 1853).

History of England, Principally in the 17th Century, trans. G. W. Kitchin and C. W. Boase, 6 vols. (London, 1875).

Universal History: Oldest Historical Group of Nations, ed. G. W. Prothero (London, 1884), only vol. I.

"A Dialogue on Politics" and "The Great Powers," in Theodore M. Von Laue, *Leopold Ranke: The Formative Years* (Princeton, 1950), pp. 152–218.

Major Literature In English On Ranke

Thomas Babington Macaulay, "Von Ranke (October 1840)," in *The Miscellaneous Works of Lord Macaulay* (New York, n.d.), IV, 365–417.

Lord Acton, "German Schools of History," *English Historical Review,* I (1886), 7–42, also in *Historical Essays and Studies* (London, 1907), pp. 344–392.

J. H. W. Stuckenberg, "Ranke and His Method," *Andover Review,* VII (1887), 117–137.

H. B. Adams, "Leopold von Ranke," *Papers* of the American Historical Association, III (1888), 101–120.

E. G. Bourne, "Leopold von Ranke," *Annual Reports* of the American Historical Association (1896), I, 65–82; Ranke and the Beginning of the Seminary Method in Teaching History," *Educational Review,* XII (1896), 359–367; both essays are reprinted in Bourne's *Essays in Historical Criticism* (New York, 1901).

George P. Gooch, *History and Historians in the Nineteenth Century* (London, 1919), reprinted as Beacon Press paperback (Boston, 1959), chap. VI: "Ranke"; chap. VIII: "Ranke's Critics and Pupils," pp. 72–121.

James Westfall Thompson, *A History of Historical Writing,* II (New York, 1942), chap. XLI: "The University of Berlin: Niebuhr and Ranke"; chap. XLII: "The Ranke School," pp. 149–204.

Friedrich Engel-Jánosi, *The Growth of German Historicism* (Baltimore, 1944).

George P. Gooch, "Ranke's Interpretation of German History," in *Studies in German History*" (London, 1948), pp. 210–266.

Theodore H. Von Laue, *Leopold Ranke: The Formative Years* (Princeton, 1950).

Ferdinand Schevill, "Ranke: Rise, Decline, and Persistence of a Reputation," *Journal of Modern History* (1952), pp. 219–234; also in Schevill, *Six Historians* (Chicago, 1956), pp. 125–155.

Pieter Geyl, "Ranke in the Light of the Catastrophe," in *From Ranke to Toynbee* in *Smith College Studies in History*, XXIX (Northampton, Mass., 1952), 1–17; reprinted in *Debates with Historians* (Cleveland, 1958), pp. 9–29.

Hans Liebeschütz, *Ranke* (London, 1954), published by the Historical Association, pamphlet, General Series: G 26.

Herbert Butterfield, *Man on His Past. The Study of the History of Historical Scholarship* (Cambridge, 1955), pp. 86–95, 100–141, 219–232; reprinted as Beacon Press paperback.

Fritz Stern, *The Varieties of History* (Cleveland, 1956), chap. III, "The Ideal of Universal History: Leopold von Ranke," pp. 54–62, brief introduction and selections from theoretical writings.

Georg G. Iggers, "The Image of Ranke in American and German Historical Thought," *History and Theory*, II (1962), 17–40.

Georg G. Iggers, *The German Conception of History. The National Tradition of Historical Thought from Herder to the Present* (Middletown, Conn., 1968), chap. IV, "The Theoretical Foundations of German Historicism, II: Leopold von Ranke," pp. 68–89.

**The Theory
and Practice
of History**

PART I

The Idealistic Theory
of Historiography

Wilhelm von Humboldt's
Classical Formulation

Karl Lamprecht has called Wilhelm von Humboldt the "greatest theorist of the *Ideenlehre*" (Doctrine of Ideas) and Ranke its "greatest practitioner." The following lecture, delivered in 1821 to the Prussian Academy of Sciences, represents the classical formulation of the *Ideenlehre* as it applies to historiography. Croce has credited the essay with containing the seminal ideas of what was to become historicism. These ideas, perhaps never again as well formulated, constitute the core of the idealistic faith of the classical German tradition of historiography from Ranke to Gerhardt Ritter.

Three ideas central to the German idealistic theory of historiography are spelled out in this essay. (1) *The doctrine of ideas:*

historical phenomena are merely the external manifestation of underlying eternal ideas. (2) *The concept of individuality:* the ideas, while timeless, are not abstract or universally valid; rather, they express themselves in concrete historical individualities. Not only every person but also every great social institution (for example, any major state or nation) constitutes such an individuality. "Every human individuality is an idea rooted in actuality." (3) *The theory of sympathetic understanding (Verstehen):* the task of the historian is to understand each historical individuality in its uniqueness, to penetrate past its "superficial appearance" to "its inner structure." There is no place for abstract deductive thinking in this process. Understanding requires two steps: first, "the exact, impartial, critical investigation of events" by the "inquiring intellect"; second, the "intuitive understanding" (*ahnen*) of the inner structure of the historical individuality under study which could not be reached by the first means.

The present translation first appeared in *History and Theory*, VI (1967), 57–71. It is based on the German version which appeared in the *Abhandlungen der Historisch-Philosophischen Klasse der Königlichen Akademie der Wissenschaften aus den Jahren 1820–21* (Berlin, 1822) and was republished in Wilhelm von Humboldt, *Gesammelte Schriften* (Berlin, 1903–1936), IV, 35–56, and in *Werke in fünf Bänden* (Darmstadt, 1960–   ), I, 585–606. It is published here with the permission of *History and Theory*.

1

WILHELM VON HUMBOLDT, "ON THE HISTORIAN'S TASK"

(1821)

The historian's task is to present what actually happened. The more purely and completely he achieves this, the more perfectly has he solved his problem. A simple presentation is at the same time the primary, indispensable condition of his work and the highest achievement he will be able to attain. Regarded in this way, he seems to be merely receptive and reproductive, not himself active and creative.

An event, however, is only partially visible in the world of the senses; the rest has to be added by intuition, inference, and guesswork. The manifestations of an event are scattered, disjointed, isolated; what it is that gives unity to this patchwork, puts the isolated fragment into its proper perspective, and gives shape to the whole, remains removed from direct observation. For observation can perceive circumstances which either accompany or follow one another, but not their inner causal nexus, on

From History and Theory, *VI (1967), 57–71. Translation copyright © 1967 by Wesleyan University. Reprinted by permission of Wesleyan University Press.*

which, after all, their inner truth is solely dependent. If one is trying to talk about the most significant fact, but at the same time attempting strictly to tell only what actually happened, one soon notices how, unless the greatest care is employed in the choice and evaluation of expressions, minute determinants will creep in beyond the actual happening, and will give rise to falsehood and uncertainty. Language itself contributes to this state of affairs since—growing out of the fullness of the soul as it does—it frequently lacks expressions which are free from all connotations. Nothing is rarer, therefore, than a narrative which is literally true; nothing is better proof of a sound, well-ordered, and critical intelligence and of a free, objective attitude. Thus historical truth is, as it were, rather like the clouds which take shape for the eye only at a distance. For this reason, the facts of history are in their several connecting circumstances little more than the results of tradition and scholarship which one has agreed to accept as true, because they—being most highly probable in themselves—also fit best into the context of the whole.

One has, however, scarcely arrived at the skeleton of an event by a crude sorting out of what actually happened. What is so achieved is the necessary basis of history, its raw material, but not history itself. To stop here would be to sacrifice the actual inner truth, well-founded within the causal nexus, for an outward, literal, and seeming truth; it would mean choosing actual error in order to escape the potential danger of error. The truth of any event is predicated on the addition—mentioned above—of that invisible part of every fact, and it is this part, therefore, which the historian has to add. Regarded in this way, he does become active, even creative—not by bringing forth what does not have existence, but in giving shape by his own powers to that which by mere intuition he could not have perceived as it really was. Differently from the poet, but in a way similar to him, he must work the collected fragments into a whole.

It may seem questionable to have the field of the historian touch that of the poet at even one point. However, their activities are undeniably related. For if the historian, as has been said, can only reveal the truth of an event by presentation, by filling in and connecting the disjointed fragments of direct observation, he can do so, like the poet, only through his imagination. The crucial difference, which removes all potential dangers, lies in the fact that the historian subordinates his imagination to experience and the investigation of reality. In this subordination, the imagination does not act as pure fantasy and is, therefore, more properly called the intuitive faculty or connective ability. But this by itself would still assign too low a place to history. The striving for the truth of events seems obvious enough. It is, however, the most difficult attainment conceivable. For if truth were ever conquered completely, all that which determines the reality of things, like a chain of necessity, would lie uncovered. The historian must therefore seek the necessity of events; he must not, like the poet, merely impose on his material the appearance of necessity; rather, he must keep constantly in mind the ideas which are the laws of necessity, because only by being steeped in them can he find evidence of them in any pure inquiry into the real in its reality.

The historian has all the strands of temporal activity and all the expressions of eternal ideas as his province. The whole of existence is, more or less directly, the object of his endeavors, and thus he must pursue all the manifestations of the mind. Speculation, experience, and fiction are, therefore, merely different manifestations of the mind, not distinct activities of it, opposed to and limiting one another.

Thus two methods have to be followed simultaneously in the approach to historical truth; the first is the exact, impartial, critical investigation of events; the second is the connecting of the events explored and the intuitive understanding of them which could not be reached by the first means. To follow only the first path is to miss the essence of truth itself; to neglect this path, however, by overemphasizing the second one is to risk falsification of truth in its details. Even a simple depiction of nature cannot be merely an enumeration and depiction of parts or the measuring of sides and angles; there is also the breath of life in the whole and an inner character which speaks through it which can be neither measured nor merely described. Description of nature, too, will be subjected to the second method, which for such description is the representation of the form of both the universal and the individual existence of natural objects. In history there is likewise no intention of finding something isolated by means of that second method, and even less are there to be any imaginative additions to the material. The historian's mind is merely supposed to understand better the genuinely intelligible material by making its own the structure of all occurrences; thus it must learn to perceive more in that material than could be achieved by the mere operation of the intellect. Everything depends on this fusion of the inquiring intellect and the object of the inquiry. The more profoundly the historian understands mankind and its actions through intuition and study, the more humane his disposition is by nature and circumstances, and the more freely he gives rein to his humanity, the more completely will he solve the problems of his profession. The chronicles prove this point. No one can deny that the better ones among them are based on the most genuine historical truth despite the fact that they contain many factual misrepresentations and many an obvious fairy tale. They are closely related to the older type of so-called memoirs, although in these the close attention paid to the individual already jeopardizes that more general concern with humanity which history requires even when it is dealing with an isolated phenomenon.

Like all other scholarly work history serves many ancillary purposes; but in itself history is no less an art, free and self-contained, than are philosophy and literature. The vast, serried turmoil of the affairs of this world, in part arising out of the nature of the soil, human nature, and the character of nations and individuals, in part springing up out of nowhere as if planted by a miracle, dependent on powers dimly perceived and visibly activated by eternal ideas rooted deeply in the soul of man—all this composes an infinitude which the mind can never press into one single form, but which incites the historian to try just that again and again and gives him the strength to achieve it in part. Just as philosophy seeks the ultimate reason of things, and art the ideal of beauty, so history strives to attain the vision of man's fate in its complete truth, its living abundance and pure clarity—a vision conceived by a soul so fixed upon its object that merely personal opinions, feelings, and standards lose themselves in it and dissolve. To achieve this state of mind and to nourish it is the historian's ultimate goal, but he can reach it only if he has faithfully pursued, as his immediate goal, the simple narration of events.

It is the historian who is supposed to awaken and to stimulate a sensibility for reality, and his activity is defined subjectively by the elaboration of that concept as it is defined objectively by the historical narrative. Every intellectual activity which affects man as a whole possesses something which might be called its essential element, its activating power, the secret of its influence on the mind; and it is so different from the objects affected by it that they often serve merely to bring it to the attention of the mind in new and different ways. In mathematics this essential element consists in isolating number and line; in metaphysics it consists in abstracting from all experience; and in art it is the wonderful manipulation of nature, so that everything in the created work appears to be taken from nature although nothing exactly like it actually exists. The element in which history operates is the sense of reality, and it contains the awareness of the transience of existence in time, and of dependence upon past and present causes; at the same time, there is the consciousness of spiritual freedom and the recognition of reason, so that reality, despite its seeming contingency, is nevertheless bound by an inner necessity. If the mind surveys only one single human life, it will be struck by the different ways in which history stimulates and captivates. Hence the historian, in order to perform the task of his profession, has to compose the narrative of events in such a way that the reader's emotions will be stirred by it as if by reality itself.

It is in this way that history is related to active life. History does not primarily serve us by showing us through specific examples, often misleading and rarely enlightening, what to do and what to avoid. History's true and immeasurable usefulness lies rather in its power to enliven and refine our sense of acting on reality, and this occurs more through the form attached to events than through the events themselves. It prevents the sense of reality from slipping into the realm of pure ideas, and yet subjects

it to ideas. And on this narrow middle path it constantly keeps
alive in the mind the notion that there is no successful intervention in the flow of events except by clearly recognizing the truth
of the predominating trend of ideas at a given time and by adhering to this truth with determination. It is this inner effect that
history must always produce, irrespective of the subject matter,
whether it be the narration of a continuous pattern of events or
of a single event. The historian worthy of his title must show
every event as part of a whole, or, what amounts to the same
thing, must reveal the form of history *per se* in every event
described

This brings us to a more precise discussion of the concept of
presentation required of the historian. The fabric of events is
spread out before him in seeming confusion, merely divided up
chronologically and geographically. He must separate the necessary from the accidental, uncover its inner structure, and make
visible the truly activating forces in order to give his presentation the form on which depends, not some imaginary or dispens-
able philosophical value or some poetical charm, but its truth and
accuracy, its first and most essential requisite. For events are only
half understood or are distorted, if one stops with their superficial
appearance; moreover, the common observer constantly imbues
this appearance with errors and half-truths. These are dispelled
only by the true form of events which reveals itself solely to the
historian whose eyesight is naturally keen and has been sharpened
by study and practice. What must he do to be thus favored in
this undertaking?

An historical presentation, like an artistic presentation, is an
imitation of nature. The basis of both is the recognition of the
true form, the discovery of the necessary, the elimination of the
accidental. We must, therefore, not disdain to apply the more
readily recognizable method of the artist to an understanding of
the more dubious method employed by the historian.

The imitation of organic form can take place in two ways:
either by direct representation of its external shape, as exact as
eye and hand will permit, or, from within, based on antecedent

study of the way in which the outward shape emerges from the idea and structure of the whole and by abstracting from the proportions of the outward shape. In this process of abstraction the form is first recognized in a way quite different from its perception by the non-artistic eye, and is then reborn through the imagination in such a way that, apart from its literal coincidence with nature, it contains yet another higher truth within itself. For it is the greatest virtue of a work of art to reveal the inner truth of forms which is hidden in their actual appearance. Both of the ways of imitation just mentioned are, for all times and all genres, the criteria of false or true art. There are two peoples, the Egyptians and the Mexicans, far removed from each other in time and place, both of which, nevertheless, represent starting-points of civilization for us, where this difference between false and true art is clearly visible. Several similarities have been shown, and I think correctly, to exist between these two peoples. Both had to overcome that terrible obstacle to all art, the use of pictures as letters; and there is not one single example of the correct perspective of the human figure to be found in the paintings or drawings of the Mexicans, whereas there is style in even the most insignificant hieroglyph of the Egyptians.[1] This is quite natural.

---

[1] My intention here was merely to support with an example the remarks about art; I am, therefore, far from making a definite pronouncement about the Mexicans. There are sculptures by them, like the head in the local Royal Museum [in Berlin—Ed.] that my brother [Alexander von Humboldt—Ed.] brought back with him, which allow a more favorable judgment about their ability to produce art. Considering that our knowledge of the Mexicans does not date back very far and that the pictures we know are comparatively recent, it would be very risky to judge their art by objects which may very well have originated during a period of extreme decadence. That monstrosities of art may exist side by side with its highest achievements was vividly brought home to me by the bronze figurines found in Sardinia, which obviously originated with the Greeks or Romans, although they yield nothing to Mexican art in their lack of proportion. There is a collection of such figurines at the Collegium Romanum in Rome. There are also other reasons to believe that the Mexicans had achieved a much higher

There is hardly any evidence of the dim perception of inner form in the Mexican drawings, nor is there any knowledge of organic structure; everything, therefore, tends to become imitative of outward appearance. Inferior art must, however, fail completely in its attempt to trace the outer contours and must consequently lead to distortions; whereas the search for proportion and symmetry shines through even the inadequacies of hand and instruments.

If you want to understand the contour of form from within, you must go back to form *per se* and to the essence of the organism, i.e. to mathematics and natural science. The latter provides the definition, the former the idea of the form. To both must be added, as a third linking element, the expression of the soul, of spiritual life. Pure form, however, as seen in the symmetry of parts and the equilibrium of proportions, is the most essential thing, as it is the first thing accessible to the mind, which, when still fresh and youthful, is more attracted by pure scientific knowledge and can more easily penetrate it than the practical knowledge which requires all kinds of preparation. This becomes apparent in works of Egyptian and Greek visual art. From all of them there first emerges a purity and rigor of form which is not afraid of severity; there emerge the regularity of circles and semi-circles, the acuteness of angles, and definiteness of lines; it is on this sure ground that the remaining outer contour rests. All this is already lucidly in evidence even where an exact knowledge of organic structure is still missing. And, when the artist had come to achieve mastery of structure and knew how to create gracefulness and to breathe divine expression into his work, he would never have dreamed of enchanting by appearances without having taken care for the underlying form. That which is essential remained for him at once of first and highest importance.

The complexity and beauty of life is, therefore, no help to the artist if it is not balanced in the solitude of his imagination by the inspiring love of pure form. One can thus understand how art

---

cultural level at an earlier time and in another region; this is also indicated by the traces of their migrations, the evidence for which is carefully collected and compared in my brother's works.

would originate with a people whose life was hardly distinguished by flexibility and charm or beauty, but whose thought turned to mathematics and mechanics at an early time, a people who had a liking for gigantic buildings, very simple but sternly regular, and who also applied the architectonics of proportions to the imitation of the human figure, battling with a resistant medium for each inch of line they carved in it. The situation of the Greeks was different in every respect. They were surrounded by exciting beauty, life which was highly and at times extravagantly versatile, and a complex and rich mythology. Their tools easily fashioned every shape from the sculpted marble, as from wood in the earliest days. All the more admirable is the profundity and seriousness of their artistic sensibility which made them even elevate Egyptian austerity by a more thorough knowledge of organic structure, without succumbing to any of the enticements of superficial charm.

It may seem strange to base art not exclusively on the richness of life but also upon the dryness of mathematical abstractions. It remains true, nevertheless; and the artist would not need the inspiration of genius if it were not his task to transform the profound seriousness of strictly determining ideas into the appearance of free play. There is, moreover, a captivating spell in the pure apperception of mathematical truths, of the eternal relationships of time and space, whether manifested in sounds, numbers, or lines. Their contemplation also offers a continually renewed satisfaction in itself, by the discovery of always new relationships and of problems which can always be completely solved. It is only the premature and multifarious application of pure science that weakens in us the sensitivity to the beauty of its form. Artistic imitation, therefore, has its origin in ideas, and truth of form appears to the artist only through these ideas. The same process must occur in historical imitation, because in both cases it is nature that has to be imitated. There remains only the question whether there are ideas capable of guiding the historian and, if so, of what kind.

Here we have to proceed with great caution lest the mere mention of ideas already impair historical accuracy in its pure form. For although both artist and historian imitate and represent, their aims are quite different. The artist merely takes away from reality its ephemeral appearance, merely touches reality in order to fly away from it; the historian is searching for reality alone and has to plunge deeply into it. It is precisely for this reason, and because the historian cannot be satisfied merely with the loose external relationships of the individual events, that he has to proceed to the center of things from which their true nexus can be understood. He has to seek the truth of an event in a way similar to the artist's seeking the truth of form. Events in history are even less obviously perceptible than appearances in the world of the senses and cannot be simply read off. An understanding of them is the combined product of their constitution and the sensibility supplied by the beholder. Here, as in art, not everything can be derived logically, one thing from another, by mere operation of the intellect, and dissected into concepts. One can only grasp that which is right, subtle, and hidden, because the mind is properly attuned to grasping it. The historian, like the draftsman, will produce only caricatures if he merely depicts the specific circumstances of an event by connecting them with each other as they seemingly present themselves. He must render strict account of their inner nexus, must establish for himself a picture of the active forces, must recognize their trends at a given moment, must inquire into the relationship of both forces and trends to the existing state of affairs and to the changes that have preceded it. To do this, however, the historian must be familiar in the first place with the conditions, the operation and interdependence of these forces, as a complete understanding of the specific always presupposes a knowledge of the general, under which it is comprehended. It is in this sense that the understanding of events must be guided by ideas. It is, of course, self-evident that these ideas emerge from the mass of events themselves, or, to be more precise, originate in the mind through contemplation of these events undertaken in a truly historical spirit: the ideas are not borrowed by history like an alien addition, a mistake so easily made by so-called philosophical history. Historical truth is, generally speaking, much more threatened by philosophical than by artistic handling, since the latter is at least accustomed to granting freedom to its subject matter. Philosophy dictates a goal to events. This search for final causes, even though it may be deduced from the essence of man and nature itself, distorts and falsifies every independent judgment of the characteristic working of forces. Teleological history, therefore, never attains the living truth of universal destiny because the individual always has to reach the pinnacle of his own development within the span of his fleeting existence; teleological history can, for that reason, never properly locate the ultimate goal of events in living things but has to seek it, as it were, in dead institutions and in the concept of an ideal totality—whether it be in the growing universality of the cultivation and population of the earth, the increasing civilization of the people and their increasing sociability, the eventual achievement of some state of perfection of human society, or some other idea of this kind. The activities and happiness of the individual may depend directly on all this; yet, whatever any generation receives of these achievements of its predecessors is no proof of its vitality and not even always immediately material for the intellectual exercise of this vitality. For even those things which are the fruit of the mind and of temperament—scholarship, art, moral institutions—lose their spirituality and become materialistic unless the mind constantly revives them. All these things partake in the nature of thought, which can only be sustained by being thought. It is to the active and productive forces, therefore, that the historian must turn. Here he stays within his proper domain. What the historian can do in order to *bring*, engraved on his soul, that form to the observation of the labyrinthine events of world history through which alone true connections will emerge, is to *abstract* that form from the events themselves. The contradiction seemingly contained in this statement disappears on closer consideration. All understanding presupposes in the person who understands, as a condition of its possibility, an analogue of that which will actually be understood later: an original, antecedent congruity between subject and object. Understanding is not merely an extension of the subject, nor is it merely a borrowing from the object; it is, rather, both simultaneously. Understanding always is the application of a pre-existent general idea to something new and specific. When two beings are completely separated by a chasm, there is no bridge of communication between them; and in order to understand each other, they must, in some other sense, have already understood each other. In the case of history that antecedent of understanding is quite obvious, since everything which is active in world history is also moving within the human heart. The more deeply, therefore, the soul of a nation feels everything human, and the more tenderly, purely, and diversely it is moved by this, the greater will be its chances to produce historians in the true sense of the word. To this condition one must add the critical practice which tests and corrects preconceived ideas against the object until both clarity and certainty emerge through this repeated interaction.

In this way, through a study of the creative forces of world history, the historian conceives for himself a general picture of the form of the connection of all events, and it is within this realm that the ideas discussed above are contained. They are not being projected into history, but are the essence of history itself. For every force, living or dead, acts according to the laws of its nature, and all occurrences are inseparably linked in space and time.

Within this context history appears like a dead clockwork moved by mechanical forces and governed by inexorable laws, no matter how variedly and vitally it moves before our eyes. For one event causes another, the extent and character of every effect are determined by its causes, and even the will of man, seemingly free, is determined by circumstances which were inexorably established long before his birth or even before the growth of the nation to which he belongs. To chart the course of the past, or even the future, on the basis of each single event seems impossible not in itself but rather because there is insufficient knowledge about a mass of connective links. Yet it has long been recognized that the exclusive pursuit of this method would lead directly away from an insight into the truly creative forces, that the central element in every activity containing something of life is precisely what defies calculation, and that seemingly mechanical determination is nevertheless fundamentally subject to free and active impulses.

In addition to the mechanical determination of one event by another, therefore, the distinctive nature of forces must receive more of our attention, and here the first level to be considered is that of physiological activity. All living forces, men as well as plants, nations as well as individuals, mankind as well as individual peoples, have in common certain qualities, kinds of development, and natural laws. This is even true for products of the mind, such as literature, art, morals, or the outward form of human society, insofar as they are based on continuous activity with a specific tradition. The same truth is evident in the step by step ascension to a peak and the gradual decline from it, or in the transition from a certain perfection to certain types of degeneracy, and so forth. There are undoubtedly many historical insights contained in such studies, yet they do not make visible the creative principle itself, but merely recognize a form to which that principle must submit unless it finds in that form a vehicle for its own upward flight.

The psychological forces of multiple, intermeshing human abilities, emotions, inclinations, and passions are even harder to chart in their course. They are little subject to discernible laws and can be captured only by certain analogies. Above all other things, they concern the historian as the most direct mainsprings of action and the most immediate causes of the events resulting from action; and they are most frequently appealed to in the explanation of events. It is precisely this point of view, however, which requires the greatest care. It is farthest from having world-historic dimensions; it diminishes the tragedy of world history to a banal drama of mediocrity, tempts one all too easily to tear individual occurrences out of their total context, and puts petty commotions of personal motives in the place of universal destiny. This viewpoint—and the line of inquiry proceeding from it—locates everything in the individual, and yet fails to recognize the uniqueness and depth, the essential nature of the individual. For the individual cannot be thus split up, analyzed and judged according to experiences which, having been derived from the multitude, are supposed to be applicable to the multitude. The unique force of the individual runs the gamut of all human emotions and passions; it also imprints upon them its own stamp and character.

One could now attempt to classify historians according to the three views indicated above. None of them by itself, not even a combination of all of them taken together, would exhaust the characterization of the truly original historian. These views do not, after all, exhaust the causes of the relationship of events, and the basic idea, which alone makes possible the understanding of all events in their complete truth, does not lie within their purview. They encompass only these intelligible phenomena of inorganic, organic, and spiritual nature which reproduce themselves in repetitive order, but not the free and independent impulse of an original force. Consequently, these occurrences bear witness only to regularly recurrent developments unfolding according to recognized laws and verifiable experience. That, however, which arises like a miracle and which may be accompanied by mechanical, physiological, and psychological explanations, though not deducible from any one of them, remains not only unexplained but unrecognized in this framework.

However one proceeds, the realm of appearances can only be understood from a point outside of it, and the circumspect stepping outside of it is as free from danger as error is certain, if one blindly locks oneself up in it. Universal history cannot be understood without world governance.

Adherence to this point of view brings with it the considerable advantage that we do not believe the understanding of events to be completely achieved by explanations taken from the realm of nature. This does little, incidentally, to make the final, most difficult, and most important part of the historian's work any easier. For he has no special faculty for inquiring directly into the plans of world governance, and every attempt to do so is only likely to lead him into errors like the search for final causes. The laws governing events, although situated outside of the process of nature, reveal themselves nevertheless in those events. They do so by means which are not themselves phenomenal objects but are attached to them and can be perceived in them, like non-corporeal beings which one never perceives unless one leaves the realm of phenomena and enters mentally into that realm where they originate. The ultimate condition for the solution of the historian's problem, then, is tied to the investigation of these laws which govern events.

The number of creative forces in history is not limited to those directly evident in events. Even after the historian has investigated them all, separately and in their inter-relationships— the nature and changes of the soil, the variations of climate, the intellectual capacity and character of nations, the even more particular characters of individuals, the influences of the arts and sciences, and the profoundly incisive and widespread influences of social institutions—there still remains an even more powerfully active principle which, though not directly visible, imparts to these forces themselves their impetus and direction: that is, ideas which by their very nature lie outside the compass of the finite, and yet pervade and dominate every part of world history.

It is beyond doubt that such ideas reveal themselves, and that certain phenomena, which cannot be explained merely as operating according to the laws of nature, owe their existence exclusively to the power of these ideas. It is equally beyond doubt that there is a point at which the historian is directed to a realm beyond the world of events in order to perceive their true configuration.

Such an idea manifests itself in two ways: on the one hand as a trend which affects many particulars, in different places and under different circumstances, and which is initially barely perceptible, but gradually becomes visible and finally irresistible; on the other hand as a creation of energies which cannot be deduced in all their scope and majesty from their attendant circumstances.

One can find examples of the former without difficulty; there has hardly been a time when they have not been recognized. It is, however, highly probable that a number of events, which at the moment are still being explained in more material and mechanical terms, will have to be viewed in this way.

Examples of the creation of energies, of phenomena for the

explanation of which attendant circumstances are insufficient, are the eruption of art in its pure form in Egypt, as mentioned above, and, perhaps even more so, the sudden development of a free and yet mutually limiting individualism in Greece, in conjunction with which language, literature, and the arts suddenly confront us in a perfection the gradual growth of which we seek in vain. It has always seemed to me the most admirable aspect of Greek culture, and also the key to understanding it, that the Greeks remained free from the tyranny of castes, although everything important which they used had come to them from nations divided into caste systems. They always retained something analogous to castes, but transformed the harsh concept of caste into the milder ones of education and free associations; they brought the differences of individuality to active co-operation through a division, more complex than that experienced by any other nation, of the original national spirit, descending into tribes, nations, and separate cities and ascending again to reunification. In this way Greece established an idea of national individuality which existed neither before it nor since; and as the secret of all existence lies in individuality, so all world-historic progress of mankind is based on the degree of freedom and on the nature of its reciprocal effects.

It is true that an idea can only appear in conjunction with nature, and thus, even in such cases, we can show a whole series of favorable causes and a transition from a lesser to a higher state of perfection; all this can justifiably be assumed despite the vast lacunae of our knowledge. But that does not lessen the miraculous element in the taking of the first step, the first flashing of the spark. Without this, favorable circumstances could not become operative, and no amount of practice or of gradual improvement, even for centuries, would lead to any fulfillment. The idea can entrust itself only to an individual spiritual force, but the fact that the seed which the idea implants in the force develops in its own way, that this way remains the same whatever other individual it is transferred to, and that the plant issuing forth from it reaches its bloom and fruition of itself and then withers and disappears no matter how the circumstances and individuals involved may develop: all this shows that it is the independent nature of the idea which completes its course in the realm of phenomena. Forms achieve actuality in this way in all the different types of existence and of mental creativity, in which some aspect of eternity is reflected and whose incursion into life brings forth new appearances. In the physical world—and it is always a safeguarding device to trace the analogies in the physical world when investigating that of the spiritual—we must not expect the creation of such important new forms. The differences of organization have already assumed their permanent shapes, and although these differences never exhaust their organic individuality within such forms, their finer nuances are not perceptible directly and are hardly visible at all in their effects on the realm of ideas. The creation of the physical world takes place in one moment in space, that of the world of ideas gradually in time, or at least the former finds its point of rest at an earlier moment where creation is superseded by uniform reproduction. Organic life is much closer to the life of the mind than is physical form or structure, and the laws governing both are more readily and mutually applicable. This is not so obvious in a state of vigorous health, although quite probably even in this state there are changes of circumstance and direction taking place which follow hidden causes and determine and re-determine, epoch by epoch, organic life. But in the abnormal states of life, as in types of disease, there is doubtless an analogy to trends, which arise suddenly or gradually without explicable causes, seem to follow their own laws, and refer to a hidden connection of all things. All of this is substantiated by many observations, but it may take a very long time before they can be made useful for history.

Every human individuality is an idea rooted in actuality, and this idea shines forth so brilliantly from some individuals that it seems to have assumed the form of an individual merely to use it as a vehicle for expressing itself. When one traces human activity, after all its determining causes have been subtracted there remains something original which transforms these influences instead of being suffocated by them; in this very element there is an incessantly active drive to give outward shape to its inner, unique nature. It is the same with the individuality of nations, and in many areas of history the inner drive is more easily recognizable in them than in individuals, since man in certain periods and under certain circumstances develops, as it were, in groups. The spiritual principle of individuality therefore remains active in the midst of the history of nations guided by needs, passions, and apparent accidents, and it is more powerful than those elements. This principle seeks to express its innate idea, and it succeeds as the most fragile plant, by the organic expansion of its cells, will succeed in splitting walls which had otherwise withstood the wear of centuries. In addition to the directions which nations and individuals impart to mankind by their actions, they leave behind them forms of spiritual individuality which are more enduring and effective than deeds or events.

There are, however, also ideal forms which, although they do not constitute human individuality, are related to it, if only indirectly. Language is one of them. For although every language reflects the spirit of its people, it also has an earlier, more independent base, and its uniqueness and internal cohesion are so powerful and determining that its independence is more influential than influenced, so that every important language appears as a unique vehicle for the creation and communication of ideas.

The original and eternal ideas of everything that can be thought achieve existence and power in a manner even more pure and complete: they achieve beauty in all spiritual and corporeal shapes, truth in the ineluctable working of every force according to its innate law, and justice in the inexorable process of events which eternally judge and punish themselves.

Human judgment cannot perceive the plans of the governance of the world directly but can only divine them in the ideas through which they manifest themselves, and therefore all history is the realization of an idea. In the idea resides both its motivating force and its goal. And thus, merely by steeping oneself in the contemplation of the creative forces one travels along a more correct route to those final causes to which the intellect naturally aspires. The goal of history can only be the actualization of the idea which is to be realized by mankind in every way and in all shapes in which the finite form may enter into a union with the idea. The course of events can end only at the point where both are no longer capable of further mutual integration.

Thus we have arrived at the ideas which must guide the historian, and we can now return to the comparison undertaken above between the historian and the artist. What knowledge of nature and the study of organic structures are to the latter, research into the forces appearing in life as active and guiding is to the former; what to the latter are proportion, symmetry, and the concept of pure form, to the former are the ideas which unfold themselves serenely and majestically in the nexus of world events without, however, being part of them. In its final, yet simplest solution the historian's task is the presentation of the struggle of an idea to realize itself in actuality. For the idea will not always be successful in its first attempt; not infrequently will it become perverted because it is unable to master completely the actively resisting matter.

There are two things which the course of this inquiry has attempted to keep firmly in mind: that there is an idea, not itself directly perceptible, in everything that happens, but that this idea can be recognized only in the events themselves. The historian must, therefore, not exclude the power of the idea from his presentation by seeking everything exclusively in his material sources; he must at least leave room for the activity of the idea. Going beyond that, moreover, he must be spiritually receptive to the idea and actively open to perceiving and appropriating it. Above all, he must take great care not to attribute to reality arbitrarily created ideas of his own, and not to sacrifice any of the living richness of the parts in his search for the coherent pattern of the whole. This freedom and subtlety of approach must become so much a part of his nature that he will bring them to bear on the investigation of every event. For no event is separated completely from the general nexus of things, and part of every occurrence lies beyond the pale of direct perception, as we have shown above. If the historian lacks this freedom of approach, he cannot perceive events in their scope and depth; if he lacks subtlety and tact, he will destroy their simple and living truth.

PART II

The Idealistic Theory
of Historiography

Leopold von Ranke's

Formulation

      Unlike Humboldt, Ranke did not publish his theoretical views regarding the character of history and historical science. The one exception was his famous inaugural lecture "On the Relationship and Difference Between History and Politics" delivered in 1836 upon his assumption of a full professorship at the University of Berlin. Ranke did, however, begin many of his lecture courses with general theoretical observations. In the winter semester of 1831–1832 he devoted an entire course to "The Study of History." His remarks on the theory of history and of historical knowledge are buried in the extensive lecture notes he left behind. We are here presenting five excerpts from those notes.

      In all five selections Ranke defends the autonomy of history against the claims of the philosophy of history. Philosophy, he explains in Selection 2 ("On the Relations of History and Philosophy"), proceeds through abstraction and history through the perception of the particular. The philosopher fails to grasp the concrete living reality of the individuals who compose history, which can never be "characterized through only one idea or one word" or "circumscribed by a concept." In contrast, the historian is filled with "a feeling for and a joy in the particular in and by itself." But while concentrating on the "original genius" that expresses itself in each individual, the historian keeps "his eyes open for the general." He will not approach the particular with preconceived ideas as would the philosopher. Rather, the particular itself will reveal the general to him because the external manifestations of every individuality (e.g., a state) rest on a spiritual basis and possess a spiritual content. In contrast to the philosopher, the historian thus keeps to the facts. But in Selection 4 ("The Pitfalls of a Philosophy of History"), Ranke rejects a purely fact-oriented method which "concentrates mainly on externals." "The particular," he suggests in Selection 6 ("The Role of the Particular and the General in the Study of Universal History"), "is always related to a larger context." Critical method and broad synthesis can and must always go together in historical inquiry and writing. "Without a general view research would become sterile."

The methodological implications of Ranke's position are spelled out in greater detail in Selection 3 ("On the Character of Historical Science"). The historian can approach the general through the particular because he "recognizes something infinite in every existence: in every condition, in every being, something eternal, coming from God," which constitutes "its vital principle." Like Humboldt, Ranke believes that the historian must go beyond the external manifestations of historical phenomena to grasp the essential principle that reveals itself to his critical contemplation. "In the last analysis every unity is a spiritual one (*geistig*)," and because it is spiritual it is capable of "spiritual apperception." The road to this apperception begins with the critical confrontation of historical reality as revealed in the available documents. But it does not end there. Ranke calls upon the historian to have a broad "universal interest" in all aspects of social and intellectual life, not merely in politics and war as too many historians have had in the past. The historian must seek the causal nexus between events, taking care however not to project an extraneous image onto the past. The observation of the events themselves will reveal their inner connectedness. Objectivity means impartiality; that is, it requires us to recognize the parties in any historical struggle in their own terms, to "understand them before we judge them." In the final analysis the task of history is the same as that of philosophy, namely, understanding the ultimate things. "If philosophy were what it ought to be, if history were perfectly clear and complete, then they would fully coincide with each other." But history approaches the problem of the coherence of universal history by *confronting* reality—not, as in philosophy, by subordinating it to a scheme. Unlike philosophy, it recognizes that the solution to the riddle of world history is known only to God: we can only divine it and approach it from a distance.

The emphasis on the individual as an irreducible entity runs through Ranke's discussion of the process of history in Selection 5 ("On Progress in History"). Here, as in the other selections, Ranke rejects a philosophy of history which sees the epochs of history as stepping stones in a great cosmic process. "Every epoch," he asserts, "is immediate to God, and its worth is not at all based on what derives from it, but rests in its own existence, in its own self." This emphasis on the objective equality of all epochs appears in contrast to Ranke's assertion in Selection 2 ("On the Relation of History and Philosophy") and in the preface to the *Universal History* (Selection 13) that only certain ages and nations deserve the historian's attention. Both in Selection 5 ("On Progress in History") and in Selection 6 ("The Role of the Particular and the General") Ranke seeks to reconcile the stress on individual spontaneity and freedom with a recognition of the role of necessity in history. Certain "leading ideas" or "great tendencies" give continuity and coherence to history. But these tendencies "can only be described"; they "cannot be

subsumed under one concept." Unlike Hegel, Ranke sees the
meaning of history not in a unified process but rather in the "multiplicity of developments" in which mankind expresses itself.
None of the following selections was published during
Ranke's lifetime, hence the titles in the present edition are our
own. Selections 2 and 6 (respectively, "On the Relations of History and Philosophy" and "The Role of the Particular and the
General in the Study of Universal History") were first published
by Alfred Dove in the introduction to Part IX, Section II, of the
Weltgeschichte (Leipzig, 1888). Selection 5 ("On Progress in
History") is taken from the introductory lecture in the series of
lectures which Ranke delivered in 1854 to King Maximilian II
of Bavaria, entitled "On the Epochs of Modern History." These
lectures were posthumously reconstructed by Alfred Dove on
the basis of stenographic notes and were published in Part IX,
Section II, of the *Weltgeschichte*. Selections 3 and 4 ("On the
Character of Historical Science" and "The Pitfalls of a Philosophy of History," respectively) were originally published by Eberhard Kessel in the *Historische Zeitschrift*, volume CLXXVIII
(1954).[1] The selections are being published with the permission
of the *Historische Zeitschrift* and of Professor Kessel. Professor
Walther Peter Fuchs, co-editor of Leopold von Ranke, *Aus Werk
und Nachlass* has graciously made available to us his own (as of
yet unpublished) readings of these two manuscripts. We have
compared Professor Fuchs's readings with Professor Kessel's versions and have indicated the divergences in the readings which
are relevant to the English translation.
All five selections have been translated by Wilma A. Iggers
for this volume.

---

[1] A part of Selection 3 ("On the Character of Historical Science")
was first published by Erich Mülbe in his doctoral dissertation, "Selbst-
zeugnisse Rankes über seine historische Theorie und Methode im
Zusammenhang der zeitgenössischen Geistesrichtungen," University
of Berlin, 1930.

2

ON THE RELATIONS
OF HISTORY
AND PHILOSOPHY

(A Manuscript of the 1830s)

Often a certain conflict has been observed between an immature philosophy and history. By way of *a priori* thinking, conclusions were drawn about what must be. Without being aware that such ideas are exposed to many doubts, men went about trying to find these ideas again in the history of the world. Out of the infinite number of facts those were then chosen which seemed to confirm these ideas. This kind of historical writing has also been called philosophy of history.

One of the ideas with which philosophy again and again confronts history as an irrefutable claim is that mankind is on an uninterrupted road to progress, in a steady development toward perfection. Fichte, one of the foremost philosophers in this field, assumes five epochs, a world plan as he says—reason ruling through instinct, reason ruling through law, emancipation from the authority of reason, reason as science, and reason as art. If this or a similar scheme were to any extent true, then general

From Alfred Dove's Vorwort *in* Weltgeschichte, Theil IX, Abt. 2, *pp. vii–xi; translated by Wilma A. Iggers.*

history would have to follow the road of progress which the human race followed in the indicated direction from one age to the next. The sole subject matter of history would then be the development of such concepts as they appear and manifest themselves in the world of phenomena. But this is by no means the case. For one thing, the philosophers themselves have extraordinarily varied opinions about the nature and selection of these supposedly ruling ideas. But they very wisely focus only on a few peoples in world history while considering the lives of all the rest as nothing, as a mere supplement. Otherwise it could not be hidden for a moment that from the beginning to this day the peoples of the world have been in the most varied conditions.

There are two ways of acquiring knowledge about human affairs—through the perception of the particular and through abstraction. The one is the way of philosophy, the other that of history. There is no other way, and even revelation encompasses both abstract doctrines and history. These two sources of knowledge are therefore to be kept clearly distinguished. Nevertheless, equally mistaken are those historians who view all of history merely as an immense aggregate of facts to be committed to memory, meaning that particulars are strung to particulars and all of these held together only by a common moral principle. I am of the opinion, rather, that historical science at its best is both called upon and able to rise in its own way from the investigation and contemplation of the particular to a general view of events and to the recognition of their objectively existing relatedness.

Two qualities are necessary to form a true historian. The first is a feeling for and a joy in the particular in and by itself. If he has a real fondness for the race of these manifold creatures of which we ourselves are a part—for this being which is always the same and yet forever different, which is so good and so evil, so noble and so beastly, so cultured and so coarse, so very much directed toward eternity and so subjected to the moment, so happy and so miserable, satisfied with little and full of desire for all—and if he has a fondness for the living phenomenon of man in general, then he will enjoy observing how man has always sought to live, regardless of the course of events. He will try to follow attentively the virtues which man has sought, the deficiencies which can be seen in him, his fortune and misfortune, the development of his nature under such diverse circumstances, and his institutions and mores. He will try to comprehend all—also the kings under whom the generations have lived, the sequence of events, and the development of major enterprises—without any purpose other than joy in individual life, as one takes joy in flowers without thinking to which of Linné's classes or of Oken's families they belong;[1] briefly put, without thinking how the whole appears in the particular.

This, however, is not all. It is necessary that the historian keep his eyes open for the general. He will not have preconceived ideas as does the philosopher, but rather while he observes the particular, the course which the development of the world in general has taken will be revealed to him. This development, however, does not relate to general concepts which may have predominated in this or that age, but to entirely different things. There is no people on earth which has remained without contact with others. In this relationship, which depends on its own peculiar character, a people enters world history, and it is this relationship which must be stressed in general history. Now some people on earth have had more power than others. They have exerted a preeminent influence on the rest. The transformations therefore which the world has experienced for good or for evil are likely to have come primarily from them. Consequently, we must direct our attention not to the concepts according to which some men appear as dominant forces but to the peoples themselves that have actively made their mark in history; to the influence they had on each other; to the struggles they waged with each other; to the way they developed in the midst of these peaceful or warlike relationships. For it would be infinitely wrong to seek in the struggles of historical powers only the work of brute force, and thus to grasp only the transitory in its external manifestation: no state has ever existed without a spiritual basis and

---

[1] Carl von Linné (1707–1778), also known as Carolus Linnaeus, Swedish botanist; Lorenz Oken (1779–1851), German naturalist.

a spiritual content. In power itself a spiritual essence manifests itself. An original genius, which has its own life, fulfills conditions more or less peculiar to itself and creates a circle of effective activity for itself. It is the task of history to observe this life, which cannot be characterized through only one idea or one word. The spirit that manifests itself in the world cannot be circumscribed by a concept. Rather, its presence fills all the limits of its existence. Nothing is accidental in it. Its appearance has its foundation in everything.

3

ON THE CHARACTER
OF HISTORICAL SCIENCE

(A Manuscript of the 1830s)

History is distinguished from all other sciences in that it is also an art.

History is a science in collecting, finding, penetrating; it is an art because it recreates and portrays that which it has found and recognized. Other sciences are satisfied simply with recording what has been found; history requires the ability to recreate.

As a science, history is related to philosophy, as an art, to poetry. The difference is that, in keeping with their nature, philosophy and poetry move within the realm of the ideal while history has to rely on reality. If one assigned philosophy the task of penetrating the image which has appeared in time, it would be involved in discovering causality and conceptualizing the core of existence: and is philosophy of history not also his-

"Idee der Universalhistorie," edited by Eberhard Kessel in Historische Zeitschrift, *CLXXVIII (1954), 290–301; translated by Wilma A. Iggers and published with the permission of Professor Kessel and the* Historische Zeitschrift. *Compared with Professor Walther Peter Fuchs's unpublished reading of the manuscript.*

tory? If philosophy of history would assign to poetry the task of reproducing past life, then it would be history.

History is distinguished from poetry and philosophy not with regard to its capacity but by its given subject matter, which imposes conditions and is subject to empiricism. History brings both together in a third element peculiar only to itself. History is neither the one nor the other, but demands a union of the intellectual forces active in both philosophy and poetry under the condition that the last two be directed away from their concern with the ideal to the real.

There are nations which do not have the ability to master this element. India had philosophy; she did not have history.

It is strange how, among the Greeks, history developed out of poetry and then emancipated itself from poetry. The Greeks had a theory of history which, while not equal by far to their practice, was nevertheless significant. Some stressed the scientific character more, others the artistic, but nobody denied the necessity of uniting the two. Their theory moves between both elements and cannot decide for either. Quintilian still said: "Historia est proxima poetis et quodammodo carmen solutum."[1]

In modern times one has, in cases of doubt, dealt only with the element of reality or has insisted on science as the sole principle. One has gone so far as to make history disappear as a part of philosophy. However, as has been said, history must be science and art at the same time. History is never the one without the other. But it is possible for the one or the other to be more pronounced. In lectures history can, of course, appear only as a science. For just this reason it is necessary that we undertake presently to deal with the idea of history.

Art rests on itself: its existence proves its validity. On the other hand, science must be totally worked out to its very concept and must be clear to its core.

Therefore, I would like to clarify the idea of world history in

---

[1] *Institutio Oratoria* X. i. 31: "History is akin to the poets and is, so to speak, a prose poem." *Solutum* in this context means free of metrical restrictions.

some preliminary lectures—by dealing in succession with the historical principle, the scope, and the unity of world history.[2]

I. Of The Historical Principle

They talk about what it is that justifies the historian's efforts in themselves. Not with regard to life. His effort is recognized as necessary, and it would be useless to speak about its utility since nobody doubts it. Society, the interrelatedness of things, demands it. But we must raise ourselves to a higher level. To justify our science against the claims of philosophy, we seek to relate to the sublime. We search for a principle from which history would receive a unique life of its own. To grasp this principle we shall consider history in its struggle with philosophy. We are speaking of that type of philosophy which has reached its results by way of speculation and which claims to dominate history.

But what are these claims? Fichte, among others, expressed them thus: "If the philosopher is to deduce the phenomena which are possible in experience from the unity of his presupposed concept, then it is clear that he needs no experience at all for his work. Remaining freely within the limits of philosophy without regard for any experience, he must be able *a priori* to describe all of time and all its possible epochs *a priori*" He demands of philosophy:[3] a unified idea of all of life which is divided into various epochs, each of which is comprehensible abstractly or through the others, just as each of these special epochs is again a unified concept of a special age—which manifests itself in manifold phenomena.

It turns out that the philosopher, starting from a truth, which has been found elsewhere and in a way peculiar to him as a philosopher, constructs all of history for himself: how it must have taken place according to his concept of mankind. Not satisfied to test whether his idea is right or wrong, without deceiving

---

[2] The passage beginning "by dealing . . ." is garbled in Kessel's reading and has been translated here from Fuchs's reading.

[3] Fuchs's reading: He demands of the philosopher.

himself, in terms of the course of events which have really occurred, he undertakes to subordinate the very events to his idea.
Indeed, he recognizes the truth of history only insofar as it subordinates itself to his idea. This is a mere construct of history.

Were this procedure correct, history would lose all independence. It would be ruled simply by a proposition derived from
pure philosophy and would stand and fall with the latter's truth.
All that which is peculiarly interesting about history would disappear. Everything worthy of knowledge would seek only to
know to what extent the philosophic principle can be demonstrated in history: to what extent the progress (*Fortgang*) of mankind, seen *a priori*, takes place. But it would be of no interest
at all to delve into the events which have taken place or even to
want to know how men lived and thought at a certain time. Only
the totality of the concept which had once been alive[4] in the observable history of man would be of interest. It would never be
possible to reach certainty about the course of universal history
through the study of history. The only possible variations would
lie in splitting concepts, in deducing the lower from the higher.
It suffices to say that history would become dependent, without
an inherent interest of its own, and that the wellspring of its life
would dry up. It would hardly be worthwhile to devote study to
history since it would already be implicit in the philosophic
concept.

These claims have in earlier times been raised by theology
which, too, on the basis of what was unquestionably a misunderstanding, wanted to divide all of human history into a few
periods based on sin, salvation, and millenium, or into the four
monarchies prophesied by Daniel. It thus sought to capture the
totality of phenomena in a few propositions contained in revelation—as theology understood revelation.

In either way, history would lose all scientific footing and
character: it would be impossible to speak of a principle of its
own from which history would derive its life.

But we notice that history remains in steady opposition to

---

[4] Fuchs's reading: which had become alive.

these claims. Indeed, even philosophy has never yet been able to exercise its rule. As far as printed works are concerned, I have not found that any philosophy has given even the slightest appearance of having taken control or succeeded in deducing the diversity of phenomena from a speculative concept; for the reality of fact eludes and escapes the concept of speculation in all respects.

Besides, we find that history has always opposed those claims with its full, undiminished strength. Hereby, it proves the unique character of principle inherent in history, opposed to that of philosophy.

Before giving expression to this principle, we ask first through what acts it manifests itself.

First of all, philosophy always reminds us of the claim of the supreme idea. History, on the other hand, reminds us of the conditions of existence. The former lends weight to the universal interest, the latter to the particular interest. The former considers the development (*Fortgang*) essential and sees every particular only as a part of the whole. History turns sympathetically also to the particular. Philosophy is forever rejecting: it places the state of which it would approve into the remote future. By its nature philosophy is prophetic, forward-directed. History sees the good and the beneficent in that which exists. It tries to comprehend them and looks to the past.

Indeed, in this opposition one science directly attacks the other. While, as we have seen, philosophy is intent on subjecting history to itself, history at times makes similar claims. It does not want to consider the results of philosophy as absolute, but only as phenomena in time. It assumes that the most exact philosophy[5] is contained in the history of philosophy, i.e., that the absolute truth recognizable to the human race is inherent in the theories which appear from time to time, no matter how much they contradict each other. History goes still one step further here; it assumes that philosophy, especially when it engages in

---

[5] Fuchs's reading: It assumes that the true (*wahrhafte*) philosophy.

definitions, is only the manifestation of national knowledge inherent in language. It thus denies philosophy any validity and comprehends it in its other manifestation.[6] In this, even the philosophers side with the historians for, as a rule, they accept all former systems only as steps, only as relative phenomena, and ascribe absolute validity only to their own systems.

I do not mean to say that the historian is right in so viewing philosophy; I only want to show that in the historic view of things there is an active principle which is always opposed to the philosophic view and which constantly expresses itself. The question is what this principle is that lies at the basis of such expression.

While the philosopher, viewing history from his vantage point, seeks infinity merely in progression, development, and totality, history recognizes something infinite in every existence: in every condition, in every being, something eternal, coming from God; and this is its vital principle.

How could anything be without the divine basis of its existence?

Therefore, as we have said, history turns with sympathy to the individual;[7] therefore it insists on the validity of the particular interest. It recognizes the beneficent, the existing, and opposes change which negates the existing. It recognizes even in error its share in truth. For this reason, it sees in the former rejected philosophies a part of eternal knowledge.

It is not necessary for us to prove at length that the eternal dwells in the individual. This is the religious foundation on which our efforts rest. We believe that there is nothing without God, and nothing lives except through God. By freeing ourselves from the claims of a certain narrow theology, we do, nevertheless profess that all our efforts stem from a higher, religious source.

The idea that even historical efforts are directed solely toward the search for that higher principle in phenomena must be re-

[6] *begreift sie unter der anderen Erscheinung*—meaning not clear.
[7] Fuchs inserts a phrase here: therefore it likes to attach itself to the conditions of appearance (*Erscheinung*).

jected. History would thereby come too close to philosophy, since it would presuppose rather than contemplate the principle. History elevates, gives significance to, and hallows the phenomenal world, in and by itself, because of what it contains. It devotes its efforts to the concrete, not only to the abstract which might be contained therein.

Now that we have vindicated our supreme principle, we have to consider what demands result from it for historical practice.

1. The first demand is pure love of truth. By recognizing something sublime in the event, the condition, or the person we want to know about, we acquire a certain esteem for that which has transpired, passed, or appeared. The first purpose is to recognize this. If we wanted to preempt this recognition with our imagination, we would counter our very purpose and would investigate only the reflection of our subjective notions and theories. By this, however, we do not mean that one should simply remain attached to the appearance, to its when, where, or how. For then we would take hold of only something external, although our own principle directs us inward.

2. Therefore, a documentary, penetrating, profound study is necessary. First of all, this study must be devoted to the phenomenon itself, to its condition, its surrounding, chiefly for the reason that we would otherwise be incapable of knowing it; then, to its essence, its content, for as in the last analysis every unity is a spiritual one, it can only be grasped through spiritual apperception. This apperception rests on the agreement of the laws in accordance with which the observing mind proceeds with those which determine the emergence of the object under observation. Here, it is already possible to be more or less gifted. All genius rests on the congruence of the individual and the species. The productive principle which formed and created nature confronts itself in the individual who recognizes her and through him becomes clear to itself and attains self-understanding.

This gift is possible to a greater or lesser degree, but to a certain extent everybody has it. Intelligence, courage, and honesty in telling the truth are sufficient. Everyone may hope to find out, to penetrate, that to which he has devoted his efforts if in his studies he remains free of prejudice and retains his humility. But what is lack of prejudice? This question leads us to the third demand issuing from our principle.

3.   A universal interest. There are those who are interested only in civic institutions, in constitutions, in scientific progress, in artistic creations, or only in political entanglements. Most of history[8] thus far has dealt with war and peace. But since these aspects of society are never present separately but always together—indeed, determining each other—and since, for instance, the attitudes of science[9] often influence foreign policy and especially domestic politics, equal interest must be devoted to all of these factors. Otherwise we would render ourselves incapable of comprehending the one aspect without the other, and would work counter to the purpose of cognition. Herein lies the freedom from prejudice which we mean. It is not a lack of interest, but rather an interest in pure cognition undulled by preconceived notions. But how? Will this penetrating truth-searching effort not merely dissect the whole field into individual parts, will we not occupy ourselves merely with a series of fragments?

4.   Penetration of the causal nexus. Basically, we should be satisfied with simple information—satisfied that it merely corresponds to the object. Our original demand would have been satisfied if there were only a sequence among the various events. But there is a connection among them. Events which are simultaneous touch and affect each other; what precedes determines what follows; there is an inner connection of cause and effect. Although this causal nexus is not designated by dates, it exists nevertheless. It exists, and because it exists we must try to recognize it. This kind of observation of history, which derives effects from causes, is called pragmatic; but we would like to understand it not in the usual manner, but according to our concepts.

Since the development of contemporary historiography, the pragmatic school of thought, as applied to actions, has introduced

----

[8] Fuchs's reading: Most histories.

[9] *die wissenschaftlichen Richtungen*—meaning not quite clear in this context.

a system according to which selfishness and lust for power are the mainsprings of all affairs. What is usually required is to explain the observable actions of individuals as the result of passions which we derive deductively from our concept of man. The resulting point of view is tinged with an aridity, irreligiosity, and lack of sensitivity which drive us to despair. I do not deny that selfishness and lust for power can be very powerful motives and have had a great influence, but I deny that they are the only ones. First and foremost, we have to investigate the genuine information as precisely as possible to determine whether we can discover the real motives. Doing so will be possible more frequently than one might think. Only when this path leads us no further are we permitted to conjecture. Let no one believe that this limitation would restrict freedom of observation; no, the more documentary, the more exact, and the more fruitful the research is, the more freely can our art unfold, which only flourishes in the element of immediate, undeniable truth! Only invented motives are dry. The true ones, derived from fresh observation, are diverse and profound. Thus, like knowledge in general, even our pragmatism is documentary.[10] It can even be very reticent and yet very essential. Where the events themselves speak, where the pure composition manifests the connection, it is not necessary to talk of this connection at length.

5. Impartiality. As a rule, two contending parties appear in world history. The struggles in which these parties are engaged, are, to be sure, very different, but closely related. We always see one develop out of the other.

Let no one believe that they will be so easily forgotten in the course of time. There is in man a happy trust in the judgment of history and of posterity which is appealed to a thousand times. But rarely is this judgment passed objectively. There is not alive within us[11] an interest similar to that of the past. We judge

---

[10] Fuchs's reading: even our pragmatism is only (*nur*) documentary.

[11] Fuchs's reading reverses the meaning: There is also alive within us.

the past too often by the present situation. Perhaps this trait was never worse than at present, when a few interests which permeate all of world history occupy general opinion more than ever and split it into a great pro and con.

This may be the way of proceeding in politics, but it is not truly historical. We, who search for truth, even in error, who view every existence as permeated with original life, must above all avoid this error. Where there is any similar struggle, both parties must be viewed on their own ground, in their own environment, so to speak, in their own particular inner state. We must understand them before we judge them.

The objection will be raised that the writer, too, the one who describes, must have his opinion, his religion, from which he cannot separate himself.

This objection would be justified if we would presume to say who is right in every dispute. It is easily possible that, even in the midst of a dispute, we already know clearly which side we would support, in favor of which opinion we would decide. It is also possible that that impartiality which, in a conflict between two divergent opinions, often sees[12] the truth in the middle, becomes impossible for the historian since he is very definitely devoted to his opinion. But this is not all that matters. We can see the error, but where is there no error? This will not lead us to deny the realities of the existence. Next to the good we recognize evil, but this is an evil which is inherent in the situation.

It is not opinions which we examine. We are dealing with existence which has often the most decisive influence in political and religious disputes. Here we rise to contemplate the essential character of the opposing, conflicting elements, and see how complex and entangled they are. It is not up to us to judge about error and truth as such. We merely observe one figure (*Gestalt*) arising side by side with another figure; life, side by side with life; effect, side by side with countereffect. Our task is to penetrate them to the bottom of their existence and to portray them with complete objectivity.

[12] Fuchs's reading: often seeks.

At present two great parties are engaged in a struggle for which the words movement and resistance have become a watchword. History marks itself off from the party who desires eternal preservation as well as from the one who favors continual movement onward. Some consider preservation to be the legitimate principle. They find a legality in the preservation of a recognized *status quo*, of a definite law. They do not want to notice that what exists is derived from reform by struggles which destroyed what existed before. But then history would cease. It would somewhere reach its goal. There would be, so to speak, no illegal condition, none which reason could attack—an impossible conclusion. But history can just as little approve of the overthrow of the old, as if it were something completely dead and unusable, without regard to locality and particular interests. If history shuns violence in observation, how much more will it shun violence in execution. This demolishing and changing and again demolishing is not the way of nature. It is a state of inner ruin which manifests itself in this way. It is an organism which has come into conflict with itself, certainly curious to observe but not pleasing. History, of course, recognizes the principle of movement, but as evolution and not as revolution. This is the very reason why it recognizes the principle of resistance. Only where movement and resistance balance each other without getting into these violent, all-devouring battles can mankind prosper. Only because history recognizes both can history be just toward both. It is not up to history even to pass judgment in theory on the struggle which the past teaches it. History knows very well that the struggle will be decided according to God's will.

6. Conception of the totality. Just as there exists the particular, the connection of the one to the other, so there finally exists totality. If it is a life, we grasp its appearance. We perceive the sequence by which one factor follows another. But that is not enough. There is also something total in each life; it becomes, it exerts an effect, it acquires influence, it passes away. This totality is as certain at each moment as every expression. We must devote all our attention to it. If we are dealing with a people, we are not interested only in the individual moments of its living expres-

sions. Rather, from the totality of its development, its deeds, its institutions, and its literature, the idea speaks to us so that we simply cannot deny our attention. The farther we go, the harder it is, of course, to get at the idea—for here, too, we can accomplish something only through exact research, through step-by-step understanding,[13] and through the study of documents. If this process proceeds through induction from the well-known, it is intuitive knowledge (*Divination*); if it proceeds from the little-known, it takes the form of abstract philosophic propositions. One sees how infinitely difficult things become with universal history. What an infinite amount of material! What diverse efforts! How difficult it is only to grasp the particular. Since, moreover, there is much that we do not know, how are we to understand the causal nexus everywhere, not to mention getting to the bottom of the essence of totality? I consider it impossible to solve this problem entirely. God alone knows world history. We recognize the contradictions—"the harmonies," as an Indian poet says, "known to the Gods, but unknown to men"; we can only divine, only approach from a distance. But there exists clearly for us a unity, a progression, a development.

So by way of history we arrive at a definition of philosophy's task. If philosophy were what it ought to be, if history were perfectly clear and complete, then they would fully coincide with each other. Historical science would permeate its subject matter with the spirit of philosophy. If historical art would then succeed in giving life to this subject matter and in reproducing it with that part of poetic power which does not think up new things but mirrors in its true character that which has been grasped and comprehended, it would, as we said in the beginning, unite in its own peculiar manner science and art at the same time.

[13] Kessel's reading: understanding (*Apprehendiren*); Fuchs's reading: approximation (*Approximieren*).

II. Of The Scope Of World History

In three ways—with regard to (1) sequence, (2) simultaneity, and (3) individual developments.[14]

1. Sequence—In the abstract, history would embrace all of the life of mankind appearing in time. But too much of it is lost and unknown. The first period of its existence as well as the connecting links are lost without any hope of ever finding them again.

We can note what significance history has. If authors of another kind are lost, one misses the expression of one single individual. In a historical book, however, not only the existence and the view of an author is expressed; the historical book rather interests us because of the lives of others it contains. Much that was described has been lost; some has never been described. All this is threatened by death. Only those whom history remembers have not entirely died; their character and their existence continue to exist insofar as they remain in the consciousness of men. Only with the extinction of memory does actual death set in.

We are fortunate where documentary traces remain. At least these can be grasped. But what happens where there are none, for instance in prehistory? I am in favor of excluding this period from history because it contradicts the historical principle, which is documentary research.

One should exclude entirely that which usually is taken over in world history from geological deduction and from the results of natural history about the first creation of the world, the solar system, and the earth. By our method we find out nothing about these topics; it is permissible to confess our ignorance.

As for myths, I do not want to deny categorically that they contain perhaps an occasional historical element. But the most important thing is that they express the view of a people of itself, its attitude toward the world, etc. They are important insofar as

---

[14] This is an incomplete sentence in the German original.

the subjective character of a people or its thoughts may have been expressed in them, not because of any objective facts they may contain. In the former respect they possess a firm foundation and are very reliable for historical research, but not in the latter.

Finally, we can devote but scant attention to those peoples who still remain today in a kind of state of nature and who lead us to assume that they have been in this state from the beginning—that the prehistoric condition has been preserved in them. India and China claim an old age and have a lengthy chronology. But even the cleverest chronologists cannot understand it. Their antiquity is lengendary, but their condition is rather a matter for natural history.

4

THE PITFALLS
OF A PHILOSOPHY
OF HISTORY

(Introduction to a Lecture
on Universal History;
A Manuscript of the 1840s)

Ⲥ

I do not want to say that it is necessary, but it is certainly useful for mutual understanding that a university lecturer, at the beginning of his course of lectures, indicate the point of view which he maintains or thinks he maintains in the realm of general ideas and that he define the position he occupies in the conflict of the leading opinions which move his scholarly discipline. Let us consider in particular the method, which not only determines the form of his lectures but has the greatest influence on the treatment of the subject matter.

So I, too, shall start out with a few remarks about the scientific conception of universal history and first of all shall mention methodological approaches with which I differ.

"Einleitung zu einer Vorlesung über Universalhistorie," edited by Eberhard Kessel in Historische Zeitschrift, CLXXVIII (1954), 304–307; translated by Wilma A. Iggers and published with the permission of Professor Kessel and the Historische Zeitschrift. Compared with the unpublished reading of the manuscript by Professor Walther Peter Fuchs.

The old traditional method or theory concentrates mainly on externals. It seeks to establish time, place, sequence—in general, that which is factual about the phenomena of the past; it also seeks to penetrate to the earliest beginnings and to progress to the most recent, noting down everything, occasionally merely collecting and registering data. But this method encounters various difficulties. Traditions are uncertain, and the mass of facts are not easily followed; the overall impression is infinitely bleak. All one gets to see again and again is how the stronger conquers the weaker until he in turn is overcome and destroyed by a still stronger adversary; until force finally reaches our times, which will fare likewise. This is the view as it is expressed in Homer: the day will come when Troy will sink down; and the same will be repeated[1] on the ruins of Carthage. As Mohammed II expressed it at the moment when he conquered Constantinople: he feels that everything is vanity, that which he destroys as well as that which he founds; he remembers the spider that spins its web in the chambers of the Constantines.[2] Nothing remains but the feeling of the vanity of all things and a revulsion against the many kinds of misdeeds with which mankind has defiled itself. One does not see for what purpose all these things happen, why these men existed and lived; even the inner connection is distorted.[3]

Now a philosophy has arisen, not in the sense of the usual[4] philosophy of the last century when only the pragmatic was considered to be philosophical, but a much freer philosophy of the

[1] Fuchs's reading: which Marius then repeats.

[2] This apparently refers to the palace of the Byzantine emperors, begun by Constantine the Great and abandoned after the sack of Constantinople in 1204. Regarding Mohammed II and the spider in the ruins of the imperial palace, see also *Weltgeschichte*, Theil IX, Abt. 1, p. 270.

[3] Kessel's reading: distorted (*verdreht*); Fuchs's reading: covered up (*verdeckt*).

[4] Kessel's reading: common, usual (*gewohnten*); Fuchs's reading: predominant (*vorwalteten*).

type already attempted by Fichte, and then with greater vigor by Hegel. This view, which has been developed in more recent times, starts from the assertion that reason rules the world. The advocates of this position, however, immediately proceed to explain more precisely that the purpose of the spiritual world, which is the substantial world—therefore the final purpose of the world altogether—is the spirit's consciousness of its freedom, the reality of its freedom. They first list the abstract definitions of the nature of the spirit and then mention the means which spirit uses to realize its idea. In order not to make the mistake which Plato criticizes in Anaxagoras, who also claimed that reason rules the world but then dealt only with external causes, they proceed at once to prove their abstract principle by reference to the concrete. They establish the steps by which the development of the spirit accomplishes itself: immersion in the natural state, partial tearing away from the latter, and elevation into pure generality; or they set down how these categories, which are logical by their nature, are more precisely grasped in their application to the concrete. The world spirit follows its course through a necessary development by sacrificing the individuals. It uses, as Hegel says, a kind of cunning against the world historical individuals; it lets them carry out their own purposes with all the force of passion while it, the spirit, thereby produces itself. This is not the place to mention all the details of this method, but even for someone who does not agree with us it is undeniable that there is something extremely grandiose in this effort—indeed something gigantic, if we consider the energy which the originator of the system applies—and which therefore deserves great respect.

But it cannot be said that this conception is adequate for historical research. This theory is probably less the result of philosophical speculation than of reflection on the facts which were known anyway and which are being daily investigated more thoroughly. But at times the best documented results of critical historical research encounter the most passionate opposition.

But the main thing is that this view runs counter to the truth of individual consciousness. If this view were correct, the world spirit alone would be truly alive. It would be the sole actor; even the greatest men would be instruments[5] in its hand and would carry out what they themselves neither understood nor wanted. History from this standpoint is actually the history of a developing God. As for myself, gentlemen, I believe in the one who was and is and will be, and in the essential immortal nature of individual man, in the living God and in the living man.

These two views constitute two opposing approaches which continually challenge each other. The inadequacy of the one calls forth the great exertion with which the other appears on the scene. Nevertheless, as often is the case with opposites, they are also related to each other. The enumeration of external conditions—men, numbers, facts—bears some similarity to the schematic organization imposed from without. Neither penetrates to the inner core of the magnificent substance (*Stoff*) of history.

The task is to a certain extent expressed in the two German words used to designate our discipline: *Geschichte* or *Historie*. *Geschichte* is merely the noun for "what happened" (*Geschehen*). "What happened" must coincide completely with science. Conversely, ἱστορία originally meant knowledge (*Wissen*) or cognition (*Erkenntnis*)—ὅτι, as Aristotle once said, but not διότι: therefore the misuse of the word in "natural history" (*Naturgeschichte*), which is merely a translation. The word *Geschichte* expresses more the objective, *Historie* more the subjective, relationship. The former raises the subject matter (*Sache*) to a science. In the latter case the science admits the subject matter (*Gegenstand*) into itself. They coincide with each other, or rather the great task consists in having them coincide.

---

[5] Kessel's reading: would be an instrument; Fuchs's reading: would only be instruments.

5

ON PROGRESS
IN HISTORY

(From the First Lecture
to King Maximilian II of Bavaria
"On the Epochs of Modern History"—1854)

I. How The Concept "Progress"
Is To Be Understood In History

If we were to assume, in common with many a philosopher, that
all of mankind is developing from a given original state to a
positive goal, we could conceive this process in two ways. Either
a general guiding will promotes the development of the human
race from one point to another or there is in mankind a vestige
of spiritual nature which of necessity drives things toward a certain goal. I would not consider these two views to be either philosophically tenable or historically demonstrable.

We cannot consider these views philosophically acceptable
because the former case goes so far as to do away with human
freedom and makes men into tools without a will of their own;
and because in the latter case men would have to be God or
nothing at all.

From "Über die Epochen der neueren Geschichte" in Weltgeschichte, *Theil IX, Abt. 2, pp. 1–9; translated by Wilma A. Iggers.*

But historically too, these views are not provable. For first of all, the greater part of mankind is still in its original state, at the very point of departure. And then the question arises: what is progress? Where is the progress of mankind noticeable? Elements of the great historical development have been incorporated in the Latin and Germanic nation. Here, to be sure, a spiritual power exists which develops step by step. Indeed, the historical power of the human spirit in all of history is unmistakable, a movement started in primeval times which continues with a certain steadiness. There is, however, but one system of populations among mankind which takes part in this general historical movement, while others are excluded from it. But in general we can also view the nationalities engaged in the historical movement as not progressing steadily. For instance, if we turn our attention to Asia, we see that culture originated there and that the continent had several cultural epochs. But there the movement has on the whole been retrogressive; for the oldest epoch of Asian culture was the most flourishing; the second and third epochs, in which the Greek and Roman elements dominated, were no longer as significant, and with the invasion of the barbarians—the Mongols—culture in Asia disappeared completely. In view of this fact the thesis of geographic progression has been offered. I must, however, from the start declare it an empty assertion to assume, as did for instance Peter the Great, that culture was making the rounds of the globe; that it had come from the East and was returning there again.

Secondly, another error is to be avoided here, namely, the assumption that the progressive development of the centuries encompasses at the same time all branches of human nature and skill. To stress only one example, history shows us that in modern times art flourished most in the fifteenth and in the first half of the sixteenth century, but in the seventeenth and in the first three quarters of the eighteenth century it declined the most. The same is true of poetry: there are also only brief periods when this art is really outstanding, but there is no evidence that it rises to a higher level in the course of the centuries.

If we thus exclude a geographic law of development and if we furthermore have to assume, as history teaches us, that peoples can perish among whom the development that has begun does not steadily encompass everything, we shall better recognize the real substance of the continuous movement of mankind. It is based on the fact that the great spiritual tendencies which govern mankind sometimes go separate ways and at other times are closely related. In these tendencies there is, however, always a certain particular direction which predominates and causes the others to recede. So, for example, in the second half of the sixteenth century the religious element predominated so much that the literary receded in the face of it. In the eighteenth century, on the other hand, the striving for utility gained so much ground that art and related activities had to yield before it.

Thus, in every epoch of mankind a certain great tendency manifests itself; and progress rests on the fact that a certain movement of the human spirit reveals itself in every epoch, which stresses sometimes the one and sometimes the other tendency, manifesting itself there in a characteristic fashion.

If in contradiction to the view expressed here, however, one were to assume that this progress consisted in the fact that the life of mankind reaches a higher potential in every epoch—that is, that every generation surpasses the previous one completely and that therefore the last epoch is always the preferred, the epochs preceding it being only stepping stones to ones that follow—this would be an injustice on the part of the deity. Such a generation which, as it were, had become a means would not have any significance for and in itself. It would only have meaning as a stepping stone for the following generation and would not have an immediate relation to the divine. But I assert: every epoch is immediate to God, and its worth is not at all based on what derives from it but rests in its own existence, in its own self. In this way the contemplation of history, that is to say of individual life in history, acquires its own particular attraction, since now every epoch must be seen as something valid in itself and appears highly worthy of consideration.

The historian thus has to pay particular attention first of all to how people in a certain period thought and lived. Then he will find that, apart from certain unchangeable eternal main ideas, for instance those of morality, every epoch has its own particular tendency and its own ideal. But although every epoch has its justification and its worth in and by itself, one still must not overlook what came forth from it. The historian must therefore, secondly, perceive the difference between the individual epochs, in order to observe the inner necessity of the sequence. One cannot fail to recognize a certain progress here. But I would not want to say that this progress moves in a straight line, but more like a river which in its own way determines its course. If I may dare to make this remark, I picture the deity—since no time lies before it—as surveying all of historic mankind in its totality and finding it everywhere of equal value. There is, to be sure, something true in the idea of the education of mankind, but before God all generations of men appear endowed with equal rights, and this is how the historian must view matters.

Insofar as we can follow history, unconditional progress, a most definite upward movement, is to be assumed in the realm of material interests in which retrogression will hardly be possible unless there occurs an immense upheaval. In regard to morality, however, progress cannot be traced. Moral ideas can, to be sure, progress extensively; and so one can also assert in cultural (*geistige*) matters that, for example, the great works which art and literature have produced are enjoyed today by larger numbers than previously. But it would be ridiculous to want to be a greater writer of epics than Homer or a greater writer of tragedies than Sophocles.

II. What Is To Be Thought Of The So-Called Leading Ideas In History

The philosophers, particularly the Hegelian school, have established certain ideas according to which the history of mankind spins itself out as a logical process in statement, counterstatement, and mediation, in positive and negative elements. However, in scholasticism life perishes; and thus also this view of history, this process of the spirit developing according to various logical categories, would lead back to that which we have already rejected above. According to this view only the idea would have an independent life, and all human beings would be mere shadows or phantoms inflated by this idea. The doctrine according to which the world spirit produces things, as it were, through deceit and uses human passions to achieve its goals is based on an utterly unworthy idea of God and mankind. Pursued to its logical conclusion consistently, this view can lead only to pantheism. Mankind is then God in the process of becoming, who gives birth to himself through a spiritual process that lies in his nature.

I can therefore understand by the "leading ideas" only the ruling tendencies in every century. These tendencies can only be described, but in the last analysis they cannot be subsumed under one concept. Otherwise we would again return to that which we have rejected above.

The historian must differentiate the great tendencies of the centuries and unroll the great history of mankind, which is just the complex of these various tendencies. From the standpoint of the divine idea, I cannot think of the matter differently but that mankind harbors within itself an infinite multiplicity of developments which manifest themselves gradually according to laws which are unknown to us and are more mysterious and greater than one thinks.

Dialogue

KING MAX: You spoke above of moral progress. Were you thinking here also of the inner progress of the individual?

RANKE: No, but only of the progress of the human race. The individual, in contrast, must always raise himself to a higher moral level.

KING MAX: But since mankind is composed of individuals, the question arises whether when the individual raises himself to a higher moral level this progress does not also encompass all of mankind.

RANKE: The individual dies. His existence is finite; that of mankind, on the other hand, is infinite. I accept progress in material matters because here one thing proceeds from the other. It is different in moral affairs. I believe that every generation is equal in moral greatness to every other generation and that there is no higher potential of moral greatness—we cannot, for example, surpass the moral greatness of the ancient world. It often happens in the spiritual world that intensive greatness stands in inverse relation to extensive greatness. We need only compare our present literature with classical literature to see this.

KING MAX: But should one not assume that Providence, without prejudice to the free self-determination of the individual, has set a certain goal for mankind toward which the latter is being led, even if not forcibly.

RANKE: This is a cosmo-political hypothesis which, however, cannot be proved historically. Indeed Holy Scripture contains a passage according to which someday there will be only one shepherd and one flock, but until now this has not shown itself to be the dominant course of world history. A proof of this is the history of Asia, which after periods of the greatest flowering fell back into barbarism.

KING MAX: But have not a greater number of individuals attained a higher degree of moral development in our time than before?

RANKE: I admit this, but not in principle; for history teaches us that many peoples are not capable of culture and that earlier epochs were often more moral than later ones. For example, France was much more moral and cultured in the middle of the seventeenth century than at the end of the eighteenth. As I said, a greater diffusion of moral ideas can be maintained, but only in certain areas. From a general human standpoint it would appear probable to me that the idea of mankind, which historically has been represented only in the great nations, will gradually embrace all of mankind, and this would then be inner moral progress. Historical science is not opposed to this view but provides no proof for it. We must especially guard against making this view into a principle of history. Our task is merely to keep to the facts.

6

THE ROLE
OF THE PARTICULAR
AND THE GENERAL
IN THE STUDY
OF UNIVERSAL HISTORY

(A Manuscript of the 1860s)

History admittedly can never have the unity of a philosophical system; but history is not without inner connection. We see before us a series of events which follow and condition each other. To say condition does not, of course, denote absolute necessity. Rather, the important point is that human freedom is everywhere brought into play. Historical writing traces the scenes of freedom; this is the source of its greatest attraction. Freedom, however, is accompanied by force—that is to say, by original force. Without this force freedom would cease in the events of the world as well as in the realm of ideas. At any moment something new can begin again which can be traced back only to the first and common source of all human activity. Nothing exists entirely for the sake of the other. Nothing is absorbed entirely in the reality of the other. But still a deep inner relationship exists from which nobody is entirely free and which enters into everything. Freedom and necessity exist side by side. Necessity lies in

From Alfred Dove's Vorwort to Weltgeschichte, Theil IX, Abt. 2, pp. xiii–xvi; translated by Wilma A. Iggers.

that which has already been formed and cannot be overturned again, which is the basis of all newly emerging activity. What has developed in the past constitutes the connection with what is in the process of becoming. But even this connection is not to be assumed arbitrarily; it exists in a certain way and in no other. It, too, is an object of cognition. A longer series of successive and concurrent events, connected in this way with each other, forms a century, an epoch. The varied character of the epochs rests on the fact that different times and different circumstances result from the struggle of the conflicting principles of freedom and necessity. If, with this in mind, we visualize the sequence of the centuries, each with its own original character, all linked to one another, we have before us universal history from the beginning to the present day. Universal history encompasses the past life of the human race in its fullness and totality, not in its individual relationships and directions.

The science of universal history is distinguished from specialized research in this way: that universal history in investigating the particular remains always aware of the great whole on which it is working. The investigation of the particular, even of a single point, is of value if it is done well. If devoted to things human, it will always reveal something worth knowing in itself. It is instructive even when applied to petty detail, for the human is always worth knowing. But the investigation of the particular is always related to a larger context. Local history is related to that of a country; a biography is related to a larger event in state and church, to an epoch of national or general history. But all these epochs themselves are, as we have said, again part of the great totality which we call universal history. The greater scope of its investigation has correspondingly greater value. The ultimate goal, yet unattained, will always remain the conception and composition of a history of mankind. Given the course which historical studies have taken in our time—and which they must continue to take if they are to portray thoroughly investigated and exactly known things—we are exposed to the danger of losing sight of the general knowledge everyone desires. For one does not study history only for school: the knowledge of the history of mankind ought to be the common property of mankind and, above all, should benefit the nation to which we belong and without which our studies would not even exist.

We need not fear to end up with the vague generalities with which an earlier age contented itself. The diligent and energetic studies which have been undertaken everywhere have been so productive and influential that such generalities can no longer be advanced today. We are also not likely to return to the systematic categories with which people occupied themselves at various times. A collection of historical notes with a superficial judgment about character and morality is just as unlikely to lead to thorough and satisfactory knowledge. In my opinion we must work in two directions: the investigation of the effective forces behind events and the perception of their general connection.

Comprehending the whole and yet doing justice to the requirements of research will, of course, always remain an ideal. It would presuppose an understanding on a firm foundation of the totality of human history. Even the investigation of the one or the other detail requires deep and extremely thorough study. Nowadays we are all agreed that criticism, objective conception, and a broad synthesis can and must go together. Relating the particular to the general cannot harm research. Without a general view, research would become sterile; without exact research, the general view would deteriorate into fantasy.

PART III

The Idealistic Theory
of the State

The following two essays first appeared in the *Historisch-Politische Zeitschrift*, which Ranke edited and largely wrote between 1832 and 1836. The essays are of particular interest because in them Ranke formulates his basic theoretical concepts regarding the nature of the state and of political power which underlie all his historical writings.

"The Great Powers" (Selection 7) contains an excellent illustration of what Ranke means by the "leading ideas" or "tendencies" in history and states succinctly the basic theme supporting all of Ranke's great works on modern history. "World history," Ranke argues, does not present a "planless succession of states." Rather, we see in history the development and conflict of "spiritual, life-giving, creative forces" and "moral energies." States, for Ranke, represent such spiritual forces. These forces "cannot be defined . . . in abstract terms, but one can behold them and observe them." The conflict of states thus represents more than a simple clash of power. Rather, in the "interaction and succession" of the spiritual forces which constitute history "lies the secret of world history." We approach this great drama through "the contemplation of the individual moments" in history, for the particular always "bears the general within itself."

Such contemplation reveals a legitimate order operating in history. The system of the balance of power is the instrument by which this order is maintained. Ranke examines the history of international relations from the age of Louis XIV to the post-Napoleonic Restoration, the recurring threats to the balance of power, and the forces within the system that led to the reestablishment of the legitimate order whenever it was temporarily threatened or disturbed. The play of power will continue indefinitely, Ranke suggests. A world government or the hegemony of one power over the rest would be disastrous for mankind. "A mixture of them all would destroy the essence of each one." The future of the world rests in continued diversity, which requires the continuation of a balance of power.

The historical approach of "The Great Powers" gives way to a more abstract analysis of the state in "A Dialogue on Politics" (Selection 8). Ranke observes that "there is an element which makes a state not a subdivision of general categories, but a living thing, an individual, a unique self." It represents a "spiritual force" which "cannot be derived from a higher principle." Politics in the abstract therefore has no meaning. Institutions can never be transplanted from one state to the other. "There is no way leading from the general theory to the perception of the particular." On the other hand, he reiterates, the particular *can* lead us to the general. "Only by comprehensive historical investigation and combination can we aspire to a divining perception of the deeply hidden, all-embracing spiritual laws." The "uniqueness" of the state makes it impossible to judge it by external moral standards. "All states that count in the world and make themselves felt are motivated by special tendencies of their own." It would be ridiculous to explain them as institutions existing for the economic benefit or the security of their citizens. Political power does not rest on a contract. States rather are "spiritual substances, original creations of the human mind—I might say, thoughts of God." But there is no real conflict between the power strivings of the states and ethics. For power, Ranke is convinced, rests on spiritual foundations. "But seriously," he comments, "you will be able to name few significant wars for which it could not be proved that genuine moral energy achieved the final victory."

"The Great Powers" was translated by Hildegard Hunt Von Laue from the edition of "Die Grossen Mächte" in the Insel-bücherei, no. 200, prepared by Friedrich Meinecke. "A Dialogue on Politics" was translated by Theodore H. Von Laue from the text in Ranke's *Sämmtliche Werke*, vol. XLIX/L, edited by Alfred Dove, 2nd ed., 1887. Both translations first appeared in Theodore H. Von Laue, *Leopold Ranke: The Formative Years*. (Princeton: Princeton University Press, 1950). They are reproduced here with the permission of Princeton University Press and the translators.

7

THE GREAT POWERS

(1833)

Introduction

It is much the same with studies and reading as with the observations of a journey or indeed with the happenings of life itself. However much the particular may attract and profit us while we are enjoying it, in time it will nevertheless retreat into the background, become obscured, and disappear. Only the general impressions which we receive in one place or another, the totality of perception which comes to us either unconsciously or through particularly careful observations, remain to increase the sum of our knowledge. The most intensely enjoyed moments of our existence are fused in our memory and make up its living content. Certainly one does well, after reading an important work, to try to list in one's mind its separate conclusions and to glance

Translated by Hildegarde Hunt Von Laue from the edition in the Inselbücherei, no. 200, prepared by F. Meinecke. From Theodore H. Von Laue, Leopold Ranke: The Formative Years *(Princeton: Princeton University Press, 1950), pp. 181–218. Reprinted by permission of Princeton University Press and the translator.*

back at the more important passages. It is also advisable sometimes to summarize a more comprehensive study. I shall go further, however, and urge the reader to visualize in their sequence
the events of a long historical period (which can first be understood only by a variety of studies), the period, namely, of the
last century and a half.

The contemplation of the individual moment in all its truth
and of the special development for its own sake doubtless has
inestimable value in history. The particular bears the general
within itself. But no one can escape the urge to survey the whole
from a detached viewpoint. Everyone strives after this in one
way or another. Out of the variety of individual perceptions a
vision of their unity involuntarily arises.

The only difficulty is to present such a view in a few pages,
with proper justification and with some hope of winning approval.
I shall nevertheless venture to do so.

For how else could I better introduce a new volume of this
periodical* than by endeavoring to dispel several almost universal
errors concerning the formation of the present era, hoping to
create a somewhat clearer and more certain perception of the
present moment in world history?

If I dare attempt this, I must not reach too far back into
the past. Otherwise it would be necessary to write a world history. I shall also deliberately limit myself to the great events, to
the development of the external relationships of the different
states. The key to the internal conditions, with which the external ones interact in a great variety of ways, will be for the
most part contained therein.

The Period Of Louis XIV

Let our starting point be the fact that in the sixteenth century
the freedom of Europe was seen to rest upon the opposition and

---

* The second volume of the *Historisch-Politische Zeitschrift*. [As-
terisked notes are by the translator.]

balance between Spain and France. Those who were overpowered by the one would find refuge with the other. The fact that France was for a long time weakened and disorganized by civil war was considered a general misfortune. That Henry IV should have been so eagerly welcomed was not only because he put an end to the anarchy in France but principally because he thereby restored a stable European order.

It happened, however, that in the course of dealing dangerous blows to her rivals everywhere, in the Netherlands, in Italy, on the Iberian Peninsula, and of defeating Spain's allies in Germany, France herself obtained a preponderance of power greater than Spain had possessed even at her height.

Let the reader imagine the condition of Europe around the year 1680. France, so suited and so long accustomed to keeping Europe in a ferment, had a king who understood perfectly how to rule her. His nobles, finally subdued after long obstinacy, served him with equal zeal at court and in the army, and his clergy had allied themselves with him against the Pope. France was more unified and more powerful than ever before.

In order to obtain some measure of her power one need only recall that when the Emperor was establishing his first two standing regiments, infantry and cuirassiers, Louis XIV already had, in peacetime, 100,000 men in his garrisons and 14,000 men in the guards. While the English navy declined steadily in the last years of Charles II (it numbered 83 vessels in the year 1678), in 1681 the French navy reached a total of 96 ships of the line, first and second class, 42 frigates, 36 feluccas, and an equal number of fireships. Louis XIV's troops were the best drilled and most experienced to be found anywhere, and his ships were extremely well constructed. No other ruler had borders so well fortified for attack and defense alike. It was not only through military power, however, but also through diplomacy and alliances that the French had succeeded in overcoming the Spaniards. They expanded their new position into a kind of supremacy.

Let us first consider the North and the East. In 1674 Sweden undertook a dangerous war, without preparation, without money, without just cause, merely at a word from France and in the confidence of receiving French subsidies. The elevation of John Sobieski to the Polish throne was hailed in an official paper as a triumph for Louis XIV, and both the Polish king and queen acted in the French interest for a long time. Since it was no longer possible to do so by way of Vienna, the discontented elements in Hungary were now supported through Poland. The French also put them in touch with the Turks, for France was continuing to exert her old influence upon the Porte by the usual means. Everything was part of the same system. One principal precaution of French diplomacy consisted in maintaining peace between Poland and Turkey; to this end they even approached the Tartar Khan. Another was to prevent Sweden from being invaded by the Russians. No sooner would the Russians give indication of attacking France's ally, Sweden, says Contarini in 1681, than the Turks would threaten to let loose their armies upon the land of the Tsar. But enough has been said. War and peace in these remote regions all depended upon France.

It is well known how this system directly affected Germany, principally through Sweden. But even without this our fatherland was already divided and weakened. Bavaria and the Palatinate were bound to the French court by marriage alliances, and almost all of the remaining rulers accepted subsidies at one time or another. By a formal treaty, which he concealed behind various feigned agreements, the Elector of Cologne delivered his fortress of Reuss over to French occupation.

Nor was it very different in central and southern Europe. At times the Swiss served in the French armies more than 20,000 strong. Under such strong open and even stronger secret influence their assemblies could no longer boast of much independence. In order to keep access to Italy Richelieu had seized Pinarolo. Still more important was Casale from which Milan and Genoa were directly threatened. Everyone perceived how dangerous it would be were this stronghold also to come into French hands. Yet despite the long duration of the negotiations which Louis XIV carried on with the Duke of Mantua, no one dared seriously to oppose him, and finally a French garrison moved in. The rest of the Italian rulers, like the Duke of Mantua,

were for the most part at the beck and call of France. The Duchess of Savoy and, on the other side of the Pyrenees, the Queen
of Portugal were Frenchwomen. The Cardinal d'Etrées exerted
so unquestionable an influence over both of them that it was
said that he despotically ruled them and thereby their countries.
Who would have thought it possible, however, that at the
same time France could even secure a decided influence over her
opponents of the House of Austria from whom she had just
wrested her predominant position? She understood how to separate the Spanish and German lines in the House of Hapsburg.
The young king of Spain married a French princess, and the
activity of the French ambassadors was soon manifest even in
the internal affairs of Spain. The most important man in that
country at the time, Don John of Austria, was, so far as I have
been able to ascertain, brought by the French into the disrepute
in which he died. In Vienna also, even in the midst of war, they
knew how to obtain a foothold, if only surreptitiously. At least
it was only by such an assumption that the vacillations of the
Austrian cabinet could be explained. As Montecuculi complained,
the orders of the imperial war council were known in Versailles
sooner than in their own headquarters.

In such a situation it was certainly England, above all other
European nations, who would have had the mission and also the
power to oppose the French. But it is well known by what strange
combination of politics and love, of luxury and religion, of personal interest and intrigue Charles II was bound to Louis XIV.
Yet these ties were not sufficiently strong to suit the French king.
At the same time he was taking pains to win over the most important members of Parliament. No matter how independent,
how republican-minded they were, he still needed to employ but
one method. "The reasons which I presented to him," says the
French envoy, Barrillon, of one of these Englishmen, "did not
convince him, but the money which I gave him, that secured
him." In this way Louis XIV first drew England into his power.
Had the English king resisted him, he would have encountered
opposition in Parliament; and as soon as Parliament gave rein
to the national antipathy toward the French, the king objected.

Louis XIV's policy, and Barrillon says explicitly that it lay close to his heart, was to keep England disunited and to prevent a reconciliation between king and Parliament. He succeeded all too well in this. England's power was completely neutralized.

In the face of France Europe was indeed divided and impotent, "without heart," as a Venetian remarked, "and without gall." One can imagine the condition of European politics if Louis XIV was suffered to set up the Chambers of Reunion at Metz at the suggestion of one of his legal councillors. He summoned mighty princes too these chambers in order that their rights to territories and populations, rights guaranteed by treaties of state, might be determined by his judges as though they were private rights. The German Empire must have been in a sorry plight that it should have allowed Strassburg to be torn from it so violently and unnaturally. Let me quote how a foreigner later described the conquest of Alsace. "When one reads its history," says Young in an account of his travels, "this does not make so deep an impression. Coming from France, however, I was impressed by the fact that I first had to cross high mountains and that I then descended to a plain (the one which had been conquered at that time), inhabited by a people who were completely different from the French in custom, speech, and descent."* Yet Germany put up with such an insult and concluded an armistice.

Where indeed was the limit to Louis XIV's presumption? I shall not dwell on how he abused Genoa nor how he had his ambassador enter Rome with an armed force in defiance of the Pope. Let us merely remember that he did not spare even his friends. He took possession of Zweibrücken although it belonged to his old ally, the king of Sweden. Although the Turks were his allies, his admiral bombarded Chios because Tripolitanian pirates had taken refuge there. He seized several forts belonging to the Hudson Bay Company during a period of the best understanding with England. He denied the afore-mentioned queen of Poland a trifling concession to her ambition. After he had made friends for

---

* Ranke paraphrased rather than quoted literally a statement in Arthur Young's *Travels in France.*

himself, by money or by support, he delighted in neglecting them, perhaps to show that he did not need them after all, perhaps in the belief that only fear of his displeasure would keep them in line. He wished his predominance to be felt in every negotiation. He himself said of one of his foreign ministers, "I had to remove him. Everything which he undertook lacked the grandeur and strength which one must show when carrying out the commands of a king of France who does not happen to be unfortunate."

One may even assume that this attitude was the principal motive behind his wars. He could hardly be called excessively greedy for land. There was really no question of widespread territorial conquest. Campaigns were merely part of the activities of the court. One assembles an army and has it parade before the ladies. Everything is prepared, the coup is successful, the king marches into the conquered city and then hurries back to the court. It was principally the triumphant splendor of the return, the admiration of the court, in which he delighted. He did not care for conquest and war so much as for the glory which they cast upon him. He did not seek universal and imperishable fame. He wanted only the homage of his entourage. To him they were both public and posterity.

But the state of Europe was no less imperiled. If there were to be a supreme authority, it should at least be a legally determined one. This arrogated supremacy, which was constantly disturbing the peace, threatened to destroy the foundations of European order and development. It is not always recognized that the European order of things differs from others that have appeared in the course of world history by virtue of its legal, even juridical nature. It is true that world agitations now and again destroy this system of law and order. But after they have subsided, it is reconstituted, and all exertions aim only at perfecting it once more.

Nor was this the only danger. A no less considerable one lay in the fact that under such decided domination by one nation, the others could hardly achieve an independent development, particularly not when this domination was supported by a preeminence in literature. Italian literature had already run its full course, English literature had not yet risen to general significance, and

German literature did not exist at that time. French literature, light, brilliant, and animated, in strictly regulated yet charming form, intelligible to everyone and yet of an individual, national character, was commencing to dominate Europe. It may seem irrelevant to point out that the dictionary of the Academy, which set the standards for speech, abounds particularly in hunting and military expressions which were current at court. But it is undeniable that French literature completely corresponded to the state and helped the latter to attain its supremacy. Paris was the capital of Europe. She wielded a dominion as did no other city, over language, over custom, and particularly over the world of fashion and the ruling classes. Here was the center of the community of Europe. Yet it is remarkable that the French should already have boasted to all the world of their constitution, calling it "the happy condition of well-protected submission in which France finds herself, under a prince who, above all others, deserves to rule the world by his courage and wisdom and to bring true unity to it."

If one puts oneself back into the mind of a contemporary, what a dismal, oppressive prospect is presented. It might well have happened that the wrong course of the Stuarts would have prevailed and that English policy would have thenceforth been forever chained to that of France. After the Treaty of Nymwegen the most strenuous efforts were made to have the choice of a Holy Roman Emperor fall upon Louis XIV himself or else upon the Dauphin. Important advocates were secured for this cause, "for the Most Christian King is alone capable of restoring its old splendor to the Empire." Nor was it wholly impossible that under favorable circumstances such a choice would have succeeded. And what if even the Spanish monarchy should fall to a prince of this house? If French literature had been cultivated in both the directions of which it was capable, the Protestant as well as the Catholic, then the French government and spirit would have subdued Europe with irresistible force. If one imagines oneself back in this period, as I have said, it would appear that nothing could check this unfortunate course of events.

But against such an increase in strength and in political predominance the lesser powers could band together. And they did indeed form alliances and associations. The concept of the European balance of power was developed in order that the union of many other states might resist the pretensions of the "exorbitant" court, as it was called. The forces of resistance gathered around Holland and William III. By a common exertion they warded off attack and waged war. One would have erred, however, in assuming that this afforded a permanent remedy. Despite the European alliance and a successful war, a Bourbon became King of Spain and the Indies. In the course of events the dominion of this House even spread over part of Italy.

In great danger one can safely trust in the guardian spirit (*Genius*) which always protects Europe from domination by any one-sided and violent tendency, which always meets pressure on the one side with resistance on the other, and, through a union of the whole which grows firmer from decade to decade, has happily preserved the freedom and separate existence of each state. As the supremacy of France rested upon the superiority of her military forces and upon her inner strength, so it could only be really challenged if other opposing powers either regained or attained inner unity, independent strength, and general importance. Let us review in a few swift strokes how this occurred.

England, Austria And Russia

England was the first to awake to a realization of her strength. We have seen how this was hitherto retarded, even prevented, by Louis XIV, who simultaneously manipulated Charles II and Parliament, using sometimes the one, sometimes the other, for his own purposes. With James II, however, Louis stood in much more intimate relationship. If nothing else, their religious convictions, their common devotion united them. The marked favor shown by James to Catholicism was gratifying to a ruler who himself was cruelly persecuting the Protestants. Louis poured forth his praise, and the English ambassador never tired of describing the cordiality with which the king offered every conceivable assistance when James took the decisive step and imprisoned the bishops. Just this action, however, turned the popular and even aristocratic forces (since the Church of England was assailed) against both their king and the French. The movement which overthrew the Stuarts was religious, national, and in the interest of threatened Europe. It was led by the man who had hitherto been at the heart of all undertakings against France, William III. Thenceforth the new king and his parliament formed a single party. There could be quarrels between them, even violent ones, but in the long run and in the most important matters they remained united, the more so because the opposition which both encountered was so strong. The parties which had hitherto gone to extremes in order to make war upon one another from their opposing positions were forced into a constitutional framework where they disagreed with one another, it is true, but at the same time compromised, so that their conflict became a creative ferment in the constitution.

It is rather interesting to contrast this situation with that in France. The two countries indeed had much in common. In France, as in England, aristocratic families were in control and enjoyed exclusive privileges. They possessed these by virtue of their religion, the French through their Catholicism, the English through their Protestantism. But despite this there was a great difference between them. Uniformity, subordination, and dependence upon a highly developed but morally corrupt court life prevailed in France. In England there was a great struggle, a political competition, between two almost equally strong parties within definite, circumscribed limits. In France the piety which had been implanted largely by force degenerated all too soon into the very opposite. In England there developed a perhaps limited but on the whole manly and confident religion, which overcame its inner differences. The former country was bleeding to death from its false ambition. The veins of the latter were bursting with youthful vigor. It was as if the stream of English national strength were now for the first time emerging from the mountains, between which it had hitherto dug its deep and full but still narrow bed, and were flowing onto the plain to rule it in proud majesty, bear ships, and see world cities founded upon its shores.

The power of the purse, over which most of the previous quarrels between king and parliament had arisen, now commenced to unite them instead. During the quarter century of his rule Charles II had collected 43 million pounds altogether. Within the space of thirteen years William received 72 million pounds; and these revenues increased tremendously thereafter. They increased for the very reason that they were voluntary, because the people perceived that they served, not the luxury of a few courtiers, but the common good. Under these conditions the predominance of the English navy did not long remain in doubt. In 1678 the flourishing condition of the royal fleet was indicated by the fact that it already numbered 83 warships, including fireships, with a complement of 18,323 men. Yet in contrast to this there were 184 ships in 1701, from first to sixth class, excluding fireships and smaller vessels, with a complement of 53,921 men. If the revenue from the postal system provides a means of measuring the internal traffic, then this must also have increased extraordinarily. The postal system is said to have yielded £12,000 revenue in 1660, and in contrast with this £90,504 in 1699.

It was already noticed that the real national motive behind the War of the Spanish Succession was the apprehension lest France and Spain should together snatch the West Indian trade back from the English and Dutch. Even if the peace which was ultimately concluded deserved the censure which the Whigs so vehemently expressed, it at least allayed this fear. Nothing better indicates the predominance of the English over the Bourbon powers than the fact that they kept Gibraltar. They now obtained by treaty the best trade with the Spanish colonies, while at the same time their own colonies expanded with tremendous progress. As Batavia had paled before Calcutta, so did the old maritime lustre of Holland give way to that of England, and Frederick the Great already found occasion to remark that Holland followed her neighbor as a dinghy its ship. And finally, the union with Hanover introduced a new continental and no less anti-French interest.

In the course of this historical development English literature first rose to an influential position in Europe and commenced to vie with the French. Science and philosophy, both schools of the latter,* produced a new and original view of the world, in which the world-dominating spirit was expressed and reflected. It would of course be claiming too much to say that the English had already created monuments of poetry and art that were perfect and imperishable in form, but they had magnificent geniuses even then and had long possessed at least one great poet, with whose works, comprehensible and effective in all ages, Europe was now for the first time becoming familiar. Whereas they had imitated French forms for a time, now one could perceive the influence of their philosophy and science upon the most distinguished Frenchmen.

In this manner Louis XIV was opposed by the rival whom he had hoped to overcome by diplomacy or the influence of religion, a more powerful, magnificent, and dangerous rival than one could ever have expected. The balance of seapower and the whole condition of western Europe were thereby radically changed.

In the meantime the East was also being transformed. I cannot share the opinion that Austria as we now know her can be called an old power. During the Middle Ages she would have amounted to little apart from the Empire. Afterwards she was both drawn along and overshadowed by the Spanish monarchy. At the end of the sixteenth century she lost all outward authority because of the religious schism and the hereditary privileges of the Estates of the Realm in her various provinces. At the beginning of the Thirty Years War German armies had to win back the Emperor's family possessions for him. Even the glory which Wallenstein's campaigns reflected upon Ferdinand II was only a passing one and provoked a powerful reaction. How often were the capitals of the Austrian provinces threatened by the Swedish armies in the latter part of the war. Yet at that very time the House of Austria succeeded in laying the permanent internal foundations of its power through the destruction of its enemies, the elevation of its satellites, and the final entrenchment of Catholicism. This was the first step towards the prestige which it has acquired in more recent times. But Austria first became an inde-

---

* Presumably Berkeley's idealism and Hume's skepticism.

pendent and important European power through the reconquest of Hungary. So long as Budapest was in the hands of the Turks, the French could threaten and gravely endanger Austria whenever they chose to exert their influence upon the Porte to this end. If they did not actually incite the expedition of Kara Mustapha in 1683, they at least knew about it. Their intention was not to ruin Germany or Christendom; they did not go that far. But they wanted to let the Turks take Vienna and even press on to the Rhine. Then Louis XIV would have appeared in the role of sole protector of Christendom. In the confusion which such an event would have produced, he could not have failed to gain control of the German crown and, if he wished, to take it for himself.

This plan was defeated outside the walls of Vienna. It was the last great effort of the Turks, which reacted the more disastrously upon them because they had thrown all their strength into it in a savage excess of effort. After that the disorderly Turkish hordes, which, according to an Italian, had advanced like "a strong, impenetrable wall," gave way everywhere before the German armies. In vain did a *fetva* of the Mufti declare Budapest to be the key to the Empire and its defense the duty of the Faithful. It was lost all the same. All of Hungary was reconquered and made into a hereditary kingdom. The discontented elements submitted. An orthodox Serbian population moved into the borderlands of lower Hungary to defend it in the future against the Turks. From then on Austria rested on a wholly different foundation. Formerly all wars in Hungary were waged by German armies, and it was said that all the rivers there were dyed with German blood. Now Hungary furnished the core of the Austrian armies in the German wars. It was no longer possible for French diplomacy to summon the Turks into the heart of the kingdom upon the slightest occasion. Only once more did France find support and help from the discontented elements. Finally all was quiet. The Emperor afterwards based his power particularly upon that very province which had hitherto been the greatest source of danger to him. It is obvious what a change must have been brought about in the condition of eastern Europe by the strengthening of this stable, rich, well-armed power, which held the Turks in check and even in awe.

Louis XIV experienced at least the beginning of another such change. The situation in Poland, which made it easy for him always to have a faction within that country, and the power of Sweden, which was at least theoretically bound to him by tradition and old alliance, readily gave him a decided predominance in the North. Charles XII made no change in this. It was one of his first resolutions, as expressed to his chancellor, "By all means to conclude the alliance with France and to be numbered among her friends." It is true that the War of the Spanish Succession and the Northern War, which commenced at almost the same time, were not connected by any previous arrangement, although this has often been suspected. But the success of the Swedish campaigns was useful to the French. The events of both wars had in fact a similar tendency. While the Spanish succession was to be the means of delivering southern Europe into the hands of the Bourbons, their old allies, the Swedes, were on the point of gaining complete supremacy in the North. After Charles XII had attacked and subdued the Danes, after he had conquered Poland and placed his own king there, after he had marched through half of Germany, which was not much better fortified in the East than in the West, and held Saxony for a long time, nothing more was needed to consolidate his supremacy but to annihilate the Tsar, whom he had already defeated once. He set out to accomplish this with his army which had been reconditioned in Saxony.

In the meantime the Tsar had made strenuous preparations. The decisive battle of 1709 took place. These two northern heroes faced each other once again, Charles XII and Peter I, original products of Germanic and Slavic nationality. It was a memorable contrast. The Teuton was highminded and simple, blameless in his conduct, every inch a hero, true to his word, bold in his undertakings, reverent, stubborn to the point of obstinacy, and steadfast. The Slav was at once good-natured and cruel, highly agile, still half barbarian but drawn towards the studies and progress of the European nations with all the impetuosity of his alert, eager nature, full of great projects and indefatigable in carrying them out. It is a sublime spectacle to observe the struggle between these two natures. One could well wonder which was the greater of the two. But this much is certain: the greater future lay with the Tsar's success. While Charles showed little understanding for the true interests of his nation, Peter had taken upon himself the development of his, had personally prepared and commenced it, and had made it his chief aim.

He carried the day. To the report on the battle of Poltava which he sent to the capital he added a postscript, "With this, the cornerstone for St. Petersburg is laid." It was the foundation for the whole edifice of his state and his politics. From then on Russia began to give orders in the North. It would be an error to believe that this required a long development. Rather did it happen on the spot. How could Augustus II of Poland, who owed his restoration solely to the Russians' arms, have withdrawn from their influence? He was forced, moreover, to avail himself again of their help in his internal conflict, the struggle with his nobility. Peter I thereby became the direct arbiter in Poland, with power over both factions, all the more so because the Poles decreased their army to one quarter of its former size while his own became ever larger, better drilled, and more to be dreaded. In 1717 a Venetian remarked that the Tsar, who had formerly taken orders from the Poles, was now giving them at will and with unlimited authority. Henceforth the French influence in Poland necessarily decreased more and more. The French were no longer able to promote their candidate for the throne, even when they had the Polish nobility on their side.

In the meantime Sweden was weakened and reduced by these events. In the last days of his reign Louis XIV had guaranteed the Swedish throne all its possessions; nevertheless it eventually lost a considerable part of these. The French still maintained their influence in Stockholm, to be sure. In 1756 people complained there that Sweden was ruled from Paris, as a French province. But, as was said before, Sweden had become completely insignificant. There were the miserable conflicts between the Caps and the Hats, of which the French made use. But if they utilized these occasionally in order to provoke a war against Russia, this only reacted to their disadvantage, Russia was merely given opportunity for new conquest and expansion.

Thus the North had come under quite another rule than the indirect one of France; a great nation was commencing a new and truly European development. In the East the French influence had not altogether disappeared, but it had nowhere near its old importance, even though Austria under Charles VI had certainly grown very weak. The sea was in the hands of France's rivals, who permitted or broke off at will the advantageous connection which France had established via Cadiz with Hispanic America.

On the other hand, through the natural agreement of the Bourbon courts, who after a short interruption had resumed their common policy, France kept the preponderance of power in southern Europe and also in Germany. Above all in Germany. There exist reflections on the state of European politics from the year 1736 which show us in concise and spirited fashion the situation, particularly of German affairs, shortly before the War of the Austrian Succession. Although their author admitted that the Emperor Charles VI endeavored to strengthen his power in the Empire and to make the constitution more monarchical, and that he even violated several articles of his Capitulation by his alliance with the Russians, who had already appeared at the Rhine, he found the danger not so great from this quarter. For he believed that the previous war had revealed the weakness of the Imperial court and that the arrogance and ruthlessness with which the Emperor sought to carry out his plans would defeat their purpose. Let us rather beware, he exclaimed, of those who by secret artifices, insinuating manners, and a feigned benevolence seek to lead us into slavery. He held that Cardinal Fleury, then prime minister of France, despite his air of extraordinary moderation, was deliberately pursuing under this very guise the schemes of a Richelieu or Mazarin. With his apparent magnanimity he was lulling his neighbors to sleep. His gentle and calm character served as a cloak for the diplomacy of his court. How shrewdly, without sensation or noise, had he won Lorraine for France! In order to gain the desired Rhine frontier, which was almost within his reach, he was only awaiting the confusion which would inevitably ensue upon the death of the Emperor.

In 1740 Charles VI died. Cardinal Fleury ventured upon even

bolder measures than one had thought him capable of. He said frankly that he did not wish Maria Theresa's husband to be her father's successor, because the former was ill-disposed towards the French. It was primarily the Cardinal who secured the German crown for Charles VII of Bavaria. He conceived the plan of establishing within Germany four states of about equal power, limiting the House of Austria principally to Hungary, linking Bohemia on the other hand to Bavaria, Moravia and Upper Silesia to Saxony, and satisfying Prussia with Lower Silesia. How easily France could have maintained a perpetual domination over four such states, who by their very nature would never have agreed with one another.

Prussia

It was a moment of seeming danger to the German fatherland, which at that time possessed neither powerful states nor distinguished men of action nor a pronounced national feeling. It had no literature, no art, no culture of its own, nothing with which it could have opposed the predominating influence of its neighbors. Just then Frederick II appeared upon the scene and Prussia emerged as a power.

This is not the place to describe either the ruler or the state which he inherited and the state which he created. Nor may we lightly venture to show the innate power of the man and of the state and the many aspects of their character. Let us only attempt to make clear their position in the world.

We must concede that Frederick's first action was supported by the turn which French policy took immediately after the death of Charles VI. But the question was whether he should align himself much more closely with it. He was the very one who, as crown prince and still removed from real affairs of state, had set down those reflections of which I have just attempted to give some idea. They are, as one can see, directed squarely against French policy. He perceived as clearly as possible the danger which threatened Germany from this quarter. For this reason he had undertaken the war entirely on his own. He did not wish the success of his arms to be advantageous to the French.* He explained in great earnest to their ambassador that he was a German prince and that he would suffer their troops to remain on German soil no longer than was stipulated by the treaties. Late in 1741 it would not have appeared so impossible to reduce Austria completely. Bohemia and Upper Austria were almost as much in enemy hands as was Silesia. Vienna was as greatly threatened as was Prague. If these attacks had been strenuously continued, who can tell what might have been the outcome? I do not wish to credit it to magnanimity on Frederick's part that he eschewed this last step. He well knew that it would not have been to his advantage to rid France of her old opponent. When he saw the Queen of Hungary [Maria Theresa] on the brink of ruin, he wished to give her a chance to recover. He said so himself. But despite his full awareness of this he deliberately paused and concluded an armistice. His aim was to be dependent upon neither France nor Austria. He wished to feel free and to assume an independent position, based upon his own strength, between the two powers. In this simple purpose lies the key to his diplomacy during the Silesian Wars. Never was an acquisition maintained with more zealous vigilance than his. He distrusted his friends no less than his enemies. He kept himself always armed and ready for battle. As soon as he believed himself to be at a disadvantage or espied danger even in the distance, he took up arms. And as soon as he had gained the advantage or won a victory, he extended his hand in peace. Of course he could not bring himself to act in behalf of a foreign interest, but he also viewed his own interest without any exaggeration or self-deception. His demands were never exorbitant. They aimed only at the

* Notice here and in the subsequent analysis the features of Count Bernstorff's foreign policy. Prussia was to make moral conquests in Germany, appearing as the true defender of German greatness and security in Europe even in the eighteenth century. For that reason Ranke stressed the German mission of Frederick the Great, not altogether for the benefit of historical accuracy.

immediate advantage. But in this he would remain firm to the very last.

At the same time such unexpected new independence, won by a bold and defiant attitude, could not help but arouse the displeasure and animosity of his neighbors. One can understand why Maria Theresa did not immediately recover from the loss of a rich province and why she viewed with uneasiness the rise of so successful and able a rival in the Empire. The prestige of Prussia also deeply affected the northern system. Prussia's conclusion of a quite harmless treaty with Sweden and France, in order to maintain a balance of power in the North, aroused the wholehearted hatred of several Russian ministers, who believed their supremacy in the North to be threatened. Frederick might all the more easily have found support in France. But the fact that he, unlike Sweden, was not to be dominated but presumed to follow a free, independent policy, provoked also the indignation of the court at Versailles. Although this court perceived very well what was at stake, it decided nevertheless to change its whole system of alliances and to ally itself henceforth with Austria. Public opinion, in one of those sudden outbursts which are so characteristic, especially in France, joyfully acclaimed the treaty. Thus the Empress succeeded in uniting both great continental powers with herself. Lesser powers, her neighbors in Saxony and Pomerania, joined with them. An alliance was at work, not very different from that which was formed against Austria after the death of Charles VI, even stronger, in fact, because of the participation of Russia. As one had talked formerly about a partition of Austria, so now of Prussia, and it was only across the sea that Frederick found an ally, the same one who had previously joined with Austria. But since he possessed only very moderate power despite this new help, and was insignificant in the face of the alliance, how should he be able or even dare to enter into conflict?

He had, as we know, sought from the Viennese court a categorical declaration as to their armaments. "If it proves even moderately satisfactory," he said to one of his ministers, "then we shall not march." At last the expected courier arrived. The answer was by no means adequate. "The die is cast," he said. "Tomorrow we march!" Thus he plunged courageously into the danger. He had sought it out. He had almost provoked it himself. But only when he was in the midst of it did he recognize its full extent. If ever an event depended upon a great personality, it was the Seven Years War. The wars of our time are usually brought to an end by a few decisive blows. Formerly they lasted longer. Yet men fought more for limited demands and claims than for their very existence or for that of the state itself. The Seven Years War differed in that throughout its long duration the existence of Prussia was at stake every moment. In that state of affairs, amidst the general hostility, only one calamitous day would have been enough to bring about Prussia's ruin. Frederick himself was completely aware of this. After the defeat at Kollin he exclaimed, "It is our Poltava!" And if this prediction was fortunately not fulfilled, it is still true that thenceforth he felt himself threatened with disaster at every moment. I shall not discuss the sources of help upon which he drew in so desperate a situation, his military genius, the bravery of his troops, the loyalty of his subjects, and accidental circumstances. The main thing is that he kept up his spirit.

French philosophy had guided him only in light intellectual exercises, superficial poetry, and academic problems. It appeared to have prepared him for the enjoyment of life while this lasted, rather than for such mighty exertions. But true genius remains unharmed even by false teachings. It is a law unto itself. It rests upon its own truth, of which it needs only to become conscious. Life and the exertion of a great undertaking take care of this. Misfortune ripens it.

Frederick II had long been a great general, but his hardships made him a hero. The resistance which he offered was not only military but at the same time an inner, moral, and spiritual one. The king waged the war with constant reflection upon the ultimate foundation of all things, with a lofty perception of the transitoriness of earthly existence.

I do not wish to praise his poems as distinguished works of poetic talent. As such they may have many defects. But those which originated during the changing fortunes of the war have an exalted sweep of simple thought. They disclose to us the agitation of a manly soul in distress, conflict, and danger. He saw himself "in the midst of a raging sea. Lightning flashes through the tempest. The thunder," he said, "bursts over my head. I am surrounded by cliffs. The hearts of the helmsmen are benumbed. The source of our fortune has dried up. The palms have vanished. The laurel has withered."

Occasionally he may have sought support and strength in the sermons of Bourdaloue. More often he turned to the philosophy of the ancients. Yet the third book of Lucretius, which he had studied so often, told him only that evil was necessary and that there was no remedy for it. He was a man to whom exalted thoughts emerged from this hard, despairing doctrine. He looked death, which he had so often wished to find on the battlefield, straight in the eye, without flinching, even when it took another form.* Just as he often liked to compare his enemies to the triumvirate, so he called upon the *manes* of Cato and Brutus and was resolved to follow their example. Yet he was not in quite the same position as these Romans. They were involved in a general world destiny—Rome was the world—with no other consideration than the importance of their own persons and of the idea for which they were fighting. But he had a country to represent and to defend. If any one special thought operated upon him, it was this thought of his country, of his fatherland.

Let us imagine him after the battle of Kunersdorf, as he fathomed the extent of his misfortune and the hopelessness of his situation. In the face of his enemies' hatred and good fortune, he thought all was lost. He saw but one single expedient for his army and his country and resolved to seize this, to sacrifice himself. But then there gradually appeared the possibility of renewed resistance, and he dedicated himself anew to his all but hopeless duty. It was impossible for him to leave his country in the state in which he had so long been forced to see it, "inundated by its enemies, robbed of its honor, with no source of help, in mortal danger." "To you," he said, "I will devote the remainder of my

* He contemplated suicide.

calamitous life. I will not be consumed by fruitless anxiety. I will throw myself once more into the field of danger." "Let us oppose fate," he exclaimed to his troops, "courageous against so many enemies, who conspire with one another and are drunk with pride and presumption." Thus he persevered. Finally he witnessed the day of peace. "Firmness is the only thing, in affairs of state," he said at the end of his history of this war, "which can save one from danger." He kept his land intact, and, from the moment that he knew he was again master of it, he made it his primary, even sole concern to heal the wounds which the war had brought to it.

If one could establish as a definition of a great power that it must be able to maintain itself against all others, even when they are united, then Frederick had raised Prussia to that position. For the first time since the days of the Saxon emperors and Henry the Lion a self-sufficient power was found in northern Germany, needing no alliance, dependent only upon itself.

It followed that from then on France was able to exert little or no influence on German affairs. The time for an opposition such as she had aroused or favored during the War of the Austrian Succession was now completely past. As Prussia had emancipated herself, so had Bavaria and Saxony allied themselves again to Austria.

And for the time being a renewal of the old relationship was unthinkable. France herself had prevented it by entering into that close alliance with Austria which had produced the Seven Years War. I shall not examine to what extent this alliance caused all the other effects which the French, not without exaggeration, ascribed to it. But it is certain that France herself thereby gave up her previous position, through which she had encouraged the German opposition, and that "from this moment on," as was said in France, "the King of Prussia, to the detriment of French supremacy on the continent, became the protector of German freedom." It is unlikely that Austria would have permitted France to exert her old influence. While he was still co-regent and from the very beginning, Joseph II proclaimed that he considered the rights of the Imperial crown to be sacred. He insisted that no one interfere with him on this point who wished to be in good standing with him. It was already recognized that the true safeguard of Germany's political independence lay in a free and solidly established union of both German powers against the outside world.*

This great change became fully significant through the fact that at the same time German literature was emancipated from French models and their false imitation. I do not mean that our nation had not hitherto enjoyed intellectual independence to a certain extent. It was found mainly in the development of theological systems, which had taken hold of all minds and were essentially of German origin. But these still represented only a part of the nation, and the pure, ideal, intuitive recognition of true religion found itself forced into a strange, scholastic form. One cannot deny the activity and partial success with which work was carried on in many other branches of learning, but they all had to submit to the same form. They were taught in complicated systems suited to delivery from a lecturer's desk but seldom to real intellectual comprehension. The universities controlled education in general, not without narrowness and compulsion. It was all the more natural that this system of education should gradually lose its hold on the upper classes, who, as was said before, let themselves be carried away by French influences.

But after the middle of the eighteenth century a new development of the national spirit began. We must not forget that it developed largely from the old system of education, although it stood in a certain contradiction to it. Dissatisfied, still influenced but no longer so limited by the dogmatic system, the German spirit achieved a fuller expression of this system through poetry.

Religion was at last brought close to people's hearts once more, with all its human implications and, most important of

---

* Here again Ranke read the policy of his masters at the Prussian Foreign Office into German history in the second half of the eighteenth century. He ignored the rivalry between Austria and Prussia and its disastrous consequences for Germany in the period of the French Revolution and Napoleonic wars.

all, without emotionalism. With a bold effort philosophy rallied to a new discussion of the ultimate foundation of all knowledge. Side by side appeared the two tendencies of German philosophy, essentially different yet closely related, the one more intuitive, the other more analytical. They have since developed next to and with one another, have attracted and repelled each other, but only in conjunction have been able to express the fullness of an original consciousness. Criticism and archeology broke through the mass of formal learning and pressed on to a grasp of living forces.

The national spirit, awakened with a start and benefiting from its own thoroughness and maturity, then developed a poetic literature, independently and with free experimentation. It thereby created a view of the world that was comprehensive, new, and, although caught in many contradictions, still more or less coherent. This literature had the inestimable quality of no longer being limited to only part of the nation. Instead it embraced the whole and made it really aware of its unity for the first time.

If new generations of great poets do not always succeed the old ones, one should not wonder too much. The great attempts are made and are successful. What one had to say has been well said, and sincere minds scorn to travel along frequented and easy roads. But the work of German genius was by no means completed. Its task was to penetrate into positive science. Many obstacles stood in the way, arising from its own development and from other influences as well. We can now hope that it will overcome them all, will become more harmonized within itself, and will then be capable of continuous new creation.

But I shall pause here since I wished to discuss politics, although all these things are very closely connected and a true political philosophy can only be inspired by a great national existence. This much is certain, that no other phenomenon contributed so much to the self-confidence with which this wave of enthusiasm was accompanied as did the life and renown of Frederick II. A nation must feel independent in order to develop freely, and never has a literature flourished save when a climax of history prepared the way for it. But it was strange that Frederick himself neither knew nor anticipated this. He labored for the emancipation of the nation, and German literature worked with him, yet he did not recognize his allies. They knew him well, however. It made the Germans proud and bold to have had a hero emerge from their midst.

As we have seen, it was a necessity of the seventeenth century that France be checked. This had now occurred in a manner that exceeded all expectation. It cannot really be said that an artificial, complex political system had been formed to this end. It merely appeared so, but the fact was that great powers had raised themselves by their own strength and that new independent national states in all their original power had taken over the world stage.

Austria, a Catholic and German nation, was in a stable military condition, full of fresh, inexhaustible vitality, rich, and, in short, a world by itself. The Graeco-Slavic principle appeared more strongly in Russia than ever before in world history. The European forms which it adopted were far from crushing this original element. They penetrated it instead, animated it, and for the first time drew forth its own strength. In England the Germanic maritime interests had developed into a colossal world power which ruled all the seas and before which all memories of earlier sea powers paled. And in Prussia the German Protestants found the support which they had long sought, at once their representation and their expression. "Even if one knew the secret," says a poet, "who would have the courage to tell it?" I shall not presume to put the character of these states into words. But we can see clearly that they were founded upon principles which had grown out of the various great developments of earlier centuries, that they were formed according to these original differences and with varying constitutions, and that they represented those historic demands which in the nature of things were made upon successive generations. In their rise and development, which, understandably enough, could not have occurred without a many-sided transformation of inner conditions, lies the principal event of the hundred years which preceded the outbreak of the French Revolution.

The French Revolution

However significant the rise of the continental powers was in itself, it cannot be denied that France was thereby restricted and that she was right in viewing the success of the other countries as her own loss. She had always vigorously opposed them. How often had she formerly tried to check the advance of Austria into Hungary and against the Turks. How often did the best Austrian regiments have to be called back from the Danube where they were opposing the Turks and sent to the Rhine against the French. Russia had wrested her influence in the north from the French. When the cabinet at Versailles became aware what position Prussia had assumed and was seeking to maintain in the world, it forgot its American interests in order not only to reduce but actually to annihilate this power. How often had the French undertaken to restore the old relationship with England, to favor the Jacobites and perhaps to foment a Stuart rebellion. In return they made enemies of the English every time, whether they stood with Prussia against Austria or with Austria against Prussia. They waged their wars upon the continent and neglected their navy. During the Seven Years War they lost America, as the elder Pitt said, in Germany.

Thus France stood nowhere near so definitely at the center of the European world as a hundred years earlier. She was forced to witness the partition of Poland without being consulted. In 1772, to her deep resentment, she had to permit an English frigate to appear at the roadstead of Toulon in order to supervise the stipulated disarmament of her fleet. Even the smaller independent states, such as Portugal and Switzerland, had admitted other outside influences.

At the same time it must be remarked that the harm was not so great as has often been represented. France still exerted her old influence over Turkey. Through the Family Compact she had linked Spain to her policy. The Spanish fleet and the riches of the Spanish colonies stood at her disposal. The remaining Bourbon

courts, among which Turin may almost be included, allied themselves with France. And the French faction finally won out in
Sweden. But this was not nearly enough for a nation who gloried
more than any other in the splendor of a universal superiority.
She was aware only of the loss of claims which she regarded as
rights. She noticed only what the others had conquered, not what
she had kept. She eyed with indignation such powerful, well-
established rivals, for whom she was no longer a match.

Much has been said about the causes of the Revolution and
they have also been sought where they can never be found. One
of the most important, in my opinion, is this change in the international position of France which had brought the government
into deep discredit. It is true that the government knew neither
how to manage the state correctly nor how to wage war properly.
It had allowed the most dangerous abuses to prevail, and the collapse of its European prestige originated in large measure from
this. But the French also blamed their government for everything
that was really only a product of the changed world situation.
They still fed on memories of the days of the all-powerful Louis
XIV. All the conditions that resulted from the rise of other vigorous states, who curtailed France's former influence, were attributed by the French to the incapacity of their foreign policy and
to the indeed undeniable degeneration of their internal situation.
Thus it came about that the reform movement in France, which
turned all too soon into a revolutionary one, was also directed
from the very beginning against the outside world.

The American Revolution at once revealed this two-fold
nature. If one did not already know, one could see from the
memoirs of Ségur what a strange mixture of zest for war and
pseudo-philosophy motivated the youth of the higher French nobility who participated in it. "Freedom," says Ségur, "presented
herself to us with all the attraction of glory. While the more mature used the opportunity to put their principles into practice and
to check arbitrary power, we younger ones marched only under
the banners of philosophy in order to wage war, to distinguish
ourselves, to win places of honor. We were philosophers out of
chivalrous conviction." But gradually these youths became philos-

ophers in real earnest. A strange combination! While they attacked England and made it their ambition to weaken her and
strip her of her colonies, yet it was the independence of an English
peer, the dignified position of a member of the House of Commons, which they particularly wished to achieve.

The American Revolution now became a turning-point, not
so much through a change in the general balance of power as
through its indirect effects. For although the English colonies had
been torn loose from the mother country, it was soon apparent
that England was in so well-established a position that she did
not feel their loss very keenly. And although the French navy had
regained a certain prestige, England had still been victorious in
the decisive battles and had maintained supremacy over her combined rivals.

By indirect effects I refer not only to the rise of republican
tendencies. There was also a more immediate result. Turgot had
opposed the war with great energy. Only in time of peace could he
hope to restore by thrifty economy the finances, which were
already then suffering from a deficit, and at the same time to put
through the necessary reforms. But he had to yield to the tide of
youthful enthusiasm.

War was declared and waged at an extravagant cost. Necker
knew how to raise new loans with all the banker's talent which he
possessed to so high a degree. The more these accumulated, however, the higher the deficit rose. In 1780 Vergennes already declared to the King that the condition of the finances was truly
alarming, that it made peace necessary, and without delay. In the
meantime the war dragged on, and only after its conclusion did the
confusion become generally apparent. Here again is a striking
contrast. England came out of the American war no less exhausted
and laden with debts, but Pitt seized the evil by the roots and restored confidence through strict measures. The French finances,
on the other hand, passed from weak into ever weaker hands,
more untried and at the same time more daring, so that matters
grew worse from month to month and not only deprived the
government of authority but threatened its very form.

One can imagine how strongly this affected foreign policy.

The French no longer had any choice; war must be avoided at all costs. Despite their bad financial situation, they preferred to buy off the demands which Austria exacted of Holland by a sum of money of which they contributed half. Had it depended only on France, the Emperor would have had a free hand to carry out his designs upon Bavaria. Closely as the French government had allied itself with the so-called Dutch patriots, it still had to let the latter be invaded and conquered by Prussia. In my opinion it cannot even be greatly blamed for this. What could it have done in that July of 1787 to prevent the Prussian ultimatum to Holland from being carried out? At that very time the *parlements* were refusing to register the new imposts without which the state could not be administered, and soon thereafter, in that famous session of August 15, the *Grand'Chambre* opened its doors and declared to the assembled crowd that in future the king could levy no new taxes without first summoning the Estates General.* At a moment when their entire internal order was in question, the French could scarcely exert any influence upon the outside world. Yet it was a very significant juncture, for just then both imperial courts decided to attack Turkey. The French were in no position to give aid to their old ally, and, if Turkey were not to perish, she had to seek help from England and Prussia.

At all events we can see that French foreign policy was suffering from an insignificance and futility neither commensurate with the natural claims of that country nor corresponding to the interests of Europe as a whole. If this weakness of policy stemmed from the internal confusion, as cannot be denied, then the latter in turn was immensely aggravated thereby. The policy of the Archbishop of Brienne was under the most violent and general censure. He was accused of cowardice and even of disloyalty because he had not supported Holland and had missed this opportunity of restoring the military prestige of the French on land. People con-

---

* Ranke's dating is incorrect. The famous session of the *Grand' Chambre* of the *Parlement* of Paris took place on August 7, 1787. On August fifteenth the whole body found itself escorted to Troyes into banishment, by authority of *lettres de cachet*.

sidered French honor to be so debased that it could only be puri-
fied by streams of blood.

However exaggerated that last statement may sound, one
cannot find fault with the sentiment which lay behind the dis-
satisfaction. The national consciousness of a great people demands
a fitting position in the European community. International relations depend not on convenience but on actual power, and the
prestige of a state will always correspond to the strength of its
internal development. Any nation will feel sensitive not to find
itself in its rightful position. How much more so the French nation
which had so often raised the singular claim of being preeminently
the great nation!

I shall not go into the multiplicity of causes which led to
the fearful development of the French Revolution. I shall only remind the reader that the decline in France's external position was
an important factor. One need think only of the role played by
an Austrian princess, the unhappy queen upon whom fell all the
hatred which this nation had so long felt for the House of Austria,
and of the unfortunate scenes occasioned by the false rumor of a
secret Austrian committee. The French not only realized that they
had lost their old influence upon their neighbors. They even persuaded themselves that the foreign powers were exerting a strong
secret influence upon their own state. They imagined that they
could detect it in all the measures of their domestic administration. This was the very thing that fanned the general indignation
and increased the ferment and fury of the populace. If we adhere
to the theory of the importance of foreign relations, we can form
the following interpretation of the Revolution.

The resources of all nations had been concentrated in unprecedented fashion in order to attain greater power. To this end
many obstacles in their internal condition had to be removed and
old privileges were often violated. This had been accomplished in
the different countries with varying degrees of planning and success. It would make an illuminating study if someone could describe how it was attempted everywhere, to what extent it succeeded, and to what it led. Finally the same task was undertaken
in France. The absolute power of previous French kings has been

much condemned, but the truth is, while it did indeed appear in occasional arbitrary acts, on the whole it had greatly declined. When the government made the attempt to modernize itself, it was already too weak to carry it through. It also did so with unsteady hands. It could not combat the opposition of the privileged orders. It appealed to the Third Estate for help, and thus to the power of the democratic ideas which had already begun to capture public opinion. Now it obtained an ally that was far too strong for it. The government wavered as soon as it recognized the strength of the Third Estate, departed from the course which it had chosen, returned to the ranks of those whom it had wished to attack, and offended the very group upon which it had called for help. It thereby aroused all the political passions of the people, came into conflict with the convictions and tendency of the century, indeed with its own tendency, and provoked a movement in which the Third Estate, or rather the revolutionary element which had developed within and around it, took a gigantic step forward, overthrowing, not only the privileged classes and the aristocracy, but the king and throne themselves and destroying the entire old regime.

The same policy had strengthened and consolidated the government of some although not of all states. But in France, because of the course which it took and because of its consequences, it led to disaster.

Yet if people sometimes assumed that the power and prestige of France must utterly perish in this great debacle, they were mistaken. So strong were the tendencies towards restoration of her power in Europe that they not only survived the fearful upheaval but were even asserted as never before, far beyond the power of other states. Whereas elsewhere the intermediary orders would have merely been limited in their independence and forced into greater participation in the common effort, here they were completely annihilated. Nobility and clergy were stripped not only of their privileges but, in the course of events, even of their possessions. It was a wholesale confiscation on the vastest scale. The ideas which Europe had hailed as salutary and liberating to mankind were suddenly transformed before its eyes into the horror of devastation. The volcanic fire, from which one had expected a nourishing, life-giving warmth for the earth, had poured forth a fearful eruption.

Yet even in the midst of this wreckage the French never abandoned the principle of unity. During the confusion of the revolutionary years France proved much more powerful than before in relation to the other European states. One can justly say that this tremendous explosion of all forces extended beyond France's borders. Between the old and the new France there existed the same contrast as between the aristocracy who had controlled the old state—spirited, to be sure, and brave by nature, but accustomed to court life, motivated often by petty ambition, effete and voluptuous—and the wild, violent Jacobins, intoxicated with a few ideas and stained with blood, who ruled the new one. In the course of events the other states had developed an aristocracy not exactly like the French one but still similar to it. Thus it was no wonder that by fiercely straining all forces the Jacobins gained the preponderance of power in Europe. The first victory, won by a coincidence of unexpected circumstances, was all that was needed to awaken the revolutionary enthusiasm which thereupon gripped the French nation and became its life principle for a long time.

It cannot be said, however, that France thus became actually stronger than the other great powers together or even than her nearest neighbors if they remained united. We are sufficiently familiar with the errors of policy and of military strategy which produced so unfavorable a result for these countries. And they could not wean themselves all at once from their previous jealousy. Even the one-sided coalition of 1799 was able to liberate Italy and to assume a very powerful military position, until an unfortunate dissension divided it. But it cannot be denied that the French state, formed in the midst of a struggle with Europe and designed to cope with it, became stronger than any one of the continental states through the new centralization of power.

Although France had always appeared to be seeking freedom, she had advanced through successive revolutions towards a military despotism which far exceeded the development of military systems elsewhere, great as these were. The successful general crowned himself emperor. He had the power to throw all available resources of the nation into the field at any moment. In this way France returned to her old supremacy. She succeeded in excluding England from the Continent, in robbing Austria of her oldest provinces in Germany and Italy during repeated wars, in overthrowing the army and the monarchy of Frederick II, in forcing even Russia into obedience, and finally in penetrating the latter's inner provinces as far as the old capital. The French emperor needed war with only these powers in order to establish direct dominion over both southern and central Europe, not excluding a large part of Germany. Thus everything which had happened in Louis XIV's time had now been far exceeded. The old liberties of Europe were submerged. Europe seemed about to be swallowed up by France. The universal monarchy, which had hitherto seemed only a remote danger, was almost realized.

Restoration

But were the energetic forces which had emerged as the great powers to be choked and destroyed at one blow?

"War," says Heraclitus, "is the father of things." Out of the clash of opposing forces, in the crucial moments of danger—collapse, resurgence, liberation—the most decisive new developments are born.

France had only attained her supremacy because, in the midst of her turbulence, she had known how to keep the feeling of national unity more alive than ever and how to strain her national resources in an extraordinary expansion for the single purpose of the war.

If anyone wished to oppose her or conceived a hope of once more breaking her predominance, the means which had previously sufficed were no longer enough. Even an improved military organization would not have helped by itself. A more thorough revival was needed in order to concentrate all available resources. It had become necessary to awaken to self-conscious activity those slumbering spirits of the nations by whom life had hitherto been carried on more unconsciously.

It would be a splendid enterprise to investigate this rejuvenation of the national spirit in the whole compass of European peoples and states, to note the events which aroused it once more, the signs which heralded its first awakening, the multiplicity of movements and institutions in which it victoriously culminated. This would be such a far-reaching undertaking, however, that we cannot even touch upon it here.

It is certain that men for the first time began to fight with some prospect of success when, in 1809, they commenced to fulfill satisfactorily these demands of world destiny; when in well-ordered empires whole sections of the inhabitants lost their hereditary dwellings to which they were tied even by religion and abandoned them to the flames; when whole populations, accustomed for generations to peaceful civilian life, took up arms, man for man; when people finally forgot their hereditary feuds and united themselves in earnest. Then for the first time, and no sooner, did they succeed in defeating the enemy, restoring the old liberties, and restraining France within her borders, driving the flooded stream back into its bed.

If the main event of the hundred years before the French Revolution was the rise of the great powers in defense of European independence, so the main event of the period since then is the fact that nationalities were rejuvenated, revived, and developed anew. They became a part of the state, for it was realized that without them the state could not exist.

It is almost generally held that our times tend towards and are capable only of dissolution. Their only significance lies in the fact that they are putting an end to the unifying or shackling institutions left over from the Middle Ages. They are striding towards this goal with the certainty of an innate impulse. It is the end-product of all great events and discoveries, of our entire civilization, in fact. It also explains the irresistible inclination towards democratic ideas and institutions, which of necessity produces all the great changes which we are witnessing. It is a general movement, in which France merely preceded the other countries.

All this is an opinion which can of course lead only to the gloomiest prospects for the future. We believe, however, that it cannot be supported against the truth of the facts. Far from being satisfied only with negation, our century has produced the most positive results. It has achieved a great liberation, not wholly in the sense of dissolution but rather in a creative, unifying sense. It is not enough to say that it called the great powers into being. It has also renewed the fundamental principle of all states, that is, religion and law, and given new life to the principle of each individual state. In just this fact lies the characteristic feature of our time.

In most epochs of world history it has been religious ties that have held the peoples together. Yet occasionally there have been other periods, which can be better compared with ours, when several larger kingdoms and free states existed side by side, linked by one political system. I shall only mention the period of the Hellenistic kingdoms after Alexander. It provides many similarities to our own, a highly developed common culture, military science, and action and interaction of complicated foreign relations, also the great importance of the trading interests and of finance, rivalry of industries, and a flowering of the exact sciences based on mathematics. But those states, produced by the enterprise of a conqueror and the dissension among his successors, had neither possessed nor been able to attain any individual principles of existence. They were based upon soldiers and money alone. It was for that very reason that they were so soon dissolved and at last entirely disappeared. It has often been asked how Rome could overcome them so quickly and completely. It happened because Rome, at least as long as she had enemies of importance, held to her principle of existence with admirable firmness.

With us it also appeared as if only the extent of our possessions, the power of the troops, the amount of wealth, and a certain share in the general civilization were of value to the state. If there were ever events qualified to dispel such an illusion, it is

7

those of our own time. They have finally made the public aware
how important moral strength and the sense of nationality are
for the state. What would have become of our states if they had
not received new life from the national principle upon which they
were based? It is inconceivable that any state could exist without it.

World history does not present such a chaotic tumult, warring, and planless succession of states and peoples as appear at
first sight. Nor is the often dubious advancement of civilization
its only significance. There are forces and indeed spiritual, life-
giving, creative forces, nay life itself, and there are moral energies,
whose development we see. They cannot be defined or put in abstract terms, but one can behold them and observe them. One can
develop a sympathy for their existence. They unfold, capture the
world, appear in manifold expressions, dispute with and check
and overpower one another. In their interaction and succession,
in their life, in their decline or rejuvenation, which then encompasses an ever greater fullness, higher importance, and wider extent, lies the secret of world history.

* As we are now attacked by a spiritual power, so must we
oppose it with spiritual force. The dominion which another nation threatens to gain over us can only be combatted by developing our own sense of nationality. I do not mean an invented, illu-
sionary nationality but the real, existing one which is expressed
in the state.

But, so people will reply, is not the world developing at this
moment into an ever closer community? Would not this tendency
be impeded and limited by the contrast between different peoples
with their national ways or different states with their individual
principles?

Unless I delude myself, there is a close analogy with literature. No one spoke of a world literature at the time that French
literature dominated Europe. Only since then has this idea been
conceived, expressed, and propagated, in other words, only after

* The subsequent conclusion was omitted by Ranke in his edition
of collected works.

most of the principal peoples of Europe had developed their own literature independently and often in sharp contrast. If I may be allowed to make a trivial comparison, I should like to remind the reader that the sort of company where one person is spokesman and leads the whole conversation affords neither pleasure nor profit, nor does the sort where all the people, being on the same level or, if you will, of the same mediocrity, only say the same thing. One only feels happy when many-sided personalities, freely developed, meet on a higher common ground or indeed produce this very meeting-place by stimulating and complementing one another. There would be only a disagreeable monotony if the different literatures should let their individual characters be blended and melted together. No, the union of all must rest upon the independence of each single one. Then they can stimulate one another in lively fashion and forever, without one dominating or injuring the others.

It is the same with states and nations. Decided, positive prevalence of one would bring ruin to the others. A mixture of them all would destroy the essence of each one. Out of separation and independent development will emerge the true harmony.

8

A DIALOGUE
ON POLITICS

(1836)

FRIEDRICH: What, visiting me in such splendor, in the uniform of a Councillor-of-State, with even your foreign decorations?

CARL: I wager, you did not even hear the carriages rumble by. But if you would come only two steps with me, I could show you the bright windows where I have been. They shine along the entire street.

FR: And from all that brilliance you stole away into the solitude of this study?

C: To offer a "Good Evening" to my Benedictine brother. Having seen the great world, I am looking for a human soul. After light conversation one wants at last to enjoy a serious talk.

Translated by Theodore H. Von Laue from the text in Ranke's Sämmtliche Werke, *vol. XLIX/L, edited by Alfred Dove, 2nd ed., 1887. From Theodore H. Von Laue,* Leopold Ranke: The Formative Years *(Princeton: Princeton University Press, 1950), pp. 152–180. Reprinted by permission of Princeton University Press and the translator.*

FR: I should feel flattered by your distinctions. Be all the more welcome.

c: Do you really believe that mingling among all these dignitaries could satisfy me—adding to the manifold opinions and bits of news that dominate the drawing room the flavor of my own?

FR: You talk like most men of the world from Byron on; you feel fatigued and uninspired.

c: The great world and its conversation only allows communication in generalities. One stays on the surface of things. One meets people whom chance or birth have raised to high society; one hears of the things in the spotlight of current interest. It is a community of the most ephemeral kind, constantly changing, and still the same, year after year. There are people who find satisfaction in it. To me this motley monotony is somewhat depressing.

FR: Still, you would not want to forego it entirely. The interests which set the wheels of the world really in motion must be revealed in high society, if only hastily and, as you say, superficially. It must be interesting for all of you in the great world to see them come to the surface, grow, dominate, and again disappear.

What did they chiefly talk about tonight?

c: Good Lord, they repeated the news as they interpret it: Tension between England and Russia, the *Portfolio*,[1] the restitution of Silistria, the journey of the French princes, Alibaud,

---

[1] *The Portfolio, or Collection of State Papers, etc., Illustrative of the History of Our Times,* ed. David Urquhart, 6 vols. (London, 1836–1837), a collection of secret Russian state papers, particularly dispatches by the diplomat Pozzo di Borge, in Russian service, dealing with the Eastern question, published by the violently anti-Russian English diplomat David Urquhart in order to drive a wedge between Austria and Russia. These papers, deposited in Warsaw, had fallen into unfriendly hands during the Polish uprising of 1831. The numbered notes are the present editors'; the asterisked notes are the translator's.

the small attention given nowadays to the sessions of the Chambre, railroads and percussion rifles, war and peace—in a word, everything you want.

FR: But some viewpoints, some opinions must have stood out . . .

C: Depending on various official positions. The eyes of the young officers gleamed at the mere mention of war, without much thought whom they would fight. They seize upon the animosities of the *Portfolio*, they believe that England seriously desires to force a rupture, they do not doubt the fire would immediately spread over the rest of Europe and the world.

FR: Indeed, what an army would not wholeheartedly wish for war . . . action, prestige, advancement—I don't blame them.

C: But it is strange: armaments were never mightier and more universal than now, and yet we have never had a longer peace.

FR: That follows quite naturally. Previously wars were waged with the excess of forces, with the people who could be spared, with money either found in the treasury or at least raised elsewhere without too great an effort. Now the nations, armed as they are, fight almost man for man, with all their might. The expenses of the initial equipment alone are nearly unbearable. One must be prepared for a struggle for life or death. No wonder then that statesmen are somewhat reluctant. But you were going to mention still another opinion.

C: The civil service, on the other hand, is pleased by the prospects of a long peace. They are losing their fear of the contrast between absolute and constitutional monarchy which beclouded the future these many years and seemed so dangerous. The "juste milieu," kept under so long, recovers its breath. They hope that everybody will become convinced that government by extremes is impossible.

FR: You, too, it seems, are siding with this opinion.

C: How could I do otherwise? Should we surrender political life to the incessant agitation of the popular party, or to the retarding tendencies of the aristocratic party? Should we not take a position between them in their conflict, if only to escape subservience to them? We do not want to be swept away by their force from what we want into what we do not want.

FR: Very wise.

C: And very necessary. Where is a state that does not face the necessity of choosing this compromise? We should have expected that after the recent French Revolution the party of movement and liberalism would have won an irresistible supremacy. But after a few days the new government was forced to call a stop to the revolution. And it is obvious what repercussions this has had on all Europe and particularly on the constitutional movement in Germany. The Whigs, too, steer between radicalism and conservative principles. However strongly they may seem to favor the former, they have not discarded the latter.

FR: Do you indeed believe that one can rule in this fashion?

C: Are you not of this opinion?

FR: I am in the peculiar position of agreeing in general, and still of disagreeing with you.

C: But what can you say against it? Explain your position.

FR: Are you really inclined, coming as you do from a gay party, to enter patiently upon the examination of a very serious question? For we might be drawn deeper than you think.

C: Why shouldn't I be? Only in this way do we advance from conversation to a serious talk, from accepted opinion to search and discovery.

FR: Then first answer me one question: have you ever found a confirmation of what you so frequently hear, that the Truth lies in the middle?

C: At least I have always noticed that it is not found in the extremes.

FR: From extremes, consequently, you will not be able to derive the truth. Truth, moreover, lies entirely outside the scope of error. You could not abstract it from all phantoms of error taken together. You must find truth and behold it by itself, in its own sphere. From all heresies in the world you could not gather what Christianity is. You must read the Gospel in order to know it. Nay, we may claim that from the praise or censure of the world no sound judgment will ever be formed, however conscientiously we try to determine the mean between them.

c: I shall let your thesis stand for the moment. But what has it to do with the "juste milieu"?

FR: In the state, too, you observe the extremes of opinion. They might not contain the correct one, I admit. But who says that it lies in the middle?

c: The state is no doctrine. The parties do not merely defend opinions. They themselves are powers, forces that oppose, fight, and displace each other, as we can see every day.

FR: And between them, now, you think the government shall hold the balance?

c: Yes, indeed; governing is guiding, directing. . . .

FR: But now I ask you: how is it able to do so? Where does it get the power?

c: There is no constitution in our time which does not grant a significant measure of power even to a limited government.

FR: Allow me: power by itself is insufficient. Power is merely an instrument. Its usefulness depends entirely on the ends for which it is employed, and whether you know how to use it at all. By itself your government would have no significance.

c: Why so? Is it not important to prevent conflict, to further the general welfare?—Listen now: however we might define state and society, there is always a contrast between superiors and subjects, between the mass of the ruled and the small number of the rulers. Let things be as they may, you will always find that ultimately the interests of the large number prevail. The ruler submits to them one way or the other. Among the masses, however, there will always be discord and divergent parties. But we should not always consider this as simply a sign of disorganization. Frequently it is only the way of life in which the public welfare thrives quite well. What more can the government do than prevent the preponderance of one or the other party, or a dangerous clash of both?

FR: You shall not escape me by this answer. In your view the political arena belongs to the parties; they are the center of life; the government is only the point of indifference. This very argument I shall not concede to you.

c: And why not?

FR: You will admit, and it is implicit in your words, that the parties of which you speak represent spiritual forces, not only a certain measure of power.

c: Yes, undoubtedly spiritual forces and tendencies.

FR: Must not the government itself be the stronger spiritual power in order to oppose these other forces and bridle them? You ascribe action to the government. But what is the "agent," the motive power? Mere goodwill for mediation will not suffice. You must have an active essence, a Self.

c: However that be, this much always remains true, that the government must hold the middle ground between the parties.

FR: At this point we agree and we disagree. There are, it seems to me, two conceptions of the "juste milieu." According to one it is of a rather negative kind: the parties constitute the state; and the ruling authority, zealous not to harm them, holds the balance between them. That seems to be your conception. According to the other, however, it is a positive idea. It excludes, I admit, the parties, the extremes, but only because it has a positive content of its own, its natural innate tendency which above all else it must realize.

c: You are indeed right, that this problem leads us into profounder regions. It is the nature of the state in general toward which—I confess to my satisfaction—our conversation now tends. I have already frequently noticed that on this matter you have formed an opinion different from my own. If you have nothing better to do tonight, give me a full account of it. What do you understand by the positive spiritual content of the state? Do not all states start from the same origin? Have they not all identical obligations? Are not their differences merely accidental?

FR: That is just the point. I answer a decided "no" to all these questions which you seem to answer affirmatively. If we want to understand each other we must now advance one step further.

Do you know the small book that lies there on the table?

C: *Les deux derniers chapitres de ma philosophie de la guerre.*[2] By whom?

FR: Read also the title page.

C: I see, by Chambray,* the diligent and penetrating historian of the Russian campaign. And the contents are even indicated on the title page. Chapter IX. *Des institutions militaires dans leur rapports avec les constitutions politiques et avec les institutions civiles.*[3] Quite a fortunate approach. I am eager to know his opinions.

FR: He finds that by inner necessity military institutions correspond to the state of society, to the civil constitution.

C: Give an example.

FR: The English army corresponds to the Unreformed Parliament. The aristocracy which sat in both Houses voted annually for its maintenance. As it was in their interest to maintain the existing order, since the aristocracy was in reality the state, they reserved the officers' commissions for themselves through some peculiar institutions, and they have kept them still. Non-commissioned officers and privates, on the other hand, are enlisted. They get better pay and more careful attention than in any other nation, which is necessary and possible on account of the high standards of that nation. It keeps their morale high. At the same time strictest discipline and harsh punishment hold them in subjection.

C: From this it seems to follow that if they changed the constitution still further, reforms in the army would not be far off.

FR: I do not doubt it, as soon as the reforms have gone still deeper.

---

* *La Philosophie de la Guerre.* Oeuvres du Marquis de Chambray, vol. III.

[2] *The Two Last Chapters of My Philosophy of War.*

[3] *On Military Institutions in Their Relationship to Political Constitutions and Civil Institutions.*

c: The difference between the English and the Prussian army also derives from this dependence of military institutions on the civil constitution.

FR: In Prussia, too, the author finds military and civil institutions in complete accord. Universal military service corresponds to individual liberty and the division of property, the institution of the *Landwehr* to municipal rights, the privileged one-year term of service of the educated classes to their social position in general. The fact that the petty officers can expect a pension ties them closely to the state. "A country," the author exclaims, "which has a militia like the *Landwehr* and institutions like the *Städteordnung* indeed possesses liberty."*

c: How utterly different were those two armies which defeated Napoleon at Waterloo: both of closely related nations, but fashioned after different inner motives, one of hired men, well-paid, tenacious, aristocratic, the other of conscripted citizens, mobile, prepared to suffer deprivations if necessary, and untiring. It is truly significant that the union of two so opposite military brotherhoods—one of which represented the old, the other the new state of Germanic Europe—won the last, decisive victory. You can understand why at that time Wellington declined the pursuit, and why he has since shown no taste to change the institutions of his army. In this, too, he is an anti-reformer. He was never able to get even an idea of what his allies were like.

Does Chambray also speak of the French army after Napoleon?

FR: He hardly admires it. He cannot stand it when a general who has won twenty battles exercises no more political rights than a grocer who pays a couple of hundred francs taxes. Advancement, he finds, is far more dependent on the recommendations of a deputy who takes only a personal interest in the

---

* "La liberté existe de fait dans un pays qui a une milice telle que la landwehr prussienne et des institutions municipales comme celles de la Prusse." *Ibid.*, 3rd ed. Paris 1839, III, p. 312. Ranke, of course, had used an earlier edition.

candidate, than on the commander-in-chief who has tested him under the most diverse conditions in competition with his fellow candidates. Even many officers seem interested in revolution, because, as you can easily foresee, in that case there will be many resignations and consequently numerous promotions.

c: Strange, how the conditions of society infuse their predominating traits into each separate institution. And it is doubly strange in the case of the armed forces which have such an autonomous purpose and are quite independent from the course of the civil administration. Everything that has proved useful to neighbor or enemy has always been eagerly appropriated for them.

fr: That is exactly my point. The idea that inspires and dominates the whole, the prevailing tendency of the minds, and conditions in general, these are what determine the formation and the character of every institution. Now you might say that an institution has an independent significance quite of its own. But as to that, I see in the abstracted frame of an institution hardly more than a postulate, a possibility. No, only through practical application does it assume a spiritual reality. But then the differences become evident at once.

c: I admit that I often thought I perceived something of the sort. We are often advised to adopt this or that institution from another country. But who will guarantee that with us it will not turn into something else? The French wished to make the German system of education their own. This system, however, is so firmly rooted in the needs, the ideas, and the development of the German protestant church, it is so strongly permeated with its spirit, so steeped in it, that probably only the merest outline, only a pale copy of the original could be reproduced. You know what a difference there is between the universities of the various countries, although they all rest on the same historical foundation.

fr: Very well. I am pleased that you agree with me. This notion is an essential part of the theory which we have to elucidate. Identical institutions, of the same purpose, resting on common historical foundations, still assume, as we saw, the most divergent forms in different countries.

What do you think is the cause of this?

c: The difference of their constitutions, no doubt. The Church of England produced the English universities, the parliamentary constitution shaped military institutions—all of our institutions are most intimately connected with our church and our state.

fr: I admit that. But I ask you further: on what does the constitution depend?

c: I suppose you are not asking how each has developed in the course of time. All that matters, I should think, is what it consists of now, the form of government, the relationship between its various branches, the predominance of one or the other, the country's entire inner economy, finally the level of civilization in that nation.

fr: Were that so, then you should be able to copy constitutions, and, after some preparation and assimilation, transplant them to foreign soil. But if, as you admit and as it seems to make sense to you in practice, it is already difficult to transplant single institutions, will it not be outright impossible in the case of a comprehensive constitution? Even if you succeeded in this beyond all expectation, you still would get something else, something different.

c: Yes, according to the modifying powers of different conditions, just as a living constitution undergoes incessant transformations on its native soil.

fr: Let us not be deceived by possibilities in which we really do not believe. External forms may be transplanted, but that element in which they have their source, not merely their historical roots but the spirit that links past and present and which also must animate the future—how would you copy that? Or rather—for even copying would not do—you would have to take hold of that spirit and breathe it into your new creation.

c: But I should say that there still exists an inner affinity. Everywhere I observe three Estates, similar constitutional forms, corresponding parties that take the warmest interest in affairs by which they are but remotely touched. There is the spirit of aristocracy, of democracy, of mixed or pure monarchy. I do not say that everything is identical, far from it. One constitution is more perfectly developed in one, and a second in another respect. But why should we be unable to select the more perfect elements and appropriate them?

FR: It seems to me that you overestimate these categories of constitutions. They are classifications like those of botany. Do you think a lover of flowers recognizes his flowers by their stamens? Those distinctions were made in antiquity and thus remained in usage. But they leave much unstated. Something besides the democratic spirit lived at Athens. Democracy has not produced the aesthetic ideals of Athenian art. Plato was a poor democrat. And think of all the formal attributes of aristocracy. Never could you imagine a Sparta from them alone, not to speak of its deeds and ethics, but only of the working of its constitution, only of the relationship between Spartiates, Lacedaemonians, and Helots.

C: Yet you will not call these distinctions unimportant. You cannot deny that the various states have something in common.

FR: It seems to me, however, that we must distinguish between formal and real aspects. The formal aspect only covers generalities, the real covers peculiarities, the living elements. Certain forms of a constitution, particularly those stipulating a limitation of personal powers and the definition of class relationships, may be necessary to all states. But they do not constitute the source of life which alone gives content to all forms. There is an element which makes a state not a subdivision of general categories, but a living thing, an individual, a unique self.

C: If I understand you correctly, your opinion differs from others in this respect: we usually start with an analysis of the differences of constitutional forms. From there we proceed to point out the peculiarities within the categories which we established. You, on the other hand, consider these forms only a secondary, subordinate element. The primary fact to you is the unique spiritual existence of the individual state, its principle.

FR: Let me elucidate my theory with examples from the field of philology. The forms by which grammar operates have a general applicability; in a certain way they recur in every language. But the spirit of each particular language creates an infinite variety of modifications. Similarly by the principle of the state we must not understand a theoretical construction, but its inner life. This principle alone imparts to those forms of human society—which, I admit, are indispensable—their characteristic modification, the concreteness of reality.

C: I see. You postulate different spiritual essences, as it were, which alone infuse life into all varieties of constitutions and societies. But do you not then defy all possibility of general laws of politics? You seem to overlook the most fundamental questions from which our political theory starts.

FR: You mean the inquiries concerning the original formation of states, the *Pactum Unionis et Subjectionis?*

C: Yes, what were the first beginnings of the state, whether from force or contract; did the government exercise a delegated or naturally inherent authority?

FR: Forgive me, this is a field which I dislike to discuss. It lies beyond our perception.

Have you perhaps visited the observatory recently and tried our new Fraunhofer telescope?

C: What brings you to that?

FR: When you have surveyed the entire firmament, even the immense stellar systems which constitute the Milky Way, and advance your gaze still deeper into the infinite space, then in the ultimate distance you encounter a second night, as it were, still more profound and dark, on the bottom of which you perceive a new world of more marvelous phenomena.

C: The nebulae, you mean?

FR: Dimly radiating, liquid meteors, sometimes like disks, sometimes like arcs, sometimes like rings, and yet a stellar system

which you might consider still in its formative stage. Now I
ask you, should we base our astronomical knowledge on the
hazy observations we can gather from this distant field?

c: Do you really think you can compare the theories of the origin of the state, which seem so strictly reasoned, with such
a chimerical enterprise?

FR: They overlook what is nearest, and from the darkest distance gather disconnected facts to apply them to the immediate problem. But Kepler discovered the laws which bear his
name only after the most exact and painstaking observation of a celestial body that could be readily watched and
calculated.

c: But would you deny the validity of the general laws of politics as they are now formulated?

FR: To me they are as doubtful as the value of the so-called philosophical grammar. It, too, never achieved anything by a
logical analysis of general linguistic forms. Each language
represents a thousand different modifications of these forms.
Only by comprehensive historical investigation and combination can we aspire to a divining perception of the deeply
hidden, all-embracing spiritual laws. As with this grammar,
so with the theory of politics which starts from an empty
concept of the state. Take Fichte's statement: "As the surface
of the earth is divided by oceans, rivers, mountains, and mankind is separated by them, so," he says, "it became necessary
that different states originated." Do you really believe that
you can obtain from this starting point a true perception and
appreciation of uniqueness and spiritual differences?

c: But still the discussion of general problems will always remain indispensable. The individual must know why he is a
member of a state and why he obeys its authority.

FR: You are right. Political theory starts from that need. It is the
mediator between private law and public law. The former
seeks protection under the latter, its final guarantee. The latter absorbs in itself the elements of the former.

c: And, indeed, is it not this mediation that matters? Is not the general security one of the chief results of modern government?

FR: I do not deny it. But from this general axiom, which, after all, reflects but the needs of private life, you can only derive the necessity of certain limited forms and institutions, just as in our nebulae the volatile, liquid schemes appeared here and there more compact and grouped around a nucleus. It may be possible to explain the first beginnings of growth in this way; but you cannot attain perception and estimation of the fully developed individual phenomena.

c: You deny then that the general concept of the state can be of much help?

FR: I am of the opinion that the mastery of politics must be based on history; it must be founded on the study of the powerful states that have reached a high degree of inner development.

c: But is it then impossible to advance from the general to the particular?

FR: Without a leap, without a new start you never can progress from the general to the particular. The spiritual force which suddenly arises as concrete phenomenon before your eyes in unimagined uniqueness cannot be derived from a higher principle. From the particular, perhaps, you can ascend with careful boldness to the general. But there is no way leading from the general theory to the perception of the particular.

c: Yet in what do you perceive the particular?

FR: Let us begin with the very simplest example. Look at our Jacques, a kind of cosmopolitan valet, who has already tried his fortune in service in Italy, Constantinople, and St. Petersburg before ill luck finally blew him into the hermitage of a German scholar. Isn't he every inch an old Frenchman?

c: He swings his arms like one when he walks on the street, he puts his hands on the lamp like one, he behaves like one if something unexpected happens. He feels, perhaps he thinks like one.

FR: Our mother country is not where we find happiness at last.

Our mother country, on the contrary, is with us, in us. Germany is alive in us, we represent it, willy-nilly, in every country to which we go, in each climate. We are rooted in it from the beginning, and we can never emancipate ourselves from it. This mysterious something that animates the lowliest as well as the greatest, this spiritual atmosphere in which we breathe, precedes every constitution. It invigorates and swells all its forms.

c: It seems that you identify nationality and state.

FR: Yet this is less the case than we should believe. Nations have a tendency to be states; but I do not know of a single one which really is. France, which perhaps closest approaches this ideal, does not comprise all Frenchmen by any means, neither those Canadians who in their remoteness and isolation reputedly still continue to represent the old feudal France, nor its next-door neighbors in Savoy and Switzerland. England is still further from it. Her colonies have turned from her in great numbers and entered upon a course quite opposite to that of their mother country. Of Germany we will not speak at all. Even if we wanted to consider the German Confederation a kind of state, which would hardly do justice to the term, it would still be far from including all Germans.

c: How do you explain this phenomenon? Nationality, if I follow your theory, should be the basis of the state.

FR: The sphere of the state is inherently far narrower than that of the nation. The state is a modification not only of human, but also of national existence.

c: And how does this modification arise?

FR: We cannot descend into the fathomless depths of the past. Our history covers only a brief span of time, and how incompletely and doubtfully even that! How would it help us to return to epochs when different ideas of heaven and earth and different religions prevailed, when different needs, failings, and virtues created their own appropriate institutions? We are facing a world of middle-class constitutions. But evolution does not stop for a minute. From insignificant origins grandiose structures arise by a new inspiration. Even from destruction new forms grow, under torments, it is true, but with lasting results. The observation of this process and the discovery of the laws of growth seem more important, and to me at least, more interesting, than all abstract speculation.

c: You must already have started to gather your facts. I shall not ask you for them tonight. But, in general, what do you think is the origin of these new formations?

FR: The nature of things and opportunity, genius and good fortune, all conspire.

c: Good fortune? You mean the verdict of events, victory?

FR: Yes, the moment when independence was achieved and secured.

c: In your political philosophy, it seems, foreign affairs will play a great part.

FR: The world, as we know, has been parceled out. To be somebody, you have to rise by your own efforts. You must achieve genuine independence. Your rights will not be voluntarily ceded to you. You must fight for them.

c: Is it not brute force alone, then, that matters?

FR: Not so much as the word "fight" might seem to imply. With independence a foundation has been laid, a community achieved. But should it rise to universal significance, it needs moral energy above all else. Only through this can the rivals, the enemies in world competition, be overcome.

c: Then you consider the bloody profession of arms a struggle of moral energies. Beware lest you become over-sublime.

FR: You know very well that our ancestors, who were certainly not sublime, thought so too. For instance, those Tencterians, those Amivarians, offered the Romans competition by arms for the possession of vacant territory. But seriously, you will be able to name few significant wars for which it could not be proved that genuine moral energy achieved the final victory.

c: And from war, from victory, you now want to derive also the forms of internal political organization?

FR: Not exactly, not directly, but their modifications. The position of a state in the world depends on the degree of independence it has attained. It is obliged, therefore, to organize all its internal resources for the purpose of self-preservation. This is the supreme law of the state.

c: You seem to favor a military tyranny.

FR: How could a magnificent position ever be acquired without the voluntary and perfect cooperation of all citizens? By the invisible activity of unifying ideas the great communities are gradually formed. Fortunate if there is a man of genius to guide them. He would never have the power to command them.

c: I see. Your military state would then at the most be based on voluntary discipline.

FR: You seem to reproach me with a charge which Aristotle laid to some ancient lawgivers: I thought more of making a state great and powerful than its citizens wise and good; I legislated more for times of struggle and crisis than for peace and leisure. You are not wrong as to the beginnings of existence when independence must be fought for. Gradually, however, the need for peace in human nature will assert itself; then a balance will be struck. But let us speak of that later. For the moment let us stop at our present conclusions and summarize them. It is not the distant origins as much as the matured facts before our very eyes that attract our attention.

c: And what do you see?

FR: All states that count in the world and make themselves felt are motivated by special tendencies of their own. It would be ridiculous to explain them as ever so many police departments for the benefit of those individuals who, let us say, have made a contract for the protection of private property. Rather, these tendencies are of a spiritual nature, and the personalities of all citizens are determined, nay ineradicably molded by them. In this way differences arise. They in turn diversify everywhere the forms of constitutions, which, I admit, are born of a common necessity. Everything depends on the supreme idea. That is the meaning when we say that states, too, derive their origin from God. For the idea is of divine origin. Each independent state has its own original life, which may have different stages and may perish like all living matter. But while it lives it penetrates and dominates its entire environment, identical only with itself.

c: In this sense, you mean that states are individuals?

FR: Individualities, analogous one to another, but basically more independent of each other. Instead of the passing conglomerations which the contractual theory of the state creates like cloud formations, I perceive spiritual substances, original creations of the human mind—I might say, thoughts of God.

c: I do not want to contradict you. You are too firm in your opinion. And I confess I feel attracted by it. But now let us descend a little from these general reflections. Tell me, do you hold that the present states, too, have this origin and substance?

FR: My theory is based just on them. It can be most perfectly proved, I think. But the evening is too short for that.

c: But let me ask you an important question. Were it as you say, each state should follow its own course, and we should not see the European states divided into two hostile, incessantly menacing camps, mainly over the issue of internal institutions.

FR: Yes, there is a sense of European unity. But nevertheless, each state was well advanced in its peculiar development before the Revolution, and everyone will, no doubt, resume it as soon as the after-effects of the revolutionary wars subside.

c: But these very wars seem to refute your theory. Has not the entire Europe waged war against the Revolution? How could they have agreed on it, had they not been animated by common interests?

FR: You will clearly remember how difficult it was to reach an agreement. Nor, if you will think back still further, was the case just as you described it. For one, they were attacked. Secondly, how much time passed before they allied themselves! Only the huge danger of a newly-risen power, which threatened independence everywhere, finally created, in the face of annihilation as it were, a common defense.

c: But witness even today the animosity between the protagonists of the liberal and absolutist principles. Tonight again they talked of the recent issues of the *Portfolio*. Do you know it?

FR: It is right here. But now, since we apparently want to return from universal reflections to the concrete material before us and link them both together, frankly, I conclude the opposite from what the papers generally see in it.

C: Do you find it conciliatory?

FR: It is without doubt the most vindictive and most hostile publication that has come out for a long time. But I cannot see that the great continental powers are put under suspicion by it.

C: What do you say about the dispatches of Pozzo di Borgo?

FR: Truly, they are masterpieces. I did not believe that modern diplomacy could produce such excellent work.

C: Do you also approve of their contents?

FR: They at least help us to correct some errors. The three continental powers have so often been accused of participation in the exaggerated and one-sided measures of the supporters of the monarchical principle in France and Spain, nay even of fomenting and provoking them. I know no better refutation of these charges than the dispatches of Pozzo di Borgo of the year 1826 which are published here.

C: Do you think they are genuine?

FR: We cannot decide that definitely as yet. On their face, at least, they look trustworthy. And their reasonable content speaks also for their authenticity.

C: You seem to have in mind particularly the dispatch about Ferdinand VII, in which the origins of the Spanish-Portuguese conflict really come quite clearly to light. It is at last admitted in it that the expedition of the Marquis de Chaves into Portugal, which has been the source of so much mischief, originated with a faction that dominated Ferdinand VII.

FR: Be just, not only that, but also that it took place against the explicit counsel of the great powers, nay even against a given pledge.

c: You cannot claim, however, that they have been favorably inclined toward the constitution of Dom Pedro.

FR: Certainly not. But has this constitution so far really proved able to make Portugal happy? Anyway, as you read here, the great powers wanted to let time reveal its true nature, in the opinion, I admit, that it would perish by its own flaws. But I cannot find such animosity dangerous. This very trial period could as well have proved its advantages, if it had any. In no case, however, did they approve of the violence, ill-conceived as it was, to which Ferdinand was persuaded.

c: You mentioned France too.

FR: With true mastery and penetrating insight the mistakes are described which Charles X committed against all better counsels. They are the very same to which we must still ascribe the misfortunes of that prince. He should not have closeted himself with a narrow circle of exalted congreganists.* He should not have treated France as though she had relapsed into paganism, and he should have exerted himself more to win over the tribunals, particularly the highest courts in Paris. The Chambre should not have appeared as a royal tool. Villèle† should have been more willing to accept other talents as colleagues.

c: Don't you think the ills lay even deeper, in the strong position into which the revolutionary forces were allowed to advance, and their natural opposition to the old monarchy?

FR: Everything worked together. After the royalists had entrenched their enemies and given them power, they did everything to provoke their wrath and to isolate themselves.

---

* Pozzo di Borgo described them as follows: "Un clergé exalté et encore ignorant . . . hommes designés sous le nom de congreganistes, qui allient l'ambition à une sorte de pieté affectée, et qui compromettent la personne du Roi, censé de les favoriser in secret." The *Portfolio*, as cited in the previous chapter. Vol. I., no. 5; p. 8.

† Jean Baptiste Comte de Villèle, French prime minister 1822–1828.

It was literally fulfilled, therefore, what was predicted in these pages: that in the first real crisis that approached, the government would be without all moral support and powerless, in spite of the immense resources of power at its disposal.

c: You are quite a successful arguer tonight.

FR: The other documents, which are here published, need no further explanation. Can you express yourself more reasonably than Count Bernstorff in his memorandum, which the blind zeal of hostile intention has placed at the head of these papers? In it is stated that the government should win over the majority of the intelligentsia. If it wanted voluntary and spontaneous obedience it had to create the conviction that it ruled not in the interest of a party but for the general welfare. These diplomats are far above the hatred of constitutional government which the world so readily ascribes to them. Every intimation is flatly rejected that other than legal means were to be used anywhere in Germany.

c: On that, it seems, you base your theory that the contrast between the two hostile parties in Europe really does not exist.

FR: Sympathies and antipathies do exist. They have been caused by the course of events. But the hostility of these two camps, reputedly ready to break into an open fight, is a chimerical fiction.

c: And what do you make of the friction between Austria and Russia which these documents reveal?

FR: Pardon my smile; tonight every argument seems to serve my purpose. You must be rather ignorant of the diplomatic affairs of the year 1828, that you are so greatly surprised by the vehement expression of this misunderstanding. Who did not hear of it then, and explain it roughly as we here read that it really was? It only proves that the alliance of the great continental powers, in this case the alliance between Russia and Austria, was not stronger than their respective interests. There is no trend of opinion, however dominant, which can break the force of political interests. In this respect, indeed, the *Portfolio* is a particularly remarkable case. It is the first sensational European publication which at least unconsciously transcends the differences of domestic politics and again relegates politics to the field of power and foreign affairs where it belongs.

c: Truly, you seem to be right. Do not smile now;—but I find myself almost in the role of that nice young man who was the companion of Goethe's last years, and who has just published his conversations with him. I, too, can say: I enjoyed your observations that there is a living, unique, inherent principle in each of our great states, by which all its foreign affairs and internal developments are shaped. I shall keep it in mind and examine it in my quiet moments.

Now for the time being, let us once more return to those general questions. I still have some objections which I shall raise with your permission.

FR: I shall try to clear them away.

c: You claim such a considerable part of a citizen's activities for the state. How do you remunerate him; what do you give him in return?

FR: I don't think I expressed myself as though I described the ideal state. I only tried to understand the one before our eyes. And does it not, indeed, claim a large share of everybody's energy? Taxes consume quite a significant slice of the nation's income. Many invest their fortunes and their youth in the preparation for state service. And in our parts nobody is exempt from military service. Autonomous private life no longer exists. Our activities naturally belong primarily to our community.

c: But what does the private citizen receive for all his participations?

FR: In the good state it is its own reward. No citizen thinks of withdrawing from it. He recognizes the need for it. And there is no purely private existence for him. He would not be himself, did he not belong to this particular state as his spiritual fatherland.

c: But I ask you, does this spontaneity of devotion exist in reality as strongly as you postulate?

FR: I am far from claiming that. I know countries where the duties are unwillingly and reluctantly performed. In Italy for instance. There, too, the state demands personal and material sacrifices according to European standards. Unfortunately, however, it cannot induce voluntary cooperation. The citizen feels the obligations imposed on him as a burden. He thinks himself overwhelmed and forced, and he shirks his duty as much as possible. That is just why that unity of private and public affairs which characterizes the true state, cannot be achieved. I fear that this will finally cause a break even in the moral energy of the state. Private activity, too, does not thrive as it could or should. I admit all this; but it represents an incomplete, an abnormal condition.

C: But are you able to avoid it, here as elsewhere?

FR: I admit that nothing is more urgent and necessary than to consider how to prevent it. That is the secret of a progressive power. Whatever resists its entreaties is not yet completely its own. The unification of all members by voluntary cooperation must be the primary aim of its internal policy.

C: But will that be possible?

FR: That is the problem. You must preserve the peculiarities of a province, or of a section of the country, and yet unite it by indestructible ties with the whole.

C: And on what do you think rests this connection of a province and of each individual citizen with the whole?

FR: Ultimately, undoubtedly, on the fact that the idea of the state permeates every citizen, that he feels in himself some of its spiritual force, that he considers himself a member of the whole with an affection for it, and that the feeling of community in him is stronger than the feeling of provincial, local, and personal isolation.

C: What means does a state have to attain this goal?

FR: Nowadays every government must be benevolent. Its powers, as we all agree, are based on the general welfare of the people anyway. But it also must show that it is benevolent in the proper way. It must take care to be recognized. People should know what it does. And every single citizen must see that his own affairs, as far as they are connected with the public affairs, are dealt with as efficiently as possible. If their reluctance is finally overcome, this invisible, penetrating, unifying motive will have seized them all. Compulsion will be transformed on a higher level into voluntary individual initiative. Duty will become liberty.

c: You would ask for patriotism also in the days of tranquillity?

FR: Then particularly must it be cultivated lest it be lacking in times of stress. In a certain sense it must be the guiding principle of all human activity.

c: You make the entire man a political being.

FR: I am convinced that the development even of a man's personality depends on the sincerity of the inner interest which he takes, not necessarily in the forms of a constitution, but in the progress of public welfare, in the common good.

c: Then you would think formal participation in counsel and decision not even necessary?

FR: I don't deny that it might be helpful. But if we consult our experience, we must admit that it is not so everywhere. I even fear that it would not be uniformly applicable. There is something in the spirit of our monarchies that resists it.

c: I am eager to know what you consider to be the spirit of our monarchies.

FR: Let us not discuss it too extensively. We would have to bring in too many factors of politics, law, and history. But to stay in our familiar field of administration, and still to give you an answer, I say that the meaning of monarchical institutions is to put the right man in the right place.

c: But do you not have to admit that just this is not always the case?

FR: The actual performance depends on a variety of conditions. This still remains their intention and tendency, however.

c: Again I am afraid you favor despotism. Why should not everybody, as far as possible, be called to share in the deliberations? Why should you be condemned to obey?

FR: Not everybody, as you will recall from Plato, must do everything. There are innumerable branches of human activity, and it is nature's fascinating miracle that it always creates new talents for each. The common advantage requires that everybody do what he is best fitted for. You would crush a poet if you consulted him on matters of tithes which won't be a bit better in consequence. That is the advantage of a commonwealth that there are private pursuits which, though animated by the spirit of the state, are not weighed down by the desire to share in the government.

c: You are avoiding the question of obedience.

fr: That is sometimes spoken of just as though a horde of foreigners had pushed its way into the government. But let me ask you: who are the men that govern and administer? Do they not rise directly from the nation? I do not see how it offends anybody's pride, if among a number of brothers and relatives, let us say one chooses industry, another commerce, a third scholarship, a fourth agriculture, and so on, and if finally one of them rises to the capacity of participating in the government, where in the last analysis he still carries on the common affairs of the others? It is hard enough for him to get there. Governing does not consist in giving orders, or in any satisfaction which petty vanity might find it in. It is the most difficult art of doing a good job in conducting public affairs; without innate capacity, without previous training and long practice nobody can attain it. Compared with other human activities it is perhaps the most difficult of all. It requires both profoundest insight into existing relationships and perfect freedom of mind in order to give shape to the yet shapeless future. Do you think it is a misfortune that this task is left to those who alone understand it? They represent the choice of the most skillful experts among the entire nation who have trained themselves for this purpose.

c: But will you always find men who deserve to be obeyed?

fr: Nature, which is always complete, guarantees that they are there. All that matters is to find them.

c: But then there must also be some limitation, considering the human tendency of abusing power.

fr: For once, you don't have to regulate everything from the top. There are so many deeper spheres in which nothing is more welcome than spontaneity of expression. And I do not say that this form of administration is absolutely perfect. It can degenerate in a thousand ways. Only that much seems obvious to me: it is founded in the nature of things, it is inherent in the idea of our monarchies and capable of the most grandiose development.

c: And you would demand of the private citizen voluntary subordination based on the conviction that this is the best arrangement?

FR: This spontaneity is the compensation for all service to the state. At all events, private and public affairs again coincide on a higher level. Private pursuits are propelled by the flywheel of public concerns, and the common weal rises from private prosperity. The spiritual force of the state must animate every single citizen.

c: You say that it must. Yet it happens with many that it does not.

FR: That depends on whether or not a state has taken a live hold of all its members. Here, too, are degrees and gradations.

c: Here you yourself touch upon another question I was going to ask you: how can you assume there are gradations? Should not all states be equally perfect according to your view?

FR: Only in so far as we consider solely the idea to which we, as I said, ascribe divine origin, but not in its realization, its actual form in the world.

c: Which gradations are there between life and life?

FR: Analogy may lead us to it. I find only the difference between health and sickness. A healthy body is in full possession of all its powers and all its limbs. It does not feel the effects of the elements, or at least it resists them without effort. A diseased or feeble body, however, is affected or even perishes by them. It is not its own master. Similarly, a healthy commonwealth inspires all its members. It rests safely on its principle. The conflicts of the faction-torn world outside affect it, of course, on its border but not in its internal life. You are already infected and no longer your proper self, if you are too eagerly interested in what happens in your neighbor's yard.

c: In this respect then it is possible that the state becomes still more perfect. It admits of progress.

FR: Admits only? The state is a living being which by its nature incessantly grows and irresistibly progresses.

c: After what model, toward which ideal?

FR: All life carries its ideal in itself. The innermost urge of spiritual life is movement toward its idea, toward greater perfection. This urge is innate in it, implanted in it at its origin.

c: You will not deny that frequently obstacles, failures, and, let us admit, even retrogression occur.

FR: How could they be lacking in human affairs? But we should not be discouraged by them. If we are otherwise healthy, they are of a passing nature.

c: But I cannot see how they can be rendered innocuous, because there is no formal counterbalance to the government in your theory.

FR: Nonetheless, there is the spirit of the community, which cannot so easily be overcome. It can be obscured, but as long as there is still some vital energy left, it will reappear, gain the upperhand, and finally hold all in its sway. It is a great thing, anyway, how the interest of the public is personified in the prince and appears necessarily as his own cause in his self-esteem.

c: But why don't you give the spirit of the community complete reality and representative expression? Why do you shun the deliberative bodies?

FR: Implicit harmony, says Heraclitus, is better than harmony on the surface. Also do not misunderstand me. I do not condemn these institutions. Wherever they exist I wish they would develop as salutarily and brilliantly as possible. But I do not believe them altogether indispensable. I am of the opinion that public opinion has still other organs which often serve it even better.

c: You mean that the inner unity is better than any form of the social contract?

FR: What belongs together by nature does not need the latter. Among parents and children no compact is necessary.

c: I have one more question on my mind. You ascribe to your
state many attributes of spiritual unity, and the devotion
which you demand is so complete that I fear you encroach
upon the domain of the church.

fr: I should think not. State and church are eternally separate.
The church unites man in the highest and supremest community. She, indeed, dictates an unchanging rule of conduct,
the rules of this mysterious community, of religion. She tries
to hold off everything that might violate it. But there also is
the limit of her authority. In a positive way she does not have
any influence on things human. Whatever degree of secular
power she claims, that much she loses in spiritual power. As
I said, she has no immediate connection with the institutions
of the state.

c: But still they are both of a spiritual nature. Where do you
draw the borderline?

fr: The spirit of the church applies without exception to all
mankind. It is the universal spirit. By nature each church
claims at least to be the universal one. The idea of the state,
however, would be destroyed if it were to include the entire
world. Of states there are many. The spirit of the state contains a trace of the divine, but at the same time it is propelled
by human nature. It represents a community of a more limited nature, above which, more removed from practical needs,
that higher community arises.

c: Now I believe I grasp your thoughts in a general way. States
are spiritual substances, by necessity and idea different from
each other. The forms of the constitution and the different
institutions are necessitated by the general conditions of human existence; they are, however, modified by this idea, and
develop their fullest reality only through it. Hence they are
necessarily divergent. Up to a certain point private and public affairs are identical. Private life, too, is dependent on the
idea which animates the state. These manifold creations of
spiritual life are subordinated to the highest community of
the church.

fr: But grasp also these entities in their full significance: these many separate, earthly-spiritual communities called forth by genius and moral energy, growing irresistibly, progressing amidst all turmoil of the world toward the ideal, each in its own way! Behold them, these celestial bodies, in their cycles, their mutual gravitation, their systems!

c: Enough for tonight. I already hear the carriages rumble by on their way home from the party. We shall discuss the doubts that arise in my mind some later day.

fr: I should have expressed myself far more clearly and completely. Be thanked, however, for your acceptance of my theories, without rejecting them at once. It is so calming and reassuring to have provoked a congenial conviction in a kindred spirit.

PART IV

The Prefaces

Ranke introduces each of his major works with a preface in which he briefly describes his sources and outlines his basic conception of the subject matter. We have chosen five of these prefaces that are of particular interest. In all of them Ranke reiterates his deep conviction concerning the relatedness of all national history to universal—or, more accurately, Western—history. In the preface to the *Histories of the Latin and Germanic Nations* (Selection 9) he explains his conception that the Germanic and Latin peoples form a unity much more meaningful historically than the geographic concept of Europe or the religious one of a Christian or a Roman Catholic civilization. The core of all modern history, he argues, is to be found in the histories of what he calls the Germanic and Latin peoples, and the book sets out to study the crucial years in the development of these nations which mark the beginnings of modern history. In the preface to the *History of the Popes* (Selection 10) he observes that papal history must be seen as "a portion of general history, of the overall development of the world." He is not interested in "petty details," he explains, but rather in the great moving "forces of history and their results." What interests him in the history of the separate nations, he notes in the preface to the *History of England* (Selection 12), are "those epochs which have had the most effectual influence on the development of mankind." He wishes to portray the crucial periods in which the unique character of the major nations was formed, whether the completion of absolutism in France or constitutionalism in England. This character, he points out in the preface to the *Universal History* (Selection 13), is never a product of nature, "an offspring of the soil and the race," but rather of the great events through which the nations have passed.

Ranke's often quoted statement that "every epoch is immediate to God" has been interpreted to mean that he regarded all phases of history to be of equal interest to the historian. The prefaces indicate that Ranke did not intend this meaning. Ranke clearly distinguished between epochs of greater and lesser interest to the historian. Not unlike Hegel, he is concerned only with periods of world historical significance. Similarly, he is interested only in the world historical peoples, which in the modern period populate the great European nations. His universal history is thus, strictly speaking, the history of Western civilization. The non-Western world, at least in the modern age, is of little interest to him.

Two sets of ideas that permeate all of Ranke's historical writings are expressed in the preface to the *Universal History*. (1) Universal history, Ranke warns, can never be merely a compilation of national histories. Rather, the history of the nations must be related to the broader course of world history. On the other hand, world history would deteriorate into mere fantasy and speculation were it to desert the firm ground of national history. (2) The history of civilization and culture, no matter how central the national and universal history, is in a sense less decisive to the development of world history than the "rivalry of nations engaged in conflict with each other for the possession of the soil or for political supremacy," which affects the whole realm of culture. Hence, Ranke's prime interest is politics and international relations.

Throughout the prefaces runs Ranke's faith that the historian who honestly confronts the documents can, as he explains in the preface to the *History of France* (Selection 11), attain "a view of the objective nature of the great facts . . . free from the mutual accusations of the contemporaries and the often restricted view of their posterity."

The preface to the *Histories of the Latin and Germanic Nations* has been newly translated by Wilma A. Iggers from the version appearing in the *Sämmtliche Werke*. The other prefaces are taken from the nineteenth-century translations mentioned in the source notes at the beginning of each selection. These translations have been checked and revised for accuracy by the editors.

9

PREFACE
TO THE FIRST EDITION
OF HISTORIES
OF THE LATIN
AND GERMANIC NATIONS

(October 1824)

The present book, I readily admit, seemed to me more perfect before it was printed than it does now that it is in print. However, I count on favorably inclined readers to pay less attention to its faults than to its possible virtues. Since I do not entirely trust it to make its own way, however, I shall preface it with a brief explanation about its purpose, subject, and form.

The intention of a historian depends on his viewpoint, about which two things must be said here. First of all, I regard the Latin and the Germanic nations as a unit. I reject three analogous concepts: one, the concept of a universal Christendom (which would embrace even the Armenians); two, the concept of the unity of Europe, for since the Turks are Asiatics and since the Russian Empire comprises the whole north of Asia, their situations could not be thoroughly understood without penetrating and drawing in the total Asian situation. Finally, my point of view also excludes the almost exactly analogous concept, that of a Latin Chris-

From Sämmtliche Werke, *XXIII, v–viii; translated by Wilma A. Iggers.*

tendom. Slavic, Latvian, and Magyar tribes belonging to the latter have a peculiar and special nature which is not included here. The author remains close to home with the tribally related peoples of either purely Germanic or Germano-Latin origin, whose history is the nucleus of all recent history, and touches on what is foreign only in passing as something peripheral.

In the following introduction an attempt will be made to show, mainly by tracing the thread of foreign undertakings, to what extent these nations have evolved in unity and kindred movement. This is one aspect of the viewpoint on which this book is based. The other aspect is directly expressed by the content of the book, which embraces only a small part of the history of these nations, what might well be called the beginning of the modern history—only histories, not history. This book considers, on the one hand, the founding of the Spanish monarchy and the end of Italian freedom; on the other hand, the creation of a dual opposition, a political one by the French, an ecclesiastical one by the Reformation—in other words, the division of our nations into two hostile parts on which all our history rests. My account starts from the moment when Italy, united in herself, enjoyed at least external freedom and may perhaps be considered as a ruling force, since she supplied the Pope. It seeks to portray the division of Italy, the invasion of the French and the Spaniards, the end in some states of all freedom and in others of self-determination, and finally the victory of the Spaniards and the beginning of their domination. Furthermore, my book starts with the political insignificance of the Spanish kingdoms and continues to their unification—to the alignment of the united kingdom against the infidels and its influence on the internal development of Christianity. It seeks to make clear how the struggle against the infidels led to the discovery of America and the conquest of great kingdoms there, but above all how the attempt to strengthen Christianity led to Spanish domination over Italy, Germany, and the Netherlands. Thirdly, my chronicle continues from the time when Charles VIII sets out in the vanguard of Christendom in its struggle against the Turks through all the changing fortunes and misfortunes of the French up to the time, forty-one years later, when Francis calls these very Turks to aid against the Emperor. Finally, in tracing the beginnings of the opposition of a political party in Germany against the Emperor and of an ecclesiastical party in Europe against the Pope, this chronicle seeks to pave the way for a more complete insight into the history of the great schism brought about by the Reformation. This very schism is to be observed in its early course. This book tries to comprehend in their unity all these and the other related histories of the Latin and Germanic nations. To history has been given the function of judging the past, of instructing men for the profit of future years. The present attempt does not aspire to such a lofty undertaking. It merely wants to show how, essentially, things happened.

But from what sources could this be newly investigated? The foundations of the present writing, the origins of its subject matter, are memoirs, diaries, letters, reports from embassies, and original narratives of eyewitnesses. Other writings were considered only when they seemed either to have been immediately deduced from the former or to equal them through some kind of original information. Every page shows which these works were; a second book to be published simultaneously with the present one will present the method of research and the critical results.

Form results from intent and subject matter. One cannot demand of a historical work the same free development which at least in theory is sought in a poetic work, and I do not know if one is right in believing such free development to have been found in the works of the Greek and Roman masters. Strict presentation of facts, no matter how conditional and unattractive they might be, is undoubtedly the supreme law. The development of the unity and progress of the events came next in order of importance. Therefore instead of starting, as might have been expected, with a general description of public conditions in Europe—which would have diffused, if not confused, my point of view—I preferred to discuss every people, every power, every individual in greater detail only at the moment when they appeared in a pronouncedly active or leading role. I was unconcerned about the fact that occasionally I had already mentioned them previously. For how could I avoid mentioning their existence? In this way the general line of their development, the direction they took, the ideas which motivated them could be grasped all the better.

Finally, what will be said of the treatment of particulars, which constitutes such an important part of historical work? Will it not often seem hard, fragmentary, colorless, tiring? There are noble models for this procedure, ancient ones and—let us not fail to recognize this—also modern ones. But I did not dare imitate them. Their world was different from mine. A lofty ideal does exist: to grasp the event itself in its human comprehensibility, its unity, and its fullness. It should be possible to attain this goal. I know how far I am from having achieved it. One tries, one strives, but in the end one has not reached the goal. Only let no one become impatient about this failure! The main thing is always what we deal with: as Jakobi says, our subject is mankind as it is, explicable or inexplicable, the life of the individual, of the generations, of the peoples, and at times the hand of God over them.

10

PREFACE TO HISTORY
OF THE POPES
(1834)

The power of Rome in the early years and Middle Ages
is universally known; in modern times, Rome has also experienced
a great epoch of rejuvenated dominance over the world. After the
decline of her importance in the first half of the sixteenth century,
she once more succeeded in becoming the center of faith and opinion of the Romanic nations of southern Europe, making bold and
at times successful attempts to recover her dominion over those
of the North.

This period of a revived church-temporal power—its renovation and internal development, its progress and decline—I intend
to describe, at least in outline; an undertaking which, however
imperfectly it may be performed, could never have been attempted
had I not found opportunity to avail myself of certain materials
hitherto unknown. My first duty is to give a general indication of
these materials and their sources.

In an earlier work I have already stated the contents of our

From History of the Popes: Their Church and State, *trans.* E.
Fowler (New York, 1901), v–xi; revised by Konrad von Moltke.

Berlin manuscripts; but Vienna is incomparably richer than Berlin in treasures of this kind.

Besides its essentially German character, Vienna possesses also an element more extensively European: the most diversified manners and languages meet in all classes, from the highest to the lowest, and Italy in particular is fully and vividly represented. Even the collections in this city present a comprehensiveness of character, attributable to the policy of the state and its geographical position: its ancient connection with Spain, Belgium, and Lombardy and its proximity to, and ecclesiastical relations with, Rome. The Viennese have from the earliest times displayed a taste for collecting, possessing, and preserving, whence it arises that even the original and purely national collections of the imperial library are of great value; to these, various foreign collections have since been added. A number of volumes similar to the Berlin Informazioni were purchased at Modena from the house of Rangone; from Venice were acquired the invaluable manuscripts of the Doge Marco Foscarini, including his materials for a continuation of his literary undertaking, the "Italian Chronicles," of which no trace is elsewhere to be found; and the bequest of Prince Eugene added a rich collection of historical and political manuscripts that had been gathered together, with comprehensive judgment, by that distinguished statesman. The reader is animated by feelings of pleasure and hope on examining the catalogues and perceiving in them the unexplored knowledge that will enable him to supply the deficiencies manifest in almost all printed works of modern history. A whole futurity of study! And at the distance of a few steps only, Vienna presents literary support still more important. The Imperial Archives contain, as might be expected, the most authentic and valuable records for the elucidation of German history in general, but particularly also of Italian history. It is true that the greater part of the Venetian archives have been restored, after many wanderings, to Venice; but there still remains in Vienna a mass of Venetian manuscripts far from unimportant: dispatches, in the original or as copies, and abstracts thereof made for the use of the state, called "Rubricaries"; reports which, in many instances, are the only copies extant; official registers of public functionaries, chronicles, and diaries. The reports relating to Gregory XIII and Sixtus V to be found in the present volumes are for the most part derived from the archives of Vienna. I cannot sufficiently praise the unconditional liberality with which I was permitted to have access to these.

And perhaps I ought here to particularize the many and various aids afforded me in furtherance of my work, both at home and abroad; but I feel restrained by a scruple (whether well founded or not, I am unable to decide) that I should have to mention so many names, some of them of great eminence, as would give my gratitude the appearance of vainglory—and a work that has every reason to present itself modestly might assume an air of pretension ill suited to its purposes.

Next to Vienna, my attention was principally directed to Venice and Rome.

It was formerly the most invariable practice of great houses in Venice to form a cabinet of manuscripts as an adjunct to the library. It was in the nature of things that these would relate principally to the affairs of the republic. They represent the part taken by the respective families in public affairs and were preserved as records and memorials of the house for the instruction of its younger members. Some of these private collections still remain, and I had access to several; but much the larger number were destroyed in the general ruin of 1797 or since then. If more have been preserved than might have been expected, the gratitude of the world is due chiefly to the librarians of St. Mark, who labored to save from the universal wreck whatever the utmost resources of their institution would permit them to secure. Accordingly this library possesses a considerable store of manuscripts, indispensable to the history of the city and state, and which are even valuable aids toward that of Europe. But the inquirer must not expect too much from it: it is a somewhat recent acquisition gathered, almost at random, from private collections, incomplete and without unity of plan. It is not to be compared with the riches of the State archives, especially as these are now arranged. I have already given a sketch of the Venetian archives in my inquiry into the conspiracy of 1618 and will not repeat what

I there said. For my Roman investigations the reports of the ambassadors returning from Rome were above all desirable; but I had good reason to use other collections for this study, because gaps are always unavoidable, and these archives must necessarily have sustained losses in their many wanderings. In different places I gathered together forty-eight reports relating to Rome, the oldest dating from the year 1500. Nineteen were of the sixteenth century and twenty-one of the seventeenth century; these formed an almost complete series, having only a few breaks here and there. Of the eighteenth century there were, it is true, only eight, but these, too, were very instructive and welcome. In the majority of cases I saw and used the originals. They contained a great number of interesting observations derived from immediate experience that would otherwise have been lost with the passing of contemporaries. These first gave me hopes of a coherent narrative.

It will be obvious that Rome alone could supply the means for verifying and extending these materials.

But was it to be expected that a foreigner, and one professing a different faith, would there be permitted to have free access to the public collections for the purpose of revealing the secrets of the papacy? This would not perhaps have been so ill-advised as it may appear since no research can bring to light anything worse that what is already assumed by unfounded conjecture and received by the world as established truth. But I cannot boast of having had any such experience. I was enabled to take cognizance of the treasures contained in the Vatican and to use a number of volumes suited to my purpose; but the freedom of access which I could have wished was by no means accorded.

Fortunately, however, other collections were thrown open to me from which I could acquire information, which, if not complete, was nonetheless very extensive and authentic. In the times of flourishing aristocracy, more particularly in the seventeenth century, it was customary throughout Europe for the great families who had administered the affairs of state to retain possession of some of the public documents. This practice prevailed in Rome to a greater extent, perhaps, than in any other state. The reigning kinsmen of the pontiff, who in all ages exercised considerable power, usually bequeathed a large part of the state papers accumulated during their administration to the perpetual possession of the princely houses they founded. These constituted a part of the family endowments. In the palaces which they erected, a few rooms, usually in the upper part of the building, were always reserved for books and manuscripts, to which each succeeding generation contributed. Thus, to a certain extent the private collections of Rome may be regarded as the public ones, as the archives of state were dispersed among the descendants of reigning houses without any objection being made to the practice, much in the same manner as the redundancy of public wealth was suffered to flow into the coffers of the papal kindred; and certain private galleries, such as the Borghese or Doria, became greatly superior to the Vatican both in extent and historical importance, though the latter is distinguished by its selection of masterpieces. The manuscripts preserved in the Barberini, Chigi, Altieri, Albani, and Corsini palaces are accordingly of inestimable value for the aid they give toward a history of the popes, their State, and their Church. The State archives, recently established, are particularly important for their collection of registers illustrative of the Middle Ages; part of the history of this period still awaits a discoverer here; but, as far as my knowledge extends, I do not believe that much is to be gained from it for later centuries. Its value is small, unless I have been purposely deceived, when compared with the wealth and magnificence of private collections. Each of these comprises, as may be readily supposed, the papers of that epoch in which the pope of the family reigned; but as the kindred of each pontiff usually retained an eminent station; as men are in general desirous of extending and completing a collection once begun, and as opportunities were frequent in Rome, from the literary traffic in manuscripts established there; so the whole of these private collections possess many valuable documents illustrating other periods, both proximate and remote. The richest of all (in consequence of important bequests) is the Barberiniana; that of the Corsini Palace has been remarkable from its commencement for the care and judgment with which it has been formed.

I was fortunate enough to be permitted to use all these collections, as well as others of less importance, and in some instances with unrestricted freedom. An unexpected harvest of authentic and suitable materials thus lay before me as, for example: the correspondence of the nuncios with the instructions given to them and the reports which were brought back; detailed biographies of several popes, written with greater freedom because they were not intended for the public; accounts of the lives of distinguished cardinals; official and private journals; discussions of particular circumstances and transactions; memoranda and deliberations; reports on the administration of the provinces, their trade and manufactures; statistical tables and accounts of receipts and disbursements. These documents, for the most part entirely unknown, were prepared by men acquainted with their subject in practical terms and were of a credibility which, though it does not supersede the necessity for a searching and critical examination, is equal to that usually accorded to the testimony of well-informed contemporaries. The oldest of these manuscripts of which I made use related to the conspiracy of the Porcari against Nicholas V. Of other manuscripts on the fifteenth century I met with only a few, but on entering the sixteenth century, they became more numerous and more comprehensive at every step. Through the whole course of the seventeenth century, during which so little is known with certainty respecting Rome, they afford information all the more valuable because of its previous dearth. After the commencement of the eighteenth century, the documents decrease in number and intrinsic value; but at that time the Roman State and Court had already lost much of their influence and importance. I shall discuss these Roman manuscripts, as well as the Venetian, in detail at the end of the work, and will there note whatever I may find deserving attention, and which I could not well introduce in the course of the narrative. The large mass of materials, both manuscript and printed, lying before me renders a stringent condensation indispensable.

An Italian or Roman, a Catholic, would undertake the subject in a very different manner. Through expressions of personal veneration—or, perhaps, in the present state of opinion, of personal hatred—he would give to his work a peculiar, and, no doubt, more brilliant coloring; on many points he would be more elaborate, more ecclesiastical, more local. In these respects a Protestant, a North German, cannot be expected to compete with him. He regards the papal power with feelings of more indifference and must, from the first, renounce that warmth of expression which arises from partiality or hostility and which might, perhaps, produce a certain impression in Europe. In the last resort, we lack the true sympathy for such matters of ecclesiastical or canonical detail; on the other hand, our position affords us different—and, if I am not mistaken, more purely historical—perspectives. For what is there in the present day that can make the history of the papal power of importance to us? Not its particular relation to ourselves; for it no longer exercises any essential influence, nor does it create in us solicitude of any kind; the times are past in which we had anything to fear; we now feel ourselves perfectly secure. It must be its world historical development and influence. The papal power was, however, not so unchangeable as is commonly supposed. If we consider the question apart from those principles upon which its existence depends and which it cannot abandon without consigning itself to destruction, we shall find it affected, quite as deeply as any other government and to the very essence of its being, by the various destinies to which the nations of Europe have been subjected. As the history of the world has varied; as one nation or another has gained the ascendancy; as the fabric of social life has been disturbed; so also has the papal power been affected: its maxims, its objectives, and its pretensions have undergone essential changes; and its influence, above all, has been subjected to the greatest variations. If we consider the long list of names so frequently repeated through successive ages, from Pius I in the second century to our contemporaries, Pius VII and VIII, in the nineteenth, we receive an impression of uninterrupted stability; but we must not permit ourselves to be misled. The popes of different periods are, in fact, distinguished by differences as strongly marked as those existing between the various dynasties of a kingdom. To us who are outsiders precisely these mutations present the most interesting subject of contemplation. We see in them a portion of general history, of the overall development of the world; and this is true not only of periods when Rome held undisputed rule but also, and perhaps even more remarkably, of those periods shaken by the conflicting forces of action and counteraction, such as the times which the present work is intended to encompass—the sixteenth and seventeenth centuries—times when the papacy was menaced and endangered, yet maintained and fortified itself, nay, even reextended its influence, striding onward for a period but at last receding again and tottering to its fall; times in which the mind of the western nations was pre-eminently occupied by ecclesiastical questions and when the power, which, abandoned and assailed by one party, was upheld and defended with fresh zeal by the other, necessarily assumed a great universal importance. It is from this point of view that our natural position invites us to consider this history, and this I will now attempt.

I think it appropriate to commence by recalling to the memory of my reader the situation of the papal power in the beginning of the sixteenth century and the course of events which led thereto.

11

PREFACE TO HISTORY
OF FRANCE

(1852)

As a German I venture to say a word upon the history of France. Great peoples and states have a double character—one national and the other in the context of world history. Their history, in a similar manner, presents a twofold aspect. So far as it forms an essential feature in the development of humanity generally or records a prevailing influence exercised upon that development, it awakens a curiosity which extends far beyond the limits of nationality; it attracts the attention and becomes an object of study even to those who are not natives of the lands whose story is narrated.

Perhaps the main difference between the Greek authors who have treated the history of ancient Rome in its flourishing period and the Romans themselves consists in the fact that the Greeks have regarded the subject as it affected the whole world while

From Civil Wars and Monarchy in France in the Sixteenth and Seventeenth Century: A History of France Principally During That Period, trans. M. A. Garvey (London: R. Bentley, 1852), pp. i–v. Revised by Georg G. Iggers and Konrad von Moltke.

the Romans have looked at it nationally. The object is the same: the writers differ in the positions from which they view the history, but together they inform posterity.

Among modern nations none has exercised a more manifold and enduring influence upon others than the French. It has been said that the history of France—at least that of modern times—is the history of Europe. I am myself very far from sharing this opinion. France has by no means shut herself off from the impulses springing out of the four great civilized nations of Europe by whom she is surrounded. From Italy she has received literary and artistic culture. The chief founders of her monarchy in the seventeenth century took Spain for their model. The tendencies of religious reform were derived from Germany and those of political reform from the example of England.

It is, however, indisputable that the general ferment, at least throughout the Continent, has for a long period risen principally in France. The French have always taken the liveliest interest in the great problem of the State and the Church, expounding it to all others with a peculiar power of expression; it has ever been their manner to centralize the free impulses of the intellect, so to speak, and to give a practical application to theory, once conceived. But the realm of opinion is not the only one in which they have sought to rule. Ambitious, warlike, and incited by feelings of national pride, they have kept their neighbors in a state of constant excitement and armed exercise, for causes springing from the claims of their system—or even without them; assuming now an attitude defiant and aggressive, now one of defense against actual or imaginary dangers; sometimes liberating the oppressed, still more frequently oppressing the free. There have occasionally been epochs in which the national history of France has, through the importance of the events whose occurrence it details and the extent of their operation, acquired in itself a world historical character.

Such an epoch is that which I have undertaken to depict in the following pages.

Personalities like those of Francis I, Catherine de' Medici and her sons, Admiral Coligny, the two Guises, the great Bourbon

Henry IV, Maria de' Medici, Richelieu, Mazarin, and Louis XIV belong as much to universal history as to that of France. All these personages, whether distinguished by great and good qualities or by the opposite, derive their distinctive character from their relationship to the politico-religious contest that extended generally through the sixteenth and seventeenth centuries. This contest did not arise so much from the conflict of the two doctrines (for within the boundaries of France neither on the one side nor the other was there much addition made) as it did from their relationship to the state and to the parties struggling for power. The supreme authority was often disputed and nearly overwhelmed; it was limited less by law than by insubordinate threatenings, until at length by inconceivable efforts it secured and fortified itself, and the kingship arose from amidst all the storms which assailed it in a fullness of power such as royalty had never before attained in any Romanic German nation. The phenomenon of absolute monarchy in itself—the imitation it excited, its pretensions and enterprises, and the resistance it called forth—made France for a long period the central point of the movements which agitated Europe and the world.

Much has been written on the history of this epoch, but to me it appears that the appropriate conception of the times has scarcely been appreciated. The contemporary writings carry in their vivid coloring the impress of the moment in which each originated; they are for the most part imbued with the peculiar views of parties or of private individuals. Learned Frenchmen have long remarked how insecure the foundation is upon which traditional history, which has been formed since Mezeray's times, and the manner in which Sismondi has extended it, is based. In a few instances this traditional authority has been departed from, but on the whole it has been submitted to.

For a closer examination of the truth of facts, I have found of the greatest value the original documentary matter published in France during the last ten years as well as that which has appeared in the Netherlands and in Italy, none of which has ever before been used. As before, I could again draw largely on unprinted documents: Italian "Relations" from the Venetian ambassadors and the papal nuncios at Paris to their respective courts, extending over the whole period; Spanish and English correspondence relating to some of the most important years, the former having reference to the sixteenth century, the latter to the seventeenth century; letters and proclamations of French kings and statesmen; rolls of the Estates and records of the parliamentary debates; diplomatic communications and many other original sources of information, much of which deserves to be published in its entirety. These documents have given me valuable information at all times and have not infrequently determined my historical convictions. I may take another opportunity to give a detailed account of them. They are to be found not in the French and English libraries alone but also in the archives of Italy, Germany, and Belgium—for all took an interest in that which affected all.

I have not desired, even had I been able, to produce a history arranged according to the models of the ancient and modern masters of narrative for such a work would require a whole life devoted to the uninterrupted study of the archives of France and neighboring countries. I was content to convince myself of having achieved a view of the objective nature of the great facts on the basis of original and reliable reports, free from the mutual accusations of the contemporaries and the often restricted view of their posterity. I have not devoted much space to less significant events; but this has enabled me to pay the greater attention to those of world-historical importance.

I am convinced that a historical work may also derive its internal logic from the intentions of the author and the nature of the task.

12

PREFACE TO HISTORY
OF ENGLAND

(1859)

Once more I come forward with a work on the history
of a nation which is not mine by birth.

It is the ambition of all nations which enjoy a literary culture to possess a harmonious and vivid narrative of their own past
history. And it is of inestimable value to any people to obtain
such a narrative, which shall comprehend all epochs, be true to
fact and, while resting on thorough research, yet be attractive to
the reader; for by this it would attain to a perfect self-consciousness and, feeling the pulsation of its life throughout the story,
become fully acquainted with its own origin and growth and character. But we may doubt whether up to this time works of such
an import and compass have ever been produced, and even
whether they can ever be written. For who could apply learned
research, such as the progress of study now renders necessary,

From History of England, Principally in the Seventeenth Cen-
tury, trans. C. W. Boase, G. W. Kitchin, et al. (Oxford: Clarendon
Press, 1875), I, v–xiv. Revised by Konrad von Moltke and Georg G.
Iggers.

to the mass of materials already collected without being lost in its immensity? Who again could possess the vivid susceptibility requisite for doing justice to the several epochs, for appreciating the actions, the modes of thought, and the moral standard of each of them, and for understanding their relations to universal history? We must be content in this area, as well as in others, if we can but approximate to the ideal we set up. The best-written histories will be accounted the best.

When then an author undertakes to make the past life of a foreign nation the object of a comprehensive literary work, he will not think of writing its national history. This would be a contradiction in terms. In accordance with his natural vantage point he will direct his attention to those epochs which have had the most effectual influence on the development of mankind; only so far as is necessary for the comprehension of these will he introduce anything that precedes or comes after them.

There is an especial charm in following, century after century, the history of the English nation, in considering the antagonism of the elements out of which it is composed and its share in the fortunes and enterprises of that great community of western peoples to which it belongs; but it will be readily granted that no other period can be compared in universal importance with the epoch of those religious and political wars which fill the sixteenth and seventeenth centuries.

In the sixteenth century the part which England took in the work of emancipating the world from the rule of the western hierarchy decisively influenced not only her own constitution but also the success of the ecclesiastical deviation throughout Europe. In England the monarchy perfectly understood its position in relation to this great renewal: while favoring the movement in its own interest, it nevertheless contrived to maintain the old historical state of things to a great extent. Nowhere have more of the institutions of the Middle Ages been retained than in England; nowhere did the spiritual power link itself more closely with the temporal. Here less depends on the conflict of doctrines, for which the classic ground is elsewhere; the main interest lies in the political transformation, accomplished amidst manifold variations of opinions, tendencies, and events, and attended at last by a war for the very existence of the nation. For it was against England that the sacerdotal reaction directed its main attack. To withstand it the country was forced to ally itself with the kindred elements on the Continent; the successful resistance of England was in turn of the greatest service to them. The maintenance of Protestantism in Western Europe, on the Continent as well as in Britain, was effected by the united powers of both. To bring out clearly this alternate action it would not be advisable to lay weight on every temporary foreign relation, on every step of the home administration, and to search out men's personal motives in them; a shorter sketch may be best suited to show the chief characters as well as the main purport of the events in their full light.

But then, through the connection of England with Scotland and the accession of a new dynasty, a state of things ensued under which the continuance of the position taken up in domestic and foreign politics was rendered doubtful. The question arose whether the policy of England would not differ from that of Great Britain and be compelled to give way to it. The attempt to decide this question and the reciprocal influence of the newly allied countries brought on conflicts at home which, though mainly arising out of foreign relations, for a long while threw those relations into the background.

If we were required to express in the most general terms the distinction between English and French policy in the last two centuries, we might say that it consisted in this: that the glory of their arms abroad lay nearest to the heart of the French nation, and the legal settlement of their domestic affairs to that of the English. How often have the French, in appearance at least, allowed themselves to be consoled for the defects of the home administration by a great victory or an advantageous peace! And the English, with a concern for constitutional questions of apparently inferior importance, have not seldom turned their eyes away from grievous perils which hung over Europe.

The two great constitutional powers in England, the Crown and the Parliament, dating back as they did to the origins of the nation, had often previously contended with each other but had harmoniously combined in the religious struggle and had both gained strength thereby; but toward the middle of the seventeenth century we see them first come into collision over ecclesiastical regulations and then engage in a war for life and death respecting the constitution of the realm. Originally disparate elements unite in attacking the monarchy; meanwhile, the old system breaks up, and energetic efforts are made to found a new one on its ruins. But none of them succeeds; the deeply felt need of a life regulated by law and able to trust its own future is not satisfied; after long storms men seek safety in a return to the old and approved forms so characteristic of Germanic and especially of English historical life. But in this there is clearly no solution of the original controversies, no reconciliation of the conflicting elements. Within narrower limits new discords break out that once more threaten a complete overthrow until, thanks to the indifference shown by England to continental events, the most formidable dangers arise to threaten the equilibrium of Europe and to menace even England herself. These European emergencies, coinciding with the troubles at home, bring about a new change of the old forms in the Revolution of 1688, the result of which is that the center of gravity of public authority in England shifts decisively to the parliamentary side. It was during this same time that France had won military and political superiority over all her neighbors on the mainland and in connection with it had concentrated an almost absolute power at home in the hands of the monarchy. England, thus reorganized, now set herself to contest the political superiority of France in a long and bloody war during which the contrast of polity came also into play; and while the first of these bore sway over the rest of Europe, the other attained to complete realization in its island-home and called forth at a later time, when the Continent was torn by civil strife, manifold imitations on the Continent also. Between these differing tendencies, these opposite poles, the life of Europe has ever since vibrated from side to side.

When we contemplate the framework of the earth, those heights which testify to the inherent energy of the original and active elements attract our special notice; we admire the massive mountains which overhang and dominate the lowlands covered with the settlements of man. So also in the domain of history are we attracted by epochs during which the elemental forces, whose joint action or tempered antagonism are the foundations of states and kingdoms, rise in sudden war against each other and amidst the surging sea of troubles heave up into the light new formations that give to subsequent ages their special character. Such a historic region, dominating the world, is formed by that epoch of English history to which these studies have been devoted, whose results I venture to publish in the present work; its importance is as great where it directly touches on the universal interests of humanity as where, on its own special ground, it develops itself apart in obedience to its inner impulses. To comprehend this period we must approach it as closely as possible: in all its general and individual spiritual life. We discern how great antagonistic principles sprang almost unavoidably out of earlier times, how they came into conflict, wherein the strength of each side lay, what caused the alternations of success, and how the final decisions were brought about; but at the same time we perceive how much, for themselves, for the great interests they represented, and for the enemies they subdued, depended on the character, the energy, and the conduct of individuals. Were the men equal to the situation, or were not circumstances stronger than they? It is from this conflict of the universal with the particular that the great catastrophes arise; yet, it sometimes happens that the impulses which seem to perish with their authors exercise a more lasting influence on the progress of events than does the power of the conqueror. In the agonizing struggles of men's minds appear ideas and designs which pass beyond what is desirable: these find a place and a future in the colonies, the settlement of which is closely connected with the struggle at home. We are far from intending to involve ourselves in juridical and constitutional controversies; nor shall we distribute censure and praise according to what prevailed at a later time or at the moment, much less according to personal sympathies; our only concern is to recognize the great moving forces and their results. And yet how can we help but recognize manifold coincidences with that conflict of opinions and tendencies in which we are involved at the present day? But it is no part of our plan to follow these out. Momentary resemblances often mislead the politician who seeks a sure foothold in the past, as well as the historian who seeks it in the present. The Muse of history has the widest intellectual horizon and the full courage of her convictions; but in forming them she is thoroughly conscientious and, we might say, jealously bent on her duty. To introduce the interests of the present time into the work of the historian usually ends in restricting its free execution.

This epoch has been already often treated of, if not as a whole then certainly in detached parts, and that by nearly the best English historical writers. A native author has this great advantage over foreigners: that he thinks in the language in which the persons of the drama spoke and lets them be seen through no strange medium, but simply in their natural idiom. But when, too, this language is employed in rare perfection, as in a work of our own time (I refer not merely to rounded sentences and euphony of cadence but to the spirit of the narrative so much in harmony with our present culture and the tone of our minds and to the style which by every happy word excites our vivid sympathy), when we have before us a description of the events in the native language with all its attractive traits and broad coloring, based on an old familiar acquaintance with the country and its condition—then it would be folly to pretend to rival such a work in its own peculiar sphere. But the results of original study may lead us to form a different conception of the events. And it is surely good that in epochs of such great importance for the history of all nations we should possess foreign and independent representations to compare with those of home growth; in the latter are expressed sympathies and antipathies as inherited by tradition and affected by the antago-nism of literary differences of opinion. Moreover, there will be a difference between these foreign representations. French histories, as in one famous instance, will hold more to the constitutional point of view and look for instruction or example in political doc-trine. The German will labor (after investigation into original documents) to comprehend each event as a political and religious whole and, at the same time, to view it in its universal historical relations.

I can in this case, as in others, add something new to what is already known, and this to a larger extent as the work goes on.[1]

In no nation has so much documentary matter been collected for its later history as in England. The leading families which have taken part in public affairs and the different parties which wished to assert their views not only in the decisions but also in their historical representation have done much to promote this; more recently, the government also has exerted itself. Yet the existing publications are far from sufficient. How incredibly deficient our knowledge still is of even the most important parliamentary transactions! In the rich collections of the Record Office and of the British Museum I have sought and found much that was unknown and which I needed for obtaining an insight into events. The labor spent on it is richly compensated by the gain such labor brings; over the originals, so injured and so hard to decipher, linger the spirits of that long-past age. Special attention is due to the almost complete series of pamphlets of the time which the Museum possesses. As we read them, there are years in which we are present, as it were, at the public discussion that went on concerning the most important questions of government and public life, at least in the capital city, from month to month, from week to week.

If anyone has ever attempted to reconstruct for himself a portion of the past from materials of this kind—from original documents, and party writings which, prompted by hate or personal friendship, are intended for defense or attack, and yet are withal exceedingly incomplete—he will have felt the need of other con-

---

[1] Note to the third edition: In the course of my researches for this work the representation of the seventeenth century has occupied a larger space than I at first thought I should have been able to give it; it forms the chief portion of the book in its present form. I have therefore allowed myself the unwonted liberty of altering the title so as to make this clear. Still the representation of the sixteenth century, which is not now mentioned in the title, has not been abridged on this account. The history of the Stuart dynasty and of William III make up the central part of the edifice; what is given to the earlier as well as the later times may, if I may be allowed the comparison, correspond to its two wings.

temporary notices, going into detail but free from such party views. A rich harvest of such independent reports has been supplied to me for this, as well as for my other works, by the archives of the ancient Republic of Venice. The "Relations," which the ambassadors of the Republic were wont to draw up on their return home, invaluable though they are in reference to persons and the state of affairs in general, are not, however, sufficient to supply a detailed and consecutive account of events. But the Venetian archives possess also a long series of continuous reports which place us, as it were, in the very midst of the courts, the capitals, and the daily course of public business. For the sixteenth century they are preserved only in a very fragmentary state as regards England; for the seventeenth they lie before us, with gaps no doubt here and there, yet in much greater completeness. Even in the first volume they have been useful to me for Mary Tudor's reign and the end of Elizabeth's; in the later ones, not only for James I's times but also far more for Charles I's government and his quarrel with the Parliament. Owing to the geographical distance of Venice from England and her neutral position in the world, her ambassadors were able to devote an attention to English affairs which is free from all interested motives and sometimes to observe their general course in close communication with the leading men. We could not compose a history from the reports they give, but, combined with the documentary materials, these reports form a very welcome supplement to our knowledge.

Ambassadors who have to manage matters of all kinds, great and small, at the courts to which they are accredited, fill their letters with accounts of affairs which often contain little instruction for posterity, and they judge a man according to the support he gives to their interests. This is the case with the French as well as with other ambassadors in England. Nevertheless their correspondence becomes gradually of the greatest value for my work. Their importance grows with the importance of affairs. The two courts entered into the most intimate relations: French politicians ceaselessly endeavored to gain influence over England, and sometimes with success. The ambassadors' letters at such times refer to the sum of weighty matters of state and become invaluable;

they rise to the rank of the most important and instructive historical monuments. They have been hitherto, in great part, unused.

In the Roman and Spanish reports also I found much which deserves to be made known to the readers of history. The papers of Germany and the Netherlands proved still more productive, as I show in detail at the end of the narrative.

A historical work may aim either at putting forward a new view of what is already known or at communicating additional information as to the facts. I have endeavored to combine both these aims.

13

PREFACE TO
UNIVERSAL HISTORY

(1880)

The earth had become habitable and was inhabited, the nations had separated and had established manifold relations with each other; they possessed the rudiments of civilization long before writing, on which history is totally dependent, had been invented. The province of history is limited by the means at her command, and the historian would be overbold who should venture to unveil the mystery of the primeval world, the relation of mankind to God and nature. The solution of such problems must be left to natural science and religious thought.

From this primeval world we pass to the monuments of a period less distant but still inconceivably remote, the vestibule, as it were, of History. These monuments have hitherto excited the admiration and defied the intelligence of successive generations, but during the last hundred years we have obtained more accurate information and a clearer understanding of them than were pos-

From Universal History, The Oldest Historical Group of Nations and the Greeks, *ed. G. W. Prothero (New York: Charles Scribner's Sons, 1884), pp. xi–xiv. Revised by Georg G. Iggers.*

sessed before. In our own day the ruins of buried cities have been disinterred, and buildings have been discovered on the walls of which the mightiest monarchs of their day caused their deeds to be inscribed. Archaeological investigation is now everywhere pursued with a sort of filial affection, while art and antiquity have become almost identical conceptions. These monuments of the past are naturally connected with the relics, unfortunately all too fragmentary, of the ancient religions, rituals, and constitutions which have survived to our time. Around the various areas of investigation have grown up fields of study, each of which forms a department by itself and demands the devoted attention of a lifetime. Lastly, a universal science of language has arisen, which, based upon knowledge as intricate as it is extensive, undertakes with success the task of distinguishing and contrasting the relationships among the nations.

For the direction of all who are interested in these researches as well as for the instruction of the public at large, nothing could be more desirable than a scientific synopsis and correlation of these fields of study. Such a work would fittingly adorn an encyclopaedia of historical knowledge, but it cannot be introduced into Universal History, which claims as its province only the ascertained results of historical research. History first begins at the point where monuments become intelligible and documentary evidence of a trustworthy character is forthcoming, but from this point onward her domain is boundless. Universal History, as we understand the term, embraces the events of all times and nations, with this limitation only: that they shall be so far ascertained as to make a scientific treatment of them possible.

The historians of bygone days were satisfied with the conception of the four great empires of the world, drawn from the prophetic books of the Bible. As late as the seventeenth century this conception prevailed, but in the eighteenth it was upset by the general progress (*Fortgang*) of public life. Through the revolution in ideas which then took place the notion of Universal History was, as it were, secularized—a result chiefly due to the publication of a voluminous record of different countries under the title of a "Universal History," which, appearing in England, was welcomed by German scholars and incited the latter to a display of similar industry.

But it was impossible to remain content with the history of individual nations. A collection of national histories, whether on a larger or a smaller scale, is not what we mean by Universal History, for in such a work the general connection of things is liable to be obscured. To recognize this connection, to trace the sequence of those great events which link all nations together and control their destinies, is the task which the science of Universal History undertakes. That such a connection exists a glance is sufficient to show.

The first beginnings of culture belong to an epoch whose secrets we are unable to decipher, but its development is the most universal phenomenon of those times concerning which trustworthy tradition is available. Its nature cannot be expressed completely by any one word. Culture embraces both religious and political life, the foundations of law and of society.

From time to time the institutions of one or another of the Oriental nations, inherited from primeval times, have been regarded as the germ from which all civilization has sprung. But the nations whose characteristic is eternal repose form a hopeless starting point for one who would understand the internal movement of Universal History. The nations can be regarded in no other connection than in that of the mutual action and reaction involved by their successive appearance on the stage of history and their combination into one progressive community.

Culture or civilization, by whichever name we choose to call it, contains one of the most powerful motives of their internal development. If we were to forecast a definite aim for their development, we would obscure the future and misunderstand the limitless scope of the movement of Universal History. The limits of historical inquiry confine our attention to the various phases in which this element appears, side by side with the opposition each of its forms encounters from the inborn peculiarities of the different nations and tribes with whom it comes in contact and who, too, have their original rights and an impregnable inner core.

But historical development does not alone rest on the tendency toward civilization. It arises also from impulses of a very different kind, especially from the rivalry of nations engaged in conflict with each other for the possession of the soil or for political supremacy. It is in and through this conflict, which always also affects the domains of culture, that the great powers of history are formed. In their unceasing struggle for dominion the peculiar characteristics of each nation are modified by universal tendencies, but at the same time resist and react upon them.

Universal History would degenerate into mere fantasy and speculation were it to desert the firm ground of national history, but just as little can it afford to cling to this ground alone. The history of mankind manifests itself within the history of the nations themselves. There is a general historical life that moves progressively from one nation or group of nations to another. In the conflict between the different national groups Universal History comes into being, and the nationalities become conscious of themselves, for nations are not entirely products of nature. Nationalities so powerful and distinct as the English or the Italian are not so much the offspring of the soil and the race as of the great events through which they have passed.

But what does it require to investigate and to understand the universal life of mankind and the peculiarities of at least the more prominent nations? In this attempt the laws of historical criticism, called for in every detailed inquiry, may on no account be neglected, for it is only the results of critical investigation which can be dignified with the title of history at all. Our gaze must indeed be always fixed on the universal, but from false premises false conclusions would be drawn. Critical inquiry, on the one hand, and intelligent synthesis can only but support each other.

In conversations with intimate friends I have often discussed the question whether it would be possible to write a Universal History on such principles as these. We came to the conclusion that perfection was not attainable but that it was nonetheless necessary to make the attempt.

Such an attempt I now lay before the public. My point of view throughout has been the following:

In the course of centuries the human race has won for itself a sort of heirloom in the material and social progress which it has made, but still more in its religious development. One portion of this heritage, the most precious jewel of the whole, consists of those immortal works of genius in poetry and literature, in science and art, which, while they originated under local conditions, yet represent what is common to all mankind. With this possession are inseparably combined the memories of the events, the institutions, and the great men of the past. One generation hands on this tradition to another, which may again and again be revived and recalled to the minds of men, as I have the courage and confidence to do.

PART V

History
of the Popes[1]

The following text of Ranke's *History of the Popes*
is based on the translation by E. Fowler in the edition of 1901.
The text has been heavily edited to accommodate it to the available space. The translation has been revised in very many details,
some of them quite extensive. The concluding two sections on
Pope Pius IX and the Vatican Council are here presented in English translation for the first time. That this is an edited version and
translation should be kept in mind. We have elected to use the
nineteenth-century translation in spite of certain inconsistencies

[1] See p. lvii for a discussion of the *History of the Popes* in the context of Ranke's work and biography.

in comparison with modern usage, as it in some ways reflects the quality of Ranke's speech more closely than a modern text might. Revisions have therefore only been made where the translation was positively inaccurate. We have, however, modernized spelling and changed punctuation to conform to current usage. A close comparison of the main body of the text with the last two sections should reveal the differences in translation that do exist. In editing the text, every effort was made to retain a coherent narrative rather than to present representative selections. This has meant that very few sections stand in their full length as written (we have retained approximately half the text). A comparison with the table of contents of the original editions will reveal that we have made more than average cuts in the sections dealing with the constitution and finance of the papal state, the history of Scandinavia and Poland in the seventeenth century and certain aspects of the counter-Reformation in Germany. As it now stands, the narrative addresses itself more exclusively to the major events of the period than did the original. The biographies of the popes have been retained as the essential framework. Hence they appear somewhat more prominently here than in the original. In no case, however, have we added to the original text to facilitate editing nor have we rearranged it to obscure cuts which we felt to be necessary. All editing took the form of simple cutting.[2] However, we have on occasion gained advantage from the slight leeway in phrasing afforded by a translation.

The only sections entirely unedited are the last two. The penultimate section was written by Ranke for the edition of 1867 and then revised slightly when he wrote the final sections for the 1871 edition of the *History of the Popes*. They are interesting examples of Ranke's approach to the historical study of contem-

---

[2] We have used two symbols to offer an indication of the extent of our editing: whenever short passages were edited out, this has been designated by an asterisk (*). Wherever we have made deletions exceeding one page, we have denoted them with a dagger (†). All major deletions have been footnoted, indicating both length of the original and content.

porary events. His ability to maintain the framework of the general study and its dispassionate diction are quite remarkable. Even his theory of ideas remains applicable to the writing of contemporary history. Only toward the very end does his bias appear. In speaking of the complex events leading to the Franco-Prussian War, he calls this "the French aggression," hardly an objective evaluation. But even in the face of the papacy's apparent demise as he had described it in the *History of the Popes*, he manages to veil and identify his Protestant point of view by use of a subjunctive construction: "a convinced Protestant would say this was the divine decision against the pretensions of the pope who claimed that he was the sole interpreter of the faith and of the divine mysteries on earth."

14

HISTORY
OF THE POPES

(1834)

BOOK I
Chapter First

EPOCHS OF THE PAPACY. A.D. 1–1500

Christianity In The Roman Empire

If we examine the condition of the ancient world in its earlier centuries we find it occupied by a great number of independent peoples. Seated along the shores of the Mediterranean, and extending themselves inland so far as their knowledge of the country permitted, they dwelt divided into various tribes, all originally confined within very narrow limits, but all purely free, and each possessing its own peculiar character and institutions. The independence enjoyed by these communities was not merely political. An independent religion also had been established by each, the ideas of God and of divine things had localized themselves, as it were; national deities of the most diversified attributes divided the worship of the world, and the law by which their votaries were governed became inseparably united with that of the state. We may safely declare that this intimate union of Church and State, this twofold freedom, limited only by the light obligations arising from identity of race, had the most important share in the civilization of the early ages. Each community was indeed surrounded by narrow limits, but within these the rich fullness of the world's vigorous youth found space to develop itself according to its own unfettered impulse.

How entirely was all this changed as the might of Rome arose! All the autonomies that had previously filled the world are seen to bend one after the other, and finally to disappear. How suddenly did the earth become desolated of her free nations!

In other times, empires have been shaken because religion had lost its power of control. In those days the subjugation of the state necessarily involved the downfall of the national religions. Of necessity they all congregated in Rome, following the lines of power—but what significance could remain to these peculiar forms of belief, once torn from the soil whence they had derived their birth? The worship of Isis was doubtless intelligible in Egypt, where it deified the powers of nature as manifested in those regions. In Rome this worship became a senseless idolatry. No sooner did the various mythologies come in contact, than their mutual destruction ensued: it was impossible to discover any theory capable of reconciling their contradictions.

But even had this been possible, it would no longer have sufficed to the necessities of the world.

However deeply we may sympathize with the fall of so many free states, we cannot fail to perceive that a new life sprang immediately from their ruins. With the overthrow of independence fell the barriers of all exclusive nationalities: the nations were conquered—they were overwhelmed together; but by that very act were they blended and united—for, as the limits of the empire were held to comprise the whole earth, so did its subjects learn to consider themselves as one people. From this moment humankind began to acquire the consciousness of its universal brotherhood.

It was at this moment of the world's development that Jesus Christ was born.

How obscure and unpretending was his life! His occupation was to heal the sick and to discourse of God in parables with a few fishermen, who did not always understand his words. He had nowhere to lay his head. Yet, even from the worldly point of view from which we consider it, we may safely assert that nothing more guileless or more impressive, more exalted, or more holy has ever been seen on earth than his life, his whole conversation, and his death. In his every word there breathes the pure spirit of God. They are words, as St. Peter has expressed it, of eternal life. The records of humanity present nothing that can be compared, however remotely, with the life of Jesus.

If the earlier forms of belief had ever contained an element of true religion, this was now entirely obscured; they no longer, as we have said, could pretend to the slightest significance. In him who united the nature of man with that of God, there shone forth, in contrast with these shadows, the universal and eternal relation of God to the world, and of man to God.

Jesus Christ was born among a nation sharply separated and distinguished from all others by ritual laws of rigid and exclusive severity, but which also possessed the immeasurable merit of holding steadfastly to that worship of the one true God in which they had persisted from their earliest existence, and from which no power could sever them. It is true that they considered this monotheism a national worship only, but it was now to receive a much wider significance. Christ abolished the law by fulfilling it. The Son of Man declared himself Lord also of the Sabbath, and rendered manifest the eternal import of those forms, which a narrow understanding has as yet but imperfectly comprehended. Thus, from the bosom of a people hitherto separated by insurmountable barriers of opinion and customs from every other, there arose, with all the force of truth, a faith which invited and received all men. The Universal Father was now proclaimed—that God, who, as St. Paul declared to the Athenians, "hath made of one blood all nations of men for to dwell on all the face of the earth." For this sublime doctrine, the appointed hour, as we have seen, had now arrived—a race of men existed who could appreciate its value. "Like a sunbeam," says Eusebius, "it streamed over the face of the earth."

But however pure and blameless the religion of Christ, it was not in the nature of things that it should escape opposition from the already established creeds. These had entwined themselves with the habits and wants of daily life; they were bound up with all the old memories of the world; and had moreover now received a certain modification which had brought them into harmony with the constitution of the empire.

The political spirit of the ancient religions displayed itself once again under a new aspect. All those self-governing powers that had once filled the world had become absorbed into one concentrated whole. There remained but one power that could be called self-dependent; the modified religions acknowledged this when they decreed divine worship to the Emperor.* This worship of the Caesar and the doctrines taught by Christ had a certain resemblance when viewed with relation to the various local religions, but they nevertheless presented the strongest possible contrast with each other.

The Emperor conceived religion only in its most worldly aspect, as bound to earth and the things of earth. "To him be these surrendered," says Celsus; "whatever each man possessed, let it come from him." Christianity regarded religion in the fullness of the spirit, and of superhuman truth.

The Emperor united Church and State: Christianity separated, before all things, that which is Caesar's from that which belongs to God.

The offering of sacrifice to the Emperor was an acknowledgment of the most abject thralldom. In that very union of Church and State wherein consisted the perfection of independence under the self-governing powers, might now be found the seal and completion of man's subjection. Thus the prohibition of this worship by Christianity was an act of emancipation. Finally, the adoration paid to the Emperor was restricted by the limits of the empire—then believed to comprise the whole earth—while the true faith was destined to reach to the world's real limits and to embrace the whole human family. Christianity sought to reawaken the primitive consciousness of religious truth (if it be granted that such consciousness preceded all idolatries), or at least to infuse a belief complete in its purity, obscured by no inevitable connection with the state, and opposed to the exactions of that all-grasping power which, not content with earthly dominion, was seeking to extend its influence over things divine also. It was from Christianity that man derived the spiritual element with which he could once again become self-sustaining, free, and personally invincible. A new vitality awoke in the bosom of the freshened earth, she became fructified for the development of new productions.

This was the contrast: between the earthly and the spiritual, between freedom and servitude—a gradual decay and a life-breathing and vigorous renovation.

It is not here that we can describe the long struggle between these opposing principles: all the elements of life throughout the Roman Empire became involved in the movement, all were gradually penetrated and influenced by the essential truth of Christianity, and were borne forward by this great effort of the spirit. "By its own act," says Chrysostom, "has the error of idolatry been extinguished"; already Paganism appeared to him as a conquered city, whose walls were beaten down, whose halls, theatres, and public buildings had been destroyed by fire, whose defenders had fallen by the sword, and among whose ruins remained only old men or helpless children. These, too, were soon dispersed, and a change without example ensued.

From the depths of the catacombs arose the adoration of the martyrs. On those sites where the gods of Olympus had been worshipped—on the very columns that had supported their temples—shrines were erected to the memory of those who had rejected their divinity and died for refusing to yield them worship. The religion of Christ, coming forth from the desert and the dungeon, took possession of the world.* The rulers of the world, themselves considered as deities, gave place to the Son of God arrayed in the nature of man. The local deities passed away, and were seen no more. In every highway, on the steep summits of the hills, in the deep ravines and remote valleys, on the roofs of houses, and in the mosaic of the floors was seen the cross: the victory was complete and decisive.*

Considered in this aspect also, how all-embracing is the influence, how immense the importance of the Roman Empire! In the ages of its elevation all nations were subjugated, all independence destroyed by its power; the feeling of self-reliance, resulting from the division of interests, was annihilated. But, on the other hand, its later years beheld the true religion awake in its bosom—the purest expression of a common consciousness extending far beyond its limits—the consciousness of a community in the one true God. May we not venture to say that by this development the empire had fulfilled its destiny—that it had rendered its own existence no longer necessary? The human race had acquired the knowledge of its true nature—it had found its unity in religion.

This religion now also received its external forms from the Roman Empire.* This did not take place, as I think, without a certain innate necessity. The rise of Christianity involved an emancipation of religion from all political elements, and this was inevitably followed by the establishment of a distinct ecclesiastical body in opposition to the state with a constitution peculiar to itself. In this separation of the Church from the State consists, perhaps, the most important and most effectually influential peculiarity of Christian times. The spiritual and temporal powers may come into close contact—they may remain in the most intimate communion; but they may coincide only under exceptional circumstances and for a limited time. In their reciprocal relations and position with regard to each other, has since then been involved one of the most important questions presented by all history.

It was nevertheless imperative for the ecclesiastical body to form their constitution on the model of that of the empire; and accordingly, the hierarchy of the bishops—metropolitan patriarchs—was formed in close correspondence with the gradations of the civil power. Little time had elapsed before the bishops of Rome acquired the supremacy. It is, indeed, a vain pretence to assert that this supremacy was universally acknowledged by East and West, even in the first century, or indeed at any time. But it is equally certain that they quickly gained a pre-eminence, raising them far above all other ecclesiastical dignitaries.* In a law that became decisive for the predominance of Rome as well as of Christianity, Theodosius the Great commands that all nations claiming the protection of his grace should receive the faith as propounded by St. Peter to the Romans. Valentinian III also forbade the bishops, whether of Gaul or of other provinces, to depart from the received customs of the Church without the sanction of that venerable man, the Pope of the Holy City. Thenceforth the power of the Roman bishops advanced beneath the protection of the Emperor himself, but in this political connection lay also a restrictive force. Had there been but one emperor, a universal primacy might also have established itself; but this was prevented by the partition of the empire. The emperors of the East were too eagerly tenacious of their ecclesiastical rights to make it possible that they should promote that extension of power desired by the western patriarchs in their dominions. In this respect also the constitution of the Church presents the closest resemblance to that of the empire.

The Papacy In Connection With The Frankish Empire

Scarcely was this great change completed—the Christian religion established, and the Church founded—when new events of universal importance took place. The Roman Empire, so long conquering and paramount, was now to see itself assailed by its neighbors: in its turn it was invaded and overcome.

Amidst the general convulsion that ensued, great Christianity itself received a violent shock. In their terror, the Romans bethought themselves once more of the Etruscan mysteries, the Athenians hoped to be saved by Achilles and Minerva, the Carthaginians offered prayers to the genius Coelestis; but these were only temporary waverings, for even though the empire was shattered in the western provinces, the entire structure of the Church remained firm and undisturbed. But she fell, as was inevitable, into many embarrassments, and found herself in an entirely altered condition.*

The Roman bishops, beset on all sides, exerted themselves, with all the prudence and pertinacity which have remained their peculiar attributes, to regain mastery at least in their ancient patriarchal diocese. But a new and still heavier calamity now assailed them. The Arabs—not conquerors merely as were the Germans, but men inspired even to fanaticism by a positive and proud creed in direct opposition to the Christian faith—now poured themselves over the West as they had previously done over the East. After repeated attacks, they gained possession of Africa: one battle made them masters of Spain, their general, Musa, boasting that he would march into Italy by the passes of the Pyrenees and across the Alps and cause the name of Mahomet to be proclaimed from the Vatican.

This position was all the more perilous for the western portion of Roman Christendom, from the fact that the iconoclastic dissensions were at that moment raging with the most deadly animosity on both sides. The Emperor of Constantinople had adopted the opposite party to that favored by the Pope of Rome; in fact, the life of the Pope was more than once in danger from the Emperor's machinations. The Lombards did not fail to perceive the advantages derivable to themselves from these dissensions. Their king, Astolphus, took possession of provinces that till then had always acknowledged the dominion of the Emperor, and again advancing toward Rome, he summoned that city also to surrender, demanding payment of tribute with vehement threats.

The Roman See was at this moment in no condition to help itself, even against the Lombards. Still less could it hope to contend with the Arabs, who were beginning to extend their sovereignty over the Mediterranean and were threatening all Christendom with a war of extermination.

Happily, the faith was no longer confined within the limits of the Roman Empire.

Christianity, in accordance with its original destiny, had long overpassed these limits—specifically it had taken deep root among the German tribes of the West. Indeed, a Christian power had already arisen among these tribes, and toward this the Pope had but to stretch forth his hands to find the most effectual succor and earnest allies against all his enemies.

Among all the Germanic nations, the Franks alone had become Catholic from their first rise in the provinces of the Roman Empire. This acknowledgment of the Roman See had secured important advantages for the Frankish nation. In the Catholic subjects of their Arian enemies—the western Goths and Burgundians—the Franks found natural allies. We read so much of the miracles by which Clovis was favored—how St. Martin showed him the ford over the Vienne by means of a hind, how St. Hilary preceded his armies in a column of fire—that we shall not greatly err if we conclude that these legends reflect the material succors afforded by the natives to those who shared their creed, and for whom, according to Gregory of Tours, they desired victory "with eager inclination." But this attachment to Catholicism, thus confirmed from the beginning by consequences so important, was afterward renewed and powerfully strengthened by a very peculiar influence arising from a totally different quarter.

It chanced that certain Anglo-Saxons exposed for sale in the slave market of Rome attracted the attention of Pope Gregory (I) the Great. He at once resolved that Christianity should be preached to the nation whence these beautiful captives had been taken, and never, perhaps, was a resolution adopted by any pope from which results more important ensued. Together with the doctrines of Christianity, a veneration for Rome and for the Holy See such as had never before existed in any nation found place among the Germanic Britons.* The Anglo-Saxons appear to have transferred to Rome and the Christian saints the old Teutonic superstition by which the gods were described as nearer to some spots of earth than to others, and more readily to be propitiated in places thus favored.

But more important results ensued when the Anglo-Saxons transplanted their modes of thought to the mainland, and imbued the whole empire of the Franks with their own opinions. Boniface,

the apostle of the Germans, was an Anglo-Saxon; this missionary, largely sharing in the veneration professed by his nation for
St. Peter and his successors, had from the beginning voluntarily
pledged himself to abide faithfully by all the regulations of the
Roman See, and to this promise he most religiously adhered. He
founded the German church and imposed upon it an extraordinary
obligation to obedience. Every bishop was required expressly to
promise that his whole life should be passed in unlimited obedience to the Roman Church, to St. Peter, and to his representative.
Nor did he confine this rule to the Germans only. The bishops of
Gaul had hitherto maintained a certain independence of Rome;
Boniface, who occasionally presided in their synods, availed himself of these occasions to impress his own views on this western
portion of the Frankish Church. Thenceforward the Gallic archbishops received their pallium from Rome, and thus did a sub-
missiveness akin to that of the Anglo-Saxons extend itself over
the whole realm of the Franks.

This empire had now become the central point for all the
germano-Western world. The fact that the reigning family, the
Merovingian race, had brought about its own destruction by its
murderous atrocities had not affected the strength of the empire.
Another family had risen to supreme power—men of great energy,
exalted force of character, and indomitable vigor. While other
realms were sinking and the world seemed about to become the
prey of the Moslem, it was this race, the house of Pepin of Heristal
(afterward called the Carolingian), by which the first effective resistance was offered to the Mahometan conquerors.

The religious development then in progress was also equally
favored by the house of Pepin: we find it early maintaining the
best understanding with Rome, and it was under the special protection of Charles Martel and Pepin le Bref that Boniface proceeded in his apostolic labors.

Let us consider the position of the papal power in the world.
On the one side the East Roman Empire, weakened, falling into
ruin, incapable of supporting Christendom against Islam, or of
defending its own domains in Italy against the Lombards, yet continuing to claim supremacy even in spiritual affairs; on the other

hand, the German nations full of the most vigorous life, victorious over the Moslems, attached with all the fresh ardor and trusting enthusiasm of youth to that authority of whose protecting and restrictive influences they still felt the need, and filled with an unlimited and most freely rendered devotion.

Already Gregory II perceived the advantages he had gained. His successors became ever more impressed with the conviction that it was necessary to separate themselves from a power by which many duties were imposed on them, but which could offer them no protection in return. They could not safely permit the suggestiveness of the Roman name and empire to fetter them, but turned themselves rather toward those from whom alone help and aid might also be expected. Thus they entered into strict alliance with those great captains of the West, the Frankish monarchs. This alliance became closer and closer from year to year, procured important advantages to both parties, and eventually exercised the most active influence on the destinies of the world.*

Relation To The German Emperors
—Internal Progress Of The Hierarchy

We now pass over some centuries in order to arrive at that point of view from which the various events they produced may most profitably be considered.

The Empire of the Franks has fallen; that of the Germans has arisen into full and vigorous life. Never did the German name count for more in Europe than during the tenth and eleventh centuries, under the Saxon and first Salian emperors.*

If we now ask on what basis a power so extended in its influence and claiming supremacy throughout Europe essentially reposed, we find in it a most active and important ecclesiastical element—the Germans also conquered by converting. Hand in hand with the Church their marches advanced, over the Elbe toward the Oder on the one hand, and the Danube on the other. Monks and priests prepared the way for German influence in Bohemia and Hungary; thus did a great increase of importance everywhere ac-

crue to the ecclesiastical power. Baronial and even ducal rights
were held in Germany by the bishops and abbots of the empire,
not only within their own possessions, but even beyond them.
Ecclesiastical estates were no longer described as situated in certain counties, but these counties were described as situated in the
bishoprics. We may not infer from this that an entire independence was already conceded to the clerical body. The appointment
to all ecclesiastical offices still resting with the sovereign, it was
generally advantageous to the prince that the man of his choice,
one on whose devotion to himself he could rely, should be invested
with temporal authority.* Nor was the endowment of bishops permitted to diminish the resources of the state. Church property was
neither exempted from civil imposts nor from feudal service, and
bishops were frequently found taking the field at the head of
their vassals.*

If, then, the ecclesiastical element was of such paramount importance to the institutions of the German Empire, it is manifest
that much would depend on the relations existing between the
Emperor and the head of the whole clerical body, the Pope of
Rome.

The papacy was not less closely allied with the German emperors than it had been with the Roman, and with the successors
of Charlemagne. The political subordination of the pope was unquestionable. It is true, that while the empire remained in weak
and incapable hands, and before it passed definitively to the Germans, certain acts of sovereign authority had been exercised by
popes over the imperial sceptre. But no sooner did the vigorous
German princes attain to that dignity, than they became, if not
without dispute, yet, in fact, as completely liege lords of the popedom as the Carolingian monarchs had been. With a powerful hand
Otto the Great maintained the Pope whom he had raised to the
throne; his sons followed the example. The circumstance of the
Roman factions once more rising into activity, seizing the papal
chair, and again resigning it, or making it an article of traffic and
barter as their family interests required, shows even more clearly
the necessity for some higher intervention. The vigor with which
this was exercised by Henry III is well known. His synod at Sutri

deposed such popes as he considered irregularly chosen; and scarcely had the patrician ring been placed on his finger, and the crown of the empire on his brow, than he nominated the individual who should ascend the papal throne by his unrestricted will. Four German popes were successively appointed by him; and when the supreme ecclesiastical dignity became vacant, the ambassadors from Rome presented themselves at the imperial court to receive the announcement of a successor, as did the envoys of other bishoprics.

In this order of things, it was a matter of personal interest to the Emperor that the Pope should hold an important place in the eyes of the world.* But this state of affairs involved a great danger to the empire. The ecclesiastical body was very differently constituted under the Germanic and Germanized states from what it had been under the Roman Empire. The clergy now possessed a large share of political power; they had risen to princely stature. The Church still depended on the Emperor, the supreme temporal authority, but suppose this authority again fell into weak and incapable hands. Suppose, then, that the head of the Church, wielding the triple force arising from his dignity—the object of universal reverence, from the devotion of his own subjects, and from his influence over other states—should seize the favorable moment and place himself in opposition to the imperial power.

The nature of things offered more than one inducement to such a course. There was a principle inherent in the ecclesiastical constitution which opposed itself to a secular influence so widely extended, and this would inevitably make itself felt should the Church become strong enough to bring it into effective action. There is also, as it appears to me, an inconsistency in the fact that the Pope should exercise on all sides the supreme spiritual power, and yet remain himself subjected to the Emperor. The case would have been different had Henry III really brought about his purpose of exalting himself to be the head of all Christendom. But as he failed in this, there needed but a certain complication of political affairs, and the Pope might have been prevented, by his subordination to the Emperor, from performing the duties imposed on him by his office as common father of the faithful.

It was under these circumstances that Gregory VII ascended the papal throne.* Gregory had a cool, one-sided, aspiring spirit: logical, one might say, as a scholastic system is; unshakable in its logical consequence and at the same time skillful and pliant in the face of well-founded objection. He perceived the end to which things were tending, and amidst the trifling occurrences of everyday life, he saw the possibilities for changing the course of universal history. He resolved to free the pontificate from the authority of the empire. Having fixed his thoughts on this object, he soon seized the decisive means for attaining it. The resolution that he caused to be adopted by one of his councils, namely that no clerical office should in future be conferred by a layman, was equivalent to altering the constitution of the empire in its very essence. This reposed, as we have already said, on the connection between the spiritual and temporal institutions and the bond that held these together was the investiture. To deprive the Emperor of this his ancient right was to declare a revolution.

It is obvious that Gregory could not have ventured to think of this measure, much less to put it in practice, had he not been favored by the convulsions that shook the empire during the minority of Henry IV, and by the frequent insurrections of the German princes and people against that monarch. Among the great vassals he found natural allies. They also felt oppressed by the overwhelming power of the Emperor; they also desired to become free. In a certain sense, the Pope might be considered one of the vassals of the empire. It is not then surprising that when the pontiff declared Germany an electoral monarchy—a doctrine tending greatly to augment the power of the princes—these last should offer no opposition to the efforts he made for his own emancipation from the imperial power.

Even in the contention for the investiture, their interests went hand in hand. The Pope was still far from claiming the direct nomination of the bishops; he referred the choice to the chapters, and over these the higher German nobility exercised the most commanding influence. In one word, the Pope had the aristocratic interests on his side.

But even with these allies, how long and how bloody were

the conflicts maintained by the popes before they could bring their enterprise to a fortunate issue!* At length, however, the task was accomplished. After long centuries of confusion, after other centuries of often doubtful strife, the independence of the Roman See and that of its essential principle was finally attained. In effect, the position of the popes was then most exalted; the clergy were wholly in their hands. It is worthy of remark that the most firm-minded pontiffs of this period—Gregory VII for example—were Benedictines. By the introduction of celibacy they converted the whole body of the secular clergy into a kind of monastic order.* While this closely knit order, so compact in itself yet so widely extended through all lands—influencing all by its large possessions, and controlling every relation of life by its ministry—was concentrating its mighty force under the obedience of one chief, the temporal powers were crumbling into ruin.* The power of the Emperor seems to have become superfluous after Frederick I had conceded the essential attributes of sovereignty to the princes of the empire. Italy, as well as Germany, was occupied by numerous independent powers; the only self-centered and comprehensive sovereignty was that of the Pope. Thus it came to pass that the independence of the ecclesiastical principle resolved itself into a new kind of hierarchical principle; the politico-religious character that life had everywhere assumed, and the general course of circumstances, all tended to this result. When countries long lost to the Church, as Spain had been, were regained from Mahometanism; when provinces like Prussia, hitherto buried in the darkness of paganism, were brought over to the faith and filled with a Christian population; when even the capitals of the Greek Church conformed to the Latin ritual; and when hundreds of thousands poured forth to plant the banner of the cross on the holy sepulchre—is it not here manifest that the crowned priest, whose hand was in all these enterprises and at whose feet was offered the fealty of the subdued, must have enjoyed unbounded influence and honor? In his name, and under his guidance, the western nations poured themselves forth as one people and sought to gain possession of the whole world.* Extraordinary aspect of those times—which no one has hitherto placed before us in all its completeness and truth! The most wonderful combination of internal discord with the most brilliant external progress of independence and subjection, of spiritual and temporal existences! Even piety herself adopted a contradictory character. At one time we see her withdrawn amidst rugged mountains, or retiring to the lonely forest where her harmless days are devoted to divine contemplation. Awaiting death, she denies herself every enjoyment that life presents her; or appearing in the homes of man, she proceeds with youthful enthusiasm to exhibit, in profound and suggestive forms, the mystery which she senses, the idea in which she lives. But a moment after and we find another piety—it is she who has invented the Inquisition and who fulminates the terrible judgment of the sword against all who reject her creed.* Sometimes she presents these widely differing aspects at the same moment of time. At sight of Jerusalem the crusaders descend from their horses— they bare their feet, to the end that they may approach the holy walls in the guise befitting pilgrims. In the midst of carnage they believe themselves aided by the visible presence of saints and angels. Yet scarcely have they passed the walls than they rush into the wildest excesses of pillage and bloodshed.* In this contradiction may be found a picture eloquently illustrative of those times, and of that politico-religious government. It is an inconsistency that will be seen to pervade their whole being.

Contrasts Between The Fourteenth And Fifteenth Centuries

There are certain periods of history that tempt us to anxiously scrutinize, if we dare thus to express ourselves, the plans of God in his government of the world, and earnestly to examine the forces that are in action for the education of the human race.

However defective may have been the development that we have sought to describe, it was indispensable to the complete naturalization of Christianity in the West. The task of bending the refractory spirits of the northern tribes to the pure laws of Christian truth was no light one. Wedded, as these nations were, to their long-cherished superstitions, the religious element required a long predominance before it could gain entire possession of the German character—but by this predominance, that close union of Latin and German elements was effected on which is based the character of Europe in later times. There is a spirit of community in the modern world which has always been regarded as the basis of its entire development, whether in religion, politics, manners, social life, or literature. To bring about this community, it was necessary that the western nations should, at one period, constitute what may be called a single politico-ecclesiastical state.

But this, also, was to be no more than a moment in the grand course of events; the necessary conversion once effected, new necessities supervened.

The advent of another epoch already announced itself in the simultaneous and almost universal rise of the vernacular in all countries. Slowly, but with unceasing effort, it pressed itself into the manifold branches of intellectual activity. Step by step the idiom of the church gave way before it; universality retired, and in its place appeared a new species of partition, founded on a higher principle. The ecclesiastical element had up to this time overborne every distinguishing nationality. Now, modified and transformed but again asserting individual existence, these nationalities displayed themselves in a new light.

We are forced irresistibly to the conviction that all the purposes and efforts of humanity are subjected to the silent and often imperceptible, but invincible and ceaseless march of events. Papal authority was furthered by the earlier moments of universal history; the later ones were averse to it. The impulse given by the ecclesiastical power was no longer as necessary as before to the well being of nations; it was consequently at once opposed. All had awakened to a sense of their own independence.*

In addition to this, the popedom itself had at this period fallen into a state of debility and confusion, so that the secular princes, who had hitherto sought only to defend themselves, were enabled to become in their turn the movers.

Schism was the result. Let us observe the consequences that ensued. For a long period of time each prince had the option of attaching himself to one pope or the other, as might best suit his political interests. The Church possessed no means within herself by which this division could be remedied; by the secular power alone could this be done. When a council was held in Constance for that purpose, the members no longer voted individually as had formerly been the practice, but by the four nations—each nation exercising the right of deliberating in preliminary assemblies on the vote to be given. Together they decided the deposition of a pope, and the newly elected pontiff was called on to accede to concordats with each separate nation. These concordats were of great importance, if only by the precedent they afforded. During the Council of Basle, many states even remained neutral; it was by the immediate intervention of the princes alone that this second breach in the Church could be closed. There could arise no state of things better calculated to promote the preponderance of the temporal power and the independence of the several states.

And now the Pope was again in a position of great splendor. He was obeyed universally, but in spite of these appearances, the old relations of things were no longer in force.*

Other interests occupied the world at that time. It was now the period when the European kingdoms were finally consolidating their forces after long internal struggles. The central authorities, having succeeded in suppressing the factions that had endangered the security of the throne, were gathering their subjects around them in renewed allegiance. The papacy, interfering in all things and seeking to dominate all, very soon came to be regarded in a political light; the temporal princes now began to put forth higher claims than they had hitherto done.

It is commonly believed that the papal authority was almost unrestricted up to the time of the Reformation, but the truth is that no inconsiderable portion of the rights and privileges of the clergy had been appropriated by the civil power during the fifteenth and in the early part of the sixteenth centuries.†

A universal tendency to the circumscription of papal power was at this time manifested throughout Christendom, in the South as in the North. The civil power most especially desired a participation in ecclesiastical revenues and the right of promotion to church benefices and offices. Nor did the popes attempt any strenuous opposition. Of their privileges and possessions they maintained what they could; the rest they resigned. It was remarked of Ferdinand of Naples by Lorenzo de' Medici in relation to a dispute of the former with the Roman See—"He will make no difficulty of promising, but when it comes to the fulfillment his deficiencies will be overlooked, as those of kings always are by the popes." This spirit of opposition had penetrated even into Italy.*

We shall be mistaken if we consider these movements as but so many acts of self-will: the life of the European nations was no longer pervaded and impressed as it had formerly been by ecclesiastical influence. The development of national character, and the separate organization of the various monarchies, were making important advances. It thus became indispensable that the relation of the ecclesiastical to the secular powers should be thoroughly modified. A very remarkable change had become obvious, even in the popes themselves.

Chapter Second
THE CHURCH AND ITS TERRITORIES
IN THE BEGINNING OF THE SIXTEENTH CENTURY

Extension Of The Papal States

Whatever judgment may be formed of the popes of the earlier ages, it is certain that they always had important interests in view—the duty of upholding an oppressed religion, that of contending with paganism, of diffusing Christianity among the nations of the North, and of establishing an independent hierarchical government. To will, and to achieve some great object, is proper to the dignity of human nature; and while such was their tendency, the popes were sustained in their lofty efforts; but this spirit had passed with the times by which it had been awakened.

Schism had been suppressed, but it had become obvious that no hope remained of effecting a combined action against the Turks. It thus followed that her spiritual head now devoted himself to the interests of his temporal sovereignty, and pursued these with an avidity hitherto unknown.

For quite some time this had been in accord with the tendencies of the times. "I had once thought," remarks one of the speakers in the Council of Basle, "that the secular power should be wholly separate from that of the Church; but I have now learned that virtue without force is but slightly respected, and that the pope, without the patrimony of the Church, would be merely the servant of kings and princes." This speaker, who had yet sufficient influences in the assembly to determine the election of Pope Felix (V), declares it not so very objectionable that a pope should have sons, who might defend him against the aggressions of tyrants.

This question was afterward considered from a different point of view among the Italians. It was held to be in order that a pope should provide for his own family and promote its interests; in fact, a pontiff neglecting to do this would have exposed himself to criticism. "Others," writes Lorenzo de' Medici to Innocent VIII, "have not so long postponed their efforts to attain the papal chair, and have concerned themselves little to maintain the retiring delicacy so long evinced by your holiness. Now is your holiness not only exonerated before God and man, but this honorable conduct may cause you to incur blame, and your reserve may be attributed to less worthy motives. Zeal and duty lay it on my conscience to remind your holiness that no man is immortal. Be the pontiff as important as he may in his own person, he cannot make his dignity and that importance hereditary; he cannot be said absolutely to possess anything but the honors and emoluments he has secured to his kindred." Such were the counsels offered by him who was considered the wisest man of Italy. It is true that he had himself a direct interest in the matter, having given his daughter in marriage to a son of the Pope, but he would never have dared to express himself thus boldly and without reserve, had not the views he was propounding been admitted without question among the higher classes of his country.

There is a certain internal coherence in the fact that at this period the temporal princes were regularly seeking possession of the papal privileges, and in the circumstance that manifold secular enterprises now began to occupy the most earnest attention of the Pope. He felt himself above all an Italian prince.*

Pope Sixtus IV was the first pontiff by whom this purpose was undertaken with a fixed will and effectual results. He was strenuously, and most successfully, followed by Alexander VI. From Julius II this plan received a direction wholly unexpected, and of which the effect was permanent.†

The great object of Alexander VI throughout his whole life was to gratify his inclination for pleasure, his ambition, and his love of ease. When at length he had attained the supreme spiritual dignity, he seemed also to have reached the summit of happiness. Despite his advanced years, the exultation he felt seemed to rejuvenate him daily. No painful thought was permitted to disturb his repose for a single night. His only care was to seize on all means that might aid him to increase his power, and advance the wealth and dignity of his sons: on no other subject did he ever seriously bestow a thought.

This one consideration was exclusively at the base of all his political alliances, by which the events of the world were so powerfully influenced. How the Pope would proceed in regard to the marriages, endowments, and advances of his children became a question affecting the politics of all Europe.*

The ecclesiastical states had hitherto been divided by the factions of the Guelfs and the Ghibellines, the first represented in Rome by the family of Orsini, the second by the house of Colonna. The popes had usually taken part with one or the other of these factions. Sixtus IV had done so, and his example was followed by Alexander and his son Caesar, who at first attached themselves to the Guelf, or Orsini, party. This alliance enabled them very soon to gain the mastery of all their enemies. They drove the house of Sforza from Pesaro, that of Malatesta from Rimini, and the family of Manfredi from Faenza. They seized upon those powerful, well-fortified cities and thus commenced the foundation of an extensive lordship. But no sooner had they attained this point, no sooner had they freed themselves from their enemies, than they turned every effort against their friends. And it was in this that the practice of the Borgias differed from that of their predecessors, who had ever remained firmly attached to the party they had chosen. Caesar, on the contrary, attacked his own confederates, without hesitation or scruple. The Duke of Urbino, from whom he had frequently received important aid, was involved, as in a network, by the machinations of Caesar. The duke saved his life with difficulty to become a persecuted fugitive in his own dominions. Vitelli, Baglioni, and other chiefs of the Orsini faction resolved to show him that at least they were capable of resistance. But Caesar Borgia, declaring that "it is permitted to betray those who are the masters of all treasons," decoyed them into his snares with profoundly calculated cruelty and mercilessly deprived them of life. Having thus destroyed both parties, he stepped into their place, gathered the inferior nobility who had been their adherents around him, and took them into his pay. The territories he had seized on were held in subjection by force of terror and cruelty.

The brightest hopes of Alexander were thus realized—the nobles of the land were annihilated, and his house was about to found a great hereditary dominion in Italy. But he had already begun to acquire practical experience of the evil which passions, aroused and unbridled, are capable of producing. With no relative or favorite would Caesar Borgia share his power. His own brother had stood in his way: Caesar caused him to be murdered and thrown into the Tiber. His brother-in-law was assailed and stabbed, by his orders, on the steps of his palace. The wounded man was nursed by his wife and sister, the latter preparing his food with her own hands to protect him from poison; the Pope set a guard upon the house to protect his son-in-law from his son. Caesar derided these precautions. "What cannot be done at noonday," said he, "may be brought about in the evening." When the prince was on the point of recovery, Caesar burst into his chamber, drove out the wife and sister, called in the common executioner, and caused his unfortunate brother-in-law to be strangled. Toward his father, whose life and station he valued only as a means to his own aggrandizement, he displayed not the slightest respect or feeling. He slew Peroto, Alexander's favorite, while the unhappy man clung to his patron for protection and was wrapped within the pontifical mantle. The blood of the favorite flowed over the face of the Pope.

For a certain time the city of the apostles and the whole state of the Church were in the hands of Caesar Borgia. He is described as possessing great personal beauty, and was so strong that in a bullfight he would strike off the head of the animal at a single blow. He was liberal and not without certain features of greatness, but given up to his passions and deeply stained with blood. How Rome did tremble at his name! Caesar required gold and possessed enemies. Every night the corpses of murdered men were found in the streets, yet none dared move, for who but might fear that his own turn would be next? Those whom violence could not reach were poisoned.

There was but one place on earth where such deeds were possible—that, namely, where unlimited temporal power was united to the highest spiritual authority, where the laws, civil and ecclesiastical, were held in one and the same hand. This place was occupied by Caesar Borgia. Even depravity may have its perfection. The kindred of popes have often distinguished themselves in the career of evil, but none attained to the eminence of Caesar Borgia. He may be called a virtuoso in crime.

Was it not in the first and most essential tendencies of Christianity to render such a power impossible? And yet, Christianity itself and the very position of the supreme head of the Church were made subservient to its existence.

Luther was not needed to prove to the world that these things were in direct opposition to the spirit of Christianity. Even at that time men complained that the Pope was preparing the way for antichrist, and laboring for the interest of Satan rather than the kingdom of God.†

Prevalence Of Secular Views And Interests In The Church

It is not otherwise conceivable than that the whole institution of the Church would bend in the direction taken by its head, contributing to its emergence or engulfed by its force.

Not only the supreme dignity of the pontiff, but all the offices of the Church, were regarded as mere secular property. The Pope nominated cardinals from no better motive than personal favor, the gratification of some potentate, or even (and this was not an infrequent occurrence) for actual payment of money! Could there be any rational expectation that men so appointed would fulfill their spiritual duties?†

A large amount of worldly power was at this time conferred, in most instances, together with the bishoprics; they were held more or less as sinecures according to the degree of influence or court favor possessed by the recipient or his family. The Roman Curia thought only of how it might best derive advantage from the vacancies and presentations.* For every favor obtained from the datary's office, a stipulated sum was paid. Nearly all the disputes occurring at this period between the several states of Europe and the Roman Court arose out of these exactions, which the Curia sought by every possible means to increase, while the people of all countries as zealously strove to restrain them.

This principle necessarily acted on all ranks affected by the system based on it, from the highest to the lowest. Many ecclesiastics were found ready to renounce their bishoprics, but they retained the greater part of the revenues, and not unfrequently the presentation to the benefices depended on them also.* It followed of necessity that the performance of ecclesiastical duties was grievously neglected. In this rapid sketch, I confine myself to remarks made by conscientious prelates of the Roman Court itself. "What a spectacle," they exclaim, "for a Christian who shall take his way through the Christian world, is this desolation of the churches! All the flocks are abandoned by their shepherds, they are given over to the care of hirelings."†

Intellectual Tendency

Could we open the books of history just as they happened, could that which is fleeting converse with us as does nature, how often we would see life spring from death, just as we now perceive the new offshoot in the decay which we lamented!

Much as we may decry the materialism of spiritual things and the disintegration of the religious institution, the spirit of man could hardly have entered upon one of its most distinctive directions, most heavily fraught with consequences, without it.

We cannot deny the fact that, ingenious, diversified, and profound as are the productions of the Middle Ages, they are yet based on views of the world, visionary in character and but little in accordance with the reality of things. Had the Church remained in full and conscious force, she would have adhered firmly to these views, narrowing and restricting as they were; but as she now was, the human intellect was left at liberty to seek a new development in a totally altered direction.

We may safely assert that during those ages the mind of man was necessarily held within the limits of a closely bounded horizon. The renewed acquaintance with antiquity removed this barrier and opened a loftier, a more comprehensive, and a grander prospect.*

We would, however, be going too far if we were immediately to speak of the development of an independent spirit of research, of the discovery of new truths, and of the production of great thoughts. As yet men sought only to comprehend the ancients; none thought of going beyond them. The efficacy of the classic writers lay not so much in the impulse given to a productive scientific activity as in the imitation they incited.*

Meanwhile it was not possible that things could remain stationary. Once arrived at this point, to whatever extent the direct imitation of the ancients in their own language might be carried, it was utterly insufficient to occupy the whole field of intellect. There was something in it incomplete and unsatisfactory, and it was so widely practiced that this defect could not long escape the general notice. The new idea gradually arose of imitating the ancients in the vernacular. The men of that day felt that they stood in the same position with regard to the classic authors as did the Romans with regard to the Greeks: they determined no longer to confine themselves within the bounds of a contest in mere details. They now resolved to vie with their masters in all fields of literature, and with youthful enthusiasm rushed forward on this new career.*

And was it not profoundly significant that a pope should himself resolve to demolish the ancient basilica of St. Peter, the metropolitan church of Christendom, every part of which was hallowed, every portion crowded with monuments that had received the veneration of ages, and determine to erect a temple, planned after those of antiquity, on its site? This was a purpose exclusively artistic. The two factions then dividing the jealous and contentious world of art united in urging Julius II to this enterprise. Michael Angelo desired a fitting site for that monument to the Pope which he proposed to complete on a vast scale, and with that lofty grandeur which he has exhibited in his Moses. Yet more pressing was Bramante. It was his ambition to have space for the execution of that bold project, long before conceived, of raising high in the air on colossal pillars an exact copy of the Pantheon, in all the majesty of its proportions. Many cardinals remonstrated, and it would even appear that there was a general opposition to the plan; so much of personal affection attaches itself to every old church; how much more then to this, the chief sanctuary of Christendom! But Julius was not accustomed to regard contradiction. Without further consideration he caused one-half of the old church to be demolished, and himself laid the foundation stone of the new one. Thus rose again, in the heart and center of the Christian worship, those forms in which the spirit of the antique rites had found so eloquent an expression.*

If this involved a contradiction, it was one that pervaded the whole existence and affected all the habits of the times.

Men frequented the Vatican, less to kneel in devotion on the threshold of the apostles than to admire those great works of ancient art that enriched the dwelling of the pontiff—the Belvedere Apollo and the Laocoön.*

In this exuberance of effort and production of intellect and art, and in the enjoyment of increasing temporal power attached to the highest spiritual dignity, lived Leo X.† One must forever

loath the debasing sensuality of Alexander VI; in the court of
Leo X there were few things deserving blame in themselves, although we cannot but perceive that his pursuits might have been
more strictly in accordance with his position as supreme head of
the Church.

Easily does life veil its own incongruities as they pass, but no
sooner do men set themselves to ponder, examine, and compare,
than at once they become fully apparent to all.

Of true Christian sentiment and conviction there could be no
question in such a state of things; they were, on the contrary,
directly opposed.†

We thus see how all is enchained and connected—how one
event calls forth another. The pretensions of temporal princes to
ecclesiastical power leads to the secular ambition in the popes, the
corruption and decline of religious institutions leads to the development of a new intellectual tendency, until at length the very
foundations of the faith become shaken in the public opinion.

Opposition In Germany

There appears to me something especially remarkable in the relationship which Germany, in particular, adopted toward this spiritual development, participating in it, albeit in a manner which
deviated substantially.

In Italy, the promoters of classical study, and those from
whom the age received its impulse toward it, were poets—as, for
example, Boccaccio and Petrarch. In Germany, the same effect was
due to a religious fraternity, the Hieronymites—a community
united by a life of labor passed in sequestration from the world.
It was one of this brotherhood, the profound and blameless mystic
Thomas à Kempis, from whose school proceeded all those earnest
and venerable men who, first drawn to Italy by the light of ancient
learning, newly kindled there, afterward returned to pour its beneficent influence over the breadth of Germany.

The difference thus observable in the beginning was equally
apparent in the subsequent progress.

In Italy the works of the ancients were studied for the sciences they contained; in Germany one took them to school. The Italians sought a solution of the highest problems that can occupy the human intellect, if not by independent thought, at least with the help of the ancients. The Germans devoted the best books to the education of their youth. The Italians were attracted toward the ancients by the beauty of form, which they sought to imitate, and thence proceeded to the formation of a national literature. Among the Germans, these same studies took a more spiritual direction. The fame of Erasmus and Reuchlin is familiar to all; if we inquire what constitutes the principal merit of the latter, we find it to be his having written the first Hebrew grammar—a monument of which he hoped, as did the Italian poets of their works, that "it would be more durable than iron." As by Reuchlin the study of the Old Testament was first facilitated, so was that of the New Testament indebted to Erasmus. To this it was that his attention was devoted; it was he who first caused it to be printed in Greek, and his paraphrases and commentaries on it have produced an effect far surpassing the end he had proposed to himself.

While the public mind of Italy had become alienated from and even opposed to the Church, an effect in some respects similar had taken place in Germany. There that freedom of thought which can never be wholly suppressed gained admission into the literary world and occasionally displayed itself in decided scepticism. A more profound theology had also arisen from sources but imperfectly known, and though discountenanced by the Church, had never been put down. This now formed an essential part of the literary movement in Germany.*

Thus, on either side of the Alps, the progress of the age was in direct opposition to ecclesiastical ascendancy. In Italy this tendency was associated with science and literature; in Germany it arose from biblical studies and a more profound theology. There it was negative and incredulous; here it was positive and full of an earnest faith. There it destroyed the very foundations of the Church; here the desire was to construct the edifice anew. In Italy it was mocking and sarcastic, but ever pliant and deferential to power; in Germany, full of a serious indignation, and deeply determined on a stubbornness of assault such as the Roman Church had never before experienced.

The fact that this was first directed against the abuses arising from the sale of indulgences has sometimes been regarded as a mere accident. But as the alienation of that which is most essentially spiritual, implicit in the doctrine of indulgences, laid open and made visible the weakest point in the whole system—the worldliness of spirit now prevalent in the Church—so it was, of all things, best calculated to shock and offend the convictions of those earnest and profound thinkers, the German theologians. A man like Luther—whose religion was sincere and deeply felt, whose opinions of sin and justification were those propounded by the early German theologians and confirmed in his mind by the study of Scripture which he had drunk in with a thirsting heart—could not fail to be revolted and shocked by the sale of indulgences. Forgiveness of sins to be purchased for money! This must of necessity be deeply offensive to him, whose conclusions were drawn from profound contemplation of the eternal relation existing between God and man and who had learned to interpret Scripture for himself.

He opposed individual abuses, but the ill-founded and prejudiced opposition he encountered, leading him on from step to step, presently made him aware of the connection between this monstrous abuse and the general disorders of the Church. His was not a nature to shrink from or tremble at the most extreme measures. With unhesitating boldness he attacked the head of the Church himself. From the midst of an order hitherto the most submissive adherents and devoted defenders of the papacy, that of the Friars-Mendicant, now rose the most determined and most vigorous opponent the pontificate had yet known. And as Luther, with the utmost precision and acuteness, held up its own declared principles in the face of that power which had so widely departed from them—as he did but express truths of which all men had long been convinced—as his opposition, the full import of which had not yet become apparent, was acceptable to those who rejected the faith, and yet, because it was undertaken in defense of

those principles, was consonant to the mind of the earnest be-
liever—so had his writings an incalculable effect and were rapidly
disseminated, not in Germany alone, but through the whole world.

Chapter Third
POLITICAL COMPLICATIONS
AND THE REFORMATION

The secular spirit that had now taken possession of the papacy
had occasioned a twofold movement in the world. The one was
ecclesiastical in the proper sense; a falling off from the Church
had begun which entailed a vast future. The second movement
was of a political nature; the elements which the pope had put in
conflict were still in ferment, which gave rise to the expectation
of new developments in affairs in general. These two movements,
their effect on each other, and the contests to which they gave
rise, imposed their influence on the history of the papacy for
centuries.

Well would it be for states and princes, should all be convinced that no essential good can result to them except from their
own exertions—that no benefit is real unless acquired by their
own strength and effort!

While the Italian powers were laboring to conquer each other
with foreign aid, they had in effect destroyed that independence
which they had enjoyed during the fifteenth century and exposed
their country to becoming the prize of a foreign victor. A large
share in this result must be imputed to the popes.* Two great
powers arose, and these contended, if not for universal supremacy,
at least for the foremost position in Europe. No pontiff could cope
with them any longer, and it was in Italy that they sought their
battleground.

The French were the first to show themselves. Soon after the
accession of Leo X they appeared, in greater force than any with

which they had ever before crossed the Alps, to regain possession of Milan. Francis I, in all the ardor of his chivalrous youth, was their leader. Everything depended on whether the Swiss could resist him or not; therefore it was that the battle of Marignano was so important, for here this question was resolved. The Swiss were totally routed, and since that defeat they have exercised no independent influence in Italy.*

In effect, the French acquired a decided preponderance in Italy by this victory. Had it been vigorously followed up, neither Tuscany nor the States of the Church, both so easily incited to revolt, could have offered them resistance, and the Spaniards would have found it sufficiently difficult to maintain themselves in Naples. "The King," says Francesco Vettori explicitly, "might become lord of Italy." How much was at this moment depending on Leo!*

Contrary to the advice of his cardinals, he betook himself to Bologna to confer with the King. They concluded the concordat,* in which they divided between them the rights of the Gallican Church. Leo was compelled to give up Parma and Placentia, but he succeeded in dispersing the storm that had threatened him, persuaded the King to return, and himself remained secure in the possession of his dominions.*

The second great power had meanwhile consolidated itself. How extraordinary it seems that one and the same prince should hold the sceptre in Vienna, Brussels, Valladolid, Saragossa, and Naples! Nor was this all—his rule extended even to another continent, yet this was brought about almost imperceptibly by a series of family alliances. This aggrandizement of the house of Austria, which linked together so many different countries, was one of the most important and eventful changes that Europe had yet witnessed. At that moment when the nations were diverging from the point that had hitherto been their common center, they were again gathered, by their political circumstances, into new combinations and formed into a new system. The power of Austria instantly opposed itself to the preponderance of France. With his imperial dignity, Charles V acquired legal claims to supremacy, at least in Lombardy. On account of these Italian affairs the battle was soon joined.

The popes, as we have before remarked, had hoped to secure entire independence by the extension of their states; they now found themselves hemmed in between two greatly superior powers. A pope was not so insignificant that he could remain neutral in a strife between them, neither was he sufficiently powerful to secure preponderance for that scale into which he should cast his weight; his safety could only be found in the dexterous use of passing events. Leo is reported to have said that when a man has formed a compact with one party, he must nonetheless take care to negotiate with the other. This double-tongued policy was forced on him by the position in which he was placed.

But the pontiff could not seriously doubt which party it was his interest to adopt, for had he not felt it of infinite importance to regain Parma and Placentia—had the promise of Charles V, that an Italian should hold possession of Milan, a thing so much to his advantage, been insufficient to determine his choice—there was still another consideration, and one that appears to me entirely conclusive; this was a motive connected with religion.

Throughout the whole period of time that we are contemplating, there was no assistance so much desired by the temporal sovereigns in their disputes with the popes as that of a spiritual opposition to the papal decrees. But when had the Pope so bold or so prosperous an opponent as Luther? The mere fact that so fearless a foe to the papacy had made his appearance, the very existence of such a phenomenon, was highly significant and imparted to the person of the reformer a decided political importance. It was thus that Maximilian considered it, nor would he permit injury of any kind to be offered to this monk. He caused him to be specially recommended to the Elector of Saxony—"there might come a time when he would be needed"—and from that moment the influence of Luther increased day by day. The Pope could neither convince nor alarm this opponent, neither could he get him into his hands. One resource yet remained to him. Might he not hope that by an alliance with the Emperor, he could secure the aid of that sovereign for the repression of so dangerous religious innovations? It is certain that they would be protected and even promoted by the Emperor, should Leo declare against him.

Religious and political matters were the subject of discussion in the Diet of Worms (1521). The Pope entered into a league with the Emperor for the recovery of Milan. On the day when the alliance was concluded, the edict of outlawry proclaimed against Luther is said to have been also dated. There may have been other motives operating to produce this act of proscription, but no one will persuade himself that there was not an immediate connection with the political treaty.

And little time elapsed before the twofold effect of this league became manifest.* It was a moment of infinite importance: new developments had arisen in politics, and a great movement had commenced in the Church. The aspect of affairs permitted Leo to flatter himself that he was directing the first, and had succeeded in repressing the second. He was still young enough to indulge in the anticipation of fully profiting from the results of this auspicious moment.

Strange and delusive destiny of man! The Pope was at his villa of Malliana when he received intelligence that his party had triumphantly entered Milan. He abandoned himself to the exultation arising naturally from the successful completion of an important enterprise, and looked cheerfully on at the festivities his people were preparing on the occasion.

He paced back and forth until deep in the night, between the window and a blazing hearth—it was the month of November. Somewhat exhausted, but still in high spirits, he arrived in Rome, and the rejoicings celebrated there for his triumph were not yet concluded, when he was attacked by a mortal disease. "Pray for me," said he to his servants, "that I may yet make you all happy." We see that he loved life, but his hour was come; he had not time to receive the sacrament nor extreme unction. So suddenly, so prematurely, and surrounded by hopes so bright!—he died—"as the poppy fadeth."*

We have called him fortunate. At the moment of his death, the purposes he had proposed to himself in the policy he had pursued were all tending toward the happiest results. It may be considered a further proof of his good fortune that his life was not prolonged. Times of a different character succeeded, and it is difficult to believe that he could have opposed a successful resistance to their unfavorable influences. The whole weight of them was experienced by his successors. On a worthier man, however, the choice of the conclave could scarcely have fallen. The reputation of Adrian was without a blemish; laborious, upright, and pious, he was of so earnest a gravity that a faint smile was his nearest approach to mirth, yet benevolent withal, full of pure intentions, a true servant of religion. What a contrast when he entered that city where Leo had held his court with so lavish a splendor!†

No one could be more earnest than was Adrian VI (he chose to retain his own name) in his desire to ameliorate the grievous condition into which Christendom had fallen at his accession.*

He was determined to anticipate the demands of the Germans with regard to the abuses that had made their way into the Church. His avowal that such existed was most explicit. "We know," he observes in the instructions for the Nuncio Chieregato, whom he sent to the Diet, "that for a considerable period many abominable things have taken place beside the holy chair—abuses in spiritual matters—exorbitant straining of prerogatives—evil everywhere. From the head, the malady has proceeded to the limbs; from the Pope, it has extended to the prelates; we are all gone astray, there is none that hath done rightly—no not one." On his part he proceeds to promise all that may be expected from a good pope: he will promote the learned and upright, suppress abuses, and if not all at once, yet gradually, bring about a reformation both in the head and members such as men have so long desired and demanded.

But to reform the world is not so light a task; the good intentions of an individual, however high his station, are insufficient. Too deeply do abuses strike their roots. With life itself they grow and become entwined, so that it is at length difficult to eradicate the one without endangering the other.*

The Germans were not now to be conciliated by what would once have been hailed as a reformation of head and members, and even had they been, how difficult, how almost impracticable, would such reform have been found!

If the Pope attempted to reduce those revenues of the Curia

in which he detected an appearance of simony, he could not do so without alienating the legitimate rights of those persons whose offices were founded on these revenues; offices that, for the most part, had been purchased by the men who held them.

If he contemplated a change in the dispensations of marriage, or some relaxation of existing prohibitions, it was instantly represented to him that such a step would infringe upon and weaken the discipline of the Church.

To abate the crying abuse of indulgences, he would gladly have revived the ancient penances; but the Penitenziaria at once called his attention to the danger he would thus incur; for, while he sought to secure Germany, Italy would be lost.

Enough is said to show that the Pope could make no step toward reform, without seeing himself assailed by a thousand difficulties.*

Thus it came to pass that in affairs of vital importance to the general interest, nothing effectual was accomplished.* Luther was more than ever active in Germany; and in Rome, which was, besides, afflicted with the plague, a general discontent prevailed.

Adrian once said, "How much depends on the times in which even the best of men are cast!" The painful sense he entertained of his difficult position is eloquently expressed in this sorrowing outburst. Most appropriately it was engraved on his monument in the German church at Rome.

And here it becomes obvious, that not to Adrian personally must it be solely attributed that his times were so unproductive in results. The papacy was encompassed by a host of coercive circumstances with universal implications that would have furnished infinite occupation, even to a man more familiar with the medium of action, better versed in men, and more fertile in expedients than Adrian VI.

Among all the cardinals, there was no one who seemed so peculiarly fitted to administer the government successfully, no one who appeared so well prepared to support the weight of the popedom, than Giulio de' Medici. He had already managed a large share of the public business under Leo—all the details were in his hands—and even under Adrian he had maintained a certain degree of influence. This time he did not permit the supreme dignity to escape him, and he ascended the papal throne under the name of Clement VII.

The faults and mistakes of his immediate predecessors were carefully avoided by the new Pope. The instability, prodigality, and pleasure-seeking habits of Leo, and that ceaseless conflict with the tastes and opinions of his court into which Adrian had suffered himself to be drawn, were all eschewed by Clement VII. Everything was arranged with the utmost discretion, and his own conduct was remarkable for the blameless rectitude and moderation of its tenor. The pontifical ceremonies were performed with due care. Audience was given with untiring application from early morning to night. Science and the arts were encouraged in that direction toward which they had now become decidedly bent. Clement was himself a man of extensive information. He spoke with equal knowledge of his subject, whether that were philosophy and theology, or mechanics and hydraulic architecture. In all affairs he displayed extraordinary acuteness. The most perplexing questions were unravelled, the most difficult circumstances were penetrated to the very bottom by his extreme sagacity. No man could debate a point with more address: under Leo he had already manifested a prudence in counsel and a circumspect ability in practice that none could surpass.†

How closely the bygone course of events and his personal position seemed to bind Clement both by necessity and inclination to the Spanish cause in Italy. Yet how many were the reasons that now presented themselves, all tending to make him execrate the power he had so largely contributed to establish, and place himself in opposition to the cause for which he had hitherto so zealously labored!

There is, perhaps, no effort in politics so difficult to make as that of retracing the path we have hitherto trodden, of reversing successes which we ourselves had achieved. And how much was now depending on such an effort! The Italians were profoundly sensible to the fact that the acts of the present moment would decide their fate for centuries. A powerful feeling of community had arisen and prevailed throughout the nation. I am fully persuaded that this may be in great part ascribed to the literary and artistic progress of Italy, a progress in which it left other nations so far behind.†

We may state that the temper of Germany now also became decisive for Italy. As a nation the Italians were far from being zealous for their great enterprise against Spain, and even among those who desired its success, unanimity did not prevail. Able as he was and thoroughly Italian in spirit, the Pope was yet not one of those men who calmly control the current of circumstances and seem to hold fortune enchained. His keen perception of realities seemed injurious rather than serviceable to him. His conviction that he was the weaker party was stronger than was expedient. All possible contingencies, every form of danger, presented themselves too clearly before him; they bewildered his mind and confused his decisions. There is a practical and inventive faculty by which some men intuitively perceive the simple and practicable in affairs, and guided by this, they rapidly seize on the best expedient. This he did not possess; in the most critical moments he was seen to hesitate, waver, and waste his thoughts in attempts to save money. His allies having failed in their promises, the results he had hoped for were far from being obtained. In November 1526, George Frundsberg crossed the Alps with a formidable body of German soldiers to bring the contest to an end. This army was altogether Lutheran—leader and followers. "When once I make my way to Rome," said Frundsberg, "I will hang the Pope."*

With anxious thought the gathering storm is seen on the narrowing and lowering horizon. Rome, loaded perhaps with vices, yet nonetheless teeming with the noblest effort, the most exalted intellect, the richest culture; powerfully creative, adorned with matchless works of art such as the world has never since produced; replete with riches, ennobled by the impress of genius, and exercising a vital and imperishable influence on the whole world, this Rome is now threatened with destruction. As the masses of the imperial force drew together, the Italian troops dispersed before them, the only army that yet remained followed them from afar. The Emperor had long been unable to pay his troops and could not alter their direction even had he desired to do so. They marched beneath the imperial banner but were guided only by their own stormy will and impulse. Clement still hoped, negotiated, offered concessions, retracted them; but the sole expedient that could have saved him—namely contenting these hordes with all the money they believed was owed them—this, he either could not, or would not adopt. Will he then at least make a stand against the enemy with such weapons as he has? Four thousand men would have sufficed to secure the passes of Tuscany, but the attempt was not even thought of. Rome contained within her walls some thirty thousand inhabitants capable of bearing arms; many of these men had seen service. They wore swords by their sides, which they used freely in their feuds among each other, and then boasted of their exploits. But to oppose the enemy, who brought with him certain destruction, five hundred men were the most that could ever be mustered to leave the city. At the first onset the Pope and his forces were overthrown. On the sixth of May 1527, two hours before sunset, the imperialists poured their unbridled numbers into Rome. Their former general, Frundsberg, was no longer at their head. In a disturbance among his troops, he had been unable to repress them as was his wont, and being struck by apoplexy, he remained behind in a state of dangerous illness. Bourbon, who had led the army so far, was killed at the first fixing of the scaling-ladders. Thus, restrained by no leader, the bloodthirsty soldiery, hardened by long privations and rendered savage by their trade, burst over the city. Never richer booty fell into more violent hands, never was plunder more continuous or more destructive. How vivid a luster was cast over the beginning of the sixteenth century by the splendor of Rome! It designates a period most influential on the development of the human mind. This day saw the light of that splendor extinguished forever.*

No less important was another occurrence: before Rome was captured and when it was merely seen that the march of Bourbon was in that direction, the enemies of the Medici in Florence had availed themselves of the confusion of the moment and once more expelled the family of the Pope. The revolt of his native city was more painful to Clement than even the downfall of Rome. With astonishment men beheld him, after so many indignities, again connect himself with the imperialists. He did so because he saw that with the help of the Spaniards alone could his kindred and party be reinstated in Florence; the domination of the Emperor was at least more endurable to Clement than the disobedience of his rebels. As the fortunes of the French were seen to decline, the Pope made approaches to the Spaniards; and when the former were at length entirely defeated, he concluded the Treaty of Barcelona with the latter. He so completely changed his policy that the very army by which Rome had been sacked before his eyes, and he himself so long held captive, was now called to his assistance. Reinforced and strengthened, it was led to the reduction of his native city.

Thenceforth Charles was more powerful in Italy than any emperor had been for many centuries. The crown that he received at Bologna had now regained its full significance; Milan gradually became as entirely subjected to his authority as was Naples. His restoration of the Medici to their seat in Florence secured him a direct and permanent influence in Tuscany. The remaining states of Italy either sought his alliance or submitted to his power. With the might of Germany and Spain, united by the force of his victorious arms and in the rights of his imperial dignity, he held all Italy in subjection, from the Alps to the sea.

To this point it was then that the Italian wars conducted the country; from that period never has she been freed from the rule of the stranger. Let us now examine the progress of the religious dissensions that were so intimately entwined with the political events.†

It was generally believed, whether justly or not I will not inquire, that a general council of the Church alone could settle differences so important and remove errors so fatal. Church councils had maintained their credit precisely because a very natural repugnance to them had been evinced by the popes, and all opposition to them by the papal chair had tended to raise them in public estimation. In the year 1530, Charles applied his thoughts seriously to this matter, and promised to call a council within a brief specified period.

In the different complications of their interests with those of the pontificate, the princes had always desired to find some spiritual backing for their point of view. Charles might thus assure himself of most zealous allies in a council assembled under existing circumstances. Convened at his instigation, it would be held under his influence and to him also would revert the execution of its edicts. These decrees would have to bear upon two important questions—they would affect the Pope equally with his opponents, the old idea of a reformation in head and members would be realized, and how decided a predominance would all this secure to the temporal power, above all to that of Charles himself!

This mode of proceeding was most judicious. It was, if you will have it so, inevitable; but it was, at the same time, for the best interest of the Emperor.

On the other hand, no event could be better calculated to awaken anxiety in the pontiff and his court. I find that at the first serious mention of a council, the price of all the salable offices of the court declined considerably. The danger threatened by a council to the existing state of things is obvious from this fact.

In addition to this, Clement VII had personal motives for objecting to the measure. He was not of legitimate birth, neither had he risen to the supreme dignity by means that were altogether blameless. Again, he had been determined by considerations entirely personal to employ the resources of the Church in a contest with his native city, and for all these things a pope might fairly expect heavy reckoning with a council. Thus it inspired him with a just terror, and Soriano tells us that he would not willingly utter its very name.

He did not reject the proposal outright—this he could not do without implicating the honor of the Papal See—but one can easily imagine how reluctant he was to receive it.

He submitted, certainly. He was compliant but he did not fail to set forth the objections to the measure, and that in the most persuasive forms. He represented all the dangers and difficulties inseparable from a council, declaring its success to be very much in doubt. Next he stipulated the concurrence of all other princes, as well as a previous subjection of the Protestants—demands that were perfectly in accordance with the papal system and doctrine, but utterly impracticable in the existing state of affairs.* He doubtless still hoped to evade the necessity that hung over him.

But it clung to him fast and firm. When Charles returned to

Italy in 1533 still impressed with what he had seen and heard in Germany, he pressed the Pope in person and with increased earnestness during a conference held at Bologna on the subject of the council, which he had so frequently demanded in writing. Their opinions were thus brought into direct collision—the Pope held fast by his conditions, the Emperor declared their fulfillment impossible—they could come to no agreement. In the documents respecting these matters, a certain discrepancy is perceptible—the Pope appearing more supporting of the Emperor's wishes in some than in others; however this may be, he had no alternative—a fresh proclamation had to be issued. He could not so effectually blind himself as not to perceive that when the Emperor (who was gone to Spain) should return, mere words would be insufficient to content him—that the danger he dreaded, and with which a council summoned under such circumstances certainly did menace the Roman See, could then be no longer averted.

The situation was one in which the possessor of a power, of whatever kind, might well be excused for resorting even to audacious measures if these were the only means that could insure his own safety. The political preponderance of the Emperor was already excessive, and although the Pope had resigned himself to this state of things, he could not but feel his own depressed condition. In arbitrating the long-standing disputes of the Church with Ferrara, Charles V had decided for the latter; this mortified the pontiff, and though he acquiesced in the decision, he complained of it to his friends. How much more afflicting was it now when this monarch, from whom he had hoped the immediate subjugation of the Protestants, was preferring his claim under pretext of religious dissension to a predominance in ecclesiastical affairs such as no emperor had enjoyed for centuries. Nay, that he was proceeding without scruple to acts that must compromise the spiritual authority and dignity of the Holy See. Must Clement indeed endure to see himself sink utterly into the Emperor's hands, and wholly given up to his tender mercies?

His resolution was taken even while in Bologna. More than once Francis had proposed to cement his political alliances with Clement by means of a family connection. This the pontiff had hitherto declined—in the desperate position of his present affairs, he decided to accept. It is expressly affirmed that the real cause of Clement's once again lending an ear to the French King was the demand of Charles for a council.

The Pope would most probably never more have attempted to establish a balance of power between these two great monarchs and to divide his favor equally between them from purely political motives; but it was on this course that he now determined, in consideration of the dangers threatening the Church.

Shortly thereafter Clement met with Francis I at Marseilles, where a very close alliance was concluded. Precisely as Clement had confirmed his friendship with the Emperor during the Florentine difficulties by accepting a natural daughter of Charles as wife to one of his nephews, so did he now cement the bond which the embarrassments of the Church compelled him to form with Francis by the betrothal of his young niece, Catherine de' Medici, to the King's second son. In the first instance, it was against the French, and their indirect influence on Florence, that he sought to defend himself; on this occasion, the Emperor and his intentions with regard to a council were the cause of fear.

He now took no further pains to conceal his purpose. We have a letter addressed by him to Ferdinand I, wherein he declares that his efforts to procure the concurrence of the Christian princes to the assembling of a council had been without effect. King Francis I, to whom he had spoken, thought the present moment unfavorable for such a purpose and refused to adopt the suggestion. But Clement still hoped for some other opportunity to obtain a more favorable decision from the Christian sovereigns. I cannot comprehend the doubt that has existed in regard to the real intentions of the Pope. It was but in his last communication with the Catholic princes of Germany that he had repeated his demand for universal concurrence as a condition to the proposed council. Is not his present declaration that he cannot bring about this general agreement equivalent to the positive assertion that he recalls his announcement of the council? In his alliance with France, he had found alike the courage to pursue this line of conduct and the pretext for it. I cannot convince myself that the council ever would have been held in his pontificate.†

The papacy was in an utterly false and untenable position;

its worldly tendencies had produced a degeneracy that had in its turn called forth innumerable opponents and adversaries. These tendencies being persisted in, the increasing complications and antagonism of temporal and ecclesiastical interests, promoted its decadence, and at length bore it wholly to the ground.†

The schism of England filled the last year of Clement's life; his last years were rendered all the more bitter by the consciousness that he was not altogether blameless, and that his misfortunes stood in a sorry relationship to his personal qualities. Day by day the course of things became more threatening. Already Francis was preparing to make a new descent on Italy; and for this design he declared himself to have had the verbal, if not the written, sanction of Clement's approval. The Emperor would no longer be put off with pretences and urged the assembling of the council more pressingly than ever. Family discords added their bitterness to these sufferings; after his labors and sacrifices for the reduction of Florence, the Pope had to watch his two nephews enter into dispute for the sovereignty of that city and proceed to the most savage hostilities against each other. His anxious reflections on all these calamities, coupled with the fear of coming events, sorrow, and secret anguish, says Soriano, brought him to the grave.

We have pronounced Leo fortunate. Clement was perhaps a better man, certainly he had fewer faults, was more active, and, as regarded details, even more acute than Leo. But in what he did and what he neglected Clement was unfortunate—without doubt the most ill-fated pontiff that ever sat on the papal throne. To the superiority of the hostile powers pressing on him from all sides, he opposed only the most uncertain policy, ever depending on the probabilities of the moment. This brought about his utter downfall. Those efforts for the establishment of an independent temporal power, to which his more celebrated predecessors had devoted their best energies, he was doomed in his own case to find resulting in perfect subjugation; he had to see those from whom he had hoped to rescue his native Italy establish their dominion over her soil forever. The great secession of the Protestants proceeded unremittingly before his eyes, and the measures he adopted in the hope of arresting its progress did but serve to give it wider and more rapid extension. He left the Papal See immeasurably lowered in reputation and deprived of all effectual influence, whether spiritual or temporal. Northern Germany, for long so important to the papacy, to whose conversion in remote times the power of the popes was principally indebted for its establishment in the West, and whose revolt against Henry IV had so largely aided them in the completion of their hierarchy, had now risen against them. Our fatherland has the undying merit of having restored Christianity to a purer form than it had presented since the first ages of the Church—of having rediscovered the true religion. Armed with this weapon, Germany was unconquerable. Her convictions made themselves a path through all the neighboring countries. Scandinavia had been among the first to receive them; they had diffused themselves over England contrary to the purposes of the King, but under the protection of the measures he had pursued. In Switzerland they had struggled for, and with certain modifications, had attained a secure existence; they progressed into France; we find traces of them in Italy, and even in Spain, while Clement yet lived. These waves roll ever onward. In these opinions there is a force that attracts and enthralls all minds; and that struggle between the spiritual and temporal interests, in which the papacy suffered itself to become involved, would seem to have been designed expressly for their progress and the establishment of their universal dominion.

BOOK II
Chapter First
BEGINNING OF A REGENERATION
OF CATHOLICISM

We are not to believe that the influence of public opinion on the world has begun to make itself felt for the first time in our own day; through every age of modern Europe it has constituted a vital element of life. Who shall say whence it arises or how it is formed? It may be regarded as the most peculiar product of that identification of interests which holds society together, as the most intelligible expression of those internal movements and revolutions by which life, shared in common, is agitated. Its sources are as secret as its sustenance; requiring little support from evidence or reason, it obtains mastery over men's minds by the force of involuntary convictions. But only in its most general outline is it in harmony with itself; within these it is reproduced in innumerable greater or smaller circles and with modifications varied to infinity. And since new observations and experiences are perpetually flowing in upon it, since there are always original minds that, though affected by its course, are not borne along by its current but rather themselves impress on it a powerful reaction—it is thus involved in an endless series of metamorphoses; transient and multiform, it is sometimes more, sometimes less, in harmony with truth and right, being rather a tendency of the moment than a fixed system. It is often the attendant only of the event that has contributed to produce it, and from which it derives form and extension. There are times, nevertheless, when encountering a rugged will that refuses to be overcome, it extends to coercive demand. That its perception of defects and deficiencies is frequently the just one must needs be confessed, but it cannot, by its very nature, produce a pure, firm consciousness of what is operable and what is not. Hence it can be seen to be at opposite extremes at different times; as it aided to found the papacy, so did it help to overthrow that power. In the times under consideration, it was at one period utterly profane, at another as entirely spiritual. We have seen it inclining toward Protestantism throughout the whole of Europe; we shall also see that in a great portion of the world it will assume an entirely different coloring.[1]

---

[1] The section "Opinions Analogous to Those of the Protestants Entertained in Italy" has been omitted (pages 92–100 of the original).

Attempts At Internal Reform
And A Reconciliation With The Protestants

Possibly the most honorable act of Paul III, that indeed by which he signalized his accession to the papal throne, was the elevation of many distinguished men to the College of Cardinals without any consideration but that of their personal merits. The first of these was the Venetian Contarini, by whom, it is said, the others were afterward proposed. They were men of irreproachable character, in high repute for learning and piety, and well acquainted with the requirements of different countries—Caraffa, for example, had long resided in Spain and the Netherlands; Sadolet was bishop of Carpentras in France; Pole was a refugee from England; Giberto, after having long taken active part in administering, was then ruling his bishopric of Verona with exemplary wisdom; Federigo Fregoso, who was archbishop of Salerno—almost all, be it observed, were members of the Oratory of Divine Love, and many of them held opinions inclining to Protestantism.

It was these same cardinals who now prepared a plan for the reform of the Church by command of the Pope. This became known to the Protestants, who rejected it, not without derision. They had indeed meanwhile advanced far beyond its most liberal provisions. But we are not on that account permitted to deny the extreme significance of such an act on the part of the Catholic Church. Here we have the evil grappled with in Rome herself. In the presence of the Pope, former popes were accused of misgovernment, and in the introduction to the document now laid before him, his predecessors were accused of having "frequently chosen servants, not as desiring to learn from them what their duties demanded, but rather to procure the declaration that those things were lawful toward which their desires led them." This abuse of the supreme power was declared to be the most prolific source of corruption.†

It may be readily comprehended that a complete reformation of abuses, in which were involved so many personal rights and conflicting claims and which had become so closely interwoven with all the habits of life, was of all things the most difficult that could be undertaken. Nevertheless, Pope Paul did gradually seem disposed to enter earnestly into the task.*

And now, supposing ameliorations really to have been made —the Roman Court reformed and the abuses of the constitution done away with—if then that same dogma from which Luther had started had been taken as the principle of renovation in life and doctrine, might not a reconciliation have been possible? For even the Protestants did not tear themselves hastily or without reluctance from the communion of the Church.

To many minds this seemed possible, and earnest hopes were founded on the results of the religious conference.†

Never were parties closer to one another than at the conference of Ratisbon in the year 1541; political relations looked extremely favorable, and the Emperor, who desired to employ all the forces of the empire in a war with the Turks or with France, wished for nothing more earnestly than a reconciliation. He chose the most sagacious and temperate men he could find among the Catholic theologians, namely Gropper and Julius Pflug, to proceed to the conference. On the other side, the Landgrave Philip was again on good terms with Austria and hoped to obtain the command in the war for which he was preparing. With admiration and delight the Emperor beheld this warlike chief ride into Ratisbon on his stately charger, the rider no less vigorous than his steed. The pacific Bucer and gentle Melanchthon appeared on the Protestant side.

The earnest desire of Paul for an amicable result from this conference was made manifest by his choice of the legate whom he sent to it—no other than that Gaspar Contarini, whom we have seen so profoundly attached to the new modes of thought that were prevalent in Italy and so active in devising measures of general reform.* Adorned with such qualities, moderate, nearly approaching the Protestant tenets in their most important characteristics, Contarini appeared in Germany; by a regeneration of Church doctrines from this point, and by the abolition of abuses, he hoped to reconcile the existing differences.

But had not these already gone too far? Had not the dissident opinions taken root too deeply? I refrain from deciding these questions immediately.

There was also another Venetian, Marino Giustiniano, who left shortly before this Diet and who seemed to have examined the situation with great care. To him the reconciliation appears very possible, but he declares that certain important concessions are indispensable. The following he particularizes: "The Pope must no longer claim to be the viceregent of Christ in temporal as well as spiritual things. He must replace the profligate and ignorant bishops and priests, appointing men of blameless lives capable of guiding and instructing the people in their places; the sale of masses, the plurality of benefices, and the abuse of compositions must no longer be suffered; a violation of the rule as regards fasting must be visited by very light punishment at the most. If in addition to these things, the marriage of priests be permitted, and the communion in both kinds be allowed, Giustiniano believes that the Germans would at once abjure their dissent, yield obedience to the Pope in spiritual affairs, resign their opposition to the mass, submit to auricular confession, and even allow the necessity of good works as fruits of faith—insofar, that is, as they are the consequence of faith. The existing discord having arisen because of abuses, so there is no doubt that by the abolition of these it may be done away with."†

This, if I do not mistake, was a moment of most eventful import, not for Germany only, but for the whole world. With regard to the former, the points we have intimated tended in their consequences to change the whole ecclesiastical constitution of the land, to secure a position of increased liberty as regarded the Pope, and a freedom from temporal encroachment on his part. The unity of the Church would have been maintained, and with it that of the nation. But infinitely farther than even this would the consequences have extended. If the moderate party, from whom these attempts proceeded and by whom they were conducted, had been able to maintain predominance in Rome and in Italy, how entirely different an aspect must the Catholic world necessarily have assumed!

A result so extraordinary was, however, not to be obtained without a vehement struggle.*

A reconciliation such as that contemplated would have given Germany an unaccustomed unity and would have greatly extended the power of the Emperor, who would have been at no loss to avail himself of this advantage. As chief of the moderate party, he would inevitably have obtained predominant influence throughout Europe, especially in the event of a general council. All the accustomed hostilities were necessarily awakened at the mere prospect of such a result.†

Suffice it to say that in Rome, France, and Germany there arose among the enemies of Charles V—among those who either were or appeared to be the most zealous for Catholicism—a determined opposition to his efforts for the conciliation of differences. An unusual degree of intimacy was observed in Rome between the pontiff and the French ambassador. It was thought that the former meant to propose a marriage between Vittoria Farnese, his relative, and one of the house of Guise.

A powerful effect was inevitably produced by these agitations on the different theologians. "The enemies of the Emperor, whether in or out of Germany," says the secretary of Contarini, "dreading the power he would obtain in the union of all Germany, began to sow discord among these theologians. Carnal envy hath interrupted the conference." If we consider how many difficulties were involved in the very nature of such an attempt, it cannot surprise us that agreement as to any one article was no longer possible.

Those who attribute the whole or indeed the greater share of the blame for this failure to the Protestants pass beyond the limits of justice.

After the first encouraging discussions in Ratisbon, the Pope soon announced his firm resolve to the legate that neither in his official capacity, nor as a private person, should the legate tolerate any resolution in which the Catholic faith and opinions were expressed in words admitting the possibility of ambiguous interpretation. The formulas in which Contarini had thought to reconcile the conflicting opinions regarding the supremacy of the Pope and the power of councils were rejected at Rome unconditionally. The legate was compelled to offer explanations that seemed in flagrant contradiction to his own previous words.

So that the conference might not be altogether without result, the Emperor desired that both parties would, for the present at least, abide by the articles mutually assented to, and that with regard to those still in dispute, each should tolerate the differences of the other; but neither Luther nor the Pope could be moved to agree to this, and the cardinal was given to understand that the sacred college had resolved unanimously not to extend tolerance under any conditions whatever in regard to articles so vitally essential.

After hopes so great, after a beginning so propitious, Contarini saw himself compelled to return without effecting any part of his purpose. He had wished to accompany the Emperor to the Netherlands, but neither was this permitted to him. Returning to Italy, it was his lot to endure the slanders that from Rome had been circulated all over the country regarding his conduct and the concessions he was supposed to have made to Protestantism. He had the loftiness of spirit that rendered the failure of plans so comprehensive still more grievous and more permanently painful to him.

How noble and impressive was the position that moderate Catholicism had assumed in his person! But, having failed in securing its world-embracing design, it now became a question whether it would even maintain its own existence. Every great tendency carries with it the ineluctable task of rendering itself effective, of achieving its purpose. If it cannot achieve mastery, this implies its impending ruin.

New Ecclesiastical Orders

Meanwhile another direction had already developed, originally closely related to that which we have described, but ever more divergent and although intending reform, directly opposed to Protestantism.

As the priesthood as heretofore existing had been repudiated by Luther in its very concept and principle, so there arose a movement in Italy to reinstate this principle and to restore it to the respect of the Church by more rigid adherence. Both parties were sensible to the decadence of ecclesiastical institutes; but while the Germans were content with nothing less than the abolition of monasticism, the Italians sought to restore and regenerate it. While in Germany the churchman was throwing off so many of the restraints that had bound him, men were seeking in Italy to make these fetters yet more stringent. On this side of the Alps we entered on a new path; beyond them, attempts were repeated that had already been made from time to time for centuries past.

There is no period in church history unprovided with examples of a decline of the ecclesiastical institutions toward worldliness, but they had always appeared to recall their origin and had returned to habits of a more blameless purity. The Carolingians already had found it necessary to enforce the rule of Chrodegang on the clergy, compelling them to community of life and to voluntary subordination. Nor did the simple rule of Benedict of Nursia long suffice in the eyes of the religious houses. During the tenth and eleventh centuries, small secluded congregations with special rules after the model of Cluny were found to be requisite. This produced an instant effect on the secular clergy; by the enforcement of celibacy, they also, as before remarked, became in a manner subjected to the forms of monastic life. In spite of the powerful religious impulse given by the crusades to all Europe— an impulse so extensively influential that even the knights and nobles submitted their profession of war to forms of monastic law—these institutions had sunk into the utmost decay when the mendicant orders arose. On their first appearance, they doubtless did much to restore things to their primitive simplicity and severity; but we have seen how they too became gradually degenerate and tainted by the world's disorders, until at length the most glaring evidence of decadence in the Church might be found among these Friars-Mendicant.

From the year 1520, a conviction had been gaining ground through all those countries into which Protestantism had not yet penetrated that renewed improvement was deeply needed by the institutes of the hierarchy. This conviction became more and more confirmed as the new tenets progressed in Germany. It found place even among the orders themselves; sometimes appearing in one order, sometimes in another.*

Nothing of real value could, however, be effected by a reform of the monastic orders alone, because the secular clergy were so utterly estranged from their vocation. To mean anything, improvement must involve them too.

Here we encounter members of the Roman "Oratory of Divine Love": two of these—men, as it would seem, of contrasting character—undertook to propose such improvements. The one: Gaetano da Thiene, peaceful and retiring, of gentle manner and few words, devoted to the delights of a spiritual enthusiasm, and of whom it was said that he wished to reform the world but without letting anyone notice that he was of this world. The other: John Peter Caraffa, of whom we shall have occasion to speak at length, turbulent, impetuous, and a zealot. But Caraffa also perceived, as he said, that his heart was only more heavily oppressed the more it followed its own desire and that it would only find peace in reliance upon God, in converse with heavenly things. Thus these two men agreed in their desire for seclusion. Convinced that reform was needed, they combined to found an institution—it has since been called the Order of Theatines—having for its purpose at once the reformation of the clergy and a life of contemplation.*

They did not call themselves monks, but regular clergy—they were priests with the vows of monks. Their intention was to establish a kind of seminary. The charter of their foundation expressly allowed them to receive secular clergy. They did not originally adopt any prescribed color or form of dress, leaving these to be determined by the local customs of their inmates; they suffered even the services of the Church to be performed everywhere according to the national usages; they were thus freed from many restraints under which monks labored, expressly declaring that neither in the habits of life nor in the service of the Church should any custom be permitted to become binding on the conscience;

but on the other hand, they devoted themselves rigidly to their clerical duties—to preaching, the administration of the sacraments, and the care of the sick.*

The great point gained by all these efforts was this, that the useful purpose of conjoining the clerical duties and consecration of the secular clergy with the vows of monks gained extensive approval and imitation.*

The effect produced by such congregations, each in its separate circle, was doubtless very considerable. But either from the exclusive end that they had proposed to themselves, as in the case of the Barnabites, or from the restriction of their means, as by the very nature of their constitution was inevitable in that of the poverty-vowed Theatines, they were restrained from carrying out a deep-searching reform. They are remarkable because the voluntary character of their efforts exemplifies a great tendency that largely contributed to the regeneration of Catholicism; but the force that was to stand against the bold advance of Protestantism had to be of a totally different character. This was developing along similar lines but in a most unexpected and peculiar fashion.

Ignatius Loyola

The chivalry of Spain was the only one that had preserved a certain remnant of its religious character. The war with the Moors (but just arriving at its conclusion in the peninsula and still proceeding in Africa), the vicinity of the subjugated Moriscoes still remaining (with whom all contact continued, but fraught with religious antagonism) and the adventurous expeditions yet undertaken against infidels beyond the seas, all combined to perpetuate this spirit. In such books as the "Amadis de Gaul," full of a simple, enthusiastic loyalty and bravery, that spirit was idealized.

Don Iñigo Lopez de Recalde, the youngest son of the house of Loyola, was born in a castle of that name, between Azpeitia and Azcoitia, in Guipuscoa. He was of a race that belonged to the noblest in the land—"de parientes mayores"—and its head claimed the right of being summoned to do homage by special writ. Educated at the court of Ferdinand the Catholic, and in the service of the Duke of Navarre, Iñigo was deeply imbued with this spirit. He aspired to knightly renown, and for none of his compatriots had the glitter of arms, the fame of valor, the adventures of single combat and of love, more attraction than for him; but also the spiritual tendency was represented in him. He celebrated the first of the apostles in a romance of chivalry at this early period of his life.

It is, nevertheless, probable that his name would have become known to us only as one of those many brave and noble Spanish captains to whom the wars of Charles V gave so much opportunity for distinguishing themselves, had he not been wounded in both legs at the defense of Pamplona against the French in 1521. Twice the wounds were reopened, and such was his fortitude that the only sign of pain he permitted to escape him was the firm clenching of his hands. His sufferings were unavailing— the cure remained deplorably incomplete.

He was much versed in, and equally attached to, the romances of chivalry, more especially to the Amadis. During his long confinement, he also read the life of Christ, and of some of the saints.*

The more his recovery was protracted and his hope of ultimate cure deferred, the more also did the spiritual revery gain ascendancy over the worldly vision. Shall we do him wrong if we impute this result to the increased conviction that his former vigor could not be restored, that he could not hope again to shine in military service or a knightly career?

Not that the transition was so abrupt or to so opposite an extreme as it might, on the first view, appear to be. In his spiritual exercises, the origin of which has always been considered coincident with the first ecstatic meditations of his awakened spirit, he imagines two camps—one at Jerusalem, the other at Babylon; the one belonging to Christ, the other to Satan; in the one are the Good, in the other the Bad—prepared for combat.*

These fanciful imaginations probably facilitated his transition from the chivalry of arms to that of religion, for it was indeed to a sort of spiritual knighthood that his aspirations now tended. The ideal perfection of religious chivalry was to consist in emulation of the achievements performed and the privations endured by the saints. Tearing himself from home and kindred, he now sought the heights of Montserrat, not driven to this by remorse for his sins, nor impelled by any reality of religious feeling, but, as he has himself declared, merely by the desire to achieve deeds as great as those which make the renown of the saints. His weapons and armor he hung up before an image of the Virgin; kneeling or standing in prayer with his pilgrim's staff in his hand, he passed the night here—holding a vigil somewhat different from that of knighthood, but expressly suggested by the Amadis where all the rites proper to it are minutely described. The knightly dress in which he had arrived at Montserrat he gave away, assuming the coarse garb of the hermits whose lonely dwellings are scooped among those naked rocks. After having made a general confession, he set off toward Jerusalem, not going direct to Barcelona lest he should be recognized on the highways, but making a round by Manresa, whence, after new penances, he meant to gain his port of embarkation for the holy city.

But in Manresa he was met by other trials; the direction which he had taken, not so much from conviction as caprice, began here to assume positive mastery over him. He devoted himself to the severest penances in the cell of a convent of Dominicans; he scourged himself thrice a day, rose to prayer at midnight, and passed seven hours of each day on his knees. He found these severities so difficult to endure that he greatly doubted his own ability to persevere in them for his whole life, but what was still more serious, he felt that they did not bring him peace. He had spent three days on Montserrat confessing the sins of all his past life; but not satisfied with this, he repeated it in Manresa, recalling many faults before forgotten, permitting none of the most trifling errors to escape him; but the more laborious his exploration, the more painful became the doubts that assailed him. He did not believe that he had been either accepted by or justified before God. Having read in the works of the fathers that a total abstinence from food had once moved the compassion and obtained the mercy of the Almighty, he kept rigid fast from one Sunday to another, but his confessor forbade him to continue this attempt, and Iñigo, who placed the virtue of obedience above all others, thereupon desisted. Occasionally it appeared to him that his melancholy had been removed, falling away as does a heavy garment from the shoulders, but his former sufferings soon returned. His whole life seemed to him but one self-perpetuating series of sins, and he not infrequently felt tempted to throw himself from the window.

This experience cannot fail to remind us of the nearly similar sufferings endured by Luther some twenty years before, when he also was assailed by similar doubts. The great demand of religion, a perfect reconciliation with God and its full conscious assurance, could never be obtained in the ordinary manner prescribed by the Church with such certainty as to satisfy the unfathomable longings of a soul at odds with itself. But out of this labyrinth Ignatius and Luther escaped by very different paths: the latter attained to the doctrine of reconciliation through Christ without works; this it was that laid open to him the meaning of the Scriptures which then became his strong support. But of Loyola we do not find that he examined the Scriptures or became impressed by any particular dogma. Living in a world of internal emotion, and amid thoughts arising forever within him, he believed himself subjected to the influence now of the good, and now of the evil spirit. He finally arrived at the power of distinguishing the inspirations of the one from that of the other, perceiving that the soul was cheered and comforted by the first, but harassed and exhausted by the latter. And one day he seemed to have awakened from the dream and thought he had tangible evidence that all his torments were assaults of Satan. He resolved to resign all examination of his past life from that hour, to open those wounds no more, never again to touch them. This was not so much the restoration of his peace as a resolution; it was an engagement entered into by the will rather than a conviction to which the submission of the will is inevitable. It required no aid from Scripture; it was based on the belief he entertained of an immediate communion with the world of spirits. This would never have satisfied Luther. No inspirations, no visions would Luther admit. All were in his opinion alike injurious. He would have the simple, written, indubitable word of

God alone. Loyola, on the contrary, lived wholly in fantasies and inward apparitions. The person best acquainted with Christianity was, as he thought, an old woman who had told him in the worst of his mental anguish that Christ must yet appear to him. Originally this made no sense to him; but at length he believed not only to have the Saviour in person before his eyes, but the Virgin Mother also. One day he stood weeping aloud on the step of the church of St. Dominick, at Manresa, because he believed himself to see the mystery of the Trinity at that moment standing before his sight. He spoke of nothing else through the whole day and was inexhaustible in similes and comparisons respecting it. Suddenly also the mystery of the creation came over him in mystic symbols. In the host he beheld the God and the man. Proceeding once along the banks of the Llobregat to a distant church, he sat down and bent his eyes earnestly on the deep stream before him, when he was suddenly raised into an ecstasy wherein the mysteries of the faith were visibly revealed to him. He believed himself to rise up a new man. Thenceforth he needed neither testimony nor Scripture. Had none such existed he would have gone without hesitation to death for the faith which he had before believed, but which he now saw with his eyes.*

In the state in which he then was, without learning, profound theological knowledge, or political support, Loyola's existence must have passed and left no trace. He would have been fortunate to convert two or three Spaniards. But being enjoined by the universities of Alcala and Salamanca to study theology for four years before attempting to expound or teach the more obscure points of doctrine, he was compelled to enter on a path which gradually led him forward to an unexpected field for the exertion of his religious activity.

He proceeded to Paris, which at that time was the most celebrated university of the world.

His studies were at first surrounded by unusual difficulties, he had to begin with the class of grammar—on which he had entered in Spain—and with those of philosophy, before he could be admitted to that of theology; but his grammatical inflections and the analysis of logical forms were alike interrupted by and intermingled with the ecstasies of those religious significations with which he had been accustomed to connect them. There is something grandiose in his immediate condemnation of these as inspirations of the evil spirit, which was seeking to lure him from the path of rectitude; he subjected himself to the most rigorous discipline in the hope of combating them.

But while his studies now opened a new world to his gaze—the world of reality—he did not for a moment depart from his spiritual direction, nor fail to share them with others. It was indeed at this time that he effected those first conversions by which the future world was destined to be so powerfully and permanently influenced.

Of the two companions who shared the rooms of Loyola in the college of St. Barbara, one, Peter Faber, a Savoyard, proved an easy conquest; growing up among his father's flocks, he had one night devoted himself solemnly beneath the canopy of heaven to study and to God. He went through the course of philosophy with Ignatius (the name that Iñigo took among foreigners), and the latter communicated to him his own ascetic principles.* They lived in the closest intimacy.* His second companion, Francis Xavier of Pamplona in Navarre, was by no means so easily won; his most earnest ambition was to ennoble still further the long series of his ancestors, renowned in war for five hundred years, by adding to their names his own, rendered illustrious by learning. He was handsome and rich, possessed high talent, and had already gained a footing at court. Ignatius was careful to show him all the respect to which he laid claim, and to see that others paid it also. He procured him a large audience for his first lectures, and having begun by these personal services, his influence was soon established by the natural effect of his pure example and imposing austerity of life. He at length prevailed on Xavier, as he had done on Faber, to join him in the spiritual exercises. He was by no means indulgent; three days and three nights he compelled them to fast. During the severest winters, when carriages might be seen to traverse the frozen Seine, he would not permit Faber the slightest relaxation of discipline. He finished by making these two young men entirely his own, and shared with them his most intimate thoughts and feelings.*

Let us examine the more important features in the development of this association. After having won over certain other Spaniards to whom Ignatius had rendered himself indispensable either by good counsels or other aid, such as Salmeron, Lainez, and Bobodilla, they proceeded one day to the church of Montmartre. Faber, who was already in orders, read the mass. They took the vow of chastity and swore to proceed to Jerusalem, after the completion of their studies, there to live in poverty and dedicate their days to the conversion of the Saracens. Or, should they find it impossible to reach that place or to remain there, they were next to offer their services to the Pope, agreeing to go whithersoever he might assign them their labors, without condition and without reward. Having taken this oath, each received the host, which Faber also took himself. This completed, they proceeded in company to a repast at the fountain of St. Denis.

Here we see a league formed between enthusiastic young men, of which the purposes were absolutely unattainable but still in accordance with the original ideas of Ignatius, or departing from them only so far as, on a calculation of probabilities, they might find themselves unable to carry them into effect.

In the beginning of the year 1537, we find them assembled in Venice, with three other companions, prepared for the commencement of their pilgrimage. We have already observed many changes in Loyola: from a military knighthood, we have seen him pass to a religious chivalry; we have marked his subjection to the most violent mental conflicts, and we have seen him force his way through them by the aid of a visionary asceticism; he became a theologian and the founder of a mystical society, and now at length his purposes assumed their final and permanent character. His departure for Jerusalem was first deferred by the war just then commencing between Venice and the Turks, and the prospect of his intended pilgrimage was rendered more remote; but the institution of the Theatines, with which he became acquainted in Venice, may be said to have first opened his eyes to his true vocation. For some time Ignatius lived in the closest intimacy with Caraffa, taking up his abode in the convent of Theatines which had been established in Venice. He served in the hospitals which Caraffa superintended, and wherein he exercised his novices. But not entirely content with the institution of the Theatines, he proposed to Caraffa certain changes in its mode of action, and this is said to have caused the dissolution of their intimacy. But even this fact makes it obvious how deep an impression had been produced on him by that society; he there saw an order of priests devoting themselves zealously and strictly to their true clerical duties. Should he, as seemed ever more probable, have to remain on this side of the Mediterranean and find the scene of his activity in Western Christendom, he perceived clearly that this must be his course also—that there was no other alternative.

In pursuit of this conviction, he took priest's orders in Venice with all his companions; and after a fortnight of days of prayer, he began to preach in Vicenza together with three others of his society. On the same day and at the same hour, they appeared in different streets, mounted stones, waved their hats, and with loud cries exhorted the people to repentance. Preachers of a very unwonted aspect—their clothing in rags, their looks emaciated, and their language a mixture of Spanish and Italian well-nigh unintelligible.

Having determined to make the journey to Rome by different roads, they were now about to separate; but first they established certain rules by means of which they might observe a fixed uniformity of life, even when apart: next came the question what reply should be made to those who might inquire their profession. They pleased themselves with the thought of making war as soldiers against Satan, and in accordance with the old military fantasies of Loyola, they assumed the name of the Company of Jesus, exactly as a company of soldiers takes the name of its captain.

Their situation in Rome was in the first instance by no means free from difficulty. Ignatius thought he saw every door closed against them, and they had once more to defend themselves from suspicions of heresy. But soon the mode of their lives, with their zeal in preaching, instructing youth, and tending the sick, attracted numerous adherents, and so many showed a disposition to join them that they felt themselves in a condition to prepare for a formal institution of their society.

They had already taken two vows; they now assumed the

third, that of obedience. But as this had always been held by Loyola to be the first of virtues, so they desired to surpass all other orders in that particular. It was already going very far to elect, as they resolved to do, their general for life; but even this did not satisfy their enthusiasm—they added the special obligation "to perform whatsoever the reigning pontiff should command them, to go forth into all lands, among Turks, heathens, or heretics, wherever he might please to send them, without hesitation or delay, as without question, condition, or reward."

How entirely is all this in contrast to the tendencies hitherto manifested by that period! While from every other side the Pope met only opposition or defection and had only continued desertions to expect, here was a body of men, earnest, enthusiastic, and zealous, uniting to devote themselves exclusively to his service; there could be no hesitation in such a case for the pontiff. In the year 1540, he gave his sanction to their institute, at first with certain restrictions, but afterward, in 1543, unconditionally.

And now its members also made their final arrangements. Six of the oldest associates met to choose their president, who, according to the first sketch of their plan presented to the Pope, "should dispense offices and grades at his own pleasure, should form the rules of their constitution with the advice and aid of the members, but should alone have the power of commanding in every instance, and should be honored by all as though Christ himself were present in his person." The choice fell unanimously on Ignatius, "to whom," as Salmeron expressed it on his ballot, "they were all indebted for their birth in Christ and for the milk of his word."

At length, then, the Society of Jesus had acquired its form. This association also was a company of regular clergy; its duties were likewise a combination of the clerical and monastic, but the members were nevertheless broadly distinguished from those of other congregations.

The Theatines had freed themselves from many of the less important obligations of conventional life, but the Jesuits went much further; they dispensed entirely with the monastic habit and exempted themselves from all those devotional exercises in common, by which so much time is occupied in convents. Exempted from these less important practices, they devoted all their energies and every hour of their lives to the essential duties of their office; not to one only, as did the Barnabites—although they attended sedulously to the sick as one measure toward acquiring a good name—nor with the restrictions that fettered the Theatines, but to all the greater duties equally, and with whatever force they could command; to preaching, to confession, to the education of youth.* They laid aside, in short, all secondary matters, devoting themselves wholly to such labors as were essential, of immediate result, and calculated for the extension of their influence.

Thus was a pre-eminently practical direction evolved from the visionary aspirations of Ignatius; and from the ascetic conversions he had made, there resulted an institution framed with all that skillful adaptation of means to their end which the most consummate worldly prudence could suggest.

His most sanguine hopes were now more than fulfilled—he held the uncontrolled direction of a society, among whose members his own peculiar views found cordial acceptance, and wherein the religious convictions at which he had arrived by accident or the force of his genius were made the object of profound study and the venerated basis and guide of belief. The care of souls, which he had so earnestly recommended, was entered on with a zeal that he could not have hoped for, and to an extent surpassing his highest anticipations. And lastly, he was himself the object of an implicit obedience, combining that of the soldier to his captain with that of the priest to his spiritual chief.

But before we further describe the effect which the Company of Jesus soon achieved, let us investigate one of the most important causes contributing to its successful progress.

First Sittings Of The Council Of Trent

We have already observed the interests by which the Emperor was moved to demand a council, together with those inclining the Pope to avoid and refuse it. There was, however, one aspect under which an assembly of the Church might be considered desirable even by the pontiff—that the doctrines of the Catholic Church might be inculcated with unwavering zeal and successfully extended, it was essential to remove the doubts existing in the bosom of the Church herself, doubts which touched more than one of her tenets. The authority to do this effectively was exclusively vested in a council. An important consideration for the Pope, therefore, was the choice of a time when it might be held in favorable circumstances and under his own influence.

The eventful moment in which the two religious parties had become more nearly approximate than at any other period, on the ground of a moderate opinion, was also decisive in this question. We have remarked that the Pope believed he saw symptoms of an intention on the part of the Emperor himself to call a council. At this moment, then, assured from all sides of adherence from the Catholic princes, he lost no time in anticipating the imperial purpose. The movements we have before described were still proceeding when the pontiff resolved to interpose no further delay, but at once take steps for the ecumenic assembling of the Church. He made known his intention at first to Contarini, and through him to the Emperor. The negotiations proceeded with earnest purpose; the Pope's letters of convocation were issued, and in the following year we find his legates already in Trent. They arrived on November 22, 1542.

Again, however, new obstacles presented themselves—the number of bishops who appeared was not sufficient. The times were too deeply involved in wars, nor were the circumstances altogether favorable. It was not until December 1545 that the opening of the Council actually took place. At last the old prevaricator had found the right moment.

For what moment could have been more propitious than that when the Emperor, feeling himself threatened by the advance of Protestantism both in his own reputation and in the established government of his inherited possessions, had resolved to meet them with armed might? Since he would require the aid of the Pope, he could not venture now to assert those claims which he was believed to intend bringing forward in a council. The war would keep him entirely occupied. The power of the Protestants made it impossible to foresee the extent of the embarrassments in which he might become involved, and he would thus be in no

condition to press too earnestly for those reforms with which he
had so long been threatening the papal throne. The Pope had, besides, another method of baffling his purposes: the Emperor demanded that the Council should begin with the subject of reform,
but the papal legates carried a resolution that the question of reform and the questions of the Church should be treated together.
In effect, however, the discussion of the dogmas was that first
entered on.

Again, the Pope not only succeeded in averting whatever
might have been injurious to his interests, but contrived to secure
all that could be turned to his advantage. The establishment of
the disputed doctrines was of the very first importance to him, as
we have shown. It was now to be decided whether any of those
opinions tending toward the creed of the Protestants could hold
a place within the limits of the Catholic faith.†

However closely these opinions may appear to approximate
one another, they are in fact diametrically opposed. The Lutheran
doctrine does indeed assert the necessity of inner regeneration,
points out the way to salvation, and declares that good works
must follow, but it also maintains that divine grace proceeds from
the merits of Christ alone. The Council of Trent, on the contrary,
admitted the merits of Christ, it is true, but attributed justification to these merits only so far as they promote regeneration, and
thereby good works, on which, as a final result, this Council makes
all depend.*

And thus were the Protestant opinions altogether excluded
from Catholicism; all mediation was utterly rejected. This occurred precisely at the moment when the Emperor was victorious
in Germany, the Lutherans were submitting in almost every direction, and preparations were advancing to subdue those who
still hoped to hold out.*

The Inquisition

In the meantime, measures had been adopted for the dissemina-
tion of the doctrines promulgated at Trent and for the suppression
of those which were contrary.*

The old Dominican Inquisition had long fallen into decay. The choice of inquisitors was committed to the monastic orders, and it sometimes happened that these men shared the very opinions that they were appointed to suppress. In Spain, one had already departed from the original forms by appointing a supreme tribunal of the Inquisition for that country. Caraffa and Burgos were both old Dominicans, zealots for the purity of Catholicism, holding stern views of moral rectitude, in their own lives rigidly austere, and immovable in their opinions. These men advised the Pope to establish a supreme tribunal of Inquisition in Rome, universal in its jurisdiction, and on which all others should depend. "As St. Peter," exclaimed Caraffa, "subdued the first heresiarchs in no other place than Rome, so must the successors of Peter destroy all the heresies of the whole world in Rome." The Jesuits account it among the glories of their order that their founder, Loyola, supported this proposition by a special memorial. The bull was published on the twenty-first of July 1542.†

It will be remarked that everything tends toward severity—inflexible, remorseless severity—until confession has been wrung out no mercy may be hoped for. A fearful state of things; and more especially so when opinions were not well fixed or fully developed, and many were seeking to conciliate the more profound doctrines of Christianity with the institutions of the existing Church. The weaker resigned themselves and submitted; those of firmer character, on the contrary, now attached themselves all the more to the proscribed opinions and sought to withdraw from the violence threatening them.*

Disturbances had taken place before in Modena; they now reappeared, many being denounced to the Inquisition. Filippo Valentini withdrew to Trent, and Castelvetri thought it advisable, at least for a time, to secure himself by a retreat into Germany.

Persecution and dismay were now proceeding throughout all Italy, and the rancor of contending factions came to the aid of the inquisitors. How often did he who had long waited in vain for an opportunity to destroy his enemy now compass his designs by an accusation of heresy! Now the old bigoted monks again had the weapons wherewith to combat that band of cultivated men whose literary labors had led them toward religious speculations, and whose intelligent reasonings had made them an object of hatred to the monks, who were in their turn despised and disliked by the literati.†

In this manner all the agitations of dissident opinion were subdued by force and annihilated throughout Italy. Almost the whole order of the Franciscans was compelled to recantation, and the disciples of Valdez had for the most part to retract their opinions. In Venice a certain degree of freedom was allowed to the foreigners, principally Germans, who resided there for purposes of trade or study; but the natives, on the contrary, were compelled to abjuration, and their meetings were broken up. Many took to flight, and these fugitives were to be found in every town of Germany and Switzerland. Those who would not abjure their faith and could not escape were subjected to the penalty. In Venice, they were taken beyond the lagoons by two boats. Arriving in the open sea, a plank was laid between the boats, on which the condemned was placed. The rowers pulled simultaneously in opposite directions; the plank fell: once more did the uphappy victim invoke the name of Christ, and then the waves closed over him; he sank to rise no more. In Rome, the *auto-da-fé* was held formally at certain intervals before the Church of Santa Maria alla Minerva. Many sought to escape by flying from place to place with their wives and children; we trace their wanderings for a time, then they disappear; they had most probably fallen into the toils of their merciless hunters. Others remained where they were. The Duchess of Ferrara, who, but for the Salic law, would have sat on the French throne, was not protected by her birth and high rank. Her husband was himself her accuser. "She sees no one," says Marot, "the mountains rise between herself and her friends; she mingles her wine with her tears."

Further Progress Of The Jesuit Institution

In this course of affairs, when the opponents had been removed by force, the dogmas had been redefined in keeping with the spirit of the century, and the ecclesiastical might supervised their observation with unavoidable weapons, the order of Jesuits arose in the closest union with this might.

Not only in Rome, but throughout all Italy, the most extraordinary success attended its efforts. Designed originally for the common people, it first gained acceptance from the higher classes.†

This rapid success was, of necessity, most powerfully influential in the development of the institution.† The new arrangements were perfectly well calculated in themselves and, at the same time, laid the foundations of a hierarchy, eminently proper by its several gradations, to subjugate the minds of those on whom it acted.

And now, if we examine the laws of which the code of the Jesuits came gradually to be formed, we shall perceive that an entire separation of its members from all their accustomed relationships was one of its prime considerations. Love of kindred they denounced as a carnal inclination. The man who resigned his property to enter the order was in no case to bestow it on his relations, but must distribute all to the poor. He who had once become a Jesuit could neither receive nor write a letter that was not read by his superior. The society demands the whole being; all the faculties and inclinations of the man must be held in its fetters.

It claims to share in the most intimate of his secrets; all his faults and even all his virtues must be carefully enumerated. A confessor is appointed him by his superiors, who reserve the right of granting absolution in any cases as may be deemed expedient that they should know of. They insist on this regulation as a means to their obtaining a perfect knowledge of subordinates, so that they might the better employ them at their pleasure.

For in the order of Jesuits obedience takes the place of every motive or affection that usually awakens men to activity—obedience, absolute and unconditional, without one thought or question as to its object or consequences. No man shall aspire to any rank above that which he holds. The secular coadjutor may not even learn to read or write without permission, if he does not possess these attainments. With the most unlimited abjuration of all right of judgment, in total and blind subjection to the will of his superiors, must he resign himself to be led, like a thing without life, as the staff, for example, that the superior holds in his hand, to be turned to any purpose seeming good to him. The society is to him as the representative of the divine providence.

What a power was that now committed to the general—vested in him for life was the faculty of wielding this unquestioning obedience; nor is there one to whom he is responsible for the use made of it. According to the constitution of the order submitted to the pontiff in 1543, every member of the society who might chance to be at the same place with the general was to be called to the discussion of even the most trifling affairs. But a version which was confirmed in 1550 by Julius III freed him from this restriction except when he might himself desire it. For some material change in the constitution, or for the suppression of houses and colleges alone, was a consultation mandatory; in every other case, all power is committed to him to act as may be most conducive to the good of the society. He has assistants in the different provinces, but these confine themselves strictly to such matters as he shall refer to them. All presidents of provinces, colleges, and houses, he names at his pleasure: he receives or dismisses, dispenses or furnishes, and may be said to exercise a sort of papal authority on a small scale.†

Other institutes have existed, forming a world within the world, and which, releasing their members from all exterior obligations, have sought to absorb their whole being to themselves and to inspire each individual with a new principle of life and action. This was pre-eminently the purpose of the Jesuits, and it was fully accomplished. Peculiar to the Jesuits is the fact that on the one hand they not only support but demand individual development, on the other hand they hold this development in bounds and turn it to their service. Hence all relationships are characterized by personality, subordination, mutual surveillance. But a firmly compacted and perfect unity was thus formed—a body endowed with nerve and vigorous power of action. For such reasons men made monarchical powers so supreme: one subordinates oneself entirely, unless the possessor himself departs from its principle. It was perfectly consistent with the idea of the society to permit none of its members the acceptance of ecclesiastical dignities; for these might have involved the fulfillment of duties, or the forming of relations, over which the society could no longer exercise control. In the earlier days of Jesuitism this rule was most strictly observed.*

Thus the society, regarding its members as its own exclusive property, was desirous of seeing them attain to the highest culture of their energies—physical and mental—but ever in accordance with its principle.

This careful development of the individual was, in fact, indispensable to the performance of the duties the society undertook—those of the pulpit, that is, of the school, and of the confessional. To the two latter in particular the Jesuits devoted themselves in a distinctive fashion.†

It has been said that the Jesuits profited by the experience of the Protestants, and in some few particulars this may have happened; but on the whole they present a very strong contrast to each other. Ignatius has opposed to the discursive, logical, and very close method of the Protestants (a method by its very nature polemical), one of his own which is entirely different, being short, intuitive, calculated for awakening the imaginative faculties and prompting to instant resolve.

And in this manner did those visionary elements that had characterized his commencement condense themselves at length into an extraordinary force of practical influence. Never wholly freed from the military habits of his early days, Loyola formed his society into a sort of religious standing army, selected carefully man by man, each one trained for the special service he was intended to perform, and commanded by himself: such were the cohorts that he dedicated to the service of the Pope. He lived to see them spread over the greater portion of the earth's surface.

At the time of his death in 1556, the company of Ignatius numbered thirteen provinces, exclusive of the Roman. A mere glance will serve to show where the strength of the order lay; the majority of these provinces, seven, namely, belonged to the western peninsula and its colonies. In Castile there were ten colleges. Aragon and Andalusia had each five. Portugal had gone beyond even this; houses were established there both for professed members and novices. Over the colonies of Portugal the Company of Jesus exercised almost absolute mastery. Twenty-eight members of the order were occupied in Brazil, while in East India, from Goa to Japan, not less than a hundred were employed. An attempt on Ethiopia was also made from this quarter, and a Provincial was sent there, the success of the enterprise not being doubted. All these provinces of Spanish and Portuguese languages and manners were directed by one commissary general, Francesco Borgia. The nation that had given birth to the founder, was also that where his influence was most immediately and firmly established. But the effect produced in Italy was very little inferior. There were three provinces of the Italian tongue. First, the Roman, under the immediate direction of the general; this included Naples. It was furnished with houses for novices and professed and with two colleges in the city, namely the "Collegium Romanum" and the "Collegium Germanicum." The last was erected for Germans only by the advice of Cardinal Morone, but not with any great effect as yet. Second, the Sicilian, containing four colleges completed and two begun. The first Jesuits had been introduced into Sicily by the viceroy della Vega. Messina and Palermo had vied with each other in establishing colleges, and from these it was that the others afterward arose. The third truly Italian province encompassed all the north of Italy, and contained ten colleges. The order was not equally successful in other countries, where it was either opposed by Protestantism or by a strong tendency to Protestant opinion. In France they had but one college actually in operation; and though two provinces were counted in Germany, both were as yet in their infancy. The first was to comprise Vienna, Prague, and Ingolstadt, but its condition was extremely precarious. The second was intended to include the Netherlands, but Philip II had not yet assured a legal existence to the Jesuits in that part of his dominions.

This great and rapid success was a guarantee of the power to be attained by the order. The position it had secured in those truly Catholic countries, the two peninsulas, was a circumstance of the utmost importance.

Conclusion

Thus we perceive, that while the tenets of Protestantism were enlarging their influence over the minds of men on the one hand, a new impulse had on the other been received by Catholicism and was acting vigorously in Rome, and more especially on the court of its pontiff. This new impulse, equally with its opponent, had taken rise from the spirit of worldliness pervading the Church, or rather from the necessity of a change that this corrupt spirit had forced on the general perception.

These impulses had at first displayed a tendency toward approximation. There was a certain period during which Germany had not entirely resolved to cast off the hierarchy. There was also a moment when Italy seemed to be approaching a rational modification of that hierarchy. That moment passed.

The Protestants, guided by Scripture, retraced their steps with ever increasing firmness toward the primitive forms of Christian faith and life. The Catholics, on the contrary, stood by the ecclesiastical institutions as these had been consolidated in the course of a century, and determined only on renovating all, and infusing increased energy, a more rigid severity, and deeper earnestness of purpose into each. On the one hand there rose up Calvinism, its spirit far more anti-Catholic than that of Lutheranism; on the other, whatever could but recall the idea of the Protestant doctrines was confronted by unflinching opposition and repelled with determined hostility.

In like fashion two neighboring and kindred springs arise on the summit of the mountain, but each seeks its path to the valleys in an opposite direction, and their waters are separated forever.

BOOK III
THE POPES ABOUT THE MIDDLE
OF THE SIXTEENTH CENTURY

The sixteenth century is distinguished above all else by the spirit of religious creation. To this very day we live in the conflicts of conviction which first developed at that time.

If we seek to ascertain the precise moment of universal history when the separation was consummated, we find that it was not strictly coincident with the first appearance of the reformers because opinions did not immediately assume a fixed character, and for a certain time, there was rational ground of hope that a compromise between the conflicting doctrines might be effected. It was not until the year 1552 that all prospect of this kind was utterly destroyed and that the three great forms of Christianity in the West were separated forever. Lutheranism assumed a severity, an exclusiveness, an asceticism hitherto unknown to its habits. The Calvinists departed from it in the most essential doctrines, though Calvin himself had in earlier times been considered a Lutheran. In contrast to both, Catholicism invested itself with its modern forms. Each of these theological systems sought eagerly to establish itself in the position it had assumed; each labored to displace its rivals and to subjugate the world.

At first glance it might seem that Catholicism, seeking only to renew existing institutions, would have found less difficulty than its opponents in pressing forward and establishing itself, but its advantage was not great. It was surrounded and restricted alike by many other vital impulses of secular attitudes, profane learning, and deviant theological connections; it was like a yeast, uncertain whether it would truly envelop the elements out of which it had arisen or again be suppressed by them.*

The first important obstacle was presented by the popes themselves, by their personal character and the policy they pursued.

It will have become obvious to the reader that a most un-spiritual temper had taken firm hold of the heads of the Church and had elicited that opposition from which Protestantism had received so mighty an impetus.

The question now was whether the strict ecclesiastical ten-dencies would overcome and transform this temper, and to what extent.

To me it appears that the antagonism of these two princi-ples—the conflict between the policy, whether active or passive, hitherto prevailing and now become inveterate, and the necessity acknowledged for a complete internal reform—is that which con-stitutes the paramount interest in the history of the following popes.

Paul III

It is an error prevalent in our times that we attach undue impor-tance to the purposes and influence of governments, princes, and other eminent persons; their memory is frequently loaded with the sins of the multitude, as frequently they have credit for per-forming what in fact proceeded freely from the general effort of the community.

The Catholic movement, considered in the preceding book, arose under Paul III; but we should be mistaken to ascribe its origin to that Pope. He perceived its importance to the Roman See, and not only permitted it to take its course, but in many ways promoted its success. Still we may declare without hesitation that his own feelings were at no time in sympathy with its spirit.

Alexander Farnese (this was the former name of Paul III) was quite as worldly as any of his predecessors. Born in the year 1468, his education was completed within the fifteenth century. He studied under Pomponius Laetus at Rome and in the gardens of Lorenzo de' Medici at Florence; thus imbued with the love of art and elegant literature proper to his period, he did not escape the contagion of its morals. His mother found it needful on a certain occasion to have him restricted for a time to the castle of Saint Angelo. The future pontiff seized a moment when the atten-

tion of his guard was attracted by the procession of the Corpus
Christi, and lowering himself from the walls by a rope, he succeeded in making his escape. He acknowledged a son and daughter,
both illegitimate; nevertheless we thus find him a cardinal while
still very young. His hereditary estates were situated at Bolsena,
and he there constructed a villa so inviting to the elegant tastes
of Pope Leo X that he honored the cardinal by more than one visit
to it. The Farnese palace also, the finest in Rome, was commenced
during his cardinalate; but these occupations were by no means
the sole interests of his life. From the first he had fixed his thoughts
on the supreme dignity.

It is entirely characteristic of Farnese that he sought to attain
this eminence by means of a complete neutrality. The French and
Imperial factions then divided Italy, Rome, and the College of
Cardinals. He conducted himself with so deliberate a caution, with
so fortunate a circumspection, that no one could say to which of
these parties he most inclined. He was on the verge of being
elected pope at the death of Leo, and again at that of Adrian,
and he could not live in charity with the memory of Clement VII,
whom he accused of occupying the papal chair for twelve years
during which it ought to have been his own. At length, in October
1534, the fortieth year of his cardinalate and the sixty-seventh
year of his life, he attained the end so long desired and ascended
the papal throne.

He was now to feel all the weight of those conflicts so profoundly agitating the world: the strife of those two great parties
between which he was himself to hold so important a place; the
necessity for opposing the Protestants while at the same time
being drawn into secret connection with them by their political
position; the wish he could not but feel from the situation of his
Italian principality to weaken the preponderance of Spain (and
the great danger involved in every attempt to do so); the pressing
need of reform, and the mortifying restrictions with which this
seemed to threaten the papal power.

The mode in which his character develops between these contradictory demands is most remarkable.

The habits of Paul III were easy, magnificent, and liberal;

rarely has a pope been so much beloved in Rome as he was. His choice of the distinguished men we have before alluded to for the sacred college, and that even without their knowledge, is grandiose. How well does this contrast with the littleness of personal consideration by which such appointments had usually been made. Nor was he content with merely appointing them. He granted to all an unwonted degree of liberty, endured contradiction in the consistory, and encouraged unrestricted discussion.

But thus leaving due liberty to others, and according to every man the advantages incident to his position, he would allow none of his prerogatives to fall into disuse or be neglected. Certain remonstrances being addressed to him by the Emperor on his having advanced two of his grandsons to the cardinalate at too early an age, he replied that he would do as his predecessors had done, that examples might be cited of infants in the cradle becoming cardinals. The partiality he displayed for his family was beyond what had been customary even in the head of the Church, and his resolution to raise his house to the princely dignity, as other popes had done, was early made manifest.

Not that he sacrificed every other consideration to this purpose as did Alexander VI; this could not be alleged against him. He labored earnestly, on the contrary, for the promotion of peace between France and Spain and for the suppression of the Protestants. He strove anxiously to subjugate the Turks and to advance the reformation of the Church; but also, and together with all these cares, he had it much at heart to exalt his own house.

Proposing to himself so many conflicting purposes, whether for the public service or his own private affairs, this pontiff was necessarily forced to the most circumspect, watchful, and temporizing policy, so much always depending on the favorable moment, the happy combination of circumstances. These he was compelled to prepare and mature by degrees most cautiously calculated, and when the decisive moment had arrived, it was to be seized and maintained with the utmost promptitude.

The various ambassadors found it difficult to treat with him. They were surprised to see, that though betraying no want of courage, he was ever reluctant to decide. His object was to entangle others, and to gain some promise that should fetter them, some assurance that could not be recalled; but never would he utter a word that could pledge himself. This disposition was obvious, even in minor affairs. He was disinclined either to refuse or to promise anything, but seemed always anxious to keep his hands free up to the last moment. How much more, then, in circumstances of difficulty! It would occasionally happen that he would himself suggest some means of escape from an evil, some expedient against a danger; but if anyone sought to act on this, the Pope withdrew at once, desiring to remain always master of his own negotiations.†

This pontiff was distinguished by many and varied talents; he possessed extraordinary sagacity, his position was one of supreme elevation, but how impotent, how insignificant does even the most exalted of mortals appear in the context of world history. In all that he proposes or can effect he is limited and held back by the span of time, which bounds his view, and which yet in its momentary manifestations is to him as the weight of eternity. He is fettered besides by the personal considerations incident to his position; these occupy his every hour, occasionally, perhaps, to his comfort and enjoyment, but more frequently to his sorrow and regret. He departs and the eternal destinies of the world continue.

Julius III—Marcellus II

A group of cardinals had assembled around the altar of the chapel during the conclave; they were talking of the difficulties that presented themselves in the choice of a pope. "Take me," said one of the number, Cardinal Monte, "and the next day I will choose you for my favorites and intimates from the whole College of Cardinals." "What say you? Shall we really elect him?" inquired another, Sfondrato, when they had separated. Monte was considered irascible and impetuous, in many other respects too he was an unlikely choice. "Few bets had been taken on his chances," says a writer of the day. It nevertheless did so happen that he was elected

(February 7, 1550). He had formerly been chamberlain to Julius II, and he took the name of Julius III in his memory.

Duke Cosimo had largely contributed to this election, and when it became known at the imperial court, every face was lighted up with joy. For to the high pre-eminence of power and fortune to which the Emperor had attained was now to be added the ascent of the papal throne by a man whom he might firmly calculate on finding devoted to his interests. It now seemed probable that public affairs would take a different course.

The Emperor still adhered firmly to his wish for the reestablishment of the Council at Trent, still hoping to compel the attendance of the Protestants and their submission to its authority. The new Pope assented willingly to that proposal. He set forth the difficulties that were in fact inseparable from the whole affair, but was extremely solicitous to prevent his caution from being considered a subterfuge. He made repeated declarations that this was not the case, and affirmed that having acted through his whole life without dissimulation, he would continue to do so. He decreed the reassemblage of the Council at Trent and fixed the spring of 1551 as date, intimating that he did so "without compact or condition."

With the consent of the Pope alone, however, the way was no longer immediately clear.* The death of Paul had certainly deprived his grandsons of an important support, but it had also given them freedom. No longer compelled to act in accordance with the general interest as with that of the Church, they could now act exclusively as their interests dictated.* Italy and Germany were filled with malcontents. What the Emperor had already effected in religious and political affairs, along with what it was still expected he would do, had raised him up innumerable enemies. Henry II could risk to resume the anti-Austrian purposes of his father. He gave a truce to his wars with England, formed an alliance with the Farnese, and took the garrison of Parma into his pay. French troops soon appeared in Mirandola also, and the banners of France were seen to wave in the very heart of Italy. Pope Julius adhered steadily to the Emperor in this new complication of affairs.*

It was not, however, in small hostilities that the power could be found to suppress those agitations that had indeed originated here, but were now felt throughout Europe. Troops were in action on every frontier where the dominions of France met those of the Emperor. War had broken out by land and sea. The German Protestants finally allied themselves with the French, and the weight they cast into the scale was something very different from that of the Italians. From this union there resulted an assault more determined than any that Charles had ever before sustained: the French were in force on the Rhine; the Elector Maurice appeared in the Tyrol. The veteran conqueror, who had taken up his position on the mountain region between Italy and Germany for the purpose of holding both in allegiance, suddenly found his post one of the utmost jeopardy—his enemies were victorious, and he himself on the point of becoming a prisoner.

The affairs of Italy were instantly affected by this state of things. "Never could we have believed," said the Pope, "that God would so visit us." He was compelled to make a truce with his enemies in April 1552.

Mischances sometimes occur that seem not wholly unwelcome to the man they affect. They give pause to a course of action no longer in harmony with his inclinations, and they provide him with a legitimate cause, or at least afford an obvious excuse, for departing from it.

It would almost appear that Julius felt his tribulation to be of this character. The sight of his states filled with troops and his treasury drained of its resources had already become oppressive and painful to him; nor did he always think himself well treated by the imperial ministers. The Council, too, was presenting him with matter for serious uneasiness. Since the appearance of the German deputies to whom promises of reformation had been given, the proceedings had assumed a bolder aspect. Pope Julius complained that efforts were being made to despoil him of his authority, that the Spanish bishops sought to reduce the chapters to a state of servile subjection on the one hand, while they tried to deprive the Holy See of the presentation to benefices on the other. But he affirmed his resolve to endure no invasion of his rights under the title of an abuse; he would not permit those pre-rogatives to be torn from him that were no abuse, but an essential attribute of his legitimate power. Affairs standing thus, the attack of the Protestants by which the Council was broken up could not have been altogether embarrassing to the Pope. He lost no time in decreeing the suspension of the assembly, and thus freed him-self from innumerable disputes and pretensions. From that time Julius III never applied himself earnestly to political affairs.* In the important affairs of the Church and State he took no more part than was absolutely inevitable.

Under such circumstances, it is manifest that neither Church nor State could greatly prosper. The discord between two great Catholic powers became ever more and more dangerous; the Ger-man Protestants had recovered themselves effectually from the defeat of 1547, and now displayed a more imposing aspect than they had ever before assumed. Of the Catholic reformation so often looked for, there could now be no further hope; the fact would not permit concealment—the prospects of the Roman Church were, in all directions, ambiguous and gloomy.

But if, as we have seen, there had arisen in the bosom of that Church a more severe spirit of action, a feeling intensely re-proving the whole life and conduct of so many of her chiefs, would not this at length affect the choice of the pontiff? So much was always dependent on the personal character of the pope! For this reason the supreme dignity was elective. Thus it might be hoped that a man truly representing the prevalent spirit of the Church would be placed at the head of her government.

After the death of Julius III the more strict party could for the first time influence the election of the pope. The pontiff had frequently felt himself restrained and his undignified demeanor reproved by the presence of Cardinal Marcello Cervini. It was upon this prelate that the choice fell. He was the man now elected —April 11, 1555—as Marcellus II.

The whole life of the new pontiff had been upright and free from the shadow of reproach. That reform in the Church, of which others only talked, he had exemplified in his own person. "I had prayed," says a contemporary, "that a pope might be granted to us by whom those words of fair import, church, council, reform, might be raised from the contempt into which they had fallen. By this election I believed my hopes to have been fulfilled; my wish to have become a reality."* Thus it was that Marcellus commenced his reign. All his acts were in the same spirit. He would not permit his kindred to come to Rome; he made various retrenchments in the expenditure of the court and is said to have prepared a memorial of the different ameliorations that he proposed to effect in the ecclesiastical institutions. His first effort was to restore divine worship to its due solemnity; all his thoughts were of council and of reform. In political affairs he determined on a neutrality, by which the Emperor was perfectly satisfied. "But the world," as his contemporaries remark, "was not worthy of him." They apply to the pontiff those words of Virgil relating to another Marcellus: "Fate only wanted to show him to the world." On the twenty-second day of his pontificate he died.

We can say nothing of the results produced by so short an administration. But even this commencement, this election even, suffices to show the spirit that was beginning to prevail. It continued predominant in the next conclave and was exemplified in the choice of the most rigid among all the cardinals. Giovanni Pietro Caraffa came out of that assembly as pope on May 23, 1555.

Paul IV

Frequent mention has already been made of this pontiff, who is that same Caraffa, the founder of the Theatines, the restorer of the Inquisition, and the man who so essentially contributed to the confirmation of the old dogma in the Council of Trent. If there were a party whose purpose it was to reinstate Catholicism in all its strictness, it was not only a member, but a founder and chief of that party who now ascended the papal throne. Paul IV had already completed his seventy-ninth year, but his deep-set eyes still retained all the fire of youth: he was extremely tall and thin, walked with rapid steps, and seemed all nerve and muscle. His personal habits were subjected to no rule or order. Frequently he passed the night in study, and slept in the day—woe then to the servant who should enter the apartment before his bell had rung. In all things it was his custom to follow the impulse of the moment, but this impulse was regulated by a consciousness formed in the practice of a long life, and become a second nature. He seemed to acknowledge no other duty, no other occupation than the restoration of the Catholic faith to all its original authority. Characters of this description arise from time to time and are occasionally to be seen even in the present day. Their perceptions of life and the world are gained from a single point of view. The peculiar disposition of their mind is so powerful that all their opinions are tinctured and governed by it. Indefatigable speakers, their manner derives a certain freshness from the earnestness of their souls, and the consciousness that, as if by necessity informs and rules their whole being, pours forth in an inexhaustible stream. How powerfully do such men act on all around them when placed in a position wherein their activity depends only on their opinion and the power to act is associated with the will! What might men not expect from Paul IV, whose views and opinions had never endured either concession or compromise, but were ever carried out eagerly to their utmost consequences, now that he was raised to the supreme dignity! He was himself amazed at having reached this point—he who had in no manner conciliated a single member of the conclave, and from whom nothing was to be expected but the extreme of severity. He believed that his election had been determined, not by the cardinals, but by God himself, who had chosen him for the accomplishment of his own purposes.

"We do promise and swear," says he in the bull that he published on his accession to the Holy See, "to make it our first care that the reform of the universal Church, and of the Roman Court, be at once entered on." The day of his coronation was signalized by the promulgation of edicts respecting monasteries and the religious orders. He sent two monks from Monte Cassino to Spain, with command to reestablish the discipline of the convents which had become lax and neglected. He appointed a congregation for the promotion of reforms in general. This consisted of three classes, in each of which were eight cardinals, fifteen prelates, and fifty learned men of differing ranks. The articles to be discussed by them, in relation to the appointments to clerical offices and collation to benefices, were submitted to the universities. It is manifest that the new pope proceeded with great earnestness in the work of reform. The spiritual tendency which had hitherto affected only the lower ranks of the hierarchy now seemed to gain possession of the papal throne itself and promised to assume the exclusive guidance of all affairs during the pontificate of Paul IV.

But now came the question of what part he would take in relation to the general movements of the political world.

The principle impulses once taken by a power are not easy to change: they have become part of its essence.

A desire to deliver themselves from the heavy preponderance of Spain must ever have been uppermost in the minds of the popes, and at the accession of Paul the moment seemed to have come when his wish appeared to be within the realm of possibility. The war proceeding from the movements of the Farnesi was the most unfortunate ever undertaken by Charles V. He was closely pressed in the Netherlands; Germany had deserted his interests; Italy was no longer faithful to him; he could not rely even on the houses of Este and Gonzaga; he was himself ill and weary of life. I doubt whether any pontiff not immediately attached to the imperial party could have found strength to withstand the temptations presented by this state of things.

In the case of Paul IV they were uncommonly powerful. Born in the year 1476, he had seen his native Italy in all the unrestrained freedom of her fifteenth century, and his soul clung to this remembrance. He would sometimes compare the Italy of that period to a well-tuned instrument of four strings—these last being formed by Naples, Milan, Venice, and the States of the Church. He would then utter maledictions on the memory of Alfonso and Louis the Moor: "Lost and unhallowed souls," as he said, "whose discords had disturbed that harmony." That from their time the Spaniard should have become master in the land was a thought that he could in no way learn to bear. The house of Caraffa, to which he belonged, was attached to the French party and had frequently taken arms against the Castilians and Catalonians. In 1528 they again joined the French, and it was Giovanni Pietro Caraffa who advised Paul III to seize Naples in 1547.

There were other reasons in addition to those factional ones. Caraffa had constantly affirmed that Charles favored the Protestants from jealousy of the Pope and that "the successes of those heretics were attributable to no other than the Emperor." Charles knew Caraffa well; he once expelled him from the council formed for the administration of affairs in Naples and would never permit him to hold peaceful possession of his ecclesiastical offices within that kingdom. He had, moreover, made earnest remonstrance against Caraffa's declamations in the consistory. All these things, as may readily be supposed, did but increase the virulence of the Pope's aversion. He detested the Emperor as Neapolitan and as Italian, as Catholic and as Pope. There existed in his soul no other passions than that for reform of the Church and his hatred of Charles.†

But meanwhile how different a position was this pontificate assuming from that which it had been expected to take up! All purposes of reform were set aside for the struggles of war, and these last entailed consequences of a totally opposite character.

The pontiff, who as cardinal had most sternly opposed the abuses of nepotism and had denounced them at his own peril, was now seen to abandon himself entirely to this weakness. His nephew, Carlo Caraffa, who had passed his whole life amidst the excesses and license of camps, was now raised to the rank of cardinal, though Paul himself had often declared of him that "his arm was dyed in blood to the elbow." Carlo had found means to gain over his superannuated relative. He contrived to be occasionally surprised by him in seeming prayer before the crucifix, apparently suffering agonies of remorse. But still further was the uncle propitiated by the virulent enmity of his nephew to the Spaniards. This was their true bond of union.

On his other nephews the pontiff would not for some time bestow a glance of kindness. It was not until they had evinced their participation in his anti-Spanish mania that they were received to his grace. Never could anyone have anticipated what he next did. Declaring that the Colonnas, "those incorrigible rebels against God and the Church," however frequently deprived of their castles had always managed to regain them, he now resolved that this should be amended. He would give those fortresses to vassals who would know how to hold them. Thereupon he divided the possessions of the house of Colonna among his nephews, making the elder the Duke of Palliano and the younger the Marquis of Montebello. The cardinals remained silent when he announced these purposes in their assembly; they bent down their heads and fixed their eyes to the earth. The Caraffas now indulged in the most ambitious projects: the daughters of their family should marry into that of the French king, or at least into the ducal house of Ferrara, and the sons thought of nothing less than the possession of Siena. To one who spoke jestingly concerning the jewelled cap of a child of their house, the mother of the nephews replied, "We should rather be talking of crowns than caps."

And indeed everything was now depending on the events of the war which then broke out, but which certainly assumed no very promising aspect even from the commencement.

There are moments when it would seem as if the ideas which move events, the secret foundations of life, visibly confront one another.

The Duke of Alva might, in the first instance, have conquered Rome with very little difficulty; but his uncle, Cardinal Giacomo, reminded him of the unhappy end to which all had come who had taken part in the conquest under Bourbon. Alva, being a good Catholic, conducted the war with the utmost discretion. He fought the Pope, but did not cease to pay him reverence. He would fain take the sword from his Holiness, but had no desire for the renown of a Roman conqueror. His soldiers complained that they were led against a mere vapor, a mist and smoke that annoyed them, but which they could neither lay hold on nor stifle at its source.

And who were those by whom the Pope was defended against such good Catholics? The most effective among them were Germans, and Protestants to a man! They amused themselves with the saintly images on the highways, they laughed at the mass in the churches, were utterly regardless of the fast days, and did things innumerable, for which at any other time the Pope would have punished them with death. I even find that Carlo Caraffa established a very close intimacy with that great Protestant leader, the Margrave Albert of Brandenburg.

Contradictions more perfect, a contrast more complete, than that displayed by these circumstances could be scarcely imagined. On the one side we have the most fervent spirit of Catholicism, which was at least exemplified in the leader. On the other was that secular tendency of the popedom, by which even Paul IV, however earnestly condemning it, was seized and borne forward. Thus it came to pass that the followers of his faith were attacking him, while it was by heretics and seceders that he found himself defended! But the first preserved their allegiance, even while opposing his power. The latter displayed their hostility to and contempt for his person even while in arms to protect him.[2]

Paul permitted matters to deteriorate very far. It was not until every enterprise had completely failed, his allies beaten, his States for the greater part invested by the enemy, and his capital a second time menaced with ruin, that he would bend himself to sue for peace.

This was accorded by the Spaniards in the same spirit by which they had been actuated throughout the war. They restored all such fortresses and cities of the Church as had been taken, and even promised compensation for Palliano, which the Caraffas had lost. Alva came to Rome, and with the most profound reverence did he now kiss the foot of his conquered enemy, the sworn adversary of his king and nation. He was heard to say that never had he feared the face of man as he did that of the pontiff.

This peace seemed in every way favorable to the papal interest; it was nevertheless utterly fatal to all the projects hitherto cherished by the popedom. Any further attempt to throw off the Spanish yoke must now be abandoned, and accordingly none such has ever (in the old sense and manner) been again brought forward. The influence of the Spaniards in Milan and Naples had proved unassailable. Their allies were more powerful than ever.

[2] Pages 201–204 have been omitted.

There had been hope among the Caraffas of expelling Duke Cosimo from Florence. But this prince had not only held firm his grasp, but had seized on Siena also and was now the possessor of an important sovereignty. By the restitution of Placentia, the Farnesi had been gained over to Philip II. Marc Antonio Colonna had made himself a brilliant reputation and had fully restored the ancient luster of his family. For the pontiff there was nothing left but to resign himself to this state of affairs. Even Paul IV had to accede to it; with what feelings it is not difficult to imagine. Philip II being on some occasion called his friend, "Yes," he replied, "my friend who kept me beleaguered, and who thought to have my soul!" It is true that in the presence of strangers he compared Philip to the prodigal son of the gospel, but in the circle of his intimates he took care to mark his estimation of those pontiffs who had designed to raise the kings of France to the imperial throne; for others he had no praise. His sentiments were what they had always been, but the force of circumstances controlled him. There was nothing more to be hoped for, still less to be undertaken. He dared not even bemoan himself, unless in the closest secrecy.

When once an event is indeed accomplished, it is altogether useless for a man to struggle against its consequences. Even Paul IV felt this, and after a certain time his thoughts took another direction. He experienced a reaction which was of most effective importance, both in regards to his own administration and to the general transformation brought about in the papal position and system.[3]

This change was most certainly of the highest importance, and of ever memorable effect. His hatred of the Spaniards, and the idea of becoming the liberator of Italy, had hurried even Paul IV into designs and practices utterly worldly. These had led him to the endowment of his kinsmen with the lands of the Church and had caused the elevation of a soldier to the administration even of ecclesiastical affairs. They had plunged him into deadly feuds and bloody hostilities. Events had compelled him to abandon that

---

[3] Pages 205–208 have been omitted.

idea, to suppress that hatred, and then his eyes were gradually opened to the reprehensible conduct of his relatives. Against these offenders, after a painful combat with himself, his stern justice prevailed. He shook them off, and from that hour his early plans of reformation were resumed, he began to reign in the manner that had at first been expected of him. And now, with that impetuous energy which he had previously displayed in his enmities, and in the conduct of his wars, he turned to the reform of the State, and above all to that of the Church.

All secular offices, from the highest to the lowest, were transferred to other hands. The existing podestas and governors lost their places, and the manner in which this was effected was occasionally very singular. In Perugia, for example, the newly appointed governor arrived in the night. Without waiting for daylight, he caused the *anziani* to be called together, produced his credentials, and commanded them forthwith to arrest their former governor, who was present. From time immemorial, there had been no pope who governed without nepotism. Paul IV now showed this example.* Nor were the persons only changed, the whole system and character of the administration were changed also. Important sums were economized, and taxes to a proportional amount were remitted. Matters proceeded with greater care and consideration, but without the former abuses.*

Amidst all the commotions prevailing through the early part of his pontificate, Paul IV had never lost sight of his reforming projects. He now resumed them with earnest zeal and undivided attention. A more severe discipline was introduced into the churches. He forbade all begging; even the collection of alms for masses, hitherto made by the clergy, was discontinued; and such pictures as were not, by their subjects, appropriate to the Church, he removed. A medal was struck in his name, representing Christ driving the money-changers from the temple. All monks who had deserted their monasteries were expelled from the city and States of the Church. The court was enjoined to keep the regular fasts, and all were commanded to solemnize Easter by receiving communion. The cardinals were even compelled to occasional preaching, and Paul himself preached! He did his best to set aside many

abuses that had been profitable to the Curia. Of marriage dispensations, or of the resources they furnished to the treasury, he
would not even hear mention. A host of places that, up to his
time, had been constantly sold, he would now have disposed of
according to merit only. Still more rigidly did he insist on the
worth and clerical endowments of all on whom he bestowed the
purely ecclesiastical employments. He would no longer tolerate
those compacts by which one man had hitherto been allowed to
enjoy the revenues of an office, while he made over its duties
to another. He had also formed the design of reinstating to the
bishops many rights which had been wrongfully withheld from
them, and he considered it highly culpable that everything should
be absorbed by Rome which could in any way be made to yield
either profit or influence.*

He permitted no day to pass over, as he boasts, without the
promulgation of some edict tending to restore the Church to her
original purity. Many of his decrees present the outlines of those
ordinances which were afterward sanctioned by the Council of
Trent.

In the course now adopted, Paul displayed, as might have
been expected, all that inflexibility of nature peculiar to him.

Above all other institutions, he favored that of the Inquisition, which he had himself reestablished. The days appointed for
the "segnatura" and the consistory he would often suffer to pass
unnoticed—but never did he miss the Thursday, which was that
set apart for the congregation of the Inquisition to be assembled
before him. The powers of this office he desired to be exercised
with the utmost rigor. He subjected new cases of offense to its
jurisdiction and conferred on it the barbarous prerogative of ap-
plying torture for the detection of accomplices. He permitted no
respect of persons. The most distinguished nobles were summoned
before this tribunal, and cardinals, such as Morone and Foscherari,
were now thrown in prison because certain doubts had occurred
to him as to the soundness of their opinions, although these very
men had been formerly appointed to examine the contents and
decide the orthodoxy of important books—the "Spiritual Exercises" of Loyola, for example. It was Paul IV who established the
festival of St. Dominico, in honor of that Great Inquisitor.

Thus did a rigid austerity and earnest zeal for the restoration of passive habits become the prevailing tendency of the papacy.

Paul IV seemed almost to have forgotten that he had ever pursued other purposes than those that now occupied him. The memory of past times seemed extinguished; he lived and moved in his reforms and his Inquisition, gave laws, imprisoned, excommunicated, and held *autos-da-fé*. These occupations filled up his life strength. When laid prostrate by disease such as would have caused death even to a younger man, he called his cardinals about him, commended his soul to their prayers, and the Holy See and the Inquisition to their earnest care. Once more would he have collected his energies. He sought to raise himself as the disease prevailed, but his strength had failed him—he lay back and expired (August 18, 1559).

In one respect at least are these determined and passionate characters more fortunate than men of feebler mold. They are, perhaps, blinded by the force of their feelings, the violence of their prejudices, but they are also steeled by this force; this violence it is that renders them invincible.*

Remarks On The Progress
Of Protestantism During The Pontificate Of Paul IV

It will have become obvious to the reader that the earlier representation of the papacy and the imperial or Spanish power, had contributed more than any other external cause to the establishment of Protestantism in Germany. Yet a second breach was not avoided, and this produced results still more comprehensive and important.

The recall of the papal troops from the imperial army by Paul III, and his transfer of the Council from Trent to Bologna, may be considered as the preliminary steps. Their importance was at once made evident. There was no impediment to the subjugation of the Protestants so effective as that presented by the policy, active and passive, of Paul III at that period.

The world historical results of these measures were, however, not obvious until after the death of the pontiff. That connection with France, into which he led his nephews, occasioned a universal war; and in this the German Protestants not only achieved that memorable victory by which they secured themselves eternally from the Pope, Emperor, and Council, but also gained important progress for their opinions by the contact into which the Protestant soldiers, who fought on both sides, were forced with those of France and the Netherlands. This contact caused the extensive acceptance of the new doctrines in those countries, their introduction being favored by the prevalence of a confusion occasioned by the war, which rendered vigilant precaution impossible.

Paul IV ascended the papal throne. It was for him to have taken a clear view of things as existing before his eyes, and above all, his first efforts should have been turned to the restoration of peace. But with all the blindness of passion, he plunged himself into the tumult, and it thus came to pass that he—the most vehement of zealots—was in fact a more effectual promoter of that Protestantism which he so abhorred and persecuted than any one of his predecessors.

Let us examine the influence of his conduct on England alone.

The first victory gained by the new opinions in that country was for a long time incomplete. Nothing further was required than a retrogression of the government, and the presence of a Catholic sovereign at once determined Parliament to subject the national church once more to the dominion of the Pope. But then the latter must proceed cautiously. He must not wage open war with those innovations which had arisen from the present and recent state of things. This had been at once obvious to Julius III.*

Affairs proceeded most prosperously. The accession of Paul IV to the papal throne was followed by the arrival of English ambassadors, who assured him of that nation's obedience.

Thus Paul had not to acquire the allegiance of England, he had merely to retain it. Let us see by what measures he sought to effect this.

First, he declared the restitution of all Church property to be an indispensable duty, the neglect of which entails everlasting damnation; he next attempted to reestablish the tax called "Peter's pence." But, apart from these ill-considered measures, could he have adopted any method better calculated to prevent the return of the English to the Catholic pale than the indulgence of his rancorous hostility to Philip II, who, if a Spanish prince, was also King of England? In the battle of St. Quentin, so influential in Italy as well as France, English soldiers assisted to gain the victory. Finally, he persecuted Cardinal Poole, whom he never could endure, deprived him of his dignity as legate, an office that no man had ever borne with greater advantage to the Holy See, and appointed an aged inefficient monk to succeed him, whose principal recommendation was that he shared the prejudices of the pontiff. Had it been the purpose of Paul to impede the work of restoration, he could not have adopted more effective measures.

There can be no wonder that the opposing tendencies should immediately act with renewed violence on the unexpected death of the Queen and cardinal. This result was powerfully accelerated by the religious persecutions which Poole had condemned, but which his bigoted antagonists approved and prompted.

Once more the Pope had an opportunity of deciding the question whether England should be Catholic or Protestant, and this decision demanded all the more serious consideration by the fact that it must inevitably affect Scotland also. In that country likewise the religious parties were in fierce contest, and accordingly just as matters should be regulated in England this would assuredly be the future condition of Scotland.

How significant then was the fact that Elizabeth showed herself by no means decidedly Protestant in the beginning of her reign, and that she caused her accession to be instantly notified to the Pope. There were even negotiations in progress for her marriage to Philip II, and the world of that day believed this event very probable. One would have thought that no state of things could be more satisfactory to the pontiff.

But Paul was incapable of moderation. He returned a repulsive and contemptuous reply to the ambassador of Elizabeth: "First of all," said he, "she must submit her claims to the decision of our judgment."*

Thus, had Elizabeth not been disposed to the opinions of the Protestants, the force of circumstances would have compelled her to adopt that party. This she did firmly resolve and succeeded in obtaining a Parliament having a Protestant majority, by which all those changes that constitute the essential character of the English Church were in a few months effected.

The influence of this turn of things necessarily affected Scotland also. In that country the progress of the French-Catholic interest was resisted by a party that was at once Protestant and national. Elizabeth lost no time in allying herself with the latter and was even exhorted to the measure by the Spanish ambassador himself. The Treaty of Berwick, which she concluded with the Scottish opposition, gave the predominance in Scotland to the Protestants. Before Mary Stuart could land in her own kingdom, she was compelled not only to renounce her claim to the crown of England, but also to ratify the acts of a Parliament guided by Protestant influence—one of which forbade the celebration of the mass under penalty of death.

To a reaction against the designs of France then, which the proceedings of the Pope had favored and promoted, was in a great measure to be attributed the triumph gained by Protestantism in Great Britain, and by which its ascendancy there was secured forever.

There is no doubt that the inward impulses of those who held Protestant opinions had their origin in causes much more profound than any connected with political movements, but for the most part the outbreak, progress, and decision of the religious struggle very closely coincided with the various contingencies of politics.

Even in Germany, a measure adopted by Paul IV was in one respect of peculiar importance. Incited by his old aversion to the house of Austria, he had opposed the transfer of the imperial crown, which obliged Ferdinand I to be more attentive than he had hitherto been to the maintenance of friendly relations with his Protestant allies. The affairs of Germany were thereafter governed by a union of the moderate princes belonging to both confessions, and under their influence the transfer of ecclesiastical foundations in Lower Germany to Protestant administrations was first accomplished.

It seems as if the papacy was destined to suffer no injury to which it had not itself contributed in one way or another by its political undertakings.

And now, if we survey the world from the heights of Rome, how enormous were the losses sustained by the Catholic faith! Scandinavia and Great Britain had wholly departed; Germany was almost entirely Protestant; Poland and Hungary were in fierce tumult of opinion; in Geneva there was as important a center for the schismatics of the Latin nations and of the West as there was in Wittenberg for those of Germanic race and the East; and numbers were already gathering beneath the banners of Protestantism in France and the Netherlands.

Only one hope now remained to the Catholic confession. The symptoms of dissent that had appeared in Spain and Italy had been totally suppressed, and a restorative strictness had become manifest in all ecclesiastical institutions. The administration of Paul had been doubtless most injurious from its secular policy, but it had at least achieved the introduction of a determined spirit of reform into the court and palace. The question now was, would this have force to maintain itself there, and, in that case, would it then proceed to pervade and unite the whole Catholic world?†

Pius IV

In the latter part of the pontificate of Paul IV, a council was again universally demanded, and it is certain that Pius IV would have found it very difficult to resist this call. He could not urge the pretext of war, as had previously been done, since peace was at length established throughout Europe. A general council was indeed imperative for his own interests, since the French were threatening to convoke a national council which might possibly have led to a schism. But apart from all this, my own impression is, that he honestly desired this measure.†

On January 18, 1562, so many bishops and delegates had assembled in Trent that the twice-interrupted Council could be opened for the third time. Pius IV had the most important share in bringing this about. "Without doubt," says Girolamo Soranzo, who does not usually take the side of this pontiff, "his Holiness has in this matter given proof of all the zeal that was to be expected from so exalted a pastor. He has neglected nothing that could forward so holy and so necessary a work."

Later Sessions Of The Council Of Trent

How materially had the state of the world altered since the first sittings of this Council! No more had the Pope now to fear lest a mighty emperor should avail himself of its powers to render himself lord paramount over the Holy See. Ferdinand I was entirely divested of influence in Italy, nor was any important error as to essential points of doctrine to be feared. These dogmas, retaining the form they had received from the first sessions of the Council, though not yet entirely developed, had become predominant throughout the greater part of the Catholic world. To reunite the Protestants with the Church was no longer a thing that could be seriously considered. In Germany they had now gained a wholly unassailable position. In the North their ideas as to ecclesiastical affairs had entered even into the civil policy, a change that was in process of accomplishment in England also.* Thus the influence of the Council was limited from its commencement to the now greatly contracted circle of the Catholic nations. Its purposes must be confined to the arrangement of disputes between these and the supreme ecclesiastical authority, to the precise determination of such dogmas as were not distinctly settled, to the completion of that reform in the Church which had already commenced (this most especially was its great end), and to the setting forth of rules of discipline that should possess universal authority.*

Even this was surrounded by various difficulties, and there soon arose among the assembled fathers most animated controversies and disputes.† For ten months it was found impossible even to proceed to a plenary session. But was this a wonder? Is it surprising that the first legate should dissuade the Pope from going to Bologna on the ground of the remarks that all would make if, in spite of his presence, the Council could still be conducted to no satisfactory end and must after all be dissolved? Yet a dissolution, even a suspension, or a mere translation, which had often been thought of, would have been extremely dangerous. In Rome they hoped for nothing but evil. A council was considered much too violent a remedy for the grievously debilitated constitution of the Church, and all feared that ruin must ensue, both for Italy and the hierarchy.* All the misfortunes that had ever been anticipated from a council by his predecessors, were now believed by Pius IV to hang over his own head.

The persuasion is sublime that in times of difficulty, particularly in cases of grave errors in the Church, an assembly of her principal pastors will avail to remove all evil. "Let its deliberations proceed," says Augustine, "without presumption or envy, and in Catholic peace. Having profited by wider experience, let the concealed be made obvious, and let all that was closed be brought to the light of day." But even in the earliest councils, this ideal was far from being realized. It demanded a rectitude of purpose, a freedom from all extraneous influences—a purity of soul in short that seems to be beyond man. Still less could these now be hoped for when the Church was involved in so many contradictory relations with the State. If, notwithstanding their imperfections, general councils had still retained the respect of nations, and were still looked to with hope, and demanded as remedy, this must be attributed to the necessity of imposing some restraint on the papal influence. But the present state of affairs seemed to confirm what the pontiffs had constantly maintained, namely, that in times of great perplexity, church councils tended rather to increase than remove the evil. All Italy took part in the fears of the Curia. "The Council," said the Italians, "will either be continued, or it will be dissolved. In the first case—and particularly if the Pope should die while it was in session—the ultramontanes will arrange the conclave according to their own interests, and to the disadvantage of Italy; they will lay so many restrictions on the pontiff, that he will be little more than merely bishop of Rome. Under pretence of reforms, they will render all offices worthless and ruin the whole Curia. On the other hand, should the Council be dissolved without having produced any good effect, even the most orthodox would receive great offense while those whose faith is wavering will stand in peril of being utterly lost."

That any essential change could be produced in the opinions of the Council itself seemed, as matters now stood, altogether impossible. The legates, guided by the Pope, with the Italians who were closely bound to him, were confronted by the prelates of France, Spain, and Germany, who, on their side, were led each by the ambassador of his sovereign. What arrangement of differences—what middle term could be devised? There seemed none. Even in February of 1563, the state of things appeared to be desperate. The most vehement contentions prevailed, each party obstinately adhering to the opinions it had adopted.

But when all these affairs were examined with more earnest attention, there appeared the possibility of an escape from the labyrinth.

The conflict in Trent was a conflict of opinions; their origin and guides were in Rome, and at the courts of the respective sovereigns. If these dissensions could ever be healed, it must be by proceeding to their sources. Pius IV had declared that the papacy could no longer support itself without the aid of the temporal princes: it was now the moment to act upon that principle. The Pope had once thought of receiving the demands of the different courts himself and of settling them without recourse to the Council, but this would have been a half-measure only. The best thing now to be done was to bring the Council to a close in concert with the other great powers. No other resource presented itself.

Pius IV determined on such an attempt. The most able and statesmanlike of his cardinals, Morone, gave him effective aid.†
It was therefore rather at the respective courts, and by means of political negotiations, than at Trent and by the assembled fathers, that all discords were eventually composed and all obstacles to a peaceful close of the Council removed. Cardinal Morone, to whom this was principally attributable, had besides found means to conciliate the prelates individually, bestowing on each all the deference, praise, and favor that he desired and thought his due. His

proceedings furnish a striking example of how much may be effected by an able and skillful man who has thoroughly understood the state of affairs and proposes to himself such an aim only as is compatible with that position. To him more than to any other man is the Catholic Church indebted for the successful termination of the Council.*

The difficulties arising from political considerations thus removed, the questions that had caused so much bitterness and wrangling were treated, not so much in the hope of deciding them, as with a view to evade their spirit by some dexterous compromise.

Under these circumstances the less weighty matters were very easily accommodated and the proceedings of the Council had on no occasion made more rapid progress. The important tenets respecting clerical ordination, the sacrament of marriage, indulgences, purgatory, the adoration of saints, and in fact all the principal measures of reform adopted by the assembly, were decided on in the last three plenary sessions of the latter half of the year 1563. The project of reform was discussed in five separate assemblies—one French, which met at the house of Cardinal de Guise, one Spanish, at that of the Archbishop of Granada, and three Italian.

The questions were for the most part agreed upon with little difficulty. Two only presented an exception: the first was the exemption of chapters; the second, the plurality of benefices; and as regarded both these, private interests played an important part.†

Pius IV, having successfully accomplished the preservation of the Roman Court in the form it had hitherto maintained, did not evince any great rigor as regarded the proposed reformation of the temporal sovereigns. He permitted this subject to be dropped in compliance with the suggestions of Ferdinand.

The proceedings were in fact such as those of a peace conference might have been. While questions of subordinate interest were left to be formed into general decrees by the theologians, the more important affairs were discussed by the courts. Couriers were incessantly flying in all directions, and one concession was requited by another.

And now the most earnest desire of the Pope was to bring

the convocation to an early close. For some time the Spaniards were unwilling to accede to this. They were not satisfied with the reforms that had been effected, and the envoy of Philip even made a demonstration of protesting. But the Pope declared his readiness to call a new synod in case of need, and all perceived the great inconvenience that would be caused by protracting the proceedings until a vacancy of the papal throne might occur while the Council was still sitting. And as, besides, everyone felt tired and longed to return home, even the Spaniards at length resigned their objections.

The spirit of opposition was essentially overcome. Particularly during its final period, the Council evinced an extreme subserviency. It even condescended to solicit from the Pope a confirmation of its edicts, and expressly declared that all canons of reform, whatever might be implied in their words, were prepared with the perfect understanding that no portion of them should be construed to affect the dignity of the Holy See. How far was the Council of Trent from renewing the demands of Constance or Basle to superiority over the papal power! In the proclamations by which the sessions were closed—which were prepared by Cardinal de Guise—the universal episcopacy of the Pope was expressly recognized.

Thus prosperous was the conclusion. The Council so eagerly demanded and so long evaded, twice dissolved, and agitated by so many political tempests, that even in its third assembly had been assailed by dangers so imminent, now closed amidst the universal accord of the Catholic world. It will be readily comprehended that the prelates, as they came together for the last time on the fourth of December 1563, were moved. Former antagonists were now seen offering mutual gratulation, and tears were observed in the eyes of many among those aged men.

But seeing, as we have shown, that this happy result had been secured only by the utmost pliancy, the most astute contrivance, the most dexterous policy, may we not inquire if the efficiency of the Council had not been impaired thereby?

The Council of Trent remains forever the most important council, perhaps not of all but certainly of modern times.

Its importance lies in two momentous issues.

The first, to which we have already alluded, was during the war of Smalkalde,[4] when the tenets of Rome, after many fluctuations, became separated forever from the Protestant opinions. From the doctrine of justification as then set forth, arose the whole system of dogmatic theology as it is professed even to the present day by the Catholic Church.

In the second, which we have been just considering, and after the conferences of Cardinal Morone with Ferdinand in the summer and autumn of 1563, the hierarchy was established anew, theoretically by the decrees respecting clerical ordination and practically by the resolutions touching measures of reform.

These reforms were and are of great importance.

For the faithful were again subjected to the uncompromising severity of Church discipline, and even, in extreme cases, to the sword of excommunication. Seminaries were established, wherein the youth preparing for the Church were carefully trained in habits of austerity and the fear of God. Parishes were regulated anew. Preaching and the administration of the sacraments were subjected to fixed ordinances, and the cooperation of the conventual clergy was regulated by specific laws. The most rigid performance of their duties was enjoined on the bishops, particularly that involving the supervision of the clergy, according to their different grades of consecration. It was besides of the most essential efficacy that these prelates had solemnly bound themselves, by a particular "confession of faith," subscribed and sworn to by each, in a compact of obedience to the ordinances of Trent, and of subjection to the pope.

And this was the result of a council which had originally intended to restrict the authority of the pontiff. An object far from being obtained, that authority having in effect received extension and confirmation from the acts of the assembly. Reserving to himself the exclusive right of interpreting the decrees of Trent, the Pope held the power of prescribing the rule of faith and life. Discipline was restored, but all the faculties of directing it were centered in Rome.

[4] Prior reference to the war of Smalkalde between Charles V and the German Protestants (1540) has been partially cut (pages 231–232).

But the close circumscription of her limits was now also perceived and acknowledged by the Catholic Church. On the East and the Greek confession she now resigned all claim, while she drove Protestantism from her borders with anathemas innumerable. In the bosom of the earlier Catholicism, a certain element of the Protestant creed was included. This was now cast out forever; but if the Catholic profession had received limitations, it had also concentrated its forces and braced all its energies together.

Results so effective were achieved only by the concurrence and aid of the great Catholic sovereigns, and it is in this alliance of the Church with the princes that one of the primary conditions of her subsequent development will be found. This is in some degree analogous with the tendency of Protestantism to combine the episcopal and sovereign rights. It was only by degrees that this displayed itself among Catholics. There is manifestly involved in it a possibility of new divisions, but of such a result there was then no immediate apprehension. The decrees of the Council were readily admitted in one province after another. Having effected these things has procured for Pius IV an important place in the history of the world. He was the first pontiff by whom that tendency of the hierarchy to oppose itself to the temporal sovereigns, was deliberately and purposely abandoned.[5]

Pius V

Michele Ghislieri, Cardinal of Alessandria, later pope under the name Pius V, felt an immovable conviction that the path he had chosen was the only right one. Its having conducted him to the papal throne gave him so complete a self-reliance that doubt or fear as to the consequences of his own actions was a pain unknown to his experience.

He was obstinate in adhering to his opinions; the most cogent reasons availed nothing toward making him retract or alter them. Easily provoked by contradiction, he would redden deeply on being opposed and fall into expressions of the utmost violence.

[5] Pages 241–245 have been omitted.

But slightly acquainted with the affairs of the world, or with politics, and suffering his judgment to be warped by accidental and secondary circumstances, it was extremely difficult to deal with him.

It is true that he did not permit himself to act on his first impressions regarding individuals with whom he came into contact; but having once made up his mind about any man, whether for good or evil, nothing could afterward shake his opinion. He was, nevertheless, more disposed to think people deteriorated, rather than that they became better, and there were few whom he did not regard with suspicion.

Never would he mitigate a penal sentence; this was constantly remarked of him. Rather would he express the wish that the punishment had been more severe!

He was not satisfied to see the Inquisition visiting offenses of recent date, but caused it to inquire into such as were of ten or twenty years' standing.

If there were any town wherein few punishments were inflicted, he did not believe the place any the better for that, but ascribed the fact to the negligence of the officials.

The severity with which he insisted on the maintenance of church discipline is entirely characteristic. "We forbid," he says in one of his bulls, "that any physician, attending a patient confined to his bed, should visit him longer than three days, without receiving a certificate that the sick person has confessed his sins anew." Another bull sets forth the punishments for violation of the Sabbath, and for blasphemy. These were fines for the rich, but "for the common man who cannot pay, he shall stand before the churchdoor for one whole day with his hands tied behind his back, for the first offense; for the second he shall be whipped through the city; but his tongue, for the third, shall be bored through, and he shall be sent to the galleys."

This was the general spirit of his ordinances. How frequently did it become necessary to remind him that he had to govern mere men, and not angels!

To defer to the secular powers was now acknowledged to be most necessary, but no consideration of this kind was permitted to affect the severities of Pius V. The princes of Europe had constantly complained of the bull, "In Coena Domini."[6] This he not only proclaimed anew, but even rendered it more onerous, by adding special clauses of his own, wherein there was a disposition shown to refuse the temporal sovereign all right of imposing new taxes.

It will be manifest that proceedings so violent must necessarily produce reactions. And so it happened; not merely because the demands made by a man of so rigid an austerity never can be complied with by the generality of mankind, but also because in this case a deliberate resistance was provoked and various misunderstandings arose. Even Philip of Spain, though usually so devout, was once moved to warn the pontiff that he would do well to avoid the trial of what a prince was capable of doing when driven to extremes.

Pius V, on his part, felt this very deeply. He was sometimes most unhappy in his high station and declared himself "weary of life." He complained that having acted without regard to persons had made him enemies, and that he had never been free from vexations and persecutions since he had ascended the papal throne.

But, however this may have been, and though Pius V could no more give satisfaction to the whole world than other men, it is yet certain that his demeanor and habits did exercise incalculable influence over his contemporaries and the general development of his Church. After so long a train of circumstances—all concurring to call forth and promote a more spiritual tendency—after so many resolutions had been adopted, to make this tendency universally dominant a pope of this character was needed in order to secure that it should not only be widely proclaimed, but also practically enforced. To this effect, the zeal and example of Pius V were alike efficacious.[7]

Thus the pontiff ruled both the Iberian and the Italian penin-

---

[6] "In Coena Domini," published in 1363 by Urban V, imposed ecclesiastical censures for a variety of ecclesiastical and temporal transgressions. It was discontinued in 1770 by Clement XIV.

[7] Pages 248–256 have been omitted.

sula with an authority more unlimited than had been known for long periods by his predecessors. The decrees of the Council of Trent were put in practice through all Catholic countries. Every bishop subscribed the *"professio fidei,"* wherein the substance of those dogmatic decisions promulgated by the Council was contained; and Pius published the Roman catechism, in certain parts of which these same propositions are more extensively expressed. All brevaries not expressly issued by the Papal See, or which had not been in use upward of two hundred years, were abolished, and a new one was composed on the model of that used in the earliest periods by the principal churches of Rome. This the pontiff desired to see adopted universally. A new missal was also prepared "according to the rule and ritual of the holy fathers" and appointed for general use. The ecclesiastical seminaries received numerous pupils, monastic institutions were effectually reformed, and the Court of Inquisition devoted itself with untiring vigilance and merciless severity to guard the unity and inviolability of the faith.

Governed by ordinances thus uniform, a strict alliance ensued between all these countries and states. This state of affairs was further promoted by the circumstance that France, involved in civil wars, had either renounced her former hostility to Spain or was unable to give it effect. A second consequence also resulted from the troubles in France. From the events of any given period, certain political convictions of general influence are always elicited, which convictions then became a practical and motive power throughout the world over which they extend. Thus the Catholic sovereigns now believed themselves assured that any change in the religion of a country involved the danger of destruction to the state. Pius IV had said that the Church could not support herself without the aid of the temporal princes, and these last were now persuaded that union with the Church was equally requisite to their security. Pius V did not cease to preach this doctrine in their ears, and in effect he lived to see all southern Christendom gathered around him for the purposes of a common enterprise.

The Ottoman power was still making rapid progress. Its ascendancy was secured in the Mediterranean, and its various attempts, first upon Malta, and next on Cyprus, rendered obvious the fact that it was earnestly bent on the subjugation of the yet unconquered islands. Italy herself was menaced from Hungary and Greece. After long efforts, Pius succeeded in awakening the Catholic sovereigns to the perception that there was indeed imminent danger. The idea of a league was suggested to the Pope by the attack on Cyprus. This he proposed to Venice on the one hand, and to Spain on the other. "When I received permission to negotiate with him on that subject," says the Venetian ambassador, "and communicated my instructions to that effect, he raised his hands to heaven, offering thanks to God, and promising that his every thought, and all the force he could command, should be devoted to that purpose."

Infinite were the troubles and labors required from the pontiff before he could remove the difficulties impeding the union of the two maritime powers. He contrived to associate with them the other states of Italy, and although in the beginning he had neither money, ships, nor arms, he yet found means to reinforce the fleet with some few papal galleys. He also contributed to the selection of Don John of Austria as leader and managed to stimulate alike his ambition and religious ardor. From all this resulted a battle, the most successful in which Christendom had ever engaged with the Turks, that of Lepanto. The pontiff's mind was so intensely absorbed by the enterprise that on the day of the engagement he believed himself to witness the victory in a kind of trance. The achievement of this triumph inspired him with the most lofty self-confidence and the boldest prospects. In a few years he believed that the Ottoman power would be utterly subdued.

It would have been well if his energies had always been devoted to works so unquestionably praiseworthy, but this was not the fact. So exclusive, so imperious were his religious feelings, that he bore the most bitter hatred to all who would not accept his tenets. And how strange a contradiction! The religion of meekness and humility of innocence and piety is made to persecute! But Pius V, born under the wings of the Inquisition and reared in its principles, was incapable of perceiving this discrepancy. Seeking with inexhaustible zeal to extirpate every trace of dissent that might yet lurk in Catholic countries, he persecuted with an even more savage fury the avowed Protestants who were either freed from his yoke or still engaged in the struggle. Not content with dispatching such military forces as his utmost efforts could command in aid of the French Catholics, he accompanied this with the monstrous and unheard-of instruction to their leader, Count Santafiore, to "take no Huguenot prisoner, but instantly to kill everyone that should fall into his hands." When trouble arose in the Netherlands, Philip of Spain was at first undetermined as to the manner in which he should treat those provinces. Pius recommended an armed intervention, "for," he said, "if you negotiate without the eloquence of arms, you must accept laws. With arms in your hands, it is by yourself that they are imposed." The bloody measures of Alva were so acceptable to the Pope that he sent him a consecrated hat and sword as marks of his approval. There is no proof that he was aware of the preparations for the massacre of St. Bartholomew, but he did things that leave no doubt of his approving it just as his successor did.

What a combination of simplicity, magnanimity and personal austerity with devout religiosity and strict exclusiveness, bitter hatred, bloody persecution!

Such were the dispositions in which Pius V lived and died. When he felt that death was approaching, he once more visited the seven churches, "in order," as he said, "to take leave of those holy places." Thrice did he kiss the lowest step of the Scala Santa. He had promised at one time not only to expend the whole treasure of the Church, the very chalices and crosses included, on an expedition against England, but even to appear himself at the head of the army. Certain fugitive Catholics from England presenting themselves on his way, he declared that "fain would he pour forth his own blood for their sakes." The principal subject of his last words was the League, for the prosperous continuation of which he had made all possible preparations; the last monies that he spent were destined for this purpose. His fancy was haunted to the last moment by visions of his different undertakings. He had no doubt of their success, believing that, of the very stones, God would, if necessary, raise up the man demanded for so sacred a work.

His loss was felt more immediately than he had himself anticipated. But also there was a unity established—a force called into existence, by whose inherent power the course into which he had directed the nations would inevitably be confirmed and maintained.

BOOK IV
THE TIMES OF GREGORY XIII
AND SIXTUS V

Gregory XIII

Gregory XIII, Hugo Buoncompagno of Bologna, who had raised himself to eminence as a jurist and in the civil service, was cheerful and lively in disposition. He had never married, but before the assumption of any clerical dignity he had a son born to him. Later in life his habits became serious and regular, not that he was at any time particularly scrupulous. On the contrary, he displayed a certain dislike of all sanctimonious strictness and seemed more disposed to take Pius IV as an example than his more immediate predecessor. But what happened to Gregory XIII exemplifies the force of public opinion. A hundred years earlier, he would have governed at the most as did Innocent VIII. It was now on the contrary made obvious that even a man of his disposition could no longer resist the strict ecclesiastical tendency of the times.

This tendency was maintained by a party in the court whose first object was to prevent it from declining. Jesuits, Theatines, and their adherents were its members. Those more conspicuously active were Monsignori Frumento, Corniglia, the bold and fearless preacher Francesco Toledo, and the datary Contarelli. Their influence over the Pope was acquired all the more readily and preserved the more securely by the fact that they all acted in concert. They represented to him that the high consideration enjoyed by his predecessor had derived principally from his personal character and conduct. In all the letters that they read aloud to him, the memory of Paul's holy life and virtues with the fame of his reforms was the subject principally dwelt on; whatever was not to this effect they passed over. By thus proceeding, they gave to the ambition of Gregory XIII a character most thoroughly spiritual.†

This pontiff is not chargeable with nepotism, or with advancing his own family contrary to the laws. On one occasion when a newly appointed cardinal declared that he should be ever grateful "to the family and nephews of his Holiness," Gregory struck the arms of the chair he sat on with both hands, exclaiming, "Be thankful rather to God and to the Holy See!"

To this extent he was already influenced by the religious tendency of the time. Not only did he seek to equal the piety of Pius V, he even desired to surpass it; in the early years of his pontificate he read mass three times a week, never omitting to do so on Sundays. His life and deportment were not only irreproachable but even exemplary.

There were certain duties of the papal office that no pontiff ever performed with more zeal and propriety than Gregory XIII. He kept a list of all those men, of whatever country, who were proper to the office of bishop, evinced an accurate knowledge of the character and qualifications of all who were proposed to his acceptance, and exercised the most anxious care in the nomination to these important offices.

His most earnest endeavors were especially given to securing a strict system of ecclesiastical education. His liberality in assisting the progress of Jesuit colleges was unusual. He made rich presents to the house of the "professed" in Rome, caused whole streets to be closed up, purchased many buildings, and assigned a large income to aid the completion of the college in that form in which we see it even to our days. Twenty lecture rooms and 360 cells for students were provided for in this building, which was called "the Seminary of All Nations." Even on its first foundation, measures were taken to make it clear that this college was meant to embrace the whole world—twenty-five speeches being pronounced in as many different languages, each accompanied by a Latin interpretation. The *Collegium Germanicum*, which had been founded some years before, was falling into decay from want of means; to this also, Gregory gave a palace, that of St. Apollinare, and added the revenues of San Stefano on Monte Celio, together with the sum of 10,000 scudi charged on the *Camera Apostolica*. He may indeed be regarded as the true founder of this institution, whence, year after year since his time, a steady number of champions for the Catholic faith has been sent into Germany. He found means to erect and endow an English college in Rome; he assisted the college of Vienna and Graz from his private purse; and there was not, perhaps, a single Jesuit school in the world which he did not in some way contribute to support. Following the counsels of the Bishop of Sitia, he also established a Greek college into which boys from thirteen to sixteen were admitted. And not only were they received from countries already under Christian rule, such as Corfu and Candia, but also from Constantinople, Saloniki, and the Morea. They had Greek instructors and were clothed in the kaftan and Venetian *barret*. They were upheld in all Greek customs, and never permitted to forget that it was in their native country they were preparing to act. They retained their own rites as well as language, and their religious education was conducted according to those doctrines of the Council, and in those principles, whereon the Greek and Latin churches were of one accord.

The reform of the calendar, accomplished by Pope Gregory XIII, was another proof of that assiduous care which he extended over the whole Catholic world. This had been greatly desired by the Council of Trent, and it was rendered imperative by the displacement of the high festivals of the Church from that relation to particular seasons of the year which had been imposed on them by the decrees of the Council. All Catholic nations took part in this reform. A Calabrian else little known, Luigi Lilio, has gained himself immortal renown by suggesting the most efficient method for overcoming the difficulty. All the universities, among them the Spanish—those of Salamanca and Alcala—were consulted as to his proposed plan. Favorable opinions came from all quarters. A commission was then appointed in Rome (its most active and learned member being our compatriot Clavius). It was minutely examined by this body and finally decided on. The learned Cardinal Sirleto had exercised the most important influence over the whole affair. It was conducted with a certain degree of mystery, the calendar being concealed from all, even from the ambassadors, until it had received the approval of the different courts. Gregory then proclaimed it with great solemnity, vaunting this reform as a proof of God's illimitable grace toward his Church.†

The mode in which Gregory should administer the resources of the State was a question of paramount importance. The evil of alienations had at length become clearly apparent to all. New imposts were considered impolitic and highly censured—the doubtful, nay, the pernicious consequences of such a system were clearly perceived and fully appreciated. Gregory imposed on the congregation the task of procuring him money, but they were to make no ecclesiastical concessions, lay on no new taxes, nor permit the sale of church revenues.

How, then, were they to proceed? The means devised, in reply to this question, were sufficiently remarkable, as were also the results eventually produced by them.

Gregory, who always subscribed to a most uncompromising concept of what was the law, believed to have discovered that many prerogatives of the ecclesiastical principality yet remained to be put in force. These he thought had only to be asserted in order for them to supply him with new sources of income. It was not in his character to respect the privileges that might stand in his way: thus, among others, he abolished without caution that possessed by the Venetians of exporting corn from the March and Ravenna under certain favorable conditions, declaring that it was fair to make foreigners pay equal duty with the natives. Since the Venetians did not instantly comply, he caused their magazines in Ravenna to be opened by force, the contents to be sold by auction, and the owners imprisoned. This was but a small affair, it is true, but served to intimate the path he intended to pursue. His next step was of much more lasting importance: believing that a host of abuses existed among the aristocracy in his own territories, he decided that the reform of these would be highly beneficial to his treasury. His secretary of the *Camera*, Rudolfo Bonfigliuolo, proposed a comprehensive renewal and extension of feudal rights which had hitherto scarcely been thought of. He affirmed that a large part of the estates and castles held by the barons of the State had lapsed to the sovereign, either by failure in the direct line of succession, or because the dues for which they were liable had not been paid. The Pope had already acquired some domains that had either lapsed or were purchased, and nothing could be more agreeable to him than to continue doing so. He at once set earnestly to work. From the Isei of Cesena he wrested Castelnuovo in the hills of Romagna, and from the Sassatelli of Imola he gained Coreana. Lonzano, seated on its beautiful hill, and Savignano in the plain, were taken from the Rangoni of Modena. Alberto Pio resigned Bertinoro to escape the court proceedings prepared against him by the treasury; but this did not suffice, and he was divested of Verrucchio and other places. Seeing this, he tendered his arrears of rent on every festival of St. Peter, but they were never afterward accepted. All this occurred in Romagna alone, and the other provinces did not fare better. It was not only to estates on which the feudal services remained unpaid that the court asserted a claim, there were other domains which had originally been mortgaged to certain barons, but this so long since that the mode of their tenure had been forgotten. The property had descended from hand to hand as freehold and had often largely increased in value. The Pope and his secretaries now chose to redeem the mortgages; in this manner they gained possession of Sitiano, a castle that had been pledged for 14,000 scudi. That sum they laid down, but it was greatly below the value of the property which, being considered freehold, had received extensive improvement.

Gregory congratulated himself on these proceedings. He believed he had established a new claim to the favor of heaven with every addition, were it only of ten scudi, that he succeeded in adding to the income of the Church provided it were done without new imposts. He calculated with infinite pleasure that he should soon have made an addition of 100,000 scudi to the revenues of the State, and all by legitimate proceedings. How greatly would his means for proceeding against infidels and heretics be thus increased! His measures were, for the most part, much approved by the court. "This Pope is called the 'vigilant' " (Gregorius means vigilant), says the Cardinal of Como, "by his vigilance will he recover his own." But the feeling of the provinces on this subject was altogether different from that of the court. On the aristocracy the impression produced was most unfavorable.

From all this there arose the most violent fermentation, the influence of the barons on the peasantry and on the nobles of the neighboring towns awakened extreme indignation throughout the country at the pontiff's new measures.

Equally unexpected and peculiar were the consequences that ensued from the policy that Gregory had adopted.

In all countries (but more especially in one of so pacific a character as that now displayed by the Papal States) obedience to the government is based on voluntary subordination. In the Roman territories, the elements of dissension were neither destroyed nor removed, they were simply concealed by the mantle of authority extending over them. Accordingly, the principle of subordination being disturbed on one point, these all pressed forward together and burst into open conflict. The land seemed suddenly to remember how warlike, how well skilled in arms, and how unfettered in its parties it had remained for whole centuries. It began to feel contempt for this government of priests and men of law, and returned to the condition most natural to it.

It is true that no direct opposition was offered to the government. No general revolt ensued. But the old feuds reappeared in every part of the country.

Public authority being thus enfeebled, troops of bandits assembled in the March, in the Campagna, indeed in all the provinces, and these outlaws very soon amounted to small armies. Giacomo Buoncompagno took the field, and he certainly succeeded in dispersing these bands and in clearing the country; but no sooner was his back turned than the outlaws instantly sprang up as actively as ever in his rear, and all the previous disorders recommenced.

Thus it came to pass that Gregory could never make himself

master of these bandits. The taxes remained unpaid, and the
sussidio could not be collected. A feeling of discontent took possession of the whole country; even cardinals were mooting the
question whether it would not be advisable to attach themselves
to some other state.

The further prosecution of the measures suggested by the
secretary of the *Camera* was out of the question in this state of
things. In December 1581, the Venetian ambassador made it publicly known that his Holiness had commanded the discontinuance
of all proceedings in the confiscation of lands.

Perhaps even more painful was the necessity to which the
pontiff was also reduced of permitting Piccolomini to appear in
the capital and present a petition for pardon.[8] A deep shudder
passed over him as he read the long list of murders and other
atrocities that he was called upon to forgive, and he laid the paper
from his hand. But he was assured that one of three things must
happen, either his son Giacomo would receive his death from the
hand of Piccolomini, or he must himself condemn Piccolomini to
death, or resolve on granting him a pardon. The fathers confessor
of St. John Lateran declared that though they dared not violate
the secrets of the confessional, yet they were permitted to say that
a great calamity was impending, and unless something were speed-
ily done, calamity would inevitably ensue. Piccolomini was also
publicly favored by the Grand Duke of Tuscany and was at that
moment lodged in the Medici palace. Seeing all these things, the
pontiff at last submitted, but with a deeply mortified spirit, and
the brief of absolution received his signature.

This did not, however, suffice to restore tranquillity to the
country. His own capital was filled with the outlaws, and matters
came to such a pass that the city magistracy of the *conservators*
was compelled to act in aid of the Pope's police, which could not
secure obedience. A pardon being offered to a certain bandit called
Marianazzo, he refused it, declaring that his life "was more se-

---

[8] Alfonso Piccolomini, leader of one of the bands of outlaws
making Rome insecure.

cure while remaining an outlaw, to say nothing of the increased advantage!"

Worn out and weary of life, the aged pontiff raised his hands to heaven and cried, "Thou wilt arise, O Lord, and have mercy upon Zion!"

Sixtus V

It would sometimes seem that even in confusion itself there exists some hidden force by which the man capable of containing it is formed and brought forward.

Hereditary principalities or aristocracies transmit their power from generation to generation throughout the world, but the sovereignty of the Church has this peculiarity, that her throne may be attained by men from the lowest ranks of society. It was from a station among the most humble that a pope now appeared, by whom those qualities, intellectual and moral, demanded for the suppression of the prevalent disorders were possessed in their highest perfection.

When the provinces of Illyria and Dalmatia first became a prey to the successful armies of the Ottomans, many of their inhabitants fled into Italy. Arriving in melancholy groups, they might be seen seated on the seashore and raising their hands imploringly toward heaven. Among these fugitives would most probably have been found a Sclavonian by birth, named Zanetto Peretti. This was the ancestor of Sixtus V. Sharing the frequent lot of exiles, neither Zanetto nor his descendants, who had settled in Montalto, could boast of any great prosperity in the country of their adoption. Peretto Peretti, the father of the future pope, was driven by his debts from Montalto, and it was only by marriage that he was enabled to rent a garden at Grotto a Mare, near Fermo. The place was a remarkable one. Amidst the plants of the garden were seen the ruins of a temple to Cupra, the Etruscan Juno, and rich fruits of the South grew up around it, for the climate of Fermo is milder and more beneficent than that of any

other district in the March. Here a son was born to Peretti, on
the thirteenth of December 1521; but a short time before this
birth, the father had been consoled by the voice of a divinity,
which, speaking to him in a dream as he bemoaned his many privations, assured him that a son should be granted to him, by whom
his house should be raised to high fortunes. On this hope he seized
with all the eagerness of a visionary temperament, further excited
by want, and naturally disposed to mysticism. He named the
boy Felix.

That the family was not in prosperous circumstances appears
from what is related, among other things, of the child falling into
a pond, when his aunt, "who was washing clothes at this pond,"
drew him out; it is certain that he was employed to watch the
fruit, and even to attend swine. His father was not able to spare
even the five *bajocchi* (three-pence) demanded monthly by the
nearest schoolmaster. Thus Felix had to learn to spell from the
primers that other boys left lying beside him as they passed
through the fields on their way to and from school. There was
happily one member of the family who had entered the Church,
Fra Salvatore, a Franciscan. This relative at length permitted himself to be prevailed on to pay the schoolmaster. Felix could then
go to receive instruction with the other boys. He had a piece of
bread for his dinner, and this he ate at mid-day by a stream, which
supplied him with drink for his meal. These depressed circumstances did not prevent the hopes of the father from being shared
by his son. In his twelfth year he entered the order of the Franciscans, for the Council of Trent had not then forbidden the vows
to be taken this early, but did not resign his name and continued
to be called Felix.†

Fra Salvatore kept him in very strict order, but he sent him
to school. Young Felix passed long evenings in learning his les-
sons, without supper, and with no better light than that afforded
by the lantern hanging in the cloisters; and when this failed him,
he would go to the lamp that burnt before the host in the chapel.
He was not remarked for any particular tendency to religious devotion or profound researches in science. We find only that he
made rapid progress at the school of Fermo, as well as at the uni-

versities of Ferrara and Bologna. His particular talent seemed rather for dialectics, and he became a perfect master of that monkish accomplishment, the dexterous handling of theological subtleties. At the general convention of the Franciscans in the year 1549, which commenced with an exhibition of skill in literary disputation, he was opposed to a certain Telesian, Antonio Persico of Calabria, who was at that time in high repute at Perugia. On this occasion he acquitted himself with a presence of mind and intelligence that first procured him notice and a certain degree of distinction. From this time Cardinal Pio of Carpi, protector of the order, took a decided interest in his fortunes.

But it is to another circumstance that his fortune is principally to be attributed.

In the year 1552, he was appointed Lent preacher in the Church of the Holy Apostles in Rome, and his sermons were very well received. His style was found to be animated, copious, fluent, and free from meretricious ornament. His matter was well arranged, his manner impressive, his utterance clear and agreeable. While preaching to a full congregation, he one day came to that pause in the sermon customary among Italian preachers; and when he had reposed for a time, he took up the memorials, which are usually prayers and intercessions only. While reading these, he perceived a paper lying sealed in the pulpit and containing matter of a totally different character. All the main points of the sermons hitherto preached by Peretti, especially those touching the doctrine of predestination, were here set down and opposite to each were written in large letters the words, "Thou liest." The preacher could not wholly conceal his amazement, he hurried to a conclusion, and instantly on reaching home dispatched the paper to the Inquisition. Shortly thereafter the Grand Inquisitor, Michele Ghislieri, entered his room. The most searching examination ensued. In later times Peretti often described the terror caused him by the aspect of this man, with his stern brow, deep-set eyes, and strongly marked features. But he did not lose his presence of mind, answered satisfactorily, and betrayed weakness on no point whatever. When, therefore, Ghislieri saw that there was no shadow of suspicion, that the friar was not only guiltless, but also well versed in the Catholic doctrines and firmly fixed in the faith, he became a totally different person, embraced Peretti with tears, and was his second patron.

From that time Fra Felice attached himself with a firm hold to the strict party just then beginning to gain ascendancy in the Church. With Ignazio, Felino, and Filippo Neri, all of whom received the title of saints, he maintained the most intimate intercourse. It was of particular advantage to him that he was driven out of Venice by the intrigues of his brethren for having attempted to reform the order. This greatly enhanced his credit with the representatives of the more rigid opinions, then fast acquiring the predominance. He was presented to Paul IV, and sometimes called to give an opinion in cases of difficulty. At the Council of Trent he labored with the other theologians, and was then consultor to the Inquisition. He had a considerable share in the condemnation of Archbishop Carranza, patiently submitting to the labor of seeking through the Protestant writers for all those passages which Carranza was accused of embodying in his works. He gained the entire confidence of Pius V, who appointed him vicar-general of the Franciscans, with the express understanding that his authority extended to the reformation of the order. This Peretti carried into execution with a high hand. The principal offices of the order had hitherto been controlled by the commissaries-general. These functionaries he deposed, restored the primitive constitution according to which the supreme power was vested in the provincials, and made the most rigorous visitations. The expectations of Pius were not only fulfilled, they were surpassed. He considered his inclination for Peretti as an inspiration from above, refused all credence to the calumnies by which his favorite was persecuted, bestowed on him the bishopric of St. Agatha, and in the year 1570 exalted him to the College of Cardinals.

The bishopric of Fermo was also conferred on the successful monk. Robed in the purple of the Church, Felix Peretti returned to the abode of his fathers, to that place where he had once guarded the fruit-trees and followed the swine; yet neither the predictions of his father nor his own hopes were yet entirely accomplished.

The various artifices employed by Cardinal Montalto, so was

Peretti now called, to obtain the papal tiara have been described and repeated, much and often. The affected humility of his deportment; how he tottered along leaning on his stick, bent to the earth, and coughing at every step. But to him who reflects this will seem quite improbable. It is not by such means that the highest dignities are won. Montalto lived a life of tranquil frugality and industrious seclusion. His recreations were the planting of vines and other trees in his gardens near the Church of Santa Maria Maggiore, which are still visited by the stranger, and doing such service as he could to his native town. His hours of labor he devoted to the works of St. Ambrose, an edition of which he published in the year 1580. In spite of his industrious application to this task, its treatment remained rather arbitrary. In other respects his character does not appear to have been so guileless as it is occasionally represented. As early as 1574, he is described as learned and prudent, but also crafty and malignant. He was doubtless gifted with remarkable self-control. When his nephew, the husband of Vittoria Accorambuona, was assassinated, he was himself the person who requested the Pope to discontinue the investigation. This quality, which was admired by all, very probably contributed to his election; when, having been put in nomination, principally by the intrigues of the conclave in 1585, he was nevertheless elected. The authentic narrative of the proceedings assures us also that his comparatively vigorous years were taken into account, he being then sixty-four and possessing a firm and healthy constitution. For all were persuaded that a man of unimpaired energies was imperatively demanded by the circumstances of the times.

And thus Fra Felice saw his aspirations fulfilled. It was doubtless with a feeling of proud satisfaction that he beheld the accomplishment of desires so noble and so legitimate. Every incident of his life in which he had ever believed himself to perceive an intimation of his exalted destiny now recurred to his thoughts. The words he chose for his motto were these: "Thou, O God, art my defender, even from my mother's womb."

In all his undertakings he believed himself, from this time, to possess the immediate favor of God. At his first accession to the throne, he announced his determination to exterminate all the bandits and evil-doers. He was persuaded that in the event of his own powers failing, God would send him legions of angels for so good a work.

To this difficult enterprise he at once addressed himself with deliberate judgment and inflexible resolution.[9]

Finances

The Chigi family in Rome are in possession of a small notebook kept by Sixtus, in his own handwriting, while yet but a poor monk. With the utmost interest does the reader turn over the leaves of this document, wherein Sixtus has noted all the important interests of his life: the places he preached in during Lent, the commissions he received and executed, the books that he possessed, in what manner they were bound, whether singly or together, are here noted down; finally, all the details of his small monkish household are given with the utmost exactitude. We read in these pages how his brother-in-law Battista bought twelve sheep for him; how he, monk that he was, paid first twelve florins, and afterward two florins and twenty bolognins for these sheep so that they became his own property; how the brother-in-law kept them, receiving half the profits, as was the custom of Montalto; and many other matters of like character. We perceive with how close an economy he guarded his small savings, how minutely he kept account of them, and how at length they amounted to some hundred florins. All these details one follows with interest and sympathy, remarking throughout at the same economical exactitude which this Franciscan afterward brought to bear on the government of the Papal States.* It is certain that no pope, either before or after him, administered the revenues of the Church with so good an effect.

The treasury was utterly exhausted when Sixtus V ascended

---

[9] The sections "Extirpation of the Banditti" and "Leading Characteristics of the Administration" have been omitted (pages 308–318).

the papal throne, and he complains bitterly of Pope Gregory, whom he accuses of having spent the income of his predecessor and his successor, as well as his own. He conceived so bad an opinion of this pontiff, that he ordered masses to be said for his soul, having seen him in a dream enduring the torments of the other world. The revenues of the State were found to be mortgaged up to the following October.

All the more earnestly did he set himself to the task of replenishing the public coffers, and in this he succeeded beyond his expectations. In April 1586, at the close of the first year of his pontificate he had already gathered 1,000,000 scudi in gold. To this he added a second million in November of 1587, and in the April following a third. Thus an amount of more than 4,500,000 of silver scudi was laid up by the early part of 1588. When Sixtus had got together 1,000,000, he deposited it in the castle of Saint Angelo, dedicating it, as he says, "to the Holy Virgin, the mother of God, and to the holy apostles Peter and Paul." He stipulated for what purposes these funds might be used.* They were the following: a war undertaken for the conquest of the Holy Land, or for a general campaign against the Turks; the occurrence of famine or pestilence; manifest danger of losing any province of Catholic Christendom; hostile invasion of the Ecclesiastical States; or the attempt to recover a city belonging to the Papal See. He bound his successors, by the wrath of Almighty God and of the holy apostles Peter and Paul, to confine themselves within the limits thus assigned them.

The merit of this arrangement we leave for the moment unquestioned, to inquire by what means the pontiff contrived to amass a treasure so astonishing for the times he lived in.

The direct revenues of the Papal See could not account for it; these, as Sixtus himself informs us, were not in their net product more than 200,000 scudi a year.

The savings of the Pope were considerable, but not equal to this amount. His retrenchments were certainly very close, the expenses of his table being reduced to six pauls a day (nearly three shillings of our present money). He abolished many useless offices of the court and disbanded a part of the troops. But we have the authority of the Venetian Delfino for the fact that all this did not lessen the expenditure of the *Camera* by more than 150,000 scudi; and we learn, besides, from Sixtus himself, that his reduction of expense was to the amount of 146,000 scudi only.

We find then that with all his economy and by his own showing the net revenue was increased to 350,000 scudi, and no more. This would scarcely suffice for the buildings he was engaged in; what then would it do toward the amassing of so enormous a treasure?*

In the sale of offices it was that Sixtus found one chief source of his treasures. He raised in the first instance the prices of many that had been obtained by purchase only from periods long before his own. Thus the office of treasurer to the *Camera*, for which the price until now had been 15,000 scudi, he sold for 50,000 to one of the Giustiniani family. And, having raised him to the College of Cardinals, he sold it again to a Pepoli for 72,000 scudi. This second purchaser being also invested with the purple, Sixtus appropriated one-half of the income of the office, namely 5,000 scudi, to a *monte;* and thus mulcted, he sold it once more for 50,000 golden scudi. In the next place he began to sell certain employments that up to his time had always been conferred gratuitously, as, for example, the notariates, the office of fiscal, with those of commissary-general, solicitor to the *Camera*, and advocate of the poor. For all these he now obtained considerable sums, as 30,000 scudi for a notariate, 20,000 for a commissariat-general, etc. Finally, he created a multitude of new offices, many of them very important ones, as were those of treasurer to the *dataria*, prefect of the prisons, etc., and some others. Of his invention are, besides, the "twenty-four referendaries," from which, as from notariates in the principal cities of the State and from "200 cava-lierates," he derived very large sums of money.

When all these means are taken into account, the mode by which Sixtus amassed his treasure is no longer problematical. The sale of offices is computed to have brought him 608,510 golden scudi, and 401,805 silver scudi, making together nearly a million and a half of silver scudi. But if this sale of places had before caused undue pressure on the State from their involving a share in the rights of government as collateral for a loan, which rights were most rigorously enforced against the tax-payer while the duties of these offices were never performed, how greatly was this evil now augmented! Offices were, in fact, considered as property conferring certain rights, rather than as an obligation demanding labor.†

By all these means so many new sources of income were rendered available that the pontiff was enabled to take up a loan from the *monti* of 2,500,000 scudi (or to be exact 2,424,725), and pay interest thereon.

It must be admitted, however, that in this system of finance there is something exceedingly difficult to comprehend.

The country was most oppressively burdened by these taxes and by the multitude of offices. Of the latter the salaries were made to depend on perquisites and fees, which must of necessity embarrass the course of justice and the administration. The taxes were imposed on the trade of the country, wholesale and retail, and could not but seriously impair its activity. And to what end was all this suffering inflicted?

If we add the proceeds of the *monti* to those of the offices, we shall find that the whole sum thus produced to the *Camera* was about equal to the treasure shut up by Sixtus in the castle of Saint Angelo—4,500,000 scudi—and very little more. All the undertakings for which this Pope has been so highly praised might very well have been accomplished with the amount of his savings.

To collect and hoard superfluous revenues is understandable. To raise a loan for some present necessity is quite normal, but to borrow money and impose heavy imposts merely for the purpose of locking up the proceeds in a fortress as a treasure for some future contingency, this is altogether foreign to the general practice of governments. Nevertheless this was what won most admiration for Sixtus.

There was doubtless much tyranny and many an unpopular characteristic in the administration of Gregory XIII. The reaction to these was most pernicious; but I am decidedly of opinion that if he had succeeded in rendering the papal treasury independent of new loans and imposts for the future, the result would have been highly beneficial to the Roman States and would probably have rendered their progress much more prosperous.

But Gregory was lacking the energy to implement his thoughts, particularly in his later years.

This practical force it was, this power of executing what he willed, which characterized Sixtus V. His accumulation of treasure by means of loans, imposts, and venal offices did but add burden to burden—nor shall we fail to perceive the consequence. But the world was dazzled by his success, which, for the moment, did certainly give the Papal See increased importance. Surrounded by states which were in most cases always pressed for money, and the possession of wealth inspiring the pontiffs with a more perfect confidence in themselves, procured for them a more influential position in the eyes of the others.

This mode of administering the state was indeed an essential part of the Catholic system of those times. By gathering all the financial strength of the realm into the hands of the ecclesiastical chief, it rendered him the complete and exclusive organ of spiritual influence. For to what purpose could all this treasure be applied, if not to the defense and extension of the Catholic faith? And in projects having these ends in view did Sixtus live, move, and have his being. His enterprises were sometimes directed against the East and the Turks, but more frequently against the West and the Protestants. Between these two confessions, the Catholic and Protestant, a war broke out in which the pontiffs took most earnest part.

This war we shall treat in the following book. For the present let us remain a little longer with Rome herself, which now made her influence once more felt by the whole world.[10]

The Public Works Of Sixtus V

Sixtus devoted himself with his whole spirit to his architectural undertakings. A herd-boy brought up among fields and gardens,

[10] Pages 325–333, all part of the section on the public works, have been omitted.

for him the city had peculiar attractions. He would not hear mention of a villa residence. His best recreation, as he declares himself, was "to see many roofs." He doubtless meant that his highest satisfaction was derived from the progress of his buildings.

Many thousand hands were kept constantly employed, no difficulty deterred him from his purpose.

The cupola of St. Peter's was still wanting, and the architects stipulated ten years for its completion. Sixtus was willing to give the money, but he also desired to gratify his eyes by the completed building. He set 600 men to work, allowing no intermission even at night. In twenty-two months the whole was finished, the leaden covering to the roof alone excepted; this he did not live to see.

The arbitrary and impetuous character of the pontiff was manifest even in labors of this kind. He demolished without remorse the remains of the papal *patriarchium*, which were by no means inconsiderable, and were singularly interesting. These antiquities were connected with the dignity of his own office, but he destroyed them nevertheless to erect his palace of the Lateran on their site, a building not at all wanted, and which excites a very equivocal interest solely as one of the earliest examples of the uniform regularity of modern architecture.

How complete was the revolution which then took place in the relations of the age to antiquity! As in former times men emulated the ancients, so did they now; but their earlier efforts were directed to approximating their beauty and grace of form. Now they sought only to vie with or exceed them in extent and magnitude. Formerly the slightest trace of the antique spirit was revered in however trifling a monument; now the disposition seemed rather to destroy these traces. One sole idea held predominance among the men of this day; they would acknowledge no other. It was the same that had gained ascendancy in the Church—the same that had succeeded in making the State a mere instrument of the Church. This ruling idea of modern Catholicism had penetrated throughout the being of society and pervaded its most diversified institutions.

General Change In The Intellectual Tendency
Of The Age

It is not to be supposed that the Pope alone was subjected to the dominion of the spirit we have seen to prevail. Toward the close of the sixteenth century, a tendency became obvious in every manifestation directly opposed to that which had marked its commencement.

Highly significant of this change is the fact that the study of the ancients, which in the first part of the century had been a primary condition to all knowledge, had now greatly declined. Another Aldus Manutius had indeed appeared in Rome, and was professor of eloquence; but neither for his Greek nor Latin did he find admirers. At the hour of his lectures he might be seen pacing up and down before the portal of the university with one or two hearers, the only persons who showed an interest in him. How rapid a progress was made by the study of Greek in the early part of this century! Yet there did not exist at its conclusion one single Hellenist of repute in all Italy.

Not that I would assert this change to be altogether symptomatic of decline. It was in a certain sense connected with the necessary progress of science and literature.

For if in earlier times all science had been immediately derived from the ancients, this was now no longer possible. How enormous was the mass of knowledge brought together by Ulisses Aldrovandi, for example, during the labors of his long life and extensive travels, in comparison with anything that could be possessed by the ancients! In the construction of his museum he had labored to produce completeness, and wherever the natural object was unattainable had supplied its place by drawings, carefully appending to each specimen an elaborate description. How far, too, had the knowledge of geography extended beyond what had even been imagined by those best informed in the ancient world! A more profound and searching spirit of investigation had arisen; mathematicians had in earlier days sought only to fill up the gaps left by the ancients.* But by this very process men were conducted to more extensive observations. Even while seeking to pursue the light offered by the ancients, the mind of the student became freed from their tutelage. Discoveries were made that led beyond the circle prescribed by them, and these again opened new paths to further inquiries.

Above all men applied themselves in independent zeal to the knowledge of nature. For a moment men wavered between an acquiescence in the mysteries attributed to natural phenomena and the bold, deep-searching examination of those phenomena; but the love of science soon prevailed. An attempt was already made to produce a rational classification of the vegetable kingdom. In Padua, one professor of anatomy was called "the Columbus of the human body!" Inquirers marched boldly forward in all directions, and knowledge was no longer restricted to the works of the ancients.

It followed, if I am not mistaken, as a matter of course that antiquity, being no longer studied with so exclusive an attention as regarded the subject, could no longer exert its earlier influence with reference to form.

Writers of learned works began now to think principally of accumulating material. In the beginning of the century, Cortesius had embodied the essence of the scholastic philosophy, in spite of the intractable nature of his subject, in a well-written classical work, full of wit and spirit. But now, the subject of mythology, well calculated to call forth and to repay the most genial and imaginative treatment, was handled by one Natal Conti in a dull and uninviting quarto. This author also wrote a history composed almost entirely of opinions quoted directly from the ancients; the passages whence he has borrowed being cited, but he is devoid of any sense for essential portrayal. His contemporaries thought it sufficient to amass the material as facts. We may safely affirm that a work like the Annals of Baronius, so entirely destitute of form—written in Latin, yet without one trace of beauty or elegance even in detached phrases—could not ever have been conceived of at the commencement of the century.

Nor was this departure from the track of the ancients, in

science, in form, and in expression, the only change. Others took place in all the social habits of the nation; changes by which an incalculable influence was exercised both on all literary and artistic endeavor.

Republican and independent Italy, on whose peculiar circumstances the early development of the spirit itself had depended, was now no more. All the freedom and simplicity of spiritual intercourse proper to the earlier days had departed. It is worthy of note that titles came into use at this time. As early as the year 1520, it was remarked with disgust that everybody desired to be called "Sir": this was attributed to the influence of the Spaniards. About the year 1550, the old forms of address, so noble in their simplicity, were encumbered, whether in speech or writing, by ponderous epithets of honor. At the end of the century, duke and marquis were the prevailing titles. All wished to possess them; every man would fain be "Excellency." Nor are we permitted to consider this a mere trifle. Even in the present day, when this system of titles has become outdated, they still have their effect; how much more then when all were new? In every other respect also, society became more rigid, stiff, and exclusive. The cheerful easy tone of manner, the frank intercourse of earlier times were gone.

Whatever the cause, even if it were a change founded on the nature of the soul, it is clear that as early as the middle of the century a different spirit pervaded all manifestations; new wants were making themselves felt in the external forms, as in the living essence of society.*

This essential change, this infusion of a different spirit, may be traced through most of the productions of that period.

If the longer poems of Alamanni and Bernardo Tasso are tedious and uninviting, this does not proceed entirely from the absence of talent, particularly in the case of the latter. But this very conception is cold. In compliance with the demands of a public that was certainly not very virtuous, but had put on manners of serious sedateness, both these writers chose immaculate heroes. Bernardo Tasso selected Amadis.* The hero of Alamanni was Giron le Courtoys, the mirror of all knightly virtues. His express purpose was to show youth by this example, how hunger and night-watching, cold and heat, were to be endured; how arms should be borne; how justice and piety were best to be exemplified; how enemies were to be forgiven, and mercy extended to all. Proceeding with this as their moral and didactic aim entirely after the manner of Berni, and intentionally divesting the fable of its poetic basis, the result they have gained is a work of infinite prolixity and insipid dullness.

The nation would seem, if we may venture the expression, to have worked out and used up all the poetic conceptions inherited from its bygone history and from the ideas proper to the Middle Ages. It had even lost the power of comprehending those conceptions. Something new was sought for, but the creative genius would not come forth, nor did the life of the day present any fresh material. Up to the middle of the century, Italian prose, from its nature didactic, was yet imaginative, lifelike, flexible, and graceful. Gradually prose also became rigid and cold.*

In this state of things—when antiquity was deserted, when its forms were no longer imitated, when its science was left in the background and far overpassed, when the old national poetry and all religious modes of conception were despised and rejected by literature and art—the resuscitation of the Church commenced. She obtained the mastery over the minds of men, either with their consent or in spite of their resistance, producing a radical change in all literary and artistic being.

The Church exercised, unless I am much mistaken, quite a different influence on science than on the arts.†

The investigation of physics and of natural history was at that time almost inseparably connected with philosophical inquiry. The whole system of ideas as previously accepted was called in question; there was indeed a great tendency in the Italians of this epoch to search and to advance—what noble anticipation! Who shall say where this might have led? But the Church set up a barrier over which they must not pass; woe to him who should be found beyond it!

That the restoration of Catholicism produced unfavorable effects on science it is impossible to deny. Poetry and art on the contrary received benefit from its renovation. A living subject, a prolific material was needful to them, and this they once more received from the Church.[11]

As regarded one art, only, did it long remain doubtful whether or not it could be made subservient to the purposes of the Church.

This was music, which toward the middle of the sixteenth century had become lost in the most artificial intricacies. Variations, imitations, riddles, and fugues formed the reputation of composers; the meaning of the words was disregarded. Masses of that period may be found in great number, of which the themes are furnished by well-known profane melodies. The human voice was treated as a mere instrument.

No wonder that the Council of Trent should take offense at the introduction of music thus arranged in the churches. In consequence of the discussion there commenced, Pius IV appointed a commission to inquire into the subject and to settle definitely whether music should be tolerated in the divine service, or not. The decision was very doubtful. The Church required that the words sung should be intelligible, and that the musical expression should be in harmony with the sense. The musicians asserted that this was unattainable according to the rules of their art. Cardinal Borromeo was in the commission, and the known rigor of that eminent churchman rendered an adverse decision extremely probable.

Happily the right man once more presented himself, and he appeared at the right moment.

Among the Roman composers of that day was Pier Luigi Palestrina. This master was married, and the severity of Paul IV had driven him on that account from the papal chapel. After his expulsion he lived retired and forgotten in a wretched hut among the vineyards of Monte Celio. He was a spirit who could not yield to adverse fortune. Particularly he devoted himself in this abandonment to his art with a singleness of purpose that secured the originality of his conceptions and the free action of that creative force with which he was endowed. It was here that he wrote the

[11] Pages 340–344 have been omitted.

"Improperie" which to this day ennoble the solemnities of Good Friday in the Sistine Chapel. The profound significance of a scriptural text, its symbolic import, its power to move the soul, and its application to religion have perhaps in no instance been more truly appreciated by any composer.

If the experiment whether his method were applicable to the grand and comprehensive purposes of the mass could be successfully made by any man, that man was Palestrina; to him accordingly the commission entrusted it.

Deeply conscious that the life or death of the grand music of the mass was now depending on this trial, it was with self-conscious tension of all his powers that the composer proceeded to his task. The words, "O Lord, open mine eyes," were found written on his manuscript.

His success was not immediate; the first two attempts failed. At length, however, in propitious moments the mass known as "the mass of Pope Marcellus" was completed. All expectation was far surpassed by this composition. Full of simple melody, it will yet bear comparison in rich variety with any work preceding it. Choruses separate and again blend. The meaning of the words received the most eloquent expression. The Kyrie is all submission, the Agnus humility, the Credo majesty. Pope Pius IV, before whom it was performed, was enchanted. He compared it with those heavenly melodies that St. John may have heard in his ecstatic trance.

The question was set at rest forever by this one great example; a path was opened, pursuing which, the most beautiful and most touching works, even to those who are not of the Roman creed, have been produced. Who can listen to them without enthusiasm? Nature herself seems to have acquired melody and voice. It is as if the elements spoke; and the tones, breathing through universal life, poured forth in blended harmony of adoration—now undulating, like the waves of the sea, now rising in songs of triumph to the skies. Amidst the consenting sympathies of creation, the soul is borne upward to the region of religious entrancement.

It was precisely this art, at one time alienated more completely perhaps than any other from the Church and her service, that was now to become one of her most efficient handmaids. Few things could more effectively promote the interests of Catholicism. Even in her dogmas, the Church, if we are not mistaken, had embodied some portion of that enthusiasm and reverie which form the leading characteristic of her devotional books. Spiritual sentimentality and rapture were favorite subjects for poetry and painting. Music—more direct, more penetrating, more irresistable than any other exposition or any other art—now embodied the prevailing tendency in language more pure and appropriate, fascinating and subjecting the minds of men.

The Curia

While all the elements of social life and of intellectual activity were seized and transformed by the ecclesiastical spirit, the Court of Rome, in which these varying elements met, was also greatly changed.

This change was remarked under Paul IV, and it was essentially promoted by the example of Pius V. Under Gregory XIII it became palpable to all. "Several pontiffs in succession have been men of blameless lives," says Paolo Tiepolo in 1576, "and this has contributed immeasurably to the welfare of the Church, for all other men have become better, or at least have assumed the appearance of being so. Cardinals and prelates attend diligently at the mass; their households are careful to avoid whatever might give offence. The whole city has indeed put off its former recklessness of manner. People are all much more Christian in life and habit than they formerly were. It may even be safely affirmed that in matters of religion Rome is not far from as high a degree of perfection as human nature is permitted to attain."

Nor are we by any means to conclude that the court was composed of prayerful simpletons. It was formed, on the contrary, of distinguished men; but these men had in a high degree assimilated themselves to the rigorous tone of manner and opinion prevailing in the Church. If we consider the Papal Court as it appeared under Sixtus V, we find many among its cardinals who had taken a considerable share in the politics of the world.[12] But from the very nature of this court it resulted inevitably that the most eager struggle after worldly greatness was mingled with the general effort to promote religious interests.

The Curia was not an ecclesiastical institution only; it had to rule a State of its own directly, and indirectly a large part of the world. In proportion as men acquired part in the exercise of this power, they also acquired consideration, riches, influence, and whatever else men usually desire. Human nature could not so entirely change that men should limit themselves to spiritual weapons alone in their efforts to attain the great prizes of society and of the state. Matters proceeded in Rome as at any other court, but with very peculiar modifications imposed by the nature of the arena.

The population of Rome was then more fluctuating than that of any city in the world. Under Leo X it had risen to more than 80,000 souls. The severe measures of Paul drove so many to flight, that in his pontificate it sank to 45,000. In a few years after his death it was found to be increased to 70,000, and under Sixtus V it rose to more than 100,000. The most peculiar circumstance was that the fixed residents bore no proportion to these numbers. To few of its inhabitants was the city a home; their abode in it was rather a long sojourn than a permanent citizenship. It might be said to resemble a fair or diet, without stability or duration, devoid of links of family or kindred. Many were there simply because no road to preferment was open to them in the land of their birth. Wounded pride drove one man thither, boundless ambition impelled another; some came believing they found more liberty in Rome than elsewhere. But the grand object of all was to advance their own interest in their own manner.

These varying classes did not become amalgamated into one body. The different nations were still so numerous and so distinct that the diversities of national and provincial character were clearly perceptible. The courteous and observant Lombard was

---

[12] Pages 347–351 have been omitted.

readily distinguished from the Genoese, who expected to accomplish all things by his money. Nor was it difficult to discover the Venetian, ever seeking to penetrate the secrets of others. The frugal and talkative Florentine met here with the sagacious Romagnese, whose eyes were ever bent with instinctive prudence on the path by which his interests might best be secured. The ceremonious and exacting Neapolitan came, as did the simply mannered native of the North, remarked for his love of comfort. Even the learned German Clavius was the subject of many a jest, provoked by the abundance of his two substantial breakfasts. The Frenchman kept himself much apart and relinquished his national habits with more difficulty than any others. The Spaniard, full of personal pretense and projects of ambition, stalked onward, wrapping his cloak about him and casting looks of scorn on all the rest.

In this court there was no position so eminent but the most obscure individual might aspire to hold it. People delighted to recall the words of John XXIII, who, being asked why he was going to Rome, said "he meant to be pope," and pope he became. It was from a station among the humblest that Pius V and Sixtus V had just been exalted to the supreme dignity. Each man believed himself capable of all, and hoped for everything.

It was a remark frequently made in those days, and a perfectly just one, that there was a sort of republicanism in the character of the prelacy and Curia; this consisted in the circumstance that all might aspire to all. Examples were continually presented of men whose origin was most obscure attaining to positions of the first eminence. The constitution of this republic was nevertheless very singular; to the rights of the many stood opposed the absolute power of one, from whose arbitrary decision it was that all promotion and every advantage must be derived. And who was this one? It was he who, by some combination on which it was impossible to calculate, had come forth as victor from the conflict of election. Of small importance hitherto, he was suddenly invested with the supreme authority. Persuaded that he had been raised by the Holy Spirit to this height of dignity, he was but slightly tempted to dissemble his disposition and inclination; thus the pontificate usually commenced with some profound change.

All legates and governors of provinces were replaced. There were certain appointments in the capital that fell as matters of course to the nephews or other kinsmen of the reigning pope, for even when nepotism was under restraint, as was the case in the times we are describing, there was no pontiff who did not promote his confidants and adherents. He would naturally feel indisposed to resign the society of those with whom he had previously been passing his life. The secretary who had long served the cardinal Montalto was most acceptable to that prelate when he became Sixtus V. The adherents of their opinions also were sure to be brought forward by each new pope. Thus did every accession to the papal chair cause a complete change in all prospects and expectations, in the approaches to power, and in ecclesiastical no less than in temporal dignity. Commendone says it was as if "a city in which the palace of the sovereign had been transferred to a new site, and all the streets turned toward this new center. How many abodes must be demolished? How often must the road be carried through a palace; new passages are opened, and thoroughfares hitherto unfrequented are enlivened by the crowd." The alterations taking place on these occasions, and the degree of stability possessed by the new arrangements are thus not badly described.

But from these peculiarities there necessarily resulted a consequence very singular in its character.

From the fact that a pope attained the sovereignty when much older than other monarchs, these mutations were so frequent that a new change might at any moment be expected. Power might be instantly placed in other hands. This made people live as in a perpetual game of chance, wherein nothing could be calculated but everything might be hoped for.

To attain promotion, to gain advancement, as everyone desired and trusted to do, this would depend on the degree of personal favor that each could command. But where all personal influence was in so perpetual a fluctuation, the calculations of ambition must necessarily assume a similar character, and sometimes employ very extraordinary devices.*

We have seen the dignity, the seriousness, the religious zeal prevailing in the Roman Court; we now remark its worldly aspect, ambition, avarice, dissimulation, and craft.

If it were our purpose to pronounce the eulogy of the Papal See, we should have insisted on the first only of the two elements composing it. Were we disposed to inveigh against it, we should have displayed only the second. But whoever will raise himself to the level from which a pure and unprejudiced view can be obtained will arrive at an exact perception of the whole subject. He will see both these elements, but he will also perceive that both are rendered inevitable by the nature of man and the condition of things.

The period of the world's history that we have just been considering was one in which the prevalent mode of opinion made pressing demand for propriety, purity of life, and religious fervor. This state of public feeling coincided with the principle of the court, whose position, as regards the rest of the world, is determined by these qualities. It followed of necessity that power and eminence were most certainly secured by men whose characters were in accordance with this demand. Were it otherwise, public opinion would not only be untrue to itself, it would destroy its own existence. But that the advantages of fortune should happen to be so immediately consequent on the possession of spiritual qualities is indeed the most seductive allurement that could be offered by the spirit of this world.

We cannot doubt the sincerity of these qualities and sentiments not unfrequently described by our observant and discreet authorities; but there were doubtless many by whom the mere appearance of these qualities was adopted for the furtherance of their fortunes, while in others the worldly tendency may have insinuated itself together with those of more lofty import to become intermingled in the dim uncertainty of motives imperfectly developed.

The process we have seen taking place in art and literature may be traced also in the Curia. Here also a desertion from what the Church demands was most apparent; there was a laxity approaching paganism in the prevailing modes of thought. But the development of world history which we have just described reawakened the principle of the Church, aroused the energies of society as with a new breath of life, and imparted an altered tone to the existence of the times. What a difference between Ariosto and Tasso, Giulio Romano and Guercino, Pomponazzo and Patrizi! A great epoch lies between them. They have, nevertheless, something in common, and the later is linked by certain points of contact with the earlier. With its ancient forms the Curia also retained many component parts of its old nature, yet this did not prevent it from being animated by a new spirit. What could not be wholly transferred and assimilated to itself was at least urged forward by the force of the impulse which that spirit communicated.

While contemplating these commingling elements, I recall to mind a scene of nature that may serve to bring this state of things more vividly before us by the kind of similitude it presents.

At Terni, the Nera is seen tranquilly approaching through wood and field; it proceeds across the distant valley in calm, unruffled course. From the other side comes rushing the Velino; pressed between rocks it foams onward with irresistible speed, till at length its mass of waters are dashed down headlong in magnificent falls that sparkle and glitter with a myriad changing hues. These reach the peaceful Nera; they at once communicate their own wild commotion, ranging and foaming; the mingled waters then rush forward on their eager and hurried course.

It was thus that the whole being of society, all literature, and every art, received a new impulse from the reawakened spirit of the Catholic Church. The Curia was at once devout and restless, spiritual and warlike: on the one side replete with dignity, pomp, and ceremony; on the other, unparalleled for calculating subtlety and insatiable love of power. Its piety and ambition, reposing on the idea of an exclusive orthodoxy, coincide and act in harmony for the production of one end—universal domination.

BOOK V

COUNTER-REFORMATION

FIRST PERIOD, 1563–1589

In the history of a nation or power, there is no problem more difficult than that of appreciating correctly the connection of its particular circumstances with those of the world in general.

It is true that the individual life of a nation is determined by causes peculiar to itself, inherent in its nature, and displaying a characteristic consistency through all ages. But each community is subjected to the action of general influences by which its progress is powerfully affected.

In this conflict of forces, the character presented by modern Europe may be said to have its basis. Nations and states are separated forever, but at the same time are knit together in indissoluble community. There is no national history of which universal history does not form an important portion. So necessary in itself, so all-embracing is the course of the ages, that even the most powerful of states appears but as a member of the universal commonwealth, involved in and ruled by its destinies. Whoever has earnestly sought to comprehend the history of any people as a whole, to contemplate its progress without prejudice or illusion, will have experienced the difficulties arising from this cause. In the several impulses of a nation's progressive existence we discern the different currents that form the sum of human destiny.

Occasionally, however, in the flux of the ages one or another of the powers may give its impulse to the universal course of events, representing some principle of the same in pre-eminent fashion. The power thus in action takes so influential a part in the collective operations of the century, it enters into relations so intimate with all the powers of the world, that its history, in a certain sense, expands into universal history. Such was the epoch upon which the papacy entered at the close of the Council of Trent.

Convulsed to its core, endangered in the very groundwork of its being, it had not only maintained itself, but found means to gain renewed force. In the two southern peninsulas, all influences hostile to its ascendancy had been promptly expelled, all the elements of thought and action had been once more gathered to itself and pervaded by its own spirit. It now conceived the idea of subduing those who had revolted in all other parts of the world. Rome once more became a conquering power. Projects were formed and enterprises engaged in, recalling those proceeding from the Seven Hills in ancient times and during the Middle Ages.

The history of the renovated papacy would be but imperfectly understood did we limit our attention to its center only. Its essential importance is best perceived by observing its operations on the world in general.

Let us begin by taking a review of the strength and position of its opponents.

State Of Protestantism
About The Year 1563

On this side of the Alps and Pyrenees the opinions of Protestantism had made vigorous and unceasing progress up to the time when the Council of Trent closed its last sessions; they extended their dominion far and wide over the Germanic and Slavonic and Romanic nations.

Among the Scandinavian kingdoms, the tenets of the Protestants had established themselves all the more immutably from the fact that their introduction was coincident with that of new dynasties and with the consequent remodelling of all political institutions. They were received with delight from the very first, as they bore in their nature some natural affinity with the national disposition. Bugenhagen, the founder of Lutheranism in Denmark, can find no words that suffice to depict the enthusiasm with which his sermons were listened to. "Even on work-days," as he expresses it, "before dawn the people were eagerly waiting, and on holidays they were in attendance through the whole day." Protestant tenets had now made their way to the most remote countries. It is not known by what agency the Faeroe Islands were rendered Protestant, so easily was the change effected. In Iceland the last representatives of Catholicism had disappeared by the year 1552, and a Lutheran bishopric was founded at Wyborg in the year 1554. The Swedish governors were accompanied by Lutheran preachers to the most distant shores of Lapland. Gustavus Vasa exhorts his heirs in his will, made in 1560, to hold fast by the evangelical doctrines, to inculcate the same on their most remote successors, and to admit no false teachers. He makes this almost a condition to the inheritance of the crown. On our coast of the Baltic, Lutheran opinions were also predominant, at least among such of the inhabitants as used the Germanic tongue. Prussia had given the first example of secularizing church property on a grand scale. This was followed by Livonia in 1561; the first condition made by the province on its submission to Poland was that it should be at liberty to abide by the Confession of Augsburg. The connection of the Jagellon kings with countries whose adherence to their rule was secured only by the maintenance of Protestant principles was a check on those princes which prevented their opposing any determined resistance to the progress of Lutheran tenets. The more important cities of Prussian Poland were confirmed in the exercise of their religion according to the Lutheran ritual by express charters granted in the years 1557 and 1558. The smaller towns received privileges yet more explicit some short time after; they being more exposed to attacks from the powerful bishops. A large part of the nobles in Poland proper had been won over to the Protestant confession, which they found more in harmony with that feeling of independence awakened and maintained by the constitution of their State. "A Polish noble is not subject to the king—shall he then be subject to the Pope?" was the question they asked. Things went so far in this country that Protestants gained possession of episcopal sees; and under Sigismund Augustus, they had even obtained the majority in the Senate. That sovereign was undoubtedly Catholic, but what people believed in his court or kingdom seemed but little to disturb his quiet, nor did he show any disposition to embitter the close of his life by a contest with opinions making so vigorous a progress.

An attempt at opposition of this kind had certainly produced no very encouraging results in the neighboring dominions of Hungary. The Diet had constantly refused to pass the resolutions unfavorable to Protestant opinions that were pressed on it from time to time by Ferdinand I. In the year 1554 a Lutheran was elected palatine of the empire, and concessions were soon afterward extorted in favor of the Helvetic Confession in the valley of Erlau. Transylvania was altogether separated from the Catholic Church. The ecclesiastical possessions in that country were confiscated by a formal decree of the Diet, and the princes even appropriated the greater part of the tithes.

We now come to our fatherland, where the new form of the Church had taken its origin from the peculiar constitution of the national spirit, had maintained itself through long and perilous wars, had achieved a legal existence in the empire, and was now in the act of occupying the various territories. Already this process had been in great measure accomplished. In northern Germany, where the Protestant tenets had originated, they were entirely paramount. They had gained permanent ascendancy in those districts of southern Germany where they had been early introduced and had besides extended their influence far and wide beyond these limits.† Protestantism had gained a decided ascendancy throughout Germany, from the east to the west and from the north to the south. The nobility had from the first been sympathetic; the public functionaries, already numerous and highly respected, were trained in the new creed; the common people would hear no more of certain articles once insisted on as matters of faith—the fires of purgatory, for example—nor of certain ceremonies, as pilgrimages; no convent could maintain itself, and none dared to exhibit the relics of saints. A Venetian ambassador calculated in the year 1558 that a tenth part only of the German people still adhered to the ancient religion.*

Furthermore Catholicism could not expect much from the future for itself.

Protestant opinions were predominant in the universities and other schools. The old champions of Catholicism, who had taken the field against Luther and distinguished themselves in religious controversy, were dead or far advanced in years, and no young men competent to occupy their places had arisen. Twenty years had elapsed since any student in the University of Vienna had taken priests' orders. Even in Ingolstadt, which was so pre-eminently Catholic, no qualified candidates of the faculty of theology presented themselves for important offices that hitherto had always been filled by ecclesiastics. The city of Cologne established a school with endowments, but when all the arrangements were completed it appeared that the new regent was a Protestant. A university was founded by Cardinal Otto Truchsess in his town of Dillingen for the express purpose of resisting the Protestant opinions. It flourished for some years under the care of certain eminent Spanish theologians, but when these had departed no learned Catholic could be found to take their places, which were at once occupied by Protestants. At this period the teachers in Germany were Protestant with very few exceptions. All the youth of the country sat at their feet and imbibed hatred of the pope with the first rudiments of learning.

Such was the state of things in the north and east of Europe—Catholicism was utterly banished from many places; it was subdued and despoiled in all; and while endeavoring to defend itself in these regions, still more formidable enemies were pressing forward to assail it in the west and south.

For the Calvinistic beliefs were without doubt more decidedly opposed to the Roman tenets than were the doctrines of Luther, and it was precisely at the period we are now contemplating that Calvinism took possession of the minds of men with irresistible force.

It had arisen on the borders of Italy, Germany, and France, and had extended in all directions. Toward the east, in Germany, Hungary, and Poland, it constituted a subordinate but very important element of the Protestant movement. In Western Europe it had already raised itself to independent power.†

Under these circumstances new energies were awakened in the earlier oppositions to the faith of Rome. In the year 1562 the Moravian brethren were formally acknowledged by Maximilian II, and they availed themselves of this fortunate circumstance to elect a large number of new pastors in their synods—some accounts say 188. In the year 1561 the Duke of Savoy saw himself compelled to accord new privileges even to the poor communities of Waldenses in the mountains. To the most remote and neglected corner of Europe Protestant doctrines had extended their invigorating power. How immeasurable an empire had they conquered within the span of forty years! From Iceland even to the Pyrenees—from Finland to the summits of the Italian Alps. Even on the southern side of these last mountains, opinions analogous to Protestantism had, as we have seen, once prevailed—they embraced the whole territory of the Latin Church. A large majority of the upper classes, and of the men most active in public life, were attached to them. Whole nations were devoted with enthusiasm to these tenets, which had entirely changed the constitution of states. This is all the more extraordinary because the Protestant creed was by no means a mere negation of the papacy—a simple renunciation. It was in the highest degree positive, a renovation of Christian sentiments and principles that govern human life even to the most profound recesses of the soul.

The Forces Of The Papacy

The papacy and Catholicism had long maintained themselves against these advances of their enemy—in an attitude of defense, it is true, but passive only; upon the whole they were compelled to endure them.

Affairs now assumed a different aspect.

We have considered that internal development by which Catholicism began the work of her own restoration. It may be affirmed generally that a vital and active force was again manifested, that the Church had regenerated her dogma in the spirit of the age, and had established reforms in accordance with the demands of the times. The religious tendencies which had appeared in southern Europe were not suffered to become hostile to herself. She adopted them and gained the mastery of their movements;

thus she renewed her powers and infused fresh vigor into her system. The Protestant spirit alone had hitherto filled the theatre of the world with results that held the minds of men enthralled. Another spirit—equally deserving of esteem perhaps, if regarded from an elevated point of view, though of decidedly opposite character—now entered the lists, displaying similar power to make the minds of men its own and to kindle them into activity.

The influence of the restored Catholic system was first established in the two southern peninsulas, but this was not accomplished without extreme severity. The Spanish Inquisition received the aid of that lately revived in Rome; every movement of Protestantism was violently suppressed. But at the same time those tendencies of the inward life which renovated Catholicism claimed and enchained as its own, were peculiarly powerful in those countries. The sovereigns also attached themselves to the interests of the Church.

It was of the greatest importance that Philip II, the most powerful of all, adhered so decidedly to the papacy. With the pride of a Spaniard, by whom unimpeachable Catholicism was regarded as the sign of a purer blood and more noble descent, he rejected every adverse opinion. The character of his policy was, however, not wholly governed by mere personal feeling. From remote times, and more especially since the regulations established by Isabella, the royal dignity in Spain had assumed an ecclesiastical character. In every province the royal authority was strengthened by the addition of spiritual power. Deprived of the Inquisition, it would not have sufficed to govern the kingdom. Even in his American possessions, the King appeared above all in the light of a disseminator of the Christian and Catholic faith. This was the bond by which all his territories were united in obedience to his rule; he could not have abandoned it without incurring real danger. The extension of Huguenot opinions in the south of France caused the utmost alarm in Spain. The Inquisition believed itself bound to redoubled vigilance.* The papal nuncio considered the result of the Council then assembled of equal importance to the royal as to the papal authority. "For the obedience paid to the King," he remarks, "and his whole government, depend on the Inquisition;

should this lose its authority, insurrections would immediately follow."

The power possessed by Philip in the Netherlands secured to the southern system an immediate influence over the whole of Europe. But besides this, all was far from being lost in other countries. The Emperor, the Kings of France and Poland, with the Duke of Bavaria, still adhered to the Catholic Church. On all sides there were spiritual princes whose expiring zeal might be reanimated; there were also many places where Protestant opinions had not yet made their way among the mass of the people. The majority of the peasantry throughout France, Poland, and even Hungary still remained Catholic. Paris, which even in those days exercised a powerful influence over the other French towns, had not yet been affected by the new doctrines. In England, a great part of the nobility and commons were still Catholic; and in Ireland the whole of the ancient native population remained in the old faith. Protestantism had gained no admission into the Tyrolese or Swiss Alps, nor had it made any great progress among the peasantry of Bavaria. Canisius compared the Tyrolese and Bavarians with the two tribes of Israel, "who alone remained faithful to the Lord." The internal causes on which this pertinacity, this immovable attachment to tradition, among nations so dissimilar, was founded might well repay a more minute examination. A similar constancy was exhibited in the Walloon provinces of the Netherlands.

And now the papacy resumed a position in which it could once more gain the mastery of all these inclinations and bind them indissolubly to itself. Although it had experienced great changes, it still possessed the inestimable advantage of having all the externals of the past and the habit of obedience on its side. In the Council so prosperously concluded, the popes had even gained an accession of that authority which it had been the purpose of the temporal powers to restrict and had strengthened their influence over the national churches. They had, moreover, abandoned that temporal policy by which they had formerly involved Italy and all Europe in confusion. They attached themselves to Spain with perfect confidence and without any reservations, fully returning the devotion evinced by that kingdom to the Roman Church. The

Italian principality, the enlarged dominions of the pontiff, served primarily to promote the success of his ecclesiastical enterprises, while the interests of the universal Catholic Church were for some time essentially promoted by the surplus of its revenues.

Thus strengthened internally, thus supported by powerful adherents, and by the idea of which they were the representatives, the popes exchanged the defensive position with which they had hitherto been forced to content themselves with that of assailants. The attack that resulted, its progress and consequences, it is the principal object of this work to consider.

A boundless scene opens before us. The action is proceeding in many places at the same time, and we are called on to direct our attention to the most varying and widely separated quarters of the world.

Religious activity is intimately connected with political impulses; combinations are formed which embrace the whole world and under whose influence the struggle for mastery succeeds or fails. We shall fix our attention the more earnestly on the great events of general politics, because they often coincide exactly with the results of the religious conflict.

But we must not confine ourselves to generalities. If the conquests of the sword require some native sympathies with the victor on the part of the conquered for their achievement, still more indispensable are these sympathies to spiritual conquest. We must examine the interests of the several countries to their utmost depths in order to attain full comprehension of those internal movements by which the designs of Rome were facilitated.

There is here presented to us so great an abundance and variety of events and expressions of life that we have to fear the impossibility of comprehending the whole under one view. The state of things before us has its basis fixed on kindred principles, and occasionally exhibits great crises, but it also presents an infinite variety of phenomena.[13]

---

[13] The following sections have been omitted: "The First Jesuit Schools in Germany"; "Counter-Reformation in Germany" (pages 17–38).

Troubles In The Netherlands
And In France

While the efforts of Catholicism were producing results important and extensive also in Germany, they were applied in the Netherlands and in France, though in a manner entirely different.

The principal distinction was that a powerful central authority existed in each of these last-named countries, which took immediate part in every movement, assumed the guidance of all religious enterprises, and was itself directly affected by any opposition offered to a religious undertaking.

There was, consequently, more unity in affairs, a more perfect combination of means, and more effectual energy of action.

The many and varied measures taken by Philip to enforce obedience in the Netherlands at the beginning of his reign are well known. He was compelled to abandon most of them, one after another, but he clung with stubborn tenacity and inflexible rigor to all that had been framed for the maintenance of Catholicism and religious uniformity.

By the institution of new bishoprics and archbishoprics, he completely remodelled the ecclesiastical constitution of the country. In these proceedings he would permit himself to be checked by no remonstrance or appeal to the rights which he was unquestionably invading.

These bishoprics acquired redoubled importance from the increased severity enforced on the discipline of the Church by the Council of Trent. Philip II had adopted the decrees of the Council after a short deliberation and had then proclaimed them in the Netherlands. The daily life of the people, who had hitherto found means to avoid any violent restraints, was now to be placed under the most rigorous supervision and subjected to the minute observance of forms from which they had believed themselves about to be entirely emancipated.

In addition to this came the penal laws, of which so many had been issued against the Netherlands under the preceding government, and the zeal of the inquisitors, whom the newly erected tribunal of Rome was daily stimulating to increased activity.

The people of the Netherlands left no means untried that might induce the King to moderate his rigor, and he did appear at times to be more leniently disposed. Count Egmont thought he had received assurance of this during his sojourn in Spain; it was, nevertheless, scarcely to be hoped for. We have already observed that the authority of Philip throughout his dominions reposed on a religious basis. Had he made concessions to the inhabitants of the Netherlands, they would have been demanded in Spain where he could not possibly have granted them. He, too, was subjected— a fact we must not refuse to acknowledge—to the pressure of an inevitable necessity. This was, besides, the period when the accession and first measures of Pius V were exciting increased zeal through all Catholic Christendom. Philip II felt an unusual inclination toward this pontiff and gave an attentive ear to his exhortations. The attack of the Turks on Malta had just been repulsed, and the more bigoted party, enemies to the Protestant Netherlands, may have availed themselves of the impression produced by this victory, as the Prince of Orange suspected, to lead the King into some violent resolution. Let it suffice to say that toward the end of the year 1565 an edict was promulgated surpassing all preceding ones in severity.

The penal enactments—the decrees of the Council and those of the provincial synods held subsequently—were to be enforced without remission; the inquisitors were to have sole jurisdiction over religious offenses, all civil authorities being enjoined to render them assistance. A commissioner was appointed in every province to watch over the execution of this edict with orders to give a report every three months.

The effect of these decrees was manifestly to introduce a spiritual government, if not exactly like that of Spain, yet, at least, resembling the rule of Italy.

Among the first results that ensued was that the people took up arms. The destruction of images began, and the whole country was in the wildest commotion. There was a moment when the authorities were forced to yield, but, as is usual in such cases, acts of violence defeated their own end. The moderate and peaceable inhabitants were alarmed and gave assistance to the government. Victory remained with the Governess of the Netherlands, and having taken possession of the rebellious towns, she found herself in a position to impose an oath on the public officers, and even on the feudatories of the King, by which they formally pledged themselves to the maintenance of the Catholic faith and to an armed resistance to heretics.

Even this did not suffice for Philip II. It was that unhappy moment when the catastrophe of his son Don Carlos occurred; he was more than usually severe and unbending. The Pope repeated his exhortations that no concession to the disadvantage of Catholicism should be made, and Philip assured his Holiness that he would not suffer the root of a single noxious plant to remain in the Netherlands; either he would uphold the Catholic faith in all its purity or would consent to lose those provinces altogether. For the better fulfillment of these intentions he sent his best general, the Duke of Alva, with a formidable army into the Netherlands, even after the troubles had been allayed.

Let us at least examine the moving principle by which the proceedings of Alva were regulated.

The Duke was convinced that all might be arranged in a country disturbed by revolutionary movements, when once the chiefs had been disposed of. That Charles V, after so many important victories, had been very nearly driven from the German Empire, he attributed to the forbearance of that monarch, who had spared his enemies when they had fallen into his hands. Frequent reference has been made to the alliance entered into between the French and Spaniards at the Congress of Bayonne, and to the measures concerted there, but of all that has been said of this Convention, thus much only is certain, that the Duke of Alva exhorted the French Queen to disembarrass herself of the Huguenot leaders by whatever means she could find. What he then advised, he now made no scruple of putting in practice. Philip had entrusted him with some blank warrants bearing the royal signature. The first use he made of them was to arrest Egmont and Horn, whom he assumed to have been implicated in the recent insurrections. "May it please your sacred Catholic Majesty," he begins the letter which he wrote to the King on this occasion, and which seems to imply that he had no express command for the arrest of the counts, "on my arrival in Brussels I procured the necessary information from the proper quarter, and thereupon secured the person of Count Egmont. I have also caused Count Horn and some others to be imprisoned." It will, perhaps, be asked, why a year later he sentenced these prisoners to be executed? It was not because he had received proof of their guilt from the trial; the blame attached to them was rather that of not having prevented the disturbances than of having caused them. Nor was it by command of the King, who rather left it to Alva to decide on the execution, or not, as he should consider expedient. The cause of their death was as follows: a small body of Protestants had made an incursion into the country. They had effected nothing of moment, but had gained some little advantage at Heiligerlee, and the Duke of Arenberg, a general of high reputation in the royal army, had been left dead on the field. In his letters to the King, Alva said that he had perceived the people to be thrown into a ferment by this mischance; that they were becoming bold; and he considered it expedient to show that he was in no wise afraid of them. He wished also to deprive them of any wish they might have to excite new commotions with a view to rescue the prisoners and had, therefore, resolved on permitting the execution to proceed immediately. And thus did these noble men lose their lives, though no guilt worthy of death could be found in them; their sole crime consisted in the defense of the ancient liberties of their country. They were sacrificed, not to any principle of justice, but rather to the momentary considerations of a cruel policy. The Duke remembered Charles V, whose errors he was determined to avoid.

We see that Alva was cruel from principle. Who could hope for mercy from the fearful tribunal that he erected under the name of "Council of Disturbances"? He ruled the provinces by arrests and executions. He razed the houses of the condemned and confiscated their property. He pursued his ecclesiastical designs together with his political purposes. The ancient power of the Estates was reduced to a mere name; Spanish troops occupied the country; and a citadel was erected for them in the most important mercantile city. The Duke insisted with obstinacy on the exaction of the most odious taxes; and in Spain, whence also he drew large sums, people asked with surprise what he could do with all the money. It is, however, true that the country was obedient; no malcontent ventured to move; every trace of Protestantism disappeared; and those who had been driven into neighboring districts remained perfectly still.

"Monsignore," said a member of Philip's Council to the papal nuncio during these events, "are you now satisfied with the proceedings of the King?" "Perfectly satisfied," replied the nuncio, with a smile.

Alva himself believed he had performed a masterstroke, and it was not without contempt that he regarded the French government, which had not been able to make itself master in its own territory.

After some legal concessions to the Protestants in France had been made, a strong reaction against them set in, originating with the magnates who would neither tolerate so substantial a deviation from the established system of faith and life nor give free reign to the existing government. They succeeded in gaining control of the same by persuasion or force and established a change of the leading intentions which was connected with bloody conflicts.

Certainly the Protestants also had mighty and determined leaders who met force with force.

The close connection of Protestantism with the court faction had unquestionably been the circumstance most injurious to its influence. As long as the adherents of reform maintained the peace, everything seemed to be going their way. But when, hurried on by their connection with some of the leaders of faction, they took up arms and committed those acts of violence that are inseparable from a state of warfare, they lost their advantage in public opinion. "What kind of religion is this?" men asked. "Where has Christ commanded the pillage of our neighbor and the shedding of his blood?" The population of Paris was inclined toward the Catholic regent from the very beginning, on account of the overbearing attitude of Condé, the apparent leader of the Huguenots. The population of the city capable of bearing arms was organized as a military body, and the officers appointed to command this force were required above all things to be Catholics. The members of the university and of the Parliament, with the very numerous class of advocates, were compelled to sign a confession of faith, the articles of which were purely Catholic.* All aspects of the city's life were anti-Protestant.

In general, the Catholic spirit of the Frenchmen, in its opposition to the Huguenots, again began to manifest itself vigorously when the Huguenots once again took to their weapons out of fear that they might face a similar lot as was awaiting the Netherlands, and thereby forced an advantageous edict of settlement. A large number of the French towns refused to enforce it. By now Catherine de' Medici, infuriated by the new aggression of the Huguenots, was inclined to assert her power. The example of Alva showed how much could be accomplished by inflexible determination. The Pope continually exhorted her to repress the insolence of the rebels, to arrest their progress, and no longer to endure their existence. At length he accompanied his admonitions by the permission to alienate Church property, by which the treasury gained a million and a half livres. Accordingly, Catherine de' Medici, following the example given the year before by the Governess of the Netherlands, imposed an oath on the French nobility, by which they bound themselves to abjure every engagement contracted without the previous knowledge of the King. She demanded the dismissal of all their magistrates from the cities which were suspected of favoring the new doctrines and assured Philip II in September of the year 1563 that she would tolerate no other religion but the Catholic. Her actions meant war.

The Huguenots also drew their forces together. They too were full of religious zeal. They too gave no quarter and were equally provided with foreign aid. They were nevertheless entirely defeated at Moncontour.*

As had so frequently occurred before, a revulsion of opinion now took place in the Court of France, and though occasioned by trifling circumstances of a personal nature only, this yet brought about great changes in matters of the highest importance.

The King became envious of the honor gained by his brother, the Duke of Anjou, from the defeat of the Huguenots at Moncontour where he had commanded the troops and of the influence acquired by the Duke from the repose he had thus procured for the country. He was confirmed in this feeling by those around him who were equally jealous of Anjou's followers and who feared lest power should go hand in hand with the honor they had acquired. Not only were the advantages gained followed up with the utmost indifference, and after long delay, but in opposition to the strict Catholic party led by Anjou, another and more moderate party appeared at court, which adopted an altogether different policy, made peace with the Huguenots, and invited the Protestant leaders to the court. In the year 1569, the French, in alliance with Spain and the Pope, had sought to overthrow the Queen of England. In the summer of 1572, we see them in league with that Queen to wrest the Netherlands from Spain.

Meanwhile, these changes were too sudden and too imperfectly matured to have consistency or duration. The most violent explosion followed and affairs resumed their previous direction.

There can be no doubt that Catherine de' Medici, while entering with a certain degree of warmth and earnestness into the policy and plans of the dominant party, which favored her interests, so far as they appeared likely to assist in placing her youngest son Alençon on the English throne, was yet concerting the measures requisite for executing a stroke of policy directly opposed to them. She did her utmost to draw the Huguenots to Paris; numerous as ing, but had she still felt wavering, the occurrences of the moment were such as must at once have determined her. The Huguenots were gaining over the King himself; they were apparently supplanting the authority of the Queen Mother, and in this personal they were, they were there surrounded and held in check by a population far more numerous, in a state of military organization, significant intimation to the Pope of her purpose in this proceed- and easily excited to fanaticism. She had previously given a very danger she hesitated no longer. With the irresistible and magic power that she exercised over her children, she aroused all the latent fanaticism of the King. It cost her but a word to make the people take to arms; that word she spoke. Of the eminent Huguenots, each one was pointed out to his personal enemy and given over to his vengeance. Catherine had declared that she desired the death of six men only; the death of these men she would take upon her conscience. The number massacred was fifty thousand.

Thereby all that the Spaniards had perpetrated in the Netherlands was exceeded by the French. What the first brought about gradually, with deliberate calculation and with a certain observance of legal forms, the latter accomplished in the heat of passion in defiance of all forms of law, and by the aid of a populace roused to a fury of fanaticism. The result appeared to be the same. Not one leader was left whose name might serve as a point round which the scattered Huguenots could gather. Many fled, a large number surrendered; place after place returned to attendance on the mass, the preachers were silenced. With pleasure Philip II saw himself imitated and surpassed. He offered Charles IX, who had now earned a right to be called the most Christian King, to assist the completion of his undertaking by the power of his arms. Pope Gregory XIII marked this great event by a solemn procession to the church of San Luigi. The Venetians, who seemed to have no particular interest in the matter, expressed in official dispatches to their ambassadors their satisfaction at "this favor of God."

But can it be possible that crimes of a character so sanguinary ever succeed? Are they not in too flagrant opposition to the more profound mysteries of human events, to the incomprehensible, inviolable principles of the eternal order of the universe which have effect on the inner movements? Men may blind themselves for a time, but they cannot disturb the rules on which their existence reposes, the spiritual law which governs the universe with a necessity inevitable as that which regulates the course of the stars.

Resistance Of The Protestants
In The Netherlands, France, and Germany

Machiavelli advises his prince to execute the cruelties he shall find necessary in rapid succession, but gradually to permit more lenient measures to follow.

It would almost seem that the Spaniards had sought to follow that advice to the letter in their government of the Netherlands.

They appeared to be themselves at length of the opinion that property enough had been confiscated, heads enough struck off, and that the time for clemency had arrived. In the year 1572 the Venetian ambassador at Madrid declares his conviction that the Prince of Orange would obtain his pardon if he would ask for it. The King received the deputies of the Netherlands very favorably when they arrived with a petition for the repeal of the impost of the tenth penny, and even thanked them for their pains. He had determined to recall the Duke of Alva and to replace him by a more clement governor.

But it was now too late. Immediately after the conclusion of that treaty between France and England which had preceded the Massacre of St. Bartholomew, the insurrection broke out. Alva had believed his work at an end, but the struggle was in fact only then beginning. He defeated the enemy whenever he met them in the open field, but in the towns of Holland and Zeeland, where the religious movement had been most profound and where Protestantism had attained to a more effectual organization, he encountered a force of resistance that he could not overcome.

In Haarlem, when all means of supporting life were consumed, even to the grass growing between the stones, the inhabitants resolved to cut their way through the besiegers with their wives and children. The dissensions prevailing in their garrison compelled them at last to surrender, but they had shown that the Spaniards might be resisted. The people of Alkmaar declared themselves for the Prince of Orange at the moment when the enemy appeared before their gates: their defense was as heroic as their resolution, not a man would leave his post, however severely wounded. Before the walls of Alkmaar the Spaniards received their first effective repulse. The country breathed again, and new courage entered the hearts of the people.

The men of Leyden declared that rather than yield, they would devour their left arms to enable themselves to continue the defense with their right. They took the bold resolution of breaking down their dikes and calling on the waves of the North Sea to expel the besiegers. Their misery had reached its utmost extremity when a northwest wind, setting in at the critical moment, laid the country under water to the depth of several feet and drove the enemy away.

The French Protestants had also regained their courage. No sooner did they perceive that their government, notwithstanding the savage massacre it had committed, displayed irresolution, procrastinated, and adopted contradictory measures, than they again took arms and soon war broke out again. La Rochelle and Sancerre defended themselves as Leyden and Alkmaar had done—the preachers of peace were heard exhorting men to arms—women shared in the combat with their husbands and brothers. It was the heroic age of Protestantism in Western Europe.

The acts of cruelty, committed or sanctioned by the most powerful princes, were met by a resistance proceeding from various nameless points, but which had its secret origin in the most profound religious convictions, and which no amount of force could overcome.

It is not our purpose at this time to give the details and follow the vicissitudes of the wars in France and the Netherlands—this would lead us too far from our principal object—they are besides to be found in many other books. It must suffice to say that the Protestants maintained their ground.

In the year 1573, and again in the following years, the French government was repeatedly compelled to enter into negotiations from which the Huguenots gained a renewal of former concessions.

In the Netherlands, the power of the government had fallen to ruin in the year 1576. The Spanish troops not receiving their regular pay were in open insurrection, and all the provinces had united against them, those which had hitherto maintained their allegiance with those which had revolted, the districts remaining in a great measure Catholic with those entirely Protestant. The States-General took the government into their own hands, appointed captains-general, governors, and magistrates, and garrisoned the fortified places with their own troops in place of the King's. The Treaty of Ghent was concluded, by which provinces pledged themselves to expel the Spaniards and keep them out of the country. Philip of Spain sent his brother, who might be considered a Netherlander and fellow countryman, to govern them as Charles V had done: but Don John was not even acknowledged until he had promised to fulfill the principal conditions laid before him. He was compelled to accept the Treaty of Ghent and to dismiss the Spanish troops; and no sooner did he make the first movement to free himself from the restraint that fettered him, than all parties rose against him. He was declared an enemy of the country, and the chiefs of the provinces called another prince of his house to take his place.

The principle of local government now obtained supremacy over the monarchical power, the native authority was victorious over the Spanish rule.*

How changed was the position now held by the Prince of Orange! He had but lately been an exile whose best hope was to obtain pardon; he was now possessed of a well-established power in the northern provinces, was sheriff (*Ruwart*) of Brabant, all-powerful in the Assembly of the States, and acknowledged as their chief and leader by a great religious and political party which was making rapid progress. He was, besides, in close alliance with all the Protestants of Europe, and more especially with his neighbors, the Germans.

The aggressions of the Catholics were resisted in Germany also with a force on the Protestant part which seemed to promise the most important results.

The effects of this resistance were apparent in the general transactions of the empire, in the assemblies of the electors, and in the imperial Diets, although there the German system of conducting affairs prevented any adequate results from appearing.

They were most sensibly felt, as had been the aggressions that had called forth the resistance, in the several territories and distinct sovereignties into which Germany was divided.

It was in the spiritual principalities, as we have seen, that the question was most earnestly debated. There was scarcely one wherein the prince had not attempted to restore Catholicism to its ancient supremacy. The Protestants, who felt their own strength, retorted with efforts equally comprehensive and labored with equal energy to bring the ecclesiastical sovereignties themselves to their own opinions.

In the year 1577 Gebhard Truchsess ascended the archiepiscopal chair of Cologne.* All his actions indicated his intention—later openly avowed—to convert his spiritual principality into a secular one. Gebhard Truchsess still conformed, occasionally at least, and in externals, to the Catholic faith. The adjacent bishoprics of Westphalia and Lower Saxony, on the contrary, fell immediately into the hands of Protestants. The elevation of Duke Henry of Saxe-Lauenburg was most especially important. He had been elected while yet very young, and though a firm Lutheran, to the archbishopric of Bremen; some time thereafter to the bishopric of Osnabrück; and in 1577, to that of Paderborn. Even in Münster, a large party, including all the younger members of the chapter, was attached to his interests, and but for the direct intervention of Gregory XIII, who declared a resignation actually made to be null and void, he would have been elevated to that See also, in spite of all efforts made to prevent it by the rigidly Catholic party. Indeed, these last were still unable to prevail so far as to secure the election of any other bishop.

It is obvious that a powerful impulse must have been given to Protestant opinions in Rhineland Westphalia—where they had before been widely propagated—by the disposition on the part of the ecclesiastical chiefs. There needed only some fortunate combination of circumstances, some well-directed stroke, to secure the decided predominance of Protestantism in that district.

All Germany would have felt the influence of this event. The same contingencies were probable in regard to the bishoprics of Upper Germany as those we have seen occurring in the lower part of the empire; and, even in the territories where the restoration had begun, resistance to its efforts was far from being suppressed.* But it was of much higher importance that Protestantism was making continual progress in the Austrian provinces, and was gradually acquiring an acknowledged and legalized existence.† In all the provinces of Austria of the German, Slavonic, and Hungarian tongues, with the single exception of the Tyrol, Protestantism was in 1578 the predominant religion. It thus becomes evident that throughout Germany the progress made by Catholicism was met by successful opposition and equal progress on the part of the Protestants.[14]

Crisis In The Netherlands

The general state of things in Europe was at that time such as we are about to describe. Restored Catholicism, under the form it had assumed in Italy and Spain, had made an extensive inroad upon the rest of Europe. It had gained important conquests in Germany and had made considerable advances in other countries, but in all it had encountered determined opposition. In France the Protestants were secured by extensive privileges and by the strength of their position—military and political. In the Netherlands they held the supremacy. They were triumphant in England, Scotland, and the North. In Poland they had extorted vigorous laws in their own favor and had gained extensive influence in the general affairs of the kingdom. Throughout the territories of Austria they confronted the government, armed with the ancient immunities of the provincial states. In Lower Germany the ecclesiastical institutions seemed to be on the point of suffering material change.

In this state of affairs, vast importance was attached to the issue of the struggle in the Netherlands, where the people were continually resorting to arms.

[14] The section "Contrasts Exhibited in Other Parts of Europe, Poland, Sweden, England, and Switzerland" has been omitted (pages 55–64).

It was impossible that Philip II could intend to repeat those measures which had already suffered so signal a failure; he was not, indeed, in a condition to do so. It was his good fortune to receive the assistance of friends, who presented themselves spontaneously. Protestantism, also, was arrested in its progress by an obstacle at once unexpected and insurmountable. It is well worth our while to devote some attention to the consideration of this important event.

In the first place, it was by no means agreeable to all parties in the provinces that the Prince of Orange should grow so powerful—least of all was this satisfactory to the Walloon nobility.

Under the government of the King, these nobles had ever been the first to take to horse in all wars, most especially in those with France. It thus happened that the leaders of note, whom the people were accustomed to follow, had acquired a certain independence and authority. Under the government of the Estates, they found themselves pushed into the background. Their pay was irregular, the army of the Estates consisted principally of Dutch, English, and Germans, who, being staunch Protestants, enjoyed the most confidence.

When the Walloons acceded to the Treaty of Ghent, they had hoped to obtain a leading influence in the general affairs of the country, but the result was quite the opposite—power fell almost exclusively into the hands of the Prince of Orange and his friends of Holland and Zeeland.*

But the personal disaffection thus occasioned was not all—religious animosities combined with it.

Whatever may have been the cause, the fact is certain that in the Walloon provinces but little sympathy was ever excited toward the Protestant movements.†

In the year 1578 the Walloon provinces were considered among their contemporaries to be, according to their own expression, most Catholic.

But this religious organization was endangered no less than the political claims of the provinces by the increasing predominance of Lutheran opinions.

At Ghent the form assumed by Protestantism was such as in

the present day we should call revolutionary. The ancient liberties which had been crushed by Charles V in 1539 had never been forgotten. The atrocities of Alva had excited peculiar exasperation in that city. The populace was fierce and ungovernable, much inclined to image-breaking, and violently enraged against the priests. Two daring leaders of the people, Imbize and Ryhove, availed themselves of these tumultuous feelings. Imbize conceived the idea of establishing a republic, and fancied that Ghent would become a new Rome. They commenced their proceedings at the moment when their Governor, Arschot, was holding a meeting with certain bishops and Catholic leaders of the neighboring towns, whom they took prisoners, together with the Governor. They next restored the ancient constitution, with modifications, as will be readily supposed, which secured to themselves the possession of power. They laid hands on the property of the Church, abolished the bishopric, and confiscated the abbeys. The hospitals and monasteries they converted into barracks, and finally they endeavored to introduce a similar order of things among their neighbors by force of arms.

Now it happened that some of the leaders taken prisoner with the Governor belonged to the Walloon provinces, where the troops of Ghent were already making incursions. All who were disposed to the Protestant opinions began to arouse themselves, and the democratic passions of the people were called in aid of the religious excitement, as had been done in Ghent. In Arras a tumult was raised against the town council. From Douai itself the Jesuits were expelled in a commotion of the people, despite the efforts made by the Council; and although not compelled to absent themselves more than fourteen days, yet the circumstance was one of great importance. In St. Omer they maintained their ground only by the special protection of the Council.

The civic magistracy, the provincial nobility, and the clergy were all at the same time endangered and oppressed. They saw themselves menaced by a development as destructive as that which had just occurred in Ghent; it is therefore not surprising if in this peril they should have recourse to every possible means of defense. They first sent their troops into the territory of Ghent, which they cruelly devastated, and then looked around for some alliance from which they might derive a more certain security than was afforded by their connection with the general union of the Netherlands.

Don John of Austria was not backward in turning this disposition of mind to his own purposes.

If we consider the conduct and measures of Don John in the Netherlands from a general point of view only, we are almost inclined to think that they produced no results, that his existence passed away without leaving a trace, as it had done without satisfaction to himself. But if we examine more closely what his position was, what his actions were, and what consequences resulted from his measures, we shall find that to him above all other persons must be attributed the founding of the Spanish Netherlands. Don John endeavored for some time to abide by the terms of the Treaty of Ghent, but the independent position assumed by the States, with that held by the Prince of Orange, who was much more powerful than himself—the Viceroy—and the suspicions entertained by each party against the other, made an open rupture inevitable. He therefore resolved to begin the war. This was doubtless in opposition to the will of the King, but it was unavoidable. There were no other means by which he could hope to secure a single province to the sovereignty of Spain. He retained possession of Luxembourg, he invested Namur, and the battle of Gembloux made him master of Louvain and Limburg. If the King desired to recover his power in the Netherlands, that was not to be effected by treating with the States-General, which was manifestly impracticable. It could only be done by a gradual subjugation of the separate districts, either by treaty or by force of arms. This system Don John adopted, and it soon laid open to him the most cheering prospects. He succeeded in reviving the old attachment of the Walloon provinces to the Burgundian race and had the good fortune to gain over to his party two men of great power and influence, Pardieu de la Motte, Governor of Gravelines, and Matthieu Moulart, Bishop of Arras.

These were the men who, after the early death of Don John, conducted the negotiations on which everything depended with great zeal and successful skill.*

Alexander Farnese, the successor of Don John, possessed the inestimable gift of persuading, attaching, and inspiring lasting confidence. He was assisted by François de Richardot. "A man," says Cabrera, "of keen penetration and sound judgment in various affairs, and experienced in all; he was capable of conducting every sort of business, be its nature what it might." Sarrazin, Abbot of St. Vaast, was also his zealous supporter. Of him the same Cabrera says, "He was a great politician, with an appearance of tranquil indifference; very ambitious under a show of extreme humility, and was skilled to maintain himself in the good opinion of all."

We do not follow the whole course of the negotiations until they gradually attained their end.

It must suffice to say that on the part of the Walloon provinces the interests of self-preservation and of religion pointed to the King, while on the part of Philip II nothing was omitted that priestly influence and dexterous negotiation, combined with the returning favor of the sovereign could effect. In April 1579, Emanuel de Montigny—whom the Walloon forces acknowledged as their leader—entered the service of the King. He was followed by Count de Lalaing, without whom Hainaut could never have been won. At length, on May 17, 1579, the treaty was concluded in the camp of Maastricht. But to what conditions was the King compelled to submit! It was a restoration of his authority, but was effected only under the strictest limitations. He not only promised to dismiss all foreigners from his army and to employ troops raised in the Netherlands alone, but he agreed to confirm all those in their places who had acquired office during the troubles. The inhabitants even pledged themselves to receive no garrison of which information had not previously been given to the Estates of the country; two-thirds of the Council of State were to consist of men who had been implicated in the disturbances. The remaining articles were all in a similar spirit. The provinces acquired a degree of independence exceeding anything that they had ever before possessed.

This event involved a turn of affairs that was of universal importance. Throughout the west of Europe, all attempts hitherto made for the maintenance or restoration of Catholicism had been by open force; and under this pretext, the sovereign power had labored to complete the destruction of all provincial freedom. But monarchy was now compelled to adopt a different course. If kings desired to reinstate Catholicism and to uphold their own authority, they must take their measures in firm alliance with the Estates and on the basis of their privileges.*

But these events did not bring affairs to a complete decision. The union of the Catholic provinces with the King was perhaps the very cause which compelled the northern districts, all exclusively Protestant, not only to form a closer confederation among themselves, but eventually to declare an absolute renunciation of the royal authority.

We will here take a rapid glance at the general history of the Netherlands. A contest of long standing subsisted in all the provinces between the provincial rights and the sovereign prerogative. In the time of Alva, princely power had obtained a preponderance more decided than it had ever before possessed, but which it could not long maintain. The Treaty of Ghent demonstrated the complete superiority acquired by the Estates over the government. The northern provinces possessed no advantage over those of the south in this respect. Had they been of one opinion in religion, they would have constituted one general republic of the Netherlands, but they were separated, as we have seen, by a difference of faith. From this circumstance, it followed, first, that the Catholics returned to the protection of the King, with whom they pledged themselves above all to the maintenance of the Catholic religion; and a second result was that the Protestants, after long persevering in the struggle, at length cast aside the very name of subjection and entirely renounced their allegiance to the King. We give the name of the subject provinces to the first of these parties, and designate the last as the republic. But we must not suppose the essential difference between them to have been so great as these names would imply, for the subjected provinces asserted all their rights and the privileges of their Estates with the most spirited tenacity, while the republican provinces could not dispense with an institution (the stadtholdership) which was closely analogous to that of royalty. The most important distinction consisted in their religion.

It was by this that the true principles of the contest were brought out, and that events were matured and advanced to their consummation.*

The Spanish-Italian army, already once withdrawn, then brought back and expelled again, returned once more to the country. As in Germany the colonies of Jesuits, composed of Spaniards, Italians, and some few Netherlanders, had restored Catholicism by the zealous inculcation of its dogmas and by carefully arranged education, so now in the Netherlands an Italian-Spanish army appeared to unite with the Walloon Catholics for the reinstatement of the Roman supremacy by force of arms.

At this point of the history, it is impossible to avoid some slight description of the war; in its course the destinies of religion were also involved.

In July 1583, the port and town of Dunkirk were taken in six days. They were followed by Nieuport and the whole coast, even to Ostend, Dixmuide, and Furnes.

The character of the war was at once made manifest. In everything relating to politics the Spaniards displayed forbearance, but in all that pertained to religion they were inexorable. It was not to be thought of that the Protestants should be allowed a church; they were refused even the right of private worship; all the preachers taken were hanged. The war was conducted with full consciousness and fixed design, as a war of religion; and in a certain sense, this was indeed most prudent, considering the existing state of affairs. A complete subjugation of the Protestants could never have been effected. But by so decided a mode of proceeding, whatever elements of Catholicism the provinces contained were aroused to activity and excited to aid the Spanish cause; and accordingly, their cooperation was offered spontaneously.

Alexander Farnese soon found himself sufficiently powerful to prepare for an attack on the more important cities. In the month of April, Ypres surrendered, immediately afterward Bruges, and finally Ghent, where Imbize himself had argued the cause of reconciliation. The conditions granted to the communes, in their political character, were very favorable. Their immunities were for the most part respected, but the Protestants were expelled without mercy. The principal condition in every case was that the Catholic clergy should be reinstated and the churches restored to the Catholic worship.

But with all that had been effected, nothing permanent seemed to be gained; no security was possessed while the Prince of Orange survived to give force and consistency to the opposition and to prevent hope from expiring even in the vanquished.

The Spaniards had set a price of 25,000 scudi on his head, and amidst the fierce excitement of the period there could not fail to be men whose fanaticism and avarice would prompt them to earn this reward. I do not know that the annals of humanity can furnish a more fearful blasphemy than that found in the papers of the Biscayan Jaureguy, who was taken in an attempt on the life of the prince. He carried about him, as a kind of amulet, prayers in which he besought the merciful God, who appeared to men in the person of Christ, to aid in the murder, and in which he promised a portion of the profit to the divine persons in the event of his enterprise being accomplished. To the Mother of God at Bayonne he would give a robe, a lamp, and a crown; to the Mother of God at Aranzosu, a crown; and to the Lord Jesus himself, a rich curtain! This fanatic was fortunately seized, but another was already preparing to imitate him. At the moment when the outlawry of the prince was proclaimed in Maastricht, a Burgundian named Balthaser Gerard felt himself inspired by the wish to carry the ban of the empire into execution.* He represented himself to the prince as a refugee, and having thus gained admittance, he found a favorable opportunity in July 1584, and killed the prince at one shot. He was taken, but all the tortures inflicted on him failed to extort a sigh from his lips; he persisted in declaring that if the deed were not done he would yet do it. Whilst Gerard was expiring at Delft amidst the execrations of the people, the canons of Hertogenbosch performed a solemn Te Deum in celebration of his act.

The passions of both parties were in fierce commotion, but the impulse communicated to the Catholics was the stronger—it accomplished its purpose and bore off the victory.

How completely had the times changed! At one time Philip himself had hesitated to grant the Jesuits a fixed establishment in the Netherlands, and they had since then often been menaced, attacked, and expelled. The events of this war led to their immediate return, and that under the decided protection of the government. The Farnesi, moreover, were especial patrons of the order. Alexander had a Jesuit for his confessor. He beheld in the society the most efficient instrument for restoring the half Protestant country he had conquered to the Catholic Church, and thus achieving the main purpose of the war.*

Nor was the patronage of the prince confined to the order of Jesuits. In the year 1585 a small number of Capuchins arrived in the Netherlands, and on addressing a special letter to the Pope, the prince obtained permission for their fixed residence in that country. He then bought them a house in Antwerp. They produced a powerful effect even on the different religious communities, so much that the Pope found it needful to restrain the other Franciscans from adopting the reformed rule of the Capuchins.

The most important consequences gradually resulted from all these arrangements. They transformed Belgium, which had previously been half Protestant, into one of the most decidedly Catholic countries in the world. It is also unquestionable that they contributed, at least in the commencement, to the reestablishment of the royal authority.

As one of the results of these changes, the opinion that only one religion ought to be tolerated in a state became more and more firmly established. This is one of the principal maxims in the political system of Justus Lipsius. In affairs of religion, he declares, neither favor nor indulgence is permissible; the true mercy is to be merciless; to save many, we must not scruple to remove one here and there out of the way.

This is a principle that has been received in no country with a more cordial acceptance than in Germany.

Progress Of The Counter-Reformation
In Germany

The Netherlands being still a province of the German Empire, it followed of necessity that the events occurring in the former country would be extremely influential on the affairs of Germany. The disputes in Cologne were brought to a decision as one of the first and most immediate consequences of the change in the Netherlands.

The Spaniards had not yet returned, still less had the Catholics achieved their great triumphs, when the Elector Truchsess of Cologne determined to adopt the reformed religion and to marry without, on that account, resigning his archbishopric. This occurred in November 1582. He had the greater part of the nobility on his side; the Counts of Neuenar, Solms, Wittgenstein, Wied, and Nassau, with the whole duchy of Westphalia, all professed the evangelical opinions. With the Bible in one hand and the sword in the other, the Elector entered Bonn, while Casimir of the Palatinate took the field in considerable force to reduce the city of Cologne, the chapter, and the remaining officers of the archbishopric who opposed the Elector.

In all the actions of those times we find this Casimir of the Palatinate always ready to mount his horse or draw his sword, and always followed by martial bands, disposed to Protestantism, but he rarely seemed to effect anything important. He did not carry on the war with the earnest purpose demanded by a contest for religion, because he had always some personal interest of his own before his eyes; nor did he display the expertise and energy distinguishing those who appeared against him. In the case we are considering, he did indeed lay waste the open country of his opponents, but he accomplished nothing in promotion of the general interests. He achieved no conquests, nor did he succeed in obtaining more efficient assistance among the Protestant powers of Germany.

The Catholic powers, on the contrary, gathered all their forces together. Pope Gregory would not permit the business to be subjected to the delays attendant on legal proceedings of the Curia. He considered that the urgency of the case made a simple consistory of the cardinals sufficient to decide an affair of so much importance as despoiling an elector of the empire of his archiepiscopal dignity. His nuncio, Malaspina, had already hurried to Cologne, where, with the special aid of the learned members of the chapter, he not only succeeded in excluding all the less firmly Catholic members from that body, but also in raising to the archiepiscopal throne a prince of the only house still remaining thoroughly Catholic, Duke Ernest of Bavaria, Bishop of Freising. Thereupon a German Catholic army appeared in the field, which the Duke of Bavaria had collected with the aid of subsidies from the Pope. The Emperor lost no time in threatening the Count Palatine Casimir with ban; he sent besides admonitory letters to the troops of Casimir, which eventually caused the army of the Palatinate to disperse. When affairs had reached this point, the Spaniards also appeared. They had taken Zutphen in the summer of 1583; they now marched 3,500 Belgian veterans into the archbishopric. To enemies so numerous, Gebhard Truchsess was compelled to yield. His troops would not act in opposition to the imperial mandate; his principal fortress surrendered to the united Spanish and Bavarian forces; and he was himself obliged to seek refuge with the Prince of Orange, at whose side he had hoped to stand as a defender of Protestantism.*

The effects of this great reversal could not fail to be felt in all the remaining Ecclesiastical Estates, and they were further heightened in the neighborhood of Cologne by a particular accident. Henry of Saxe-Lauenburg, Bishop of Paderborn and Osnabrück, Archbishop of Bremen, left his palace of Vohrde one Sunday in April 1585, and proceeded to church. On the way back, his horse fell with him; and although still young, in perfect health, and receiving, as it appeared, no serious injury from the fall, he yet died in consequence before the end of the month. It was believed that this prince would have followed the example of Gebhard Truchsess, had the latter been more fortunate. The elections that followed his death were greatly to the advantage of Catholicism. The new bishop of Osnabrück did not refuse to subscribe the *professio fidei*, and the new bishop of Paderborn, Theodore von Fürstenberg, was a most zealous Catholic. Even as canon he had opposed his predecessor, and as early as the year 1580, he effected the passing of a statute to the effect that Catholics only should for the future be received into the chapter. He had also brought a few Jesuits, whom he had suffered to preach in the cathedral, and to whom he had confided the upper classes of the gymnasium; the latter under the condition that they should not wear the dress of their order. How much more easily could he now promote the views of his party, being himself in possession of the bishopric! The Jesuits no longer found it necessary to conceal their presence; the gymnasium was made over to them without reserve; and they were not only permitted to preach but also to catechize. They found abundant occupation. The Town Council was entirely Protestant, and there were very few Catholics among the burghers. In the country around, things were much the same. The Jesuits compared Paderborn to a barren field, demanding infinite labor and yielding no return. We shall, nevertheless, have occasion to show hereafter that in the beginning of the seventeenth century their industry had penetrated this stubborn soil.

In Münster also the death of Henry Saxe-Lauenburg occasioned important changes. No election had hitherto been made in this See, where the younger members supported Prince Henry, while the elder opposed him. But Duke Ernest of Bavaria, Elector of Cologne and Bishop of Liège, was now chosen Bishop of Münster also.* The Elector Ernest also held the bishopric of Hildesheim. It is true that his power was much more closely restricted in that diocese; he was, nevertheless, able to promote the introduction of the Jesuits. The first who entered Hildesheim was John Hammer, a native of the town, and brought up in the Lutheran faith (his father was still living), but actuated by all the zeal of a new convert. His preaching was remarkable for clearness and force. He effected several brilliant conversions and eventually made good his position. In the year 1590 the Jesuits obtained a residence and pension in Hildesheim.

We cannot fail to observe that the attachment of the house

of Bavaria to the Catholic faith was of the first importance, even as regarded Lower Germany, where in so many dioceses at once, one Bavarian prince appears as its most earnest defender.

We are, nevertheless, not to imagine that this prince was very zealous or very devout in his personal conduct. He had natural children, and it was at one time believed that he would end by adopting a similar course to that taken by Gebhard Truchsess. The caution with which Pope Sixtus treated the Elector Ernest is quite remarkable. He carefully avoided showing the prince that his irregularities were known to him, perfectly as he was acquainted with them; for otherwise admonitions and exhortations would have been necessary, and these might have driven the self-willed Ernest to resolutions by no means desirable. It was, indeed, long before affairs in Germany could be treated as those of the Netherlands had been. They required the most delicate regard to various personal feelings and interests.*

Thus throughout a great part of Lower Germany, Catholicism, if not immediately restored, was yet maintained in the hour of danger; confirmed and strengthened, it acquired a degree of preponderance that in the course of time might be matured into absolute supremacy.

In Upper Germany a similar train of circumstances immediately ensued.†

Results so important had not been expected even in Rome. On the close of the autumn holidays in 1586, Acquaviva, general of the Jesuits, appeared before the Pope and announced the new conquests achieved by his order. Sixtus was in raptures.† But the joy of Pope Sixtus in Acquaviva's report was greatly increased by the receipt of similar intelligence from the Austrian provinces, and more especially from Styria.[15]

For all these things Pope Sixtus could find no eulogies that seemed to him sufficient. He extolled the Austrian princes as the firmest pillars of Christendom. To the Archduke Charles of Styria more particularly he sent the most obliging letters. The acquisition of a countship, which just then lapsed to the archduke as

---

[15] Pages 86–91 have been omitted.

feudal lord, was considered by the court at Graz to be a recompense sent directly by heaven for all the service he had rendered to Christendom.

The Catholic confession owed its return to supremacy in the Netherlands principally to the fact that it had accommodated itself to existing privileges; but in Germany that was by no means the case. On the contrary, the respective territorial princes extended their power and importance in proportion with their success in promoting Catholic restoration. The intimacy of this connection between the ecclesiastical and political interests, and the extent to which it proceeded, are most remarkably exemplified by Wolf Dietrich von Raittenau, Archbishop of Salzburg.

The archbishops of former days, who had lived amid the tumults of the Reformation, contented themselves with an occasional edict promulgated to oppose innovations; with rare punishment or an attempt at conversion; but all as Archbishop Jacob says, by mild, paternal, and truthful means.

Very different was the disposition of the young Archbishop Wolf Dietrich von Raittenau, when he ascended to the archbishopric in 1587. He had been educated in the *Collegium Germanicum* in Rome and was thoroughly imbued with the principles of Catholic restoration. He had seen the brilliant commencement of the administration of Sixtus V and had conceived extreme admiration for that pontiff. His zeal was further stimulated by the elevation of his uncle Cardinal Altemps, in whose house in Rome he had lived for some time, to the purple. In the year 1588, on returning from a journey which had taken him back to the Papal Court, he proceeded to the execution of the designs formed under the impressions received there. All the citizens of his capital were called upon to make public profession of the Catholic faith. Many evinced great reluctance, and he allowed them a few weeks for reflection. Then, on September 3, 1588, he commanded them to depart within one month from the city and diocese. That one month only, and, after pressing entreaties, the delay of a month longer, was allowed these recusants for the purpose of selling their property. Of this they were required to present an inventory to the archbishop, who would then permit them to sell it to such persons only as were approved by himself. Very few could resolve on deserting their faith, and those who did so were compelled to do public penance in the church with lighted candles in their hands. The greater number, including many of the most wealthy burghers, preferred to leave their country. The loss of these citizens occasioned no regret to the prince, who believed he had discovered various means of maintaining the splendor of the archbishopric. He had already much increased the taxes, had raised the tolls and duties, imposed new burdens on the salt of Hallein and Schellenberg, converted the contributions in aid of the Turkish war into a regular land tax, and introduced duties on wine, with an income tax and legacy duty. He was entirely regardless of the established liberties. The dean of the diocese was said to have committed suicide in a fit of despair at seeing the chapter deprived of its privileges. The principal object of the archbishop's enactments respecting the salt pans and the whole business of mining was the destruction of the independence enjoyed by the works before his time, and their subjection to the absolute control of his treasury. Throughout Germany no similar example of a regularly organized fiscal system was presented during that century. The young archbishop had brought the ideas of an Italian principality with him across the Alps. To have money appeared to him the most important talent of a statesman, the highest problem of political economy. He had taken Sixtus V as his model; like him he desired to have an obedient, thoroughly Catholic, tribute-paying state in his hands. The expatriation of the principal citizens from Salzburg was even a source of satisfaction to the archbishop because he considered them rebels. He ordered their deserted houses to be taken down and palaces in the Roman style to be erected on their sites.

Wolf Dietrich was above all things delighted with splendor. He never refused knightly entertainment to any foreigner, and on one occasion appeared at the Diet with a train of 400 persons. In the year 1588 he was but twenty-nine years of age; buoyant of spirit and full of ambition, he had already fixed his eyes and hopes on the highest ecclesiastical dignities.

The process adopted in the spiritual and secular principalities was repeated, wherever circumstances rendered it practicable, in the cities also. The Lutheran burghers of Gmunden complained bitterly because they had been struck off the roll of candidates for the Town Council. In Biberach the council appointed by the commissary of Charles V still maintained its ground. The whole town was Protestant, the council alone was Catholic and carefully excluded every Protestant. Heavy oppressions were endured by those of the reformed faith in Cologne and Aix-la-Chapelle. The members of the Council of Cologne declared that they had promised the Emperor and the Elector to tolerate no other religion than the Catholic, and they sometimes punished the attendance at a Protestant sermon with fines and imprisonment. In Augsburg, also, the Catholics gained the upper hand. Disturbances occurred on the introduction of the new calendar, and in the year 1586 the evangelical superintendent was expelled from the city. Eleven clergymen at one time, and a large number of the more determined citizens were also driven forth soon after. Something very similar occurred from similar causes in Ratisbon during the year 1587. Many other towns began to claim the right of reforming their religious institutions: nay, certain counts, nobles, and knights of the empire who had been converted by some Jesuit believed themselves entitled to assert a similar right, and each resolved to restore Catholicism in his small domain.

It was an immeasurable reaction. The Protestant doctrines were now repulsed with an energy equal to that with which they had formerly advanced. Preaching and the inculcation of Catholic doctrines contributed their share to the production of this result, but much more was accomplished by political measures, special ordinances, and open force.

As the Italian Protestants had formerly fled across the Alps and sought refuge in Switzerland and Germany, so now far more numerous bodies of German fugitives were seen seeking refuge in the northern and eastern districts from the oppressions that assailed them in the west and south. The Belgians in like manner retreated to Holland. It was a mighty triumph of Catholicism, which rolled on from land to land.[16]

[16] Pages 95–100 have been omitted.

The League

The great movement thus engrossing Germany and the Netherlands also extended its influence over France with irresistible force. The affairs of the Netherlands had for a long period of time been intimately connected with those of France. The French Protestants had frequently given assistance to those of the Netherlands, and the latter were equally ready to lend their aid to the Protestants of France. The ruin of Protestantism in the Belgian provinces was an immediate loss to the French Huguenots.

But in addition to this came the fact that in France, as well as in other countries, the tendency toward a restoration of Catholicism was constantly gaining extension of influence and increase of power.†

But under these circumstances the Catholic spirit assumed a new position in regard to the regal authority.

The court was living in a state of continual self-contradiction; Henry III was unquestionably a good Catholic—no one could expect favor at his hands who did not attend the mass nor would he suffer Protestants to hold the magistracy in any town of his kingdom—but notwithstanding all this, he continued now as in former times to dispose of ecclesiastical appointments in accordance with the exigencies of court favor and without the slightest regard either to worth or talent; neither did he cease to appropriate and squander the property of the Church.

Thus, the prevailing rigid spirit of Catholicism, though favored in many ways by the court, was yet in effect and essentially in direct opposition to it.*

To this cause of uneasiness was added the death of the Duke of Alençon, which took place in 1584, and as the King had no heir, nor any hope of one, Henry of Navarre became the next expectant of the crown.

The fear of future evil has perhaps more influence over the minds of men than a misfortune actually present. The prospect of Henry's accession caused the utmost agitation among the French

Catholics. Particularly the Guises, the old antagonists of Navarre, feared the influence he would acquire even as heir to the throne—let alone the power he would exercise as king. We cannot be surprised that they should look to Philip of Spain for support.*

The Guises took arms and labored to get as many provinces and fortified towns as they possibly could into their own hands.*

Henry III already felt the ground trembling beneath his feet. The proceedings of his enemies were reported to him from day to day. In the Sorbonne they had become so bold as to propose the question whether it were permitted to withdraw allegiance from a prince who neglects to perform his duty and to this question a reply was returned in the affirmative by a council of from thirty to forty doctors. The King was excessively irritated. He threatened to do as Pope Sixtus had done and chain the refractory preachers to the galleys; but he did not possess the energy of the pontiff, and contented himself with ordering the advance of the Swiss who were in his service to the neighborhood of the capital.

Alarmed by the menace implied in this movement, the citizens sent to Guise[17] entreating him to come and protect them. The King caused it to be intimated to him that a compliance with this request would be viewed unfavorably, but the Duke appeared in Paris nevertheless.

Everything now seemed ready for a great explosion.

The King commanded the Swiss to enter Paris, when it instantly burst forth. The city was immediately barricaded, the Swiss were driven back, and the Louvre was menaced. The King had no alternative but flight.

The Duke of Guise had before been master of a large portion of France; he was now in possession of Paris. The Bastille, the Arsenal, the Hotel de Ville, and all the surrounding places fell into his hands. The King was completely overpowered. He was very soon compelled to pronounce an interdict against the Protestant religion and to resign various fortified places to the Guises, in addition to those they already held. The Duke of Guise might now be considered as lord of half France, and Henry III gave him

[17] Head of the Catholic party.

legal authority over the other half, by conferring on him the dignity of lieutenant-general of the kingdom. The States were convened, and there could be no doubt but that Catholic opinions would predominate in that assembly. The most decisive measures were to be expected from it, ruinous for the Huguenots, and entirely to the advantage of the Catholic party.

Savoy And Switzerland

It will be readily perceived that the preponderance of Catholicism in the mighty realm of France would inevitably produce a corresponding effect on the neighboring kingdoms and communities.

The Catholic cantons of Switzerland attached themselves more closely than ever to the ecclesiastical principle and to the Spanish alliance.

The establishment of a permanent "nunciature" was productive of the most remarkable effects in Switzerland as well as in Germany.

In the year 1586, immediately after the adoption of this measure, the Catholic cantons united to form the Golden or Borromean League, in which they bound themselves and their descendants forever, "to live and die in the true, undoubted, ancient, apostolic Roman Catholic faith." Thereupon they received the host from the hand of the nuncio.

If the party by which the administrative power seized at Mühlhausen in the year 1587 had gone over to the Catholic creed, as they seemed on the point of doing, and if they had done so at the right moment, they would have been supported without doubt by the Catholics. Conferences had already been held on the subject at the house of the nuncio in Lucerne, but the people of Mühlhausen deliberated too long. The Protestants, on the contrary, pressed forward their expedition with the utmost promptitude, and reestablished the old government which was upon the whole favorable to themselves.

It was, however, at this moment that the three forest cantons, in concert with Zug, Lucerne, and Freiburg, took a new and most important step. After long negotiations, they concluded a treaty with Spain on May 12, 1587, in which they promised to maintain perpetual friendship with the King, conceded to him the right of raising recruits in their territories, and of marching his troops through their mountains; Philip, on his side, making corresponding concessions to them. But the most important part of their mutual engagement was that each promised to aid the other to the utmost extent of his powers in the event of either being involved in war on account of the holy apostolic religion. In this treaty the six cantons made no exception, not even in favor of the confederated cantons. On the contrary, it was against them in particular that this part of the treaty must have been arranged, seeing that there was no other power with which there was any probability of their being involved in a war from motives of religion.

Here also then, how much more powerful was the influence of religious feeling than that of national attachment! A community of faith now united the original Swiss cantons with the house of Austria! The Confederation became for the moment a secondary consideration.

It was most fortunate that no cause for immediate hostilities arose. The influence of this league was therefore confined in the first instance to Geneva.

Charles Emanuel, Duke of Savoy, a prince whose whole life had been marked by restless ambition, had often evinced a desire to seize the first favorable occasion for regaining possession of Geneva, regarding himself as the legitimate sovereign of that city. But his designs had hitherto always been defeated by opposition from the Swiss and French, from both of whom the Genevese received protection.

But circumstances were now altered. Under the influence of Guise, Henry III promised in the summer of 1588 that he would no longer impede any enterprise undertaken against Geneva. At least the Catholic cantons of Switzerland no longer had any objections. As far as I can see all that they demanded was an assurance that conquered Geneva not be turned into a fortress.

Receiving this intimation, the Duke prepared himself for the attack. The Genevese did not lose their courage, and made occasional incursions on the ducal territories. But, on this occasion, Berne afforded them but very insufficient aid. The Catholic party had insinuated their partisans into the very midst of this city, closely interwoven as it was with Protestant interests; there was a faction there which would not have been unwilling to see Geneva fall into the hands of the Duke. It thus happened that he very soon gained an advantage. He had hitherto held the counties bordering on Geneva under closely limited conditions, imposed on him by former treaties of peace with Berne. He now seized the occasion and made himself for the first time master in those districts. He expelled the Protestants, whom he had previously been obliged to tolerate, and made the whole country exclusively Catholic. Charles Emanuel had until that time been prohibited from erecting fortresses in that portion of his territories. He then built them in places where he could not only make them serve for defense, but also for harassing Geneva.

But before these affairs had proceeded further, other enterprises had been undertaken from which consequences of much more extensive importance might be expected, and which seemed not unlikely to produce a complete revolution in all the relations of Europe.

Attack On England

The Netherlands were in great part subdued, and negotiations had already commenced for the voluntary submission of the remainder. In Germany the efforts of Catholicism had prevailed in many districts, and a project was conceived, by which those remaining might be overcome. In France the Champion of Catholicism was proceeding on a path that by victories, investment of fortresses, attachment of the people, and legitimate authority seemed inevitably to lead him to the possession of exclusive sovereignty. The ancient metropolis of the Protestant faith, the city of Geneva, was no longer protected by her former alliances. At this moment the plan was formed of laying the axe to the root of the tree by an attack on England.

The central point of the Protestant power and policy was without doubt in England. The provinces of the Netherlands yet remaining unsubdued, as well as the Huguenots of France, found their principal support in Queen Elizabeth.[18]

Thus the forces of Italy and Spain, from which influence so mighty had gone forth over the whole world, aroused themselves for an attack upon England. The King had caused a collection to be made from the archives of Simancas of all the claims he possessed to the English throne. The expedition was associated in his mind with the most brilliant prospects, especially that of universal dominion over the seas.

All things now seemed to combine toward one result—the ascendancy of Catholicism in Germany, the renewed attack on the Huguenots in France, the attempt upon Geneva, the enterprise against England. At the same moment a decidedly Catholic sovereign, Sigismund III, succeeded to the crown of Poland (an event of which we shall speak further hereafter), with the prospect of future accession to the throne of Sweden.

But whenever any principle, be it what it may, tends to the establishment of absolute dominion in Europe, there is invariably opposed to it a vigorous resistance, springing from the deepest sources of human nature.

Philip found himself confronted in England by the national energies in all the vigor of their youth, inspired by the full consciousness of their destiny. The bold corsairs, who had rendered every sea unsafe, gathered around the coasts of their native land. The whole body of the Protestants, even the Puritans, although they had been oppressed as heavily as the Catholics, rallied round the Queen, who now maintained to an admirable degree that masculine courage with which she was endowed, and gave proof of her princely talent of winning, retaining, and controlling the minds of men. The insular position of the country, and even the elements, cooperated to the defense of England. The invincible Armada was annihilated even before the assault had been made: the expedition failed completely.

[18] Pages 111–116 have been omitted.

Assassination Of Henry III

Soon after the calamitous dispersion of the Spanish fleet, a reaction took place in France, unlooked for, and, as so frequently has been the case, violent and sanguinary.

At the moment when the Duke of Guise, who ruled the States of Blois at his will, seemed by virtue of his office of constable to be on the point of gathering the whole power of the kingdom into his hands, Henry III caused him to be assassinated. This King, perceiving himself beset and enchained by the Spanish and Catholic party, tore himself at once from their trammels and placed himself in direct opposition to them.*

The Pope resolved to adopt measures of the utmost severity. He cited the King to appear in person at the Court of Rome, there to render an account for having murdered a cardinal,[19] and threatened him with excommunication if he failed to release the Cardinal Bourbon and the Archbishop of Lyons, whom he had imprisoned, within a specified time.

Sixtus declared that he was bound to act thus; should he do otherwise he must answer for it to God as the most useless of pontiffs. But since he had thus fulfilled his duty, he need not fear the world. He had no doubt that Henry III would perish as King Saul had done.

The zealous Catholics and the adherents of the League abhorred the King as a reprobate and outcast, and the demonstrations of the Pope confirmed them in their violent opposition, and before it could have been expected, his prediction was fulfilled. On June 23 the *Monitorium* was published in France. On August 1 the King was assassinated by Clement.

The Pope himself was amazed: "In the midst of his army," he exclaimed, "on the point of conquering Paris, in his own Cabinet, he has been struck down by a poor monk, and at one blow."

---

[19] The Cardinal of Guise, the Duke's brother, had also been assassinated.

He attributed this to the immediate intervention of God, who thereby testified that he would not abandon France.

How is it that an opinion so erroneous can possibly have gained possession of the minds of men? This conviction prevailed among innumerable Catholics. "It is to the hand of the Almighty alone," wrote Mendoza to Philip, "that we must ascribe this happy event." At the distant University of Ingolstadt the young Maximilian of Bavaria was then pursuing his studies, and in one of his first letters still extant he expresses to his mother the joy which he had received from the intelligence that "the King of France had been killed."

This occurrence had nevertheless another and less auspicious aspect; Henry of Navarre, whom the Pope had excommunicated and whom the Guises so rancorously persecuted, now succeeded to his legitimate rights—a Protestant assumed the title of King of France.

BOOK VI
INTERNAL CONFLICTS OF DOCTRINE
AND POLITICS—A.D. 1589–1607

How different a course had the spiritual development of the world taken than might have been expected at the beginning of the century!

At that time the restraints of ecclesiastical authority were dissolving; the nations labored to separate themselves from their common spiritual chief. In the Court of Rome itself, those principles on which the hierarchy was founded were treated with ridicule. Profane tastes predominated in literature and the arts, while the maxims of a pagan morality were acted on without reserve or concealment.

How entirely was all this now changed! In the name of religion it now was that wars were undertaken, conquests achieved, and states overturned. There has been no period in which theologians were more influential than at the close of the sixteenth century. They sat in the councils of kings and discussed political affairs from the pulpit in public. They directed schools, controlled the efforts of learning, and governed the whole range of literature. From the confessional they gained opportunity for surprising the secret struggles of the soul with itself, and for giving the decisive bias to all the doubtful questions arising in private life. It may perhaps be affirmed that the eager violence with which they opposed each other, the fact that they generated their own contradictions, was precisely the cause of that comprehensive and pervading influence.

And if this might be said of both parties, it was more particularly true of the Catholics. Among them the ideas and institutions by which the minds of men are more immediately and effectually disciplined and guided were arranged with the most perfect adaptation to the end proposed; no man could now exist without a father confessor. Among Catholics, moreover, the clergy, either as members of some order, or in any case as members of the general hierarchy, constituted a corporation, combined in the strictest subordination and acting in the most perfect unity of spirit. The head of this hierarchical body, the Pope in Rome, again acquired an influence but little inferior to that which he had possessed in the eleventh and twelfth centuries. By means of the enterprises which he was continually undertaking for the furtherance of his religious purposes, the Roman pontiff kept the world in perpetual movement.

Under these circumstances the boldest pretensions of the days of Hildebrand were revived. Axioms that had hitherto been preserved in the arsenals of the canon law, rather as antiquities than for use, were now brought forth into full effect and activity.

Our European commonwealth has, however, at no time been subjected to the dominion of pure force; at all periods it has been imbued with ideas. No enterprise of importance can succeed, no power can rise to universal influence, without immediately suggesting to the minds of men the ideal of a universal order which had to be implemented. From this point proceed theories.

These reproduce spiritual import and significance of the facts, which are then presented in the light of a universal and effectual truth as deduced from reason or religion, and as a result arrived at by reflection. They thus anticipate, as it were, the completion of the event, which at the same time they most effectually promote.

Let us consider in what manner this took place at the period of which we are treating.

Theory Of Ecclesiastical Policy

The principle of the Catholic religion is not unfrequently declared to have special connection with, and natural inclination toward, the monarchical or aristocratic forms of government. A century like the sixteenth, in which this principle displayed itself in vigorous action and full self-consciousness, is particularly suitable to instruct us on this point. We find, indeed, that the Catholic religion cooperated with the existing order of things in Italy and Spain; that it further assisted the princes in Germany to establish a new preponderance over the estates of the respective territories. In the Netherlands it promoted the subjugation of the country, and in Upper Germany, as well as in the Walloon provinces, it was upheld by the nobles with peculiar attachment. But if we inquire further, we shall perceive that these were not the only sympathies awakened by the Catholic religion. If we find it maintained by the patricians in Cologne, we see it supported with equal ardor by the populace in the neighboring city of Treves. In the large towns of France it was in every case associated with the claims and struggles of the people. The principal consideration of Catholicism indeed was where the best support, the most effectual resources, were to be found. If the existing authorities were adverse to its influence, Catholicism was very far from sparing them, or even from acknowledging their power: it maintained the Irish nation in its traditional opposition to the English government. In England itself, Catholicism labored with its utmost force to undermine the allegiance demanded by the Queen, and frequently broke out into active rebellion. Finally, its adherents in France were confirmed by their religious advisers in their insurrection against their legitimate sovereigns. The religious principle in general has in fact no inherent predilection for one form of government more than another. During the short period of its renovation, Catholicism evinced the most diversified preferences: first, toward monarchy in Italy and Spain, and for the confirmation of territorial sovereignty in Germany; next, it lent itself in the Netherlands to the maintenance of the legally constituted aristocratic bodies; and at the close of the century it formed a decided alliance with the democratic tendency. This was the more important, because it now attained the most intensive activity, and the movements in which it took part represent the most influential political occurrences of the day. If the popes had succeeded at this juncture, they would have secured a perpetual predominance over the state. They advanced claims, and their adherents propounded opinions and principles, by which kingdoms and states were threatened at once with internal convulsions, and with the loss of their independence.

It was the Jesuits principally who appeared in the arena for the purpose of announcing and defending opinions of this character.[20]

The state of things here described was further promoted and favored by the fact that Spain assented to these doctrines, and that they were tolerated by a prince so jealous of his power and prerogatives as was Philip II. The Spanish monarchy was, indeed, essentially based on a combination of ecclesiastical attributes. It may be gathered from many passages of Lope de Vega, that it was so understood by the nation, that, in their sovereign, the people loved the majesty of religion, and desired to see it represented in his person.

The Spanish King, for example, had a new support in the doctrines of the Jesuits. At some future time he might have something to fear from this society, but they now upheld his policy by a justification at once religious and legitimate, from which even his consideration and dignity in Spain itself derived important advantages, and which eminently promoted his foreign enter-

[20] Pages 126–131 have been omitted.

prises. It was to this momentary utility of the Jesuit doctrines, rather than to their general purport and tendency, that Philip of Spain gave his attention.

And is not this usually the case with regard to political tenets? Do these tenets arise out of the facts, or are they the originators and creators of events? Are they cherished for their own sakes, or for the utility to which men believe they may be turned?

This, however, detracts in no way from their force. In expressing the aspirations of the reforming papacy (or, more precisely, of the moment of universal history in which it was located), the doctrines of the Jesuits gave them a new force by a systematic justification in the spirit of the predominant theological conviction. They gave direction to the senses of the very people on whom victory would depend.

Doctrinal Opposition

At no time, however, has either a power or a doctrine, least of all a political doctrine, gained pre-eminence in Europe to the extent of obtaining an absolute and undivided sovereignty. Nor can we conceive of any which, when compared with the ideal and with the highest demands, would not appear one-sided and restrictive.

A firm resistance has at all times arisen against every opinion that has labored to obtain exclusive domination, and this antagonism, proceeding from the inexhaustible depths of life in general, has invariably called new and vigorous energies into action.

Perceiving and acknowledging that no power will rise into effectual existence which does not repose on the basis of an idea, we may further assert that in this idea it also finds its limits. The great conflicts which beget new life are always also enacted on the plane of conviction, of thought.

Thus it now happened that the idea of a sacerdotal religion, supreme over all other authority, was countered by a mighty opposition from that national independence which is the proper expression of the secular element in society.

The Germanic institution of monarchy, widely diffused among the nations of Romanic or Latin origin and deeply rooted among them, has never been disturbed either by the pretensions of the priesthood or by the fiction of the sovereignty of the people, which last has in all cases been eventually proved untenable.

The extraordinary connection into which these two principles had entered at the period we are considering, was opposed by the doctrine of the divine right of monarchy.

The Protestants were the first to take this position, although they originally may have been equivocal about it. Now they embraced it with all the force of an enemy who sees his antagonist venture on a dangerous game, following a path which must lead to his ruin.

God alone, as the Protestants maintained, appoints princes over the human race. He reserves to himself the office of exalting and abasing them, of apportioning and moderating the powers they are called on to exercise. It is true that he no longer descends from heaven to point out with a visible finger the individual to whom authority shall belong, but by his eternal providence, laws and a settled order of things have been introduced into every kingdom, in accordance with which the ruler is chosen. If a prince attains his office by virtue of these appointed regulations, his right is unquestionable, as though God's voice had said, "This shall be your King." God did indeed of old point out to his people Moses, the Judges, and the first Kings; but when a fixed order had once been established, those who afterward succeeded to the throne were equally with the anointed of God.*

It would have been of much importance had the Protestants alone devised and firmly upheld these opinions. But they became of infinitely greater moment from the fact that they gained acceptance with a part of the French Catholics, or rather, that these last arrived at similar conclusions by their own independent reflections.

In spite of the papal excommunication, a band of good Catholics, of no inconsiderable numbers, maintained their allegiance to Henry III, and on his death transferred it to Henry IV. The Jesuits failed to influence this party, which was at no loss for arguments to defend their position, without, on that account, departing from Catholicism.*

Thus, there arose within the bounds of Catholicism itself an opposition to those pretensions which the papacy had been emboldened by the Restoration to put forth; and from the very first it was doubtful whether power would be found in Rome for its suppression. The tenets of the opposition were not, perhaps, entirely matured. Their defenders were less practiced than those of the Jesuit pretensions, but they were more firmly rooted in the convictions of the European world. The position assumed by those upholding them was in itself entirely just and blameless, and they derived an important advantage from the fact that the papal doctrines were in close alliance with the Spanish power.

The monarchy of Philip II seemed daily to become a greater menace to the general freedom. It awakened throughout Europe that jealous aversion which proceeds less from the acts of violence committed than from the apprehension of such violence, and from that sense of danger to freedom which seizes on the minds of men, although they cannot clearly account to themselves for its presence.*

So intimate a connection now existed between Rome and Spain that the opponents of the papal claim were also antagonists of the progress of the Spanish power. They thereby performed an office which the safety of Europe now required and thus could not fail to obtain approbation and support.

A secret sympathy united the nations; determined allies arose unsolicited and from unexpected quarters in aid of that national party of French Roman Catholics. They appeared in Italy itself before the eyes of the Pope, and first of all in Venice.

Some few years previously, in 1582, a change had taken place in Venice which was effected silently and was almost overlooked in the history of the Republic, but which was nevertheless of great influence. Up to that period, all affairs of moment had been confided to a few patricians—men advanced in years, who had been chosen from a small circle of families. But, at the time we are contemplating, a discontented majority in the Senate, consisting principally of the younger members, had instituted a successful struggle for a share in the administration, to which they were beyond doubt entitled by the letter of the constitution.

It is true that even the previous government had ever maintained a zealous guard over the Venetian independence, and had sedulously asserted it on all occasions. But it had always supported, so far as was by any means practicable, the views of the Church and of Spain. The new administration no longer adhered to this policy. They rather evinced an inclination, from the mere spirit of opposition, to throw difficulties in the path of those powers.*

Under these circumstances, men did not content themselves with mere thoughts and inclinations. The Venetians had felt confidence in Henry IV from the very commencement of his career; they had believed him capable of reviving the fortunes of France and restoring the lost balance of power. They were bound by manifold obligations to the Pope, who had excommunicated Henry, and were encompassed both on land and sea by the Spaniards, who desired to destroy that prince. The extent of their power was not such as to command great influence in the world, yet the Venetians were the first of all the Catholics who had courage to acknowledge Henry of Navarre as King of France. When his accession was communicated to them by their ambassador Mocenigo, they at once empowered that functionary to congratulate Henry on the occasion. Their example did not fail to influence others. Although the Grand Duke Ferdinand of Tuscany had not the courage for public recognition of the new sovereign, he nevertheless entered into relations of personal friendship with him. The Protestant prince suddenly beheld himself surrounded by Catholic allies—nay, received into their protection and shielded by them from the supreme head of their own church.

At all times when an important decision is to be made, the public opinion of Europe is invariably declared in a manner that admits of no doubt. Fortunate is he on whose side it takes its stand. His undertakings are accomplished with greater ease. This power now favored the cause of Henry IV. The ideas connected with his name had scarcely found expression; they were nevertheless already so influential as to make it not altogether impossible that the papacy itself might be won over to their side.

Latter Times Of Sixtus V

We return once again to Sixtus V.* We will now give some few words to the description of his policy in general. In doing this we cannot fail to remark the extraordinary fact that the inexorable justice exercised by this pontiff, the rigid system of finance that he established, and the close exactitude of his domestic economy, were accompanied by the most inexplicable disposition to political plans of fantastic extravagance.†

These were plans, or rather—for that word has too definite a meaning—these were fantasies, castles in the air, of the most extraordinary character. How flagrantly are these visions in disaccord with the stern reality, the rigid practical activity, earnestly pressing forward to its end, by which this pontiff was usually distinguished!

We may nevertheless be permitted to declare that even these had their origin in the exuberance of thoughts too lofty for implementation. The elevation of Rome to the acknowledged metropolis of Christendom, which, after a certain lapse of years, all nations, even those of America, were to visit regularly—the conversion of ancient monuments into memorials of the subjugation of heathenism by the Christian faith—the accumulation of a treasure, formed of money borrowed and paying interest, as a basis for the secular power of the Papal States—all these are purposes surpassing the limits of the practicable, which found their origin in the ardor of religious enthusiasm, but which were yet highly influential in determining the restless activity of this pontiff's character.

From youth, the life of man, active or passive, is but the reflection of his hopes and wishes. The present, if we may so speak, is encompassed by the future, and the soul never wearies of expectations of personal happiness. But as life advances, these desires and expectations become attached to more extensive interests; they aspire to the completion of some great object in science, in politics, in the more important general concerns of life. They expand, in a word, into cares for the universal interest. In the case of our Franciscan, the fascination and stimulus of personal hopes had been ever all the more powerful because he had found himself engaged in a career which opened to him the most exalted prospects: they had accompanied him from step to step and had sustained his spirit in extremity. He had eagerly seized on every word foreboding success, had treasured it in the depths of his heart, and in his anticipation, had connected with each some magnificent design suggested by monkish enthusiasm. At length his utmost hopes were realized. From a beginning the least auspicious, the most hopeless, he had risen to the highest dignity in Christendom—a dignity of which, eminent as it was, he yet entertained a conception exaggerated beyond the reality. He believed himself immediately selected by a special providence for the realization of those ideas that floated before his imagination.*

At the moment now in question, the Pope was absorbed by the grandest views connected with the undertaking against Henry IV. He anticipated a decisive victory for strict Catholicism and hoped to see the universal supremacy of the pontificate fully restored. His whole life for the moment was engrossed by these prospects. He was persuaded that all the Catholic states were entirely agreed on this point, and would turn the whole force of their united powers against the Protestant who laid claim to become King of France.

In this direction of his thoughts, and while thus ardently zealous, he was acquainted with the fact that a Catholic power—one too with which he had believed himself in particularly good intelligence, Venice, namely—had offered congratulations to that very Protestant. He was profoundly afflicted by this proceeding. For a moment he attempted to restrain the Republic from taking further steps; he entreated the Venetians to wait. Time, he assured them, brought forth marvelous fruits; he had himself learned from the good and venerable senators to permit them to mature. Notwithstanding this request, the Republic persisted and acknowledged De Maisse, the former ambassador of France, after he had received his new credentials as plenipotentiary of Henry IV. Hereupon the Pope proceeded from exhortations to menaces. He declared that he should well know what it behooved him to do, and commanded that the old *monitoria* proclaimed against the Venetians in the time of Julius II should be sought out, and the formula of a new one prepared.*

Nobody speaks without hearing an answer. The envoy-extraordinary to the Pope of the Venetians was Leonardo Donato. He was deeply imbued with the spirit of the ecclesiastical and political opposition, was a man of what would now be called the most consummate skill in diplomacy who had already successfully conducted many difficult and delicate negotiations.

The various motives by which the Venetians were influenced could not well be set forth in Rome; Donato, therefore, gave prominence to those which the Pope had in common with the Republic, and which were consequently assured of finding acceptance with his Holiness.

Was it not manifest, for example, that the Spanish predominance in the south of Europe became more decided and more perilous from year to year? The Pope felt this as deeply as any other Italian prince. He could take no step in Italy even at this time without first obtaining the consent of Spain. What then would be the state of things when the Spaniards should have gained the mastery in France? On this consideration, then, on the necessity for maintaining the balance of power in Europe, and on the means by which it might be restored, Donato principally insisted. He sought to prove that the Republic, far from seeking to offend the Pope, had rather arranged her policy with a view to defending and promoting the most important interests of the Papal See.* Some days later the Pope declared that he could not approve what the Republic had done, but he would refrain from adopting the measures he had contemplated against her. He gave Donato his blessing and embraced him.

This may be called an almost insensible change of mere personal feeling. The most important results were, nevertheless, involved in it. The Pope himself permitted the rigor with which he had persecuted the Protestant King to relax. Neither would he absolutely condemn the Catholic party attached to Henry, and by which his former policy had been opposed. A first step is always important, because it implies a whole course of action. This was instantly perceived on the part of the opposition: it had originally sought only to exculpate itself; it now proceeded to attempt to convince and gain over the Pope himself.*

How greatly must this total change have astonished the strictly Catholic world! The Pope evinced a favorable disposition toward a Protestant whom he had himself excommunicated, and who, according to the ancient ordinances of the Church, had rendered himself incapable even of receiving absolution by the commission of a double apostasy.

That from all this there should result a reaction was in the nature of things. The party holding rigid Catholic opinions was not so entirely dependent on the Pope as to make it impossible for them to oppose him, and the Spanish power supplied them with a support of which they eagerly availed themselves.†

Catholicism in its genuine forms had appeared to have but one aim—one undivided opinion. It seemed on the road to victory, and on the very point of success. But there were formed unexpectedly within itself two parties—two systems of opinion opposing each other politically and ecclesiastically—the one disposed to make aggressions, the other prepared for resistance. The struggle was commenced by each party exerting its utmost power in the effort to win over the head of the Church to its own side. The one already held possession of the Pope, and now labored to retain him by menaces, bitterness, and almost by force. Toward the other a secret feeling had disposed him at a very critical moment, and it now sought to secure him entirely for itself. Attempts were made to lure him by promises. The most attractive prospects were displayed before him. For the decision of the contest, the question to which party the pontiff should attach himself, was one of the utmost importance.

The demeanor of this Pope, so renowned for active energy and decision of character, was at that moment such as to fill us with amazement.

When letters arrived from Philip II expressing the determination of that sovereign to uphold the rightful cause and support the League with all the force of his kingdom—nay, with his own blood—the Pope was instantly full of zeal. Never would he expose himself, as he then declared, to the disgrace of not having opposed a heretic like Navarre.

He was nonetheless soon afterward inclined toward the opposite side. When the difficulties in which the affairs of France involved him were represented to the pontiff, he exclaimed that if Navarre were present he would entreat him on his knees to become Catholic.

Thus did the powerful prince of the Church, the sovereign who lived in the persuasion that he was invested with a direct authority over the whole earth, and who had amassed a treasure that might well have enabled him to perform some mighty deed, remain undecided and incapable of action when the moment for decision had arrived.

Are we permitted to reproach him with this as a fault? I fear that we should do him injustice. He had seen through the state of affairs, he perceived the dangers on both sides, he suffered himself to be subjected to the influence of conflicting opinions. No crisis presented itself by which he might have been compelled to a final decision. The elements that were dividing the world had filled his very soul with the confusion of their conflict, and neither could there obtain the decisive mastery.

It is certain that he thereby placed himself in a position wherein it was impossible that he should effectively influence the world. On the contrary, he was himself acted on by the forces then agitating society, and this effect was produced in a highly peculiar manner.

Sixtus had succeeded in suppressing the *banditti*, principally by establishing friendly relations with his neighbors. But since these were now interrupted—since opinions prevailed in Tuscany and Venice which were altogether different from those held in Naples and Milan and the Pope would declare himself decidedly for neither, he became the object of suspicion, first to one and then to the other of these neighbors, and under favor of this state of things, the *banditti* once more aroused themselves to activity.*

In this condition, surrounded by so many pressing disquietudes, and without having even attempted to announce a decision or to adopt a resolution concerning the most important affairs, Pope Sixtus V died on August 27, 1590.

A thunderstorm burst over the Quirinal at the moment when he breathed his last. The uneducated multitude persuaded themselves that Fra Felice had made a compact with the evil spirit, by whose aid he had risen from step to step, and that the stipulated period having now expired, his soul had been carried away in the tempest. It was in this manner that they signified their discontent at the number of new taxes he had imposed and expressed those doubts of his perfect orthodoxy which had for some years been frequently agitated. With impetuous fury they tore down the statues that had been erected in his earlier days, and even came to a resolution in the Capitol that no statue should ever again be erected to a pontiff during his lifetime.

Urban VII, Gregory XIV, Innocent IX, And Their Conclaves, 1590–1591

The new election was now of redoubled importance. To which of the two principles just commencing their contest the pontiff about to be chosen would attach himself must principally depend on the personal dispositions of the man selected, and it could not be doubted that his decision would involve consequences which must influence the whole world. The turmoil and electioneering of the conclave hence assume peculiar importance and require us to devote a few words to their consideration.

During the first half of the sixteenth century the College of Cardinals was powerfully influenced either by the imperial faction or by that of France. It was even remarked by one of the popes that the cardinals no longer possessed any freedom of vote. But from the middle of the century the influence thus exerted by foreign powers had materially declined. The Curia was left much more to its own decisions, and there arose from the ferment of its internal agitations a principle or custom of very singular character.

It was the habit of each pontiff to nominate a number of cardinals, who gathered round his nephews and kinsmen in the next conclave, maintained the family interests of the Pope just deceased, formed a new power, and usually sought to raise one of their own party to the papal throne. It is a remarkable fact that they never succeeded, that the opposition was victorious on every occasion, and in most cases put forward an adversary of the last Pope.

I will not attempt any close investigation of this matter. We have testimony relating to these elections which is not altogether untrustworthy, but it would be impossible to gain correct and clear views of the personal relations and motives really in action on these occasions: our best efforts would still leave some shadows.

It must suffice that we direct attention to the principle. At the period in question, the pontiff elected was invariably the antagonist, and never the adherent, of the Pope preceding. He was the creature of the last but one.* A similar practice prevailed at the election of Sixtus V, who was elevated from among the adversaries of his predecessor, Gregory XIII.

By virtue of this mode of succession, the opponents of Sixtus V, especially those of his later policy, found a cheering prospect opened before them. The creatures of Gregory succeeded in electing an opponent of the late pontiff; this was Giovanni Battista Castagnei, Urban VII.

But they were not fortunate in their choice. Urban VII died before he had been crowned, before he had nominated a single prelate, when he had worn the tiara twelve days only; the contest of election had consequently to be opened anew.†

In view of the decisive action taken by his successor, Gregory XIV, against the French King, in view of the cleverness of Philip II, the wealth of the Pope, and the influence which their united status exerted on France, it is indeed hardly calculable to what end this dual worldly-spiritual ambition might have led had not Gregory XIV died after having occupied the throne for only ten months and ten days. It was the greatest loss to the Spanish party.

Once more the Spaniards asserted themselves in the conclave. But their misfortune was that Innocent IX was also very old and weak; he hardly ever left his bed; he even held his audiences there. From the death-bed of an old man who could hardly move came incitement to war which set France and Europe in commotion. Hardly having been on the papal throne for more than two months, he also died.

Thus the election campaigns were renewed for the fourth time. Now a definite long-term decision was called for. This conclave became a moment of importance for the general history. And now it was that the Spaniards were compelled to aid in the elevation of a creature of Sixtus V to the Papal See.†

It is to be observed that on this occasion a change in the course of the papal elections was originated which we cannot consider unimportant. Men of opposite factions had for a long time invariably succeeded each other. Even now the same thing had occurred. The adherents of Sixtus V had been driven three times from the contest, but the victors had possessed only a transitory enjoyment of power, and had not been able to form any new or powerful faction. Deaths, funerals, and new conclaves had rapidly followed each other. The first who once more attained the papal throne, in the full vigor of life, was Clement VIII. The government of which he was the head was that of the same party by whom the most enduring tenure of power had of late years been held.

Attention was now universally directed to the inquiry of who the new ruler was, and what might be expected from him.

Clement VIII was born in exile. His father, Salvestro Aldobrandino, of a distinguished Florentine family but a determined and active antagonist of the Medici, was banished on the ultimate triumph of that house in the year 1531 and compelled to seek his fortune in other lands. He was a doctor of laws and had once taught in Pisa. We find him, soon after his banishment, in Venice, where he took part in the amelioration of the Venetian statutes, and in an edition of the institutes. We next meet him in Ferrara or Urbino, forming part of the council or tribunal of the duke; but more permanently in the service, first of one and then of another among the cardinals, as whose deputy he was charged with the administration of justice or of the government in one or other of the ecclesiastical cities. He is perhaps most clearly distinguished by the fact that in this uncertain mode of life he found means to educate five excellent sons. The most highly gifted among them was perhaps Giovanni, the eldest, whom they called the helmsman of the family. It was by him that their path was cleared. Entering on the judicial career, he rose from its dignities to that of cardinal in the year 1570. Had he lived longer, it is believed that he might have had well-founded hopes of the tiara. Bernardo gained renown as a soldier. Tommaso was a good philologist; his translation of Diogenes Laertius has been frequently reprinted. Pietro was reputed to be an excellent practical jurist. The youngest, Ippolito, born at Fano in the year 1536, was at first the cause of some anxiety to his father, who feared that he should be unable to provide him with an education worthy of his talents. But in the first instance Cardinal Alessandro Farnese took the boy under his protection and settled on him a yearly allowance from the revenues of his bishopric of Spoleto; the rising fortunes of his brothers were afterward sufficient of themselves to bring him forward. He soon obtained the prelacy, and next succeeded to the office of his eldest brother in the court of the Rota. He was nominated cardinal by Sixtus V, who dispatched him on an embassy to Poland. This it was that first brought him into a sort of contact with the house of Austria. All the members of that family considered themselves his debtors for helping to liberate the Archduke Maximilian from the captivity he had been held in by the Poles—a service in the performance of which he had used his authority with a prudence and foresight that could not but insure admiration as well as success. When Philip II resolved on nominating a cardinal created by Sixtus as a supernumerary, it was this circumstance that induced him to prefer Aldobrandino to others. And thus did the son of a homeless fugitive, of whom it was at one moment feared that he must pass his life as a scribe, attain to the highest dignity in Christendom.

There is a monument in the church of Santa Maria alla Minerva in Rome, the inscription on which it is impossible to read without a certain feeling of satisfaction. It was erected by Salvestro Aldobrandino to the mother of so noble a band of sons, and is inscribed as follows: "To his dear wife Lesa, of the house of Deti, with whom he lived in harmony for seven and thirty years."

The new pontiff brought to his office all that activity peculiar to a family which has contended with difficulties. He held his sessions in the early hours of the morning, his audiences in the afternoon; all reports were received and investigated, all dispatches were read and discussed, legal arguments were sought out, early precedents compared. It was no unusual thing for the Pope to display more knowledge of the subject in question than was possessed by the referendaries who laid it before him. He labored with equal assiduity when Pope as when he was auditor of the Rota. His attention was given to the details of internal policy as to those of Europe in general, or to the great interests of the ecclesiastical authority.

Nor would he permit himself the slightest negligence in his spiritual duties. Baronius received his confession every evening; he celebrated mass himself every morning. Twelve poor men dined daily in the same room with himself, at least during the early years of his pontificate, and the pleasures of the table were in his case altogether out of the question. On Fridays and Saturdays, moreover, he fasted. When he had labored earnestly through the week, his recreation on the Sunday was to send for some pious monks, or for the fathers of the Vallicella, and hold discourse with them on the more profound questions of divinity. The reputation for virtue, piety, and an exemplary life that he had always enjoyed was raised to an extraordinary degree by such modes of proceeding. He knew this, and desired it; for by this reputation he could command greater respect as sovereign pastor of the Church.*

It is manifest that the strength of the papacy itself was thereby immeasurably increased. Human institutions are strong only so long as their spirit has vital existence, and exhibits its efficacy in those who wield the powers they create.

Absolution Of Henry IV

And now everybody was wondering how this pontiff, so remarkable for talent, activity, and force, and withal so blameless in character, would consider and act upon the most momentous question of Europe—that of France.

Would he attach himself unconditionally to Spain, as his immediate predecessors had done? There was nothing in his previous life that imposed on him the necessity for this, neither was he led to it by personal inclination. He did not fail to notice that the predominance of Spain was becoming oppressive even to the papacy, and would despoil it more especially of its political independence.

Or would he decide for the party of Henry IV? It is true that this prince gave intimations of becoming Catholic, but such a promise was more readily given than fulfilled: he was still a Protestant. Clement VIII feared to be betrayed.†

Throughout his general attitude and his official pronouncements, Clement appears as the head of the hispano-ecclesiastical, strictly orthodox party; not, it is true, with the fervor and devotion by which other popes had been distinguished. If he possessed these qualities, they were effective in secret only. It was enough for him to proceed quietly and without reproach, as the order of public affairs demanded, in adherence to that party which he had once adopted and which seemed to have the closest analogy with the idea of his office. We may, nevertheless, clearly perceive that he had no wish for the perfect estrangement of the opposite party. He was careful, on the contrary, to avoid provoking it to hostilities, and by secret advances and indirect expressions inspired it with the hope of reconciliation to take place at some future day. He contented the Spaniards, but their rivals were suffered to believe that his actions were not altogether free, that their character was indeed determined by deference to the wishes of Spain and not by any harsher feeling. The indecision of Sixtus arose from the strife of opposite opinions contending within himself. Clement respected both sides and chose his line of policy with the purpose of conciliating both. His proceedings were governed by prudence and circumspection; they resulted from extensive experience and the wish to avoid exciting enmities. But it followed necessarily that he too failed to exercise any decisive influence.

The affairs of France, thus left to themselves, proceeded all the more freely in the development of their natural impulses.†

In this situation it became evident to all, and the Protestants themselves did not deny it, that if Henry desired to be king he must become Catholic. We need not investigate the claim of those who assert that they gave the final impulse to the decision. The principal part was effected by the grand combination of circumstances, the necessity of things. In undertaking his conversion to Catholicism, Henry associated himself with that national sentiment of the French Catholics, which was represented by the "tiers-parti," and the party called the "political," and which had now the prospect of maintaining the ascendancy in France.

This was in fact merely that "Catholic opposition" which had gathered round the banners of legitimacy and national independence for the purpose of resisting the ecclesiastical and Spanish interests. But how greatly had it now increased in power and importance! It had without question predominance in the public opinion of the country. The people throughout France declared for it, if not openly, at least in private. It now attained a firm internal support from the change of religion in the King, a prince moreover so warlike, so generous, and so successful. Thus enforced and extended, this party once more appeared before the Pope and implored his recognition and blessing. What glory would he obtain, and how effective an influence, if he would now at least declare himself without circumlocution in its favor! And there was still so much depending on it. The prelates who had received the King into the bosom of the Church had indeed done so only conditionally, contingent on the absolution of the Pope. This was also earnestly enforced by the most powerful members of the League, with whom Henry had commenced negotiations. Although promises are not always performed, it is yet unquestionable that the papal absolution, had it been granted at this moment, would have produced important effects on the course of events. Henry IV sent one of the great nobles of his kingdom, the Duke of Nevers, to solicit this from the Pope, and a truce was agreed on while awaiting the reply.

But Clement was distrustful and wary. As the hopes of a religious ambition had influenced Sixtus V, so did the fear of being deceived and involved in vexatious consequences restrain Clement VIII. He still felt apprehensive lest Henry should, after all, return to Protestantism as he had done once before.* Nevers was quite amazed to find himself so coldly received, and to see how indifferent an ear was turned to his proposals. When he found all his efforts fruitless, he asked the Pope at length what the King should do to merit favor from his Holiness. The Pope replied that there were theologians enough in France to instruct him on that count. "But will your Holiness be satisfied with what the theologians shall decide?" To this the Pope refused a reply.* He did not wish their conversations to be considered an official communication, but simply a private discourse, and was not to be prevailed on to give any written decision.

Man has rarely much feeling except for his own personal situation. The Roman Curia understood only what was of advantage to itself. We can find no true sympathy for the fate of France in its proceedings.

It is true that we know enough of this pontiff to believe that he did not mean absolutely to repulse the adherents of Henry IV. Least of all would he do that now, when their strength was so much greater than formerly. On the contrary, he assured a secret agent that the King had only to show himself completely Catholic, and absolution should not be wanting. It is characteristic of Clement that while in public he so stubbornly refrained from taking any part in the return of Henry to the Catholic faith, yet, in private, he intimated to the Grand Duke of Tuscany that he would make no objection to anything the clergy of France might decide on doing. The Grand Duke was also empowered to communicate favorable expressions on the part of the Pope to the chiefs of the Catholic royalists. But in all this, he thought only of securing himself, and thus the affairs of France were left to do as they could.

The truce was at an end. The sword was once more drawn—once again everything depended on the fortunes of war. But here the superiority of Henry became at once and decidedly manifest.† And herein he found occasion to show himself a good Catholic. Wherever the ritual of the Church had been departed from during the late troubles, he took care to reestablish it. And where it had maintained itself in exclusive possession, he solemnly confirmed to it the right of doing so. All this he did without having yet been reconciled with the Pope.

It had, however, now become urgently necessary to the pontiff himself to facilitate a reconciliation. If he had delayed longer, a schism might have been occasioned. An entirely separate French church might have been established.†

Preparations were accordingly made for the completion of the ceremony, which took place on the seventeenth of December 1595. The pontiff's throne was erected before the Church of St. Peter, the cardinals and Curia reverently surrounding their sovereign. The petition of Henry, with the conditions to which he had assented, were read aloud. The representatives of the most Christian King thereupon threw themselves at the feet of the Pope, who gave them absolution by a light stroke of a stick. The Papal See once more appeared on this occasion in all the splendor of its ancient authority.

And this ceremony was, in fact, the manifestation of a great success. The ruling power in France, now strong in itself and firmly founded, was again Catholic. Its interest consequently was to keep on good terms with the Pope. A new focus for Catholicism was formed in that country, and from this a most efficient influence inevitably had to proceed.

When more carefully contemplated, this event is seen to offer two distinct aspects.

It was not by the immediate influence of the Pope, nor by victory obtained by the rigidly Catholic party, that France had been recovered; it was rather by the union of opinions taking a medium between the two extremes of party. This result was brought about by the superior force of that body which had at first constituted itself in opposition. It followed that the French church assumed a position entirely different from that accorded to those of Italy, the Netherlands, or the newly established church of Germany. It submitted to the Pope, but this was done with a freedom and essential independence proceeding from its origin, the consciousness of which was never again resigned. Thus the Papal See was far from having the right to consider France a complete conquest.

But the second aspect, the political side, presented the most important advantages. The balance of power was restored. Two great sovereignties, each jealous of the other, and both involved in continual strife and conflict, kept each other within due limits. Both were Catholic and might eventually be guided into the same direction, but in any case, the Pope assumed between them a position of far greater independence than his predecessors had for a long time found it possible to attain. From those fetters, hitherto thrown about him by the Spanish preponderance, he was now, to a great extent, freed.

The political aspect was first emphasized in the immediate course of events. It was on the lapse of Ferrara to the Papal See that the French influence first again became manifest in the affairs of Italy.[21]

Commotions Among The Jesuits

The great and fortunate results obtained by Clement VIII from acting in harmony with the policy of France were manifestly calculated to bind him more and more closely to its interests. He now found the advantage of having conducted himself with so much caution in the affairs of the League; of his having opposed no obstacle to the development of events in France, and of having resolved, though it were but at the last moment, to grant the desired absolution. The war now proceeding on the frontier of France and the Netherlands awakened as lively an interest in Rome as though the cause had been their own, and all were decidedly on the French side.*

[21] The sections on "Ferrara Under Alfonso II" and "Conquest of Ferrara" have been omitted (pages 178–194).

Not that people at Rome had begun to feel any affection for those whom they had formerly combated. The chiefs of the clergy, who had been the first to attach themselves to Henry and had founded the opposition party previously described, were never allowed to forget it. Promotion was much more readily accorded to the adherents of the League if they had changed sides voluntarily—that is, when they were precisely in the same condition as the Curia itself. But there soon arose a Catholic party, even among the adherents of the King (for the opinions of men, however nearly they may be approximate, yet manifest varieties of disposition), whose determination it was to evince the most rigid Catholicism because they desired above all things to maintain a good understanding with the Court of Rome. To this party the pontiff especially attached himself, hoping to reconcile all the differences still existing between the French and Roman interests. He desired and endeavored above all to accomplish the restoration of the Jesuits, who had been driven out of France, and thus to secure a wider field for the extension of the Roman doctrines, notwithstanding the adverse disposition manifested in France.

In this design Clement was aided by a commotion in the Society of Jesus itself, and which, though taking its rise within the order, had yet a close analogy with the change of the general tendencies in the Roman Court.

So strangely are the affairs of this world sometimes complicated that at the moment when the connection of the Jesuits with Spain was charged against them by the University of Paris as their heaviest crime, when it was asserted and believed in France that every Jesuit was bound by a fifth vow to devote himself to Spain and to pray daily for King Philip—at that very moment the company was enduring the most violent assaults in Spain itself, first from discontented members of its own body, then from the Inquisition, next from another ecclesiastical order, and finally from the King himself.

This was a turn of events that had its origin in more than one cause, but of which the immediate occasion was as follows.

At the first establishment of the order, the elder and already trained men who had just entered it were for the most part Spaniards; the members joining it from other nations were chiefly young men, whose characters had yet to be formed. It followed naturally that the government of the society was, for the first ten years, almost entirely in Spanish hands. The first general congregation was composed of twenty-five members, eighteen of whom were Spaniards. The first three generals belonged to the same nation. After the death of the third, Borgia, in the year 1573, it was once more a Spaniard, Polanco, who had the best prospect of election.

It was, however, manifest that his elevation would not have been regarded favorably, even in Spain itself.* Pope Gregory XIV, who had received certain intimations on this subject, considered a change to be expedient on other grounds also.* He even proposed a candidate for election. The Jesuits opposed themselves for a moment to this suggestion, as a violation of their privileges, but concluded by electing the very man proposed by the pontiff. This was Eberhard Mercurianus.

A material change was introduced as the consequence of this choice. Mercurianus, a weak and irresolute man, resigned the government of affairs, first indeed to a Spaniard again, but afterward to a Frenchman, his official admonitor. Factions were formed, one expelling the other from the offices of importance; the ruling faction occasionally met resistance from its subordinate members.

But a circumstance of much higher moment was that on the next vacancy—in the year 1581—this office was conferred on Claudius Acquaviva, a Neapolitan belonging to a house previously attached to the French party, a man of great energy, and only thirty-eight years old.* The aged, learned, and experienced members thus saw themselves excluded, not from the supreme dignity only, but also from the official appointments in the Spanish province.† Under these circumstances, the older Jesuits in Spain became convinced that a state of things, which they felt to be a tyranny, could never be changed or amended by efforts confined to the limit of the society. They consequently resolved to look around for help from those beyond its influence.

They first had recourse to the national spiritual authority of their country—the Inquisition.* The Inquisition was, however, only empowered to punish; it could not prescribe changes. When the affair, therefore, had progressed thus far, the discontented members applied to the King, assailing him with long memorials, wherein they complained about the defects in their constitution. The character of this constitution had never been agreeable to Philip II. He used to say that he could see through all the other orders, but that the order of Jesuits he could not understand. He was particularly taken with the representations of the abuses resulting from absolute power, and the evils attendant on secret accusations. He at once commanded Manrique, Bishop of Carthagena, to subject the order to a visitation, with particular reference to these points.

It will be remarked that this was an attack against the character of the institution, and against its chief himself. It was particularly important because it originated in the country where the society had originated and first established itself.*

Acquaviva was unafraid. In view of the nature of Sixtus V, it was easy for him to excite the antipathies of that pontiff against the proceedings of the Spaniards. Pope Sixtus had formed the hope, as we know, of rendering Rome, more decidedly than it ever yet was, the metropolis of Christendom. Acquaviva assured him that Spain was trying to make itself independent of Rome. Pope Sixtus hated nothing so much as illegitimate birth, and Acquaviva had him informed that Manrique, the bishop selected as "Visitator" of the Jesuits, was illegitimate. These were reasons sufficient to make Sixtus recall the assent he had already given to the visitation. From his successor, Gregory XIV, the general succeeded in obtaining a formal confirmation of the rule of the order.

But his antagonists also were unyielding and crafty. They perceived that the general must be attacked in the Court of Rome itself. They availed themselves of a momentary absence—Acquaviva had been charged with the arrangement of a difference between Mantua and Parma—to win Clement VIII to their wishes. In the summer of 1592, at the request of the Spanish Jesuits and Philip II but without the knowledge of Acquaviva, the pontiff commanded that a general congregation should be held.

Astonished and alarmed, Acquaviva hastened back. To the generals of the Jesuits these "congregations" were no less inconvenient than were the convocations of the Church to the popes. And if his predecessors were anxious to avoid them, how much more cause had Acquaviva, against whom so active an enmity was agitating! But he was soon convinced that the arrangement was irrevocable; he therefore hastened to take his measures.*

When the congregation was assembled, he did not wait to be attacked. In the very first sitting he declared that he had had the misfortune to displease some of his brethren, and therefore begged that his conduct might be investigated before any other business was entered on. A commission was thereupon appointed and charges were formally made, but it was impossible to convict him of violating any positive law: he was much too prudent to expose himself to such an accusation, and was triumphantly acquitted.

Having thus secured himself personally, he joined the assembly in its investigation of the proposals regarding the general affairs of the institute.

Philip of Spain had demanded some changes, and had recommended others for consideration. On two things he insisted: the resignation of certain papal privileges, those of reading forbidden books, for example, and of granting absolution for the crime of heresy; and a law, by virtue of which every novice who entered the order should surrender whatever patrimonial rights he might possess, and should even resign all his benefices. These were matters in regard to which the order came into collision with the Inquisition and the civil government. After some hesitation, the demands of the King were complied with, principally through the influence of Acquaviva himself.

But the points recommended by Philip for consideration were of much higher moment. First of all came the questions whether the authority of the superiors should not be limited to a certain period, and whether a general congregation should not be held at certain fixed intervals. The very essence and being of the institute, the rights of absolute sovereignty, were here brought into question. Acquaviva was not on this occasion disposed to comply. After an animated discussion, the congregation rejected these propositions of Philip; but the Pope, also, was convinced of their necessity. What had been refused to the King was now commanded by the Pope. By the plenitude of his apostolic power, he determined and ordained that the superiors and rectors should be changed every third year, and that at the expiration of every sixth year, a general congregation should be assembled.

It is, indeed, true that the execution of these ordinances did not effect as much as had been hoped from them. The congregation could be won over, and though the rectors were changed, yet they were selected out of so narrow a circle, that the same men were soon returned to their appointments. It was, nevertheless, a very serious blow to the society that it had been compelled, by internal revolt and interference from without, to a change in its statutes.

And there was already a new storm arising from the same quarter.

At first, the Jesuits had adhered to the doctrinal system of the Thomists.* But they very soon became persuaded that with these doctrines they could not perfectly attain their end in their contest with the Protestants. They wished to be independent in their tenets as well as in their lives. It was mortifying to the Jesuits to follow in the train of the Dominicans, to whom St. Thomas had belonged and who were regarded as the natural expositors of his opinions. After they had already given so many intimations of these views and feelings that allusion had occasionally been made in the Inquisition to the free mode of thinking perceptible among the Jesuit fathers, Acquaviva came forward in the year 1584, proclaiming them openly in his "Order of Studies." He affirmed that St. Thomas was, indeed, an author deserving the highest approbation but that it would be an insufferable yoke to be compelled to follow his footsteps in all things and on no point to be allowed a free opinion; that many ancient doctrines had been more firmly established by recent theologians, who had brought forward many new arguments which served admirably in the conflict with heretics; and that in all such it was permitted to follow these doctors.

This alone was sufficient to occasion great excitement in Spain, where the chairs of theology were occupied for the most part by Dominicans. The "Order of Studies" was declared to be the boldest, most presumptuous, and dangerous book of its kind. Both the King and the Pope were applied to on the subject.

But how must the commotion have increased when the system of the Thomists was soon afterward positively abandoned in one of the most important doctrines of the Jesuits!

In all of theology, Catholic and Protestant, the disputes respecting grace and merits, free will and predestination, were still the most important and exciting. They continually occupied the minds and employed the learning and speculative powers of clergy and laity alike. On the Protestant side, a majority was secured to that severe doctrine of Calvin, of the individual decree of God, according to which "some were predestined to eternal blessedness, and others to everlasting damnation." The Lutherans, with their milder views, were here at a disadvantage, and lost ground, now in one place and now in another. A different tendency of opinions was manifested on the Catholic side.* The system of doctrine propounded by the Council of Trent—and which would never have been established but for the influence of their brethren, Lainez and Salmeron—was defended by the Jesuits against every symptom of deviation toward the tenets that had then been abjured and abandoned. Nor did even that system always suffice to content their polemical zeal.* In Trent the work of salvation had been declared to be chiefly founded on the inherent righteousness of Christ, which, being infused into us, calls forth or gives birth to love, conduces to all virtues and to good works, and finally produces justification. Luis Molina of Evara proceeded an important step further. He maintained that free will, even without the help of grace, can produce morally good works; that it can resist temptation and can elevate itself to various acts of hope, faith, love, and repentance. When man is ready, then God, for the sake of Christ's merits, grants him grace, and by means of this he experiences the supernatural operations of sanctification. But even in the reception of this grace, and in the furtherance of its growth, free will is continually in action. Everything, in fact, depends on this will. It rests with us to make the help of God effectual or ineffectual. On the union of the will and of grace it is that justification depends; they are combined, as are two men who are rowing in a boat. It is obvious that Molina could not here admit the doctrine of predestination as announced by Augustine or by Thomas Aquinas. He considers it too stern, too cruel: he will not hear of any other predestination than that which is simply and purely foreknowledge. Now God, from his supreme insight into the nature of each man's will, has previous knowledge of what each will do in given cases, although he was left free to do the contrary. Yet an event does not occur because God foreknew it, but God foresaw it because it would happen.

This was a doctrine that certainly went to the opposite extreme of Calvin's and was also the first which attempted to rationalize the mystery, if we may so speak. It is intelligible, acute, and superficial, and could therefore not fail to produce a certain effect. It may be compared with the doctrine of the sovereignty of the people, which the Jesuits promulgated about that time.

That these opinions should provoke opposition in their own church was an inevitable consequence, had it been only that they departed from St. Thomas, whose "Summa" was still the principal textbook of Catholic theologians. They were even censured, and that openly, by certain members of their own society, as Henriquez and Mariana. But much more eagerly did the Dominicans engage in the defense of their patriarch. Not content with writing and preaching against Molina, they attacked him in their lectures also. It was at length agreed that a disputation should be held between the two parties, and this took place at Valladolid on March 4, 1594. The Dominicans, who believed themselves in exclusive possession of the orthodox creed, became vehement. "Are the keys of wisdom, then," exclaimed a Jesuit, "confided to your hands?" The Dominicans burst into loud outcries—they considered this to be an attack on St. Thomas himself.

Thenceforth a complete estrangement existed between these two orders. The Dominicans would have nothing more to do with the Jesuits. Of these last the greater number, if not all, took the side of Molina. Acquaviva himself, with his "assistants," was on his side.

But here also the Inquisition prepared to interfere. The Grand

Inquisitor—it was that same Geronimo Manrique who had been selected as "visitator of the order"—showed a disposition to condemn Molina; he gave him notice that his book was not likely to escape with a mere reprobation or prohibition, but would be condemned to the flames. Of the counter-charges that Molina made against the Dominicans in return, the Grand Inquisitor refused to take cognizance.

This was a controversy by which the whole world of Catholicism was set in commotion, as well for the doctrines themselves as on account of their champions. It also greatly increased the violence of that enmity to the Jesuits which had arisen in Spain.

And from this state of things there resulted the extraordinary phenomenon that while the Jesuits were driven out of France for their attachment to Spain, they were in that country made the objects of the most perilous assaults. In either country, political and religious motives combined to produce this result; the political was in both fundamentally the same—it was a national opposition to the privileges and immunities of the order. In France it was more impetuous and fiercer, but in Spain it was more definite and better founded. In regard to doctrine, it was by their new tenets that the Jesuits had provoked hatred and persecution. Their doctrine of the sovereignty of the people, and the opinions they held as to regicide, were the causes of their ruin in France; their tenets respecting free will had produced the injury they suffered in Spain.

This was a moment in the history of the society which was of infinite importance to its future direction.

Against the assaults of the national authorities, the Parliament and the Inquisition, Acquaviva sought aid from the central point and general referee of the whole Church—from the pontiff himself.

He availed himself of the favorable moment when the Grand Inquisitor, Manrique, had just died and his place had not yet been filled, and prevailed on the Pope to summon the dispute concerning doctrine to Rome for examination.† In this controversy, Clement VIII showed a lively theological interest. Sixty-five meetings and thirty-seven disputations were held in his own presence on all the points that could be brought into question as regarded the tenets under examination. He wrote much on the subject himself, and, so far as we can judge, was inclined toward the old established doctrines, and to a decision in favor of the Dominicans. Bellarmin himself said that he did not deny the pontiff's inclination to declare against the Jesuits, but that he also knew for certain that his Holiness would not do so. It would indeed have been too dangerous, at a time when the Jesuits were the most distinguished apostles of the faith throughout the world, to break with them about one article of their creed. The French also took too decided a part. Henry IV was on the Jesuit side, either because he found their expositions convincing, which was certainly possible, or that he gave a particular support to that order which most earnestly opposed itself to Protestantism as a means of placing his own orthodoxy beyond doubt. Cardinal du Perron took part in the congregations and supported the Jesuit disputants with well-directed zeal. He told Clement VIII that a Protestant might subscribe the creed of the Dominicans and he may well have impressed him thereby.

The active rivalry between Spain and France, by which the whole world was set in commotion, became mingled with these disputes also. The Dominicans found as zealous a support from the Spaniards as did the Jesuits from the French.

From all this it resulted that Clement VIII did not, in fact, pronounce any decision. It would have involved him in new perplexities had he offended either one or the other of those influential orders or of those powerful sovereigns.

Political Situation Of Clement VIII

Precisely this became one of the prime considerations of the Papal See: never to offend one or the other of the two powers on which the balance of the Catholic world depended, to settle their disputes or at least to avoid an outbreak of war between them, and to maintain its influence with both.

The papacy here appears to us in its most praiseworthy vocation, mediating and making peace.

It was to Clement VIII that the world was principally indebted for the peace concluded at Vervins on May 2, 1598. He seized the favorable moment when the King of France was compelled by the disordered state of his finances, and the King of Spain by the increasing feebleness of his advanced age, to think of some accommodation.* The Spaniards held a large number of fortresses in France and were prepared to restore them all with the exception of Calais, but the French insisted on the restitution of Calais also; and it was by Fra Calatagirona, the general of the Franciscans, that the Spaniards were prevailed on to resign it.

This being accomplished, the negotiations at Vervins were formally opened; a legate and a nuncio presided over them. The general of the Franciscans continued to mediate with the utmost ability. The most important result was that the King of France resolved to separate himself from his allies—England and Holland. This was considered to be an advantage to Catholicism because the secession of Henry from the Protestant system appeared hereby to be completed. Henry consented after long hesitations, and the Spaniards then made an effectual restitution of all their conquests; the right of possessorship was restored to its condition of the year 1559. The legate declared that his Holiness would have more pleasure in this consummation than in the acquisition of Ferrara; that a peace bringing tranquillity to all of Christendom would be of much higher importance in his estimation than the mere temporal conquest.*

Under these fortunate circumstances, Clement VIII sometimes thought of directing the combined forces of the whole Catholic world, now united under his auspices, against its old hereditary enemy. The war against the Turks had again broken out in Hungary, but even then it was thought that an increasing weakness had become perceptible in the Ottoman Empire. The personal inefficiency of the sultans, the influence of the seraglio, and the perpetual insurrections, more especially in Asia, made it probable that something effectual might now be done against Turkey. The Pope, at least, did not fail on his part. In 1599 already the sum he had expended on this war amounted to 1,500,000 scudi, and we soon afterward find a papal army of 12,000 men on the Danube. But how much more important were the consequences that might be expected if the powers of the West could once be united on a large scale for an Eastern expedition—above all, if Henry IV would resolve to combine his forces with those of Austria. The Pope did not neglect to encourage him to this, and Henry did, in fact, write to the Venetians immediately after the peace of Vervins to the effect that he hoped shortly to embark in Venice, like the French of old times, for an expedition against Constantinople. He repeated his promise at the conclusion of peace with Savoy, but it is certain that its execution first required a much more cordial understanding than could possibly have been attained so soon after collisions of so much violence.

But on the other hand, the continuing opposition and rivalry between the two principal powers were more than once advantageous to the Papal See in its own affairs. Pope Clement had, indeed, once more occasion to avail himself of them for the interests of the States of the Church.[22]

Election And First Measures Of Paul V

Even in the next conclave, the French influence was manifest.* A cardinal whom the Spanish King had excluded by name, a Medici and near relative to the Queen of France, was raised to the papal dignity by their influence. The letters in which du Perron announced this unexpected event to Henry IV are full of exultation. The accession was celebrated in France with public festivities. But their triumph was of short duration. Leo XI, as this Pope was named, survived his election only twenty-six days. It is affirmed that the sense of his dignity, and the idea he entertained of the difficulties surrounding his office, completely extinguished the powers of a life already much weakened by age.

The tumults of an election contest were now renewed, but

[22] Pages 214–220 have been omitted.

with increased violence since Cardinal Aldobrandino was no longer in so firm an alliance with the French. Montalto opposed him powerfully and a conflict ensued, as at previous elections, between the creatures of the last pontiff and those of his predecessor. Occasionally, each of the two parties conducted the candidate of its choice, surrounded by his adherents, to one or the other of the chapels as they confronted one another. Attempts were made to elect a pope, first from one party and then another. Baronius, though resisting with all his force, was on one occasion dragged into the Pauline chapel. But the opposition displayed increased strength at each successive attempt, and neither party found it possible to carry any one of its candidates. The choice of a pontiff, like many other promotions, was gradually made to depend on who had the fewest enemies, rather than on who possessed the greatest merit.

Aldobrandino at length cast his eyes on a man among those elevated by his uncle, who had found the means to conciliate general favor and to avoid all dangerous enmities: this was Cardinal Borghese. For him Aldobrandino succeeded in securing the favor of the French, by whom an approach to reconciliation between Montalto and Aldobrandino had already been effected. Montalto, therefore, gave his vote to Borghese, who was elected before the Spaniards had heard that he was proposed. This election took place on May 16, 1605.

We find, then, that once more the nephew of the last Pope determined the election of the new one. The Borghese family was, besides, in a similar position to that of Aldobrandino. As the latter had quitted Florence to avoid submission to the rule of the Medici, so had the former left Siena for the same cause. There hence appeared a further probability that the new government would be a direct continuation of the preceding one.

But immediately after his election, Paul V evinced a peculiarly harsh disposition.

He had risen from the rank of an advocate through all the degrees of ecclesiastical dignity. He had been vice-legate at Bologna, auditor of the *Camera*, vicar of the Pope, and inquisitor. He had lived in close retirement buried in his books and law papers, and had taken no part in political affairs; thence it was that he had made his way without awakening personal enmities. No party considered him its opponent, neither Aldobrandino nor Montalto, neither the French nor the Spaniards. This, then, was the quality which had secured him the tiara.

But he considered that event in a totally different light. His elevation to the papacy, without any effort on his own part, without the employment of any arts or devices, appeared to him the direct interposition of the Holy Spirit. He felt raised above himself by this conviction. The change in his carriage and demeanor, nay, even in his countenance and the tone of his voice, was a matter of astonishment even to the Court of Rome, which was yet well accustomed to metamorphoses of every sort. But the new pontiff felt himself at the same time enchained and pledged to most important duties. With inflexibility similar to that with which he had observed the letter of the law in his previous offices, he now prepared to administer the supreme dignity.

Other popes had been accustomed to signalize their elevation to the throne by acts of clemency; Paul V, on the contrary, began his reign by passing a sentence, the remembrance of which excites horror even to the present day.

A poor author, a Cremonese by birth, named Piccinardi, impelled by some unexplained disgust had employed himself in his solitude in composing a Life of Clement VIII, wherein he compared that Pope with the Emperor Tiberius—small as was the similarity to be found between these rulers. He had not only refrained from printing this strange work, but had kept it quite to himself and had scarcely permitted its existence to be known. A woman, who had formerly resided in his house, gave information of the book. Paul V expressed himself at first very mildly on the subject, and the author seemed to have little cause for anxiety, the rather as many important persons, and even ambassadors, had interceded for him. How greatly then were all astonished when Piccinardi was one day beheaded on the bridge of Saint Angelo!*

At court this pontiff instantly renewed the regulations of the Council of Trent with respect to residence. He declared it to be a mortal sin for a bishop to remain absent from his diocese and still enjoy its revenues. From this rule he did not except the cardinals, nor would he admit holding an office in the administration as an excuse for non-residence. Many retired to their sees accordingly, others begged for some delay. But there were some who would not consent to leave Rome and yet did not wish to be accused of neglecting their duties; these, therefore, sent in the resignation of their bishoprics.

But the most serious evil of Paul's early reign was the circumstance that he had derived from his studies in canon law the most exorbitant ideas concerning the importance of the papacy. The doctrines that the Pope is the sole vicar of Jesus Christ, that the power of the keys is entrusted to his discretion, and that he is to be reverenced in humility by all nations and princes, he desired to maintain in their most extended significance. He affirmed that he had been raised to that seat, not by men, but by the Divine Spirit and with the duty imposed on him of guarding every immunity of the Church and all the prerogatives of God; that he was bound in conscience to put forth all his strength for the deliverance of the Church from usurpation and violence. He would rather risk his life to fulfill these duties than be called to account for the neglect of them when he should appear before the throne of God.

With juridical severity he assumed the claims of the Church to be identical with her rights, and regarded it as a point of conscience to revive and carry them out in their utmost rigor.[23]

Issue Of The Affairs
Of The Jesuits

The contest between the Jesuits and Dominicans was meanwhile terminated, albeit very imperfectly.

Clement died, as we have seen, before he had pronounced judgment. The question was taken up by Paul V with all the zeal

[23] The section on "Disputes with Venice" has been omitted (pages 224–242).

by which the early part of his administration was distinguished. No fewer than seventeen meetings were held in his presence, from September 1605 to February 1606. He was equally disposed as his predecessor had been toward the old system and to the side of the Dominicans. In October and November 1606, meetings were even held for the purpose of deciding on the form in which the Jesuit doctrines should be condemned. The Dominicans believed they held the victory already in their hands.

But it was about this time that some disputes with Venice had been settled, whereby the Jesuits had given proof of their attachment to the Holy See which far surpassed every other order, and for this Venice was now making them pay the penalty.

Under these circumstances it would have seemed cruelty in the Roman See to have visited these, its most faithful servants, with a decree of condemnation. When all was prepared for that purpose, the Pope paused; for some time he suffered the affair to rest. At length, on August 29, 1607, he published a declaration by which "disputatores" and "consultores" were dismissed to their respective homes. The decision was to be made known in due time; meanwhile it was the most earnest desire of his Holiness that neither party should asperse or disparage the other.

By this decision the Jesuits, after all, derived an advantage from the losses they had sustained in Venice. It was a great gain for them that their disputed doctrines, though certainly not confirmed, were yet not rejected. They even boasted of victory, and with their characteristic self-assured belief in their own orthodoxy they now pursued with unremitting ardor the course of doctrine to which they had before attached themselves.

The only question yet remaining was whether they would also succeed in settling their internal disputes.

Violent ferment still prevailed in the order. The changes made in its constitution proved insufficient, and the members of the Spanish opposition persisted in their efforts for securing their principal aim, namely the removal of Acquaviva. The procurators of all the provinces at length declared a general congregation necessary, which was a circumstance that never had occurred before. In the year 1607, the members assembled, and there was once more talk of stringent measures.

We have already more than once alluded to the close alliance into which the Jesuits had entered with Henry IV, and the favor accorded to them by that sovereign. He even took part in the internal disputes of the order and was entirely on the side of Acquaviva. In a letter written expressly for the purpose, he not only assured the general of his friendly regard, but also gave the congregation to understand his wish that no change in the constitution of the society should be proposed.

Nor did Acquaviva fail to make excellent use of so powerful a protection.

It was principally in the provincial congregations that the opposition he encountered had its seat. He now carried through a law, by virtue of which no proposition should in the first place be considered as adopted by a provincial assembly unless supported by two-thirds of the votes; and further, even when thus adopted, such proposition should not be admitted for discussion in the general assembly unless a majority of the latter had indicated provisional assent. These regulations were manifestly calculated to produce an extraordinary diminution in the authority of the provincial congregations.

Nor was this all. A formal sentence of condemnation was also pronounced on the enemies of the general, and the superiors of provinces received express command to proceed against the so-called disturbers of the peace. Tranquillity was thus gradually restored. The Spanish members resigned themselves to submission and ceased to contend against the new direction taken by their order. A more pliant generation gradually arose which was educated under the predominant influences. The general, on his side, endeavored to requite Henry IV by redoubled devotion for the favors received at his hands.

Conclusion

Thus were all these contentions once more allayed and gave promise of subsiding into peace.

But if we reflect on their progress and their results as a

whole, we perceive that the most essential changes had been thereby produced within the Catholic Church.

We started from that moment when the papal power, engaged in victorious conflict, was marching forward to the plenitude of power. In close alliance with the policy of Spain, it conceived the design of impelling all the Catholic powers in one direction and overwhelming those who had separated from it by one great movement. Had the papacy succeeded in this purpose, it would have exalted the ecclesiastical impulse to unlimited sovereignty; would have bound all Catholic states in one all-embracing unity of ideas, faith, social life, and policy; and would thus have secured to itself a paramount and irresistible influence even over their domestic affairs.

But at this precise moment the most violent internal dissensions arose.

In the matter of France, the feeling of nationality arrayed itself against the pretensions of the hierarchy. Even those who held the Catholic faith would not endure to be dependent on the ruling principles of the Church in every particular, nor to be guided on all points by the spiritual sovereign. There were other principles remaining—as of temporal policy, of national independence—all of which opposed themselves to the designs of the papacy with invincible energy. On the whole, we may affirm that these principles obtained the victory; the Pope was compelled to acknowledge them, and the French church even effected its restoration by adopting them as its basis.

But it followed from this circumstance that France again plunged herself into hostilities with the Spanish monarchy. Two great powers, naturally prone to rivalry and always disposed for battle, confronted each other in the center of the Catholic world—so little was it possible to preserve unity. The circumstances of Italy were indeed of such a character that these dissensions, and the balance of power resulting from them, produced advantages to the Roman See.

Meanwhile new theological discords also broke out. However acute and precise the definitions of the Council of Trent might be, they yet could not prevent disputes. Within the limits traced by these decisions there was still room for new controversies respecting the faith. The two most influential orders opposed each other in the lists. The two great powers even took part to a certain extent in the contest; nor had Rome the courage to pronounce a decision.

In addition to these dissensions came those regarding the limits of the ecclesiastical and secular jurisdictions—dissensions of local origin, and with a neighbor of no very important power, but conducted in a spirit and with an effect that raised them into universal importance. Justly the memory of Paolo Sarpi is held in honor through all Catholic states. He it was by whom those ecclesiastical rights, which they enjoy in common, were contended for and won. The Pope did not find himself capable of putting him down.

Conflicts thus marked between ideas and doctrines, between constitutional and absolute power, effectually impeded that ecclesiastical and secular unity which the papacy desired to establish, and even threatened to subvert it entirely.

The course of events made it nevertheless obvious that pacific and conservative ideas were once more the stronger. Internal discords were not to be prevented, but an open struggle was avoided. Peace was restored and maintained between the two great powers. Italian interests had not yet advanced to a full perception of their own strength, nor to an effectual activity in employing it. Silence was imposed on the contending orders; the differences between Church and State were not carried to extremity. Venice accepted the proffered mediation.

The policy of the papacy was to assume, as far as possible, a position above that of parties, and to mediate in their dissensions; a purpose which it still possessed sufficient authority to effect.

This policy, without doubt, was affected by that which had in part proceeded from itself, the continued progress, namely, of the great external movement, the advance of Catholic reformation, and the struggle with Protestantism, which was still proceeding without interruption.

To the further development of that struggle we must now return.

BOOK VII
COUNTER-REFORMATION,
SECOND PERIOD, 1590–1630

I think I do not deceive myself, or pass beyond the province of history, in supposing that I here discover one of the universal laws of life.

It is unquestionably true that the forces which move the very foundations of the world are always those of the living spirit; gradually prepared in the long course of bygone centuries, they arise in the fullness of time, called forth by natures of intrinsic might and vigor from the unfathomed depths of the human spirit. It is of their very essence and being that they should seek to gain possession of the world—to over-match and subdue it. But the more perfect their success, the more extended the circle of their action, so much the more certainly do they come in contact with peculiar and independent forms of life which they cannot wholly subdue or absorb into their own being. Hence it happens that being, as they are, in a state of never-ceasing development, they experience modifications in themselves. While appropriating what is foreign to their own existence, they also assume a portion of its characteristics. Tendencies are then developed within them—elements of existence—that are not infrequently at variance with their idea. These also must, however, necessarily expand and increase with the general progress. The object to be then secured is that they do not obtain the predominance; for if this were permitted, all unity, and that essential principle on which it reposes, would be utterly destroyed.

We have seen how violent internal contradictions and profound contrasts were in action during the restoration of the papacy; still the idea retained the victory. The higher unity yet preserved its ascendancy, though not perhaps with all its ancient and comprehensive power, and continually pressed forward with unremitting steps, even during periods of internal strife from which indeed it seemed to derive increased energy for new conquests. These enterprises now solicit our attention. How far they succeeded, the revolutions that were their consequences, and the opposition they encountered, whether from within or from without, are all questions of the utmost importance to the world in general.

Chapter First

PROGRESS OF THE CATHOLIC RESTORATION
A.D. 1590–1617[24]

Progress Of The Counter-Reformation In Germany

In Germany, each prince held it to be his own good right to direct the religion of his territories in accordance with his personal convictions.

The movement that had there commenced proceeded accordingly with but little interference from the imperial authority, and without attracting particular attention.

The ecclesiastical princes more particularly considered it their special duty to lead back the people of their dominions to Catholicism.

The first pupils of the Jesuits were now appearing among them. Johann Adam von Bicken, Archbishop-Elector of Mayence from 1601 to 1604, was educated at the *Collegium Germanicum* in Rome. From the castle of Königstein he once heard the hymns

[24] The sections "Enterprises of Catholicism in Poland and the Neighboring Territories"; "Attempt on Sweden"; "Designs on Russia"; "Internal Commotions in Poland" have been omitted (pages 249–272).

with which the Lutheran congregation of the place was conveying its deceased pastor to his grave. "Let them give their synagogue decent burial," exclaimed the prince. On the following Sunday a Jesuit mounted the pulpit, and from that time a Lutheran preacher was never more seen to enter it. The same things occurred in other places. What Bicken left incomplete was carried zealously forward by his successor Johann Schweikard. He was a man much addicted to the pleasures of the table, but he held the reins of government with a firm hand, and displayed remarkable talent. He succeeded in accomplishing the Counter-Reformation throughout his diocese, not excepting the Eichsfeld.*

Ernest and Ferdinand of Cologne, both Bavarian princes, proceeded in like manner, as did the Elector Lothaire of Treves. This prince was distinguished by the soundness of his understanding and by acuteness of intellect. He possessed the talent of surmounting whatever difficulties opposed him, was prompt in the execution of justice, and vigilant in promoting the interests of his country as well as those of his family. He was affable, moreover, and not particularly rigorous, provided always the matter did not affect religion; but no Protestant would he suffer at his court.*

The rapid and yet lasting change brought about in all these countries is most remarkable. Is it to be inferred that Protestantism had never taken firm root in the people, or must the change be ascribed to the method adopted by the Jesuits? It is certain that in zeal and prudence they left nothing to be desired. From every point where they obtained footing, their influence was extended in ever widening circles. They possessed the power of captivating the crowd, so that their churches were always the most eagerly frequented. With the most prominent difficulties they always grappled boldly and at once; if there was a Lutheran, confident in his biblical knowledge, and to whose judgment the neighbors paid a certain deference, this was the man whom they used every effort to win, and their practiced skill in controversy generally secured them from defeat. They were active in works of benevolence; they healed the sick and labored to reconcile enemies. The converted, those with whom they had prevailed, they bound by the most solemn oaths; under their banners the faithful were seen repairing to every place of pilgrimage. Men who but a short time before were zealous Protestants might now be seen taking part in processions.

The Jesuits had educated not only ecclesiastics, but also temporal princes. At the close of the sixteenth century, their two illustrious pupils, Ferdinand II and Maximilian I, appeared in public life.

It is affirmed that when the young Archduke Ferdinand solemnized the festival of Easter at his capital of Graz in the year 1596, he was the only person who received the sacrament according to the Catholic ritual, and that there were but three Catholics in the whole city.*

Nevertheless, Ferdinand immediately resolved on proceeding to the continuance and ultimate completion of the Counter-Reformation; political and religious motives combined to produce this determination—he declared that he also would be master in his own territories, just as the Elector of Saxony, or the Elector-Palatine. When the danger was represented to him of an onslaught from the Turks during a period of internal discord, he replied that until the perfect conversion of the people was effected, the help of God was not to be hoped for. In the year 1597 Ferdinand proceeded by way of Loreto to Rome—to kneel at the feet of Pope Clement VIII. He then vowed to restore Catholicism in his hereditary dominions, even at the peril of his life. The Pope confirmed him in this resolve, and he at once returned home to Graz to commence the work.*

This was immediately followed by more extensive proceedings affecting all the Austrian territories.

The Emperor Rudolf had at first dissuaded his young cousin from the measures he contemplated, but seeing them prove successful he proceeded to imitate them. From 1599 to 1601 we find a commission for reforms in active operation throughout Upper Austria, and in 1602–1603 these officials were at work in Lower Austria.* In Bohemia the Protestants hoped they were more effectually protected by the ancient privileges of the Utraquists. In Hungary they trusted to the independence and power of the Estates. But Rudolf now seemed disposed to respect neither the one nor the other; he had been persuaded that the old Utraquists were entirely extinct, and that the Protestants were not entitled to the enjoyment of the privileges that had been accorded to them. In the year 1602 he issued an edict forbidding the meetings of the Moravian brethren and commanding that their churches should be closed. All other Protestants felt that they were in danger of similar treatment, nor were they long left in doubt as to what they might expect. Open violence was already resorted to in Hungary.* To the complaints of the Hungarians the Emperor replied by the following resolution: "His Majesty, who profoundly believes in the holy Roman faith, is desirous of extending it throughout his empire, and especially in Hungary. He hereby confirms and ratifies all decrees that have been issued in favor of that faith from the times of St. Stephen, the apostle of Hungary."

Thus, notwithstanding his advanced age, the cautious Emperor had entirely departed from his moderation. A similar policy was pursued by the whole body of the Catholic princes, so far as they could possibly make their power extend; the stream of Catholic opinion was poured ever more widely over the land. Force and argument combined to secure its progress; the constitution of the empire supplied no means whereby to oppose it. On the contrary, the Catholic adherents felt themselves so powerful that they now began to interfere with the affairs of the empire and to endanger the rights thus far successfully defended by the Protestant party. The constitution of the supreme tribunals also received important changes, principally by the interposition of the papal nuncios, more particularly of Cardinal Madruzzi, by whom attention was first drawn to the subject.*

Even the *Kammergericht* had assumed a more decided tinge of Catholicism toward the beginning of the seventeenth century, and judgments had been pronounced by it in accordance with the Catholic interpretation of the Peace of Augsburg. Those who had suffered from these judgments had adopted the legal remedy of seeking revision, but with the visitations these revisions also were suspended. Cases accumulated, and all remained undecided.

Under these circumstances it was that the *Reichshofrat* came into being. This at least gave some hope of termination to an

affair, for the defeated party could not take refuge in a legal
process which could never be executed. But the *Reichshofrat* was
not only more decidedly Catholic than the *Kammergericht*, it was
also entirely dependent on the court.*

But what institutions of universal effect existed in the empire
except the judicial ones? To these it was that the unity of the
nation was attached. Yet even they were now subjected to the
influence of Catholic opinions and regulated by the convenience
of the court. From all quarters complaints had already arisen of
partial judgments and arbitrary executions, when the affair of
Donauwerth made obvious to all the great perils by which the
country was menaced from this state of things.

A Catholic abbot in a Protestant city, determined to celebrate his processions more publicly and with greater solemnity
than usual and the fact that he was interrupted and insulted by
the populace, was considered a sufficient pretext for the *Reichshofrat* to inflict tedious and harassing legal proceedings on the
town itself. Mandates, citations, and commissions followed in long
succession, and the town was finally laid under the ban of the
empire. Maximilian of Bavaria, a neighboring prince of rigidly
Catholic opinions, was entrusted with the execution of the sentence. Not content with taking possession of Donauwerth, he at
once invited the order of Jesuits to settle in the city, permitted
none but the Catholic service to be performed, and proceeded in
the usual manner to effect a Counter-Reformation.

This affair was regarded by Maximilian himself in the light
of its general import. He wrote to the Pope saying that it might
be considered as a test by which the decline of the Protestant influence could be judged.

But he deceived himself if he believed that the Protestants
would endure these things quietly. They saw clearly what they
had to expect if matters were permitted to proceed in that manner.*

When the Diet assembled at Ratisbon in the year 1608 the
Protestants would proceed to no deliberation until they should
receive an unequivocal confirmation of the Treaty of Augsburg.
Even Saxony, which had always before been disposed to the party
of the Emperor, now demanded that the cases instituted by the

Hofkammergericht should be done away with, so far as they were contrary to the practice of earlier times; that the judicial system should receive amendment; and not only that the Treaty of Augsburg should be renewed as concluded in 1555, but that the Jesuits, by a pragmatic sanction, should be prohibited from writing against it.

But the Catholics on their side were also very zealous and were closely united. The Bishop of Ratisbon had previously issued a circular in which he exhorted his coreligionists to impress upon their envoys the necessity for being unanimous in their defense of the Catholic religion. He admonishes all to "stand together rigid and fast as a wall"; by no means to temporize. There was now nothing to fear since they had staunch and zealous defenders in august and illustrious princely houses. If then the Catholics showed a disposition to confirm the Treaty of Augsburg, they did so with the addition of a clause to the effect "that whatever had been done in contravention of the same should be annulled and restituted"—a clause which comprehended all that the Protestants feared and which they desired to avoid.

With so decided a disagreement on the principal question, it was not to be expected that unanimity of opinion should be obtained on any separate subject of discussion, or that the Emperor should be accorded those subsidies which he was desiring, and greatly needed, for the war against the Turks.

This consideration would seem to have made some impression on the Emperor; and the court seems to have resolved at one time on a frank and fair compliance with the Protestant demands.

Such, at least, is the inference to be drawn from a very remarkable report relating to this Diet prepared by the papal envoy.

The Emperor did not appear in person—he was represented by the Archduke Ferdinand; neither was the nuncio himself at Ratisbon, but he had sent an Augustine monk thither in his place, Fra Felice Milensio, vicar-general of his order, who labored with extraordinary zeal to maintain the interests of Catholicism.

This Fra Milensio, whose report we still have, declares that the Emperor had in fact determined to publish an edict in conformity with the wishes of the Protestants. He ascribes this re-

solve to the immediate influence of Satan, and says that it had
doubtless been brought about by the agency of the Emperor's
chamberlains, of whom one was a Jew and the other a heretic.

Let us hear from himself the report he proceeds to give: "On
receiving intelligence of the edict that had arrived, and which was
imparted to myself and some others, I repaired to the archduke
and inquired if such a decree had really come. The archduke replied that it had. 'And does your imperial Highness intend to publish it?' The archduke answered, 'The imperial Privy Council has
so commanded, and you perceive yourself, reverend father, the
situation in which we are placed.' Hereupon I replied, 'Your imperial Highness will not belie the faith in which you have been
educated, and with which but a short time since you ventured, in
defiance of so many threatening dangers, to banish all heretics
from your dominions. I cannot believe that your imperial Highness will sanction the loss of church property, and the confirmation of the devilish sect of Luther, or that still worse of Calvin,
which must all come from this new concession.' The pious prince
listened to my words. 'But what is to be done?' he asked. 'I beg
your imperial Highness,' I replied, 'to bring this affair before his
Holiness the Pope, and to take no step in it until we have his
reply;' and the archduke did so, for he respected the commands
of God more than the decrees of men."

If all this occurred as described, we may readily perceive how
important a part this nameless Augustine friar performed in the
history of the German Empire. At the decisive moment he contrived to prevent the publication of a concession by which the
Protestants would apparently have been contented. In place of
this, Ferdinand now promulgated an edict of interposition, which
still left an opening for the introduction of the objectionable
clause. On April 5, 1608, the Protestants assembled and united
in passing a resolution neither to receive the edict nor to yield
obedience to it. But since the other party would also abate no
portion of their demands, and since nothing was to be obtained
from the Emperor or his representative that might have allayed
the fears of the Protestants, they adopted the extreme measure
of quitting the Diet. For the first time that assembly failed to

arrive at any conclusion, much less at any agreement—it was the moment in which the unity of the empire was in fact dissolved.

That affairs should remain in this condition was impossible. Any one of them would have been too weak alone to maintain the position that had been taken up, and the pressure of the moment now compelled them to carry into effect an alliance that had long been desired, deliberated upon, and projected. Immediately after the Diet, a meeting was held at Anhausen between two princes of the Palatinate, the Elector Frederick, and the Count Palatine of Neuburg; two princes of Brandenburg, the Margraves Joachim and Christian Ernest; the Duke of Wurtemburg, and the Margrave of Baden, by whom a league was formed known as the "Union." They pledged themselves to support and assist each other in every way—even by force of arms—and this with special reference to the grievances at the late Diet. They immediately put themselves into a state of military preparation, and each member of the Union undertook to induce such of his neighbors as he could influence to join the confederacy. Their determination was to obtain for themselves that security which, in the existing state of things, the imperial government did not afford them, and in fact to help themselves.

This was an innovation which involved the most comprehensive results, particularly since an event of very similar character just then occurred in the Emperor's hereditary dominions.†

In the Austrian provinces the Estates had consolidated their ancient privileges into a firmly grounded constitutional government. In the empire, Catholicism had once more extended itself through the territories of the Catholic princes, and it was not until it proceeded beyond due limits, until it interfered with violence in the affairs of the empire and endangered the existence of the free Estates, that resistance was opposed to its progress. In the hereditary dominions, on the contrary, it encountered invincible opposition, even within the territorial power of the imperial house, from the influence of Protestant landholders. There was nevertheless, upon the whole, a common feeling throughout the land. In Austria it was remarked with much significance that one sword must keep the other in its scabbard.

For the opposite party had also at once assumed an attitude of aggression. On July 11, 1609, an alliance was concluded between Maximilian of Bavaria and seven of the ecclesiastical princes—the Bishop of Würzburg, namely, with those of Constance, Augsburg, Passau, and Ratisbon, the Provost of Ellwangen, and the Abbot of Kempten. They formed a league for mutual defense on the model of the ancient Treaty of Landsperg. The Duke of Bavaria obtained great powers under this compact. The three ecclesiastical electors soon afterward associated themselves with this league, but retained a certain freedom of action. The Archduke Ferdinand desired to be received into the same confederacy; Spain declared its approval; the Pope gave a promise to neglect no means for promoting the objects of the compact, and without doubt the pontiff in particular became gradually more and more involved in its designs and interests, principally by means of the Spanish influence.

Two hostile parties thus confronted each other, both armed, each in constant fear of being surprised and attacked, but neither strong enough to bring the questions between them to a decisive issue.

It followed of necessity that in Germany the dispatch of all important public business, the solution of every difficulty affecting the commonweal, had become utterly impossible. In 1611 a king had to be elected; the Electors gathered in vain: they could not reach a decision.

Even after the death of Rudolf in 1612, a long time elapsed before an election could be effected. Three temporal electors insisted, by the capitulary of election, on the establishment of an imperial council, the said council to be composed equally from both parties. This demand the three ecclesiastical electors opposed, and it was only when Saxony, which in all these affairs had evinced great devotion to the house of Austria, had passed over to the Catholic side that the election was at length completed.

But that which failed to pass in the Council of Electors was insisted on with all the more violence by the Union of princes in the Diet of 1613, where it was opposed with equal pertinacity by the Catholics. No further deliberation was attempted; the Protestants would no longer subject themselves to the yoke of majority decisions.

In Juliers and Cleves, notwithstanding the vacillating weakness which characterized the government of the last native prince, effective measures had at length been adopted for the restoration of Catholicism, principally by the influence of his wife, a princess of the house of Lorraine. It seemed for a certain time that Protestantism would nevertheless obtain the supremacy, the next heirs being both Protestant, but the force of religious division prevailed here also. Of the two Protestant claimants, one passed over to the Catholic faith, and the two parties placed themselves in opposition here also. As they acknowledged no supreme arbiter, they proceeded in the year 1614 to acts of open hostility. Both seized on all around them, so far as their power could be made to reach; the one with the help of Spain, the other with that of the Netherlands. Each reformed, after its own fashion, the districts that had fallen to its share without further ceremony.

Attempts were indeed made to effect a reconciliation; a meeting of the electors was proposed, but the Elector-Palatine would not hear of this, because he had no confidence in his colleague of Saxony. The next project was a general Diet of composition, but the Catholic states had innumerable objections to oppose to this plan. Others turned to the Emperor, and recommended him to enforce his authority by the display of a large armed force. But what could have been expected from Matthias, who belonged to both parties by the very source and cause of his power, but was so trammelled by the chains he had imposed on himself, that he could not possibly attain to any freedom of action? Loud were the complaints of the Pope against him—he declared him unfit to be invested with so high a dignity, in times of so much difficulty and caused representations to be made to him, in the strongest of terms, insomuch that he was himself amazed at the Emperor's long-suffering endurance. At a later period the Catholics were not so much dissatisfied with Matthias; even the most zealous declared that he had been more useful to their Church than could have been expected. In the affairs of the empire he was, however, utterly powerless. In the year 1617 he made an attempt to dissolve both the confederacies, but the Union was immediately revived with increased strength, and the League was reestablished with all its pristine vigor.[25]

Regeneration Of Catholicism In France

The question that was now more extensively important than any other was the position that would be adopted by France in general as regarded religion.

The first glance shows clearly that the Protestants still maintained themselves there in great power and influence.

Henry IV had accorded them the Edict of Nantes which not only confirmed them in the possession of all the churches then in their hands, but even conferred on them a share in the institutions for public instruction and equality with Catholics as regarded the chambers of Parliament. They also occupied numerous strong places, and altogether possessed a degree of independence which might well have occasioned a question whether it were not incompatible with the idea of the State.* This was a power that was certain to command respect and could by no means be prudently offended.

But beside this power, and in direct opposition to it, there arose a second, the corporation of the Catholic clergy in France.

The large possessions of the French clergy secured to that body a certain degree of independence, and this was rendered more palpable to themselves, as well as more obvious to others, from their having undertaken to liquidate a portion of the public debt.

For this participation was not so entirely compulsory as to preclude the necessity for a renewal of their obligations from time to time in the form of a voluntary engagement.

Under Henry IV the assemblies which were held for that purpose assumed a more regular form; they were to be repeated

[25] The section "Papal Nunciature in Switzerland" has been omitted (pages 287–290).

every tenth year, and always in May when the days are long and give time for the transaction of much business. They were never to be held in Paris, that all distractions might be avoided. Smaller meetings were to assemble every second year for the auditing of accounts. It was not in the nature of things that these assemblies, the larger ones in particular, should confine themselves to their financial duties.*

The position of Henry IV was thus very peculiar. He stood between two corporations, both possessing a certain independence, both holding their assemblies at stated times, and then assailing him, each from its own side, with conflicting representations, while it was not easy for the King to neglect or oppose himself to either one or the other.

His wish and purpose generally were, without doubt, to maintain the balance between them, and not to suffer their becoming involved in new conflicts. But if we ask to which of the two parties he was the more inclined and which he most effectually assisted, we shall find that it was obviously the Catholic, although his own elevation was attributable to the Protestants.†

Yet this would have availed but little had not the internal regeneration of the Catholic Church, already commenced in France, made great and rapid progress at that time. She had, in fact, assumed a new form during the first twenty years of the century.†

In this course of things there was an obvious progress from austerity to moderation, from esctasy to calmness, from secluded asceticism to the performance of social duty.†

But how vast is the undertaking to remodel the religious character and feelings of a whole kingdom—to lead all into one sole direction of faith and doctrine! Among the inferior classes, the peasantry, and even the clergy of remote parishes, the old abuses might still be found to prevail. But the great missionary of the people, Vincent de Paul, appeared in the midst of the universal movement, and by him was established that Congregation of the Mission, whose members, traveling from place to place, diffused the spirit of devotion throughout the land, and penetrated to the most remote and secluded corners of France.*

These are labors that are happily ever renewed in Christian lands, whether for the nurture of infancy, the instruction of youth, or the inculcation of learning, the teaching of the people from the pulpit, or the purposes of benevolence in general; but in no place are they effectual without the combination of manifold qualities and energies with religious enthusiasm. In other regions they are usually left to the care of each successive generation, to the promptings of present need. But here an attempt was made to fix these associations on an immutable basis, to give an invariable form to the religious impulse from which they proceed, that all may be consecrated to the immediate service of the Church and that future generations may be trained imperceptibly but surely into the same path.

Throughout France the most important consequences were soon manifest. Even under Henry IV the Protestants already perceived themselves to be hemmed in and endangered by an activity so deeply searching and so widely extended as that now displayed by their opponents. They had for some time made no further progress, but they now began to suffer losses; and even during Henry's life they complained that desertion from their ranks had commenced.

And yet the policy of Henry still compelled him to accord them certain marks of favor and to reject the demands of the Pope, who desired, among other things, that they should be excluded from all public employments.

But under Maria de' Medici the policy previously pursued was abandoned. A much closer connection was formed with Spain, and a decidedly Catholic disposition became predominant both in domestic and foreign affairs. And as in the court, so also in the assembly of the Estates this supremacy was obvious.

There was at that time much life and zeal in the Protestant Church and institutions also; and most fortunate it was for them that the strength of their political situation and their force in arms made it impossible that this should be suppressed. As the government had united with their opponents, so the Protestants found support and aid from those powerful malcontents, who have never been wanting in France, and will ever be numerous in that country. Thus some time yet elapsed before it was possible to venture to attack them directly.

Chapter Second
GENERAL WAR—
VICTORIES OF CATHOLICISM
A.D. 1617–1623

War Breaks Out

However diverse the circumstances of which we have thus traced the development may have been, they yet all converged in the production of one great result. On all sides Catholicism had made vigorous advances, but it had also been opposed on all sides by a mighty resistance. In Poland it was not able to crush its opponents because they found an invincible support from the neighboring kingdoms. In Germany a closely compacted opposition had presented itself to the invading creed and to the returning priesthood. The King of Spain was compelled to grant a truce to the united Netherlands, involving little less than a formal recognition of independence. The French Huguenots were armed against all aggression by the fortresses they held, by troops well prepared for war, and by the efficiency of their financial arrangements. In Switzerland the balance of parties had long been firmly established, and even regenerated Catholicism had not sufficient power to disturb it.

We find Europe divided into two worlds, which at every point encompass, restrict, assail, and repel each other.

If we compare these two powers in general, we perceive at once that the Catholic presents a much more perfect unity. We know, it is true, that this party was not without internal dissensions, but these were for the time set at rest. Above all, there existed a good and even confidential understanding between France and Spain. There was an occasional manifestation of the old animosities of Venice or of Savoy, but they did not produce much effect. The Protestants, on the contrary, were not only without a common center, but since the death of Elizabeth and the accession of James I, they had no great leading power on their side, the last-named sovereign having observed a somewhat equivocal policy from the beginning of his reign. Lutherans and Reformed stood opposed to each other with a mutual aversion that necessarily disposed them to opposite measures in politics. The Reformed were further much divided among themselves. Episcopalians and Puritans, Arminians and Gomarists, assailed each other with furious hatred. In the assembly of the Huguenots, held at Saumur in the year 1611, a division arose which could never afterward be completely healed.

It is certain that the difference existing in this last-mentioned point between Catholics and Protestants must not be attributed to an inferior degree of religiosity on the Catholic side. We have indeed perceived that the contrary was the fact. The following cause is more probably the true one. Catholicism had no share in that energy of exclusive dogmatic forms by which Protestantism was governed. There were momentous controverted questions which the former left undetermined; enthusiasm, mysticism, and that deeper feeling or sentiment which scarcely attains to the clearness and distinctness of thought, and which must ever arise from time to time as results of the religious tendency—these Catholicism absorbed into itself, controlled, subjected to given rule, and rendered subservient to its purposes in the forms of monastic asceticism. By the Protestants, on the contrary, they were repressed, rejected, and condemned. Therefore it was that these dispositions, thus left to their own guidance, broke forth into the multiform variety of sects existing among Protestants, and sought their own partial but uncontrolled paths.*

But I will not attempt to describe the contrasts presented by these opposing spiritual worlds—to do this effectually a larger share of attention should have been devoted to the Protestant side. One portion of the subject I may be permitted to bring into more prominent notice, because this was directly influential on the events before us.

In Catholicism the monarchical tendencies were, at that period, fully predominant. Ideas of popular rights, of legitimate opposition to princes, of the sovereignty of the people, and the legality of regicide, as they had been advocated thirty years before, even by the most zealous Catholics, were no longer suited to the time. There was now no important opposition of any Catholic population against a Protestant sovereign. Even James I of England was quietly tolerated, and the above-named theories no longer found application. The result was already obvious: the religious tendency became more closely attached to the dynastic principle, and that alliance was further promoted, if I am not mistaken, by the fact that the princes of the Catholic side displayed a certain force and superiority of personal character. This may at least be affirmed of Germany. In that country the aged Bishop Julius of Würzburg was still living—the first prelate to have attempted a thorough counter-reformation. The Elector Schweikard of Mayence held the office of high chancellor; he performed his duties with an ability enhanced by his warm and earnest interest in them, and which restored to the office its ancient and effective influence. Both the other Rhenish electors were resolute active men; by their side stood the manly, sagacious, indefatigable Maximilian of Bavaria, an able administrator, full of enlarged and lofty political designs; and with him the Archduke Ferdinand, invincible from the force of his faith, to which he adhered with all the fervor of a powerful soul. Almost all were pupils of the Jesuits, who certainly possessed the faculty of awakening high impulses in the minds of their disciples; all were reformers too, in their own manner, and had indeed contributed, by earnest labors and religious enthusiasm, to bring about the state of things then existing around them.

The Protestant princes, on the contrary, were heirs rather than founders; they were already of the second or third generation. It was only in some few of them that there could be perceived intimations—I know not whether of energy and strength of mind, but, without doubt, of ambition and love of movement.

Furthermore, there now appeared among the Protestants an obvious inclination toward republicanism, or rather toward an aristocratic liberty. In many places, as in France, in Poland, and in all the Austrian territories, a powerful nobility holding Protestant opinions was in open conflict with the Catholic ruling authorities. What might be attained by such a force was clearly exemplified by the republic of the Netherlands, which was daily rising into higher prosperity. There was, without doubt, some discussion at this time in Austria as regarded emancipation from the rule of the reigning family and the adoption of a government similar to that of Switzerland or of the Netherlands. In the success of some such effort lay the only means for restoring their ancient importance to the imperial cities of Germany, and they took a lively interest in maturing them. The internal constitution of the Huguenots was already republican, and was indeed not devoid of elements of democracy. These last were already opposing themselves to a Protestant sovereign in the persons of the English Puritans. There still exists a little treatise by an imperial ambassador, who was in Paris at that time, wherein the attention of the European princes is very forcibly directed toward the common danger menacing them from the advance of such a spirit.

The Catholic world of this period was single-minded, classical, monarchical. The Protestant was divided, romantic, republican.

In the year 1617 everything already betokened the approach of a decisive conflict between them. The Catholic party appears to have felt itself the superior; it is at all events not to be denied that it was the first to take arms.*

By far the most important affairs were those in the hereditary dominions of Austria. The archdukes had been reconciled and were now reunited. With the greatness of spirit which that house has frequently displayed in moments of danger, a general resignation had been made to the Archduke Ferdinand of all claims that must devolve on them at the death of the Emperor Matthias, who had no children; that prince was in fact shortly afterward acknowledged as successor to the throne in Hungary and Bohemia. This was indeed only an adjustment and compromise of personal claims; it nevertheless involved results of important general interest.

From a zealot as determined as Ferdinand, nothing less was to be expected than an immediate attempt to secure the absolute supremacy for his own creed in the Austrian dominions. And this accomplished, it was to be supposed that he would then labor to turn the collective powers of those territories toward the diffusion of the Catholic faith.

This was a common danger, menacing alike to all Protestants, not only in the hereditary dominions of Ferdinand or in Germany, but in Europe generally.

For this reason opposition immediately arose. The Protestants, who had set themselves in array against the encroachments of Catholicism, were not only prepared for resistance—they had courage enough immediately to convert the defense into attack.

The elements of European Protestantism were concentrated in the Elector Frederick of the Palatinate. His wife was the daughter of the King of England and niece of the King of Denmark. Prince Maurice of Orange was his uncle, and the Duke de Bouillon, chief of the French Huguenots of the less pacific faction, was his near relation. Frederick himself stood at the head of the German Union; he was a prince of grave character, and had self-command enough to abstain from the dissolute habits then prevalent at the German courts. He devoted his best efforts to the sedulous discharge of his duties as a sovereign and was most diligent in attending the sittings of his Privy Council; he was somewhat melancholy, proud, and full of high thoughts. In his father's time there were tables in the dining-hall for councillors and nobles; these he caused to be removed, and would dine with princes or persons of the highest rank only. People at court had presentiments of high political vocation; innumerable connections, involving far-reaching results, were diligently formed, but so long a time had elapsed since any serious war had been waged that no very clear perception existed as to what might be attained or what the future might bring. The most daring and extravagant projects were thus considered.

Such was the prevailing mood at the Court of Heidelberg when the Bohemians, urged on by the consciousness of their religious dangers, resolved to reject Ferdinand, although he had already received their promise, and offered their crown to the Elector-Palatine.

For a moment Frederick hesitated. It was unheard of that one

German prince should wrest from another a crown devolving on him by legal right. But all his friends combined to urge him onward—Maurice, who had never liked the truce with Spain, the Duke de Bouillon, Christian of Anhalt, whose views extended over the whole arena of European politics and who was convinced that no one would have either the power or the courage to gainsay the arrangement when once accomplished—his most confidential advisers pressed his acceptance. The unbounded prospects opened before him, ambition, religious zeal, all tended to promote his compliance, and in the month of August 1619, he received the Bohemian crown. Could he have maintained his position, how vast must have been the results! The power of the house of Austria in Eastern Europe would have been broken, the progress of Catholicism limited forever.*

As the winds at times veer suddenly round in the stormy seasons of the year, so did the stream of fortune and success now suddenly flow in an altered direction.

The Catholics succeeded in gaining over one of the most powerful Protestant princes to their side: this was the Elector of Saxony, who, being a Lutheran, felt a deep hatred for any undertaking initiated by Calvinists.

This circumstance alone sufficed to inspire them with a certain hope of victory. A single battle—that of the Weissberg, fought on November 8, 1620—put an end to the power of the Palatine Frederick, and ruined all his designs.†

Gregory XV

While participating in the procession in celebration of the battle of Weissberg, Paul V was struck by apoplexy. A second stroke followed shortly thereafter from the effects of which he died—January 28, 1621.

The new election was effected, on the whole, in the manner of those preceding. Paul V had reigned so long that the whole College of Cardinals had nearly been renewed under his auspices; thus the greater part of the cardinals were dependent on his nephew, Cardinal Borghese. Accordingly, after some hesitation he found a man with regard to whom all his adherents agreed—this was Alessandro Ludovisio, of Bologna, who was forthwith elected on February 9, 1621, and took the name of Gregory XV.

He was a small, phlegmatic man, who had previously acquired a reputation for his dexterity in negotiation, and for the art he possessed of proceeding silently, and by imperceptible advances, to the attainment of all his purposes. He was, however, already bent with age at his accession, exceedingly feeble, and in bad health.

What, then, could be expected in the contest now proceeding, and which affected the whole world, from a pontiff to whom his counsellors and servants could sometimes not venture to communicate important affairs, lest they should give the last shock to his frail existence? But there stood by the side of the dying pontiff a young man, only twenty-five years old, his nephew, Ludovico Ludovisio, who at once took possession of the papal power, and who displayed a talent and boldness fully commensurate with the demands of the period.*

But if we desire to render the spirit of the new government in general, we need only remember that it was in the pontificate of Gregory XV that the Propaganda was established, that the founders of the Jesuits, Ignatius and Xavier, were canonized.†

And now, the new government took instant measures for completing the victories achieved by the Catholic arms by following them with conversions to the Catholic faith, and for justifying as well as confirming the conquests of Catholicism by the reestablishment of religion. "All our thoughts," says one of the earliest instructions of Gregory XV, "must be directed toward the means of deriving the utmost possible advantage from the fortunate transformation of affairs, and the victorious condition of things"; a purpose that was completed with the most brilliant success.*

Chapter Third
CONFLICT OF POLITICAL RELATIONS
FURTHER TRIUMPHS OF CATHOLICISM

It is not always, and solely, resistance from without which limits a rapidly progressing power in its career; reverses are for the most part occasioned by internal dissensions, which, if not the sole cause of decline, yet largely promote and accelerate it.

Had Catholicism remained of one accord, had its adherents proceeded with united forces to their aim, it is difficult to imagine how northern Germanic Europe, involved as it was to a considerable extent in the interests and hemmed in on all points by the policy of Catholicism, could eventually have resisted its domination.

But was it not inevitable that having reached this degree of power, the old elements of discord residing within Catholicism itself, and which, though stilled at the surface, had been constantly active at the center, should now burst forth anew?

The distinctive peculiarity of religious progress at this period was that it depended in all countries on the preponderance of political and military power. The successes of war preceded the progress of missions. It thus followed that the latter were associated with the most important political changes, which last were in themselves of high significance, and could not fail to cause reactions of which the particular character could not be foreseen.

Of all those changes, the most important certainly was that the German line of the house of Austria, which had hitherto been too much engrossed by the disorders in its hereditary dominions to assume any great share in the politics of Europe generally, now at once attained the independence, importance, and strength of a great European power. The elevation of German Austria awakened Spain, which had reposed in peace since the times of Philip II, but which now renewed her old warlike spirit in the assertion of her former hopes and claims. The Spanish and German sovereigns were already brought into immediate connection by the transactions in the Grisons. The Alpine passes were held by Austria on the German side, and by Spain on that of Italy. On those lofty mountains they seemed to offer each other mutual aid for enterprises embracing all parts of the world.

It is certain that in this condition of things there was involved on the one hand a magnificent prospect for Catholicism, to which both lines had devoted themselves with inviolable attachment; but on the other, it presented imminent danger of internal dissension. How much jealousy had been aroused by the Spanish monarchy under Philip II! But with much greater force and combined solidity the power of that house now reared itself, augmented as it was by the growth of its German resources. It followed that all the old antipathies against it would be called into more than ever vigorous action.

This was first made manifest in Italy.

The small Italian states, incapable of standing by their own force, were above all others at that time in need of the protection gained by all from the balance of power and were proportionately sensitive to whatever endangered its preservation. To be thus enclosed between the Spaniards and Germans, while cut off from all foreign aid by the occupation of the Alpine passes, they considered a real threat. With but slight regard to the advantages presented to their common faith by this combination, they had recourse to France, from whom alone they could hope for aid, for the purpose of destroying it. Louis XIII had also become alarmed, lest his influence in Italy should be lost. Immediately after 1622, and even before he had returned to his capital, he concluded a treaty with Savoy and Venice, in virtue of which the house of Austria was to be compelled, by the junction of their common forces, to evacuate the passes and fortresses of the Grisons.

This was an intention apparently affecting one single point only, but which might readily endanger the whole existing relations of the European powers.

The probability of such a result was clearly manifest to Gregory XV. The peril by which the peace of the Catholic world, the progress of religious interests, and consequently the renewal of the papal dignity were threatened were obvious; and with a zeal equal to that he had displayed for missions and conversions, the pontiff now labored to prevent that outbreak of hostilities, the consequences of which were to his perception so evidently menacing.

The reverence felt for the Papal See, or rather respect for the unity of the Catholic world, was still so lively that both France and Spain declared their readiness to leave the decision of this affair to the Pope. Nay, he was himself requested to take possession of those fortresses which occasioned so much jealous uneasiness, to hold them as a deposit, and to garrison them with his own troops, until the question concerning them had been fully adjusted.*

By these arrangements the danger which had been the immediate cause of the Italian anxieties appeared to be effectually removed. The chief consideration now was to provide for the safety of Catholic interests in the further arrangements. In this view it was proposed that as the Valtelline was not to fall again into the hands of the Spaniards, neither should it return to the rule of the Grisons, because the restoration of the Catholic religion would be almost inevitably interrupted by the latter arrangement. It was therefore annexed to the three ancient Rhaetian confederacies as a fourth independent state possessing equal rights. From the same motives, even the connection of the two Austrian lines was not to be entirely destroyed, that connection appearing to be still required for the progress of Catholicism in Germany. The passes of the Valtelline and the transit through Worms were always to remain open to the Spaniards, but with the understanding that this was for the passage of troops into Germany, not to facilitate their entrance into Italy.

Affairs were at this point—the treaties had not been actually concluded, but all was prepared for conclusion—when Gregory XV died (July 8, 1623). He had lived to enjoy the satisfaction of seeing dissensions that had alarmed him allayed, and of securing that the progress of his Church should remain uninterrupted. There had even been proposals in the course of those negotiations for a new alliance between the Spaniards and French for the purpose of attacking La Rochelle and Holland.

But after the death of Gregory these intentions were far from being realized.

In the first place, the new Pope, Urban VIII, did not yet enjoy that confidence which proceeds from a well-grounded presumption of perfect impartiality; and secondly, the Italians were by no means satisfied with the arrangements above described. But the most important consideration of all was that the helm of state in France was now directed by men who applied themselves to the opposition of Spain; not at the request of others, or as mere auxiliaries, but from their own impulse and as the leading principle of French policy.

But in this resolution there may possibly have been less arbitrariness than may be supposed. France, as well as the Austrian-Spanish powers, was experiencing the growth of all her forces. By victory over the Huguenots the royal power had been largely increased, together with the unity and self-confidence of the nation; and as the claims of France kept pace with her strength to enforce them, so all things now combined to produce the adoption of a bolder line of policy than had been hitherto attempted. This natural tendency inevitably called forth the organs suited to its promotion; men disposed to carry it out to its consequences and capable of doing so. Richelieu was from the first resolved to make head against the ascendancy which the house of Austria constantly asserted, and which she had but recently acquired new powers to maintain, and even to increase. He determined to engage in direct conflict with this power for supremacy in Europe.

This was a decision by which the Catholic world was menaced with a division more perilous than that which had lately been averted. The two great powers must of necessity be involved in open war.* Although Richelieu was a cardinal of the Roman Church, he did not scruple to form an undisguised league with the Protestants.†

There cannot be a doubt that this state of things immediately impeded the progress of Catholicism. It is true that the French alliance was of a political nature, but so intimate was the connection between ecclesiastical and political relations that the Protestants could not fail to perceive in this condition of affairs the opportunity for promoting their own cause. Protestantism accordingly recovered breath. A new champion, the King of Denmark, had risen for its defense in Germany, with energies fresh and unimpaired, and supported by the mighty combination of European policy—a victory on his part would have rendered all the successes of the imperial house ineffectual, and must have arrested the progress of the Catholic restoration.

But it is by the attempt that the difficulties inherent in an enterprise are made manifest. However brilliant may have been the talents of Richelieu, he had yet proceeded too rashly in this undertaking. All his desires and inclinations were attracted toward this project. He had placed it before him, whether in full and conscious perception of all its import, or in obscure presentiment, as the great aim of his life; but there arose from it dangers by which he was himself first threatened.*

Thus, even in France itself, Richelieu found himself assailed, and that by the two opposite parties at the same time. Whatever he might be able to effect against Spain by maintaining his position, it was yet one that he saw to be wholly untenable; he was compelled to abandon it with all speed.

And as in the attack he had displayed his genius for widely reaching combinations and bold, thorough-going designs, so he now exhibited that diplomatic finesse bordering on treachery, by which he made his allies mere tools and then abandoned them.†

By the time war broke out, the general alliance had ceased to exist. The French subsidies were not paid; the English support came in far too slowly. The imperial troops were more practiced in war than their opponents, and the result was that the King of Denmark lost the battle of Lutter and fell back upon his lands.

This was a result of which the effects were of necessity commensurate with the universality of their causes.†

In this moment of prosperity Urban VIII had raised his thoughts to a vast and daring design. This was no other than an attack on England; an idea that had reappeared from time to time, as if by a sort of necessity, among the grand combinations of Catholicism.†

Neither had the interests of Germany and Italy been forgotten in these calculations.

There still appeared a possibility of destroying the superiority of the naval power of England and Holland by a general combination. The formation of an armed force was suggested, and under the protection of this force a direct communication was to be established between the Baltic, Flanders, the French coasts, Spain, and Italy without the participation of the two maritime powers. The Emperor made proposals with this view to the Hanse Towns. The Infanta at Brussels desired that a port in the Baltic should be ceded to the Spaniards. Negotiations were entered into with the Grand Duke of Tuscany, who by this means might have drawn the Spanish and Portuguese trade to Leghorn.

It is true that matters were not carried so far. Controlled by the complexity of the interests involved, the event took a very different course, but yet such as eventually to produce results entirely favorable to the cause of Catholicism.

While plans of such imposing magnitude were being developed for an attack on England, it came to pass that the projectors were themselves assailed by a force from England.

In July 1627, Buckingham appeared with a noble fleet off the coasts of France; he landed on the island of Rhe and took possession of it, with the exception of the citadel of St. Martin, to which he instantly laid siege. He called on the Huguenots to arouse themselves once more in defense of their liberties and religious independence, which certainly were daily more endangered.*

To have produced results, however, Buckingham should have conducted the war with more energy and should have been better supported. Charles I acknowledges in all his letters that this was not sufficiently done. As the affair was arranged, the assailants were soon proved to be no longer equal to Cardinal Richelieu, whose genius developed its resources with redoubled power in difficult situations, and who had never given more decided proofs of steadfast resolution and unwearied persistence. Buckingham saved himself by a retreat. His expedition, which might have placed the French government in extreme peril, had in reality no other result than that of causing the whole strength of France, directed by the Cardinal, to be poured with renewed violence on the Huguenots.

The center of Huguenot power was without doubt La Rochelle. At an earlier period, when residing in the neighborhood of the city at his bishopric of Luçon, Richelieu had frequently reflected on the possibility of reducing that fortress; he now found himself called upon to direct such an enterprise, and he resolved to accomplish it, be the cost what it might.

It was a peculiar circumstance that nothing afforded him so effectual an assistance as the fanaticism of an English Puritan.

Buckingham had at length resumed his arms for the relief of La Rochelle. His honor was pledged to effect this; his position in England and the world depended on it; and he would unquestionably have strained all his powers for its accomplishment. This was the moment chosen by a fanatic, impelled by desire for vengeance and by a mistaken zeal for religion, and Buckingham was assassinated.

In a crisis of great moment, it is necessary that powerful men should make the enterprise their own personal concern. The siege of La Rochelle was as a duel between the two ministers. Richelieu alone now survived. No one was found in England to take Buckingham's place, or to be up to the defense of his honor. The English fleet appeared in the roads, but without doing anything effectual. It was said that Richelieu knew there would be nothing attempted by it. He persisted with inflexible firmness in the siege, and in October 1628, La Rochelle surrendered.

When the principal fortress had thus fallen, the neighboring places despaired of holding out: their only care now was to obtain tolerable terms.

And thus, from all these political complexities, which at first seemed so advantageous to the Protestant cause, there proceeded, at last, a further triumph for Catholicism, and a mighty promotion of its interests. Northeast Germany and southwest France, both of which had so long resisted, were alike subdued. Nothing more seemed to be required than to secure the perpetual submission of the conquered enemy by restrictive laws and institutions of permanent efficiency.

The help afforded by Denmark to the Germans, and by England to the French, had been injurious rather than advantageous. It had served to bring upon them an irresistible enemy, and these powers were now themselves endangered or attacked. The imperial forces penetrated even into Jutland, and in the year 1628, negotiations for a combined assault upon England proceeded with the most earnest activity between France and Spain.

Chapter Fourth

MANTUAN WAR—THIRTY YEARS' WAR—
REVOLUTION IN THE STATE OF AFFAIRS

The course of human affairs, the progress of a development once begun, at first glance appears immutable.

But on examining more closely, we not infrequently perceive that the fundamental cause on which the fabric of events reposes is but frail and yielding; merely some personal inclination, perhaps, whether of attachment or aversion, and which may be shaken without any great difficulty.

If we inquire by what agency the new and important advantages we have enumerated were obtained for the Catholic restoration, we shall find that it was the friendly understanding renewed between France and Spain, without which neither the generals nor the nations could have accomplished anything of moment.

The power of a self-sustained resistance had been lost to the Protestant cause from the year 1626, and it was only by the dissensions of the Catholic powers that its adherents were encouraged to attempt further opposition. The reconciliation of the governments, therefore, led to their ruin.

But none could fail to perceive how easily these friendly relations might be disturbed.

Within the confines of Catholicism were two distinct and

antagonistic impulses, each arising equally by an inevitable necessity; the one was religious, the other political. The first demanded unity of purpose, the extension of the faith, and a perfect disregard of all other considerations—the latter continually impelled the great powers to a conflict for pre-eminent authority.

It could not be affirmed that the balance of power in Europe had as yet been disturbed by the course of events. In those times the balance depended on the hostility of interests existing between France and Austrian Spain. But France, also, had greatly augmented her strength in the course of the recent occurrences.

Political action is, however, prompted and governed no less by some future prospect than by the pressure and embarrassment of the present. The natural course of things now seemed inevitably conducting to a general danger.

North Germany, the earliest home of Protestantism, was overwhelmed by the forces of Wallenstein; and this state of things seemed to present the possibility of restoring the imperial supremacy throughout the empire, where, one short period in the life of Charles V excepted, it had for ages been a shadow only, to real power and essential importance. Should the Catholic restoration proceed on the path it had entered, this was the necessary result.

France, on the other hand, could expect no advantage equivalent to this. When once the Huguenots were completely mastered, France had nothing more to gain. But it was principally among the Italians that disquietudes were awakened. They considered the revival of a mighty imperial authority, asserting so many claims in Italy and connected so immediately with the detested power of Spain, to be not only dangerous but intolerable.

The question once more recurred whether Catholic impulses were to be continued without regard to these considerations or whether political views would gain the ascendancy and impede them.[26]

[26] The section "Mantuan Succession" has been omitted (pages 363–369).

Urban VIII

Through his personal merit and by the support of others, Maffeo Barberino secured his election as successor of Gregory XV and rose to the pontifical dignity at the vigorous age of fifty-five. The Court very soon discovered a great difference between the new Pope and his immediate predecessors. Clement VIII was most commonly found occupied with the works of St. Bernard; Paul V with the writings of the holy Justinian of Venice; but on the table of Urban VIII lay the newest poems, or draughts and plans of fortifications.

It will generally be found that the time at which the character of a man receives its decided direction is in those first years of manhood which form the period when he begins to take an independent position in public affairs or in literature. The youth of Paul V (who was born in 1552) and of Gregory XV (born in 1554) belonged to a time when the principles of Catholic restoration were pressing forward with full unbroken vigor, and they were themselves accordingly imbued with these principles. The first activities of Urban's life (born in 1568) coincided, on the contrary, with that period when the papal principality was opposed to Spain—when the reestablishment of France as a Catholic power was one of the reigning topics of the day; and accordingly we find that his inclinations followed by preference the direction then chosen.*

In all these affairs Pope Urban acted with absolute and uncontrolled power. He surpassed his predecessors, at least in the early years of his pontificate, in the unlimited exercise of his authority.

If it was proposed to him to take the advice of the college he would reply that he alone knew more than all the cardinals put together. Consistories were very seldom called, and even then few had the courage to express their opinions freely. The congregations met in the usual manner, but no questions of importance were laid before them, and the decisions they arrived at were but little regarded. Even for the administration of the State, Urban formed no proper *Consulta*, as had been customary with his predecessors. His nephew, Francesco Barberino, was perfectly justified in refusing, as he did during the first ten years of Urban's pontificate, to accept the responsibility of any measure, whatever might be its nature.

The foreign ambassadors were unhappy in their dealings with this Pope; they could make no progress with him. In giving audience he himself talked most of the time; he lectured and harangued, continuing with one applicant the conversation he had commenced with another. All were expected to listen to him, admire him, and address him with the most profound reverence, even when his replies were adverse to them. Other pontiffs often refused the requests presented to them, but for some given cause—some principle, either of religion or policy. In Urban, caprice was often perceived to be the only motive for refusal. No one would conjecture whether he ought to expect a yes or a no. The quicksighted Venetians found out that he loved to contradict; that he was inclined, by an almost involuntary disposition, constantly to give the contrary decision to that proposed to him. In order to gain their point, therefore, they adopted the expedient of stating objections to their own wishes; and in seeking for arguments to oppose these, he fell of himself upon propositions to which all the persuasion in the world would not otherwise have brought him. This is a disposition which sometimes exhibits itself in a certain manner among men of subordinate station also, and was not unfrequently observed in those times among Spaniards and Italians. It would seem to consider a public office as a tribute due to its merit and personal importance; and men thus constituted are far more powerfully influenced in the administration of their duties by their own feelings and impulses than by the exigencies of the case. They are not greatly dissimilar to an author, who, occupied by the consciousness of his talents, does not so much devote his thoughts to the subject before him as give free course to the fancies of his caprice.*

But these talents, the brilliant appearance they cast about the person of the Pope, nay, even the robust health that he enjoyed, all contributed to increase that self-complacency with which his lofty position had of itself inspired him. I do not know any pope in whom this self-consciousness attained to so high a degree.*

To such a man it was, so filled with the idea of being a mighty prince; so well-disposed to France, both from his early occupation in that country and the support it had afforded him; so self-willed, energetic, and full of self-importance; to such a man, that the conduct of the supreme spiritual power over Catholic Christendom was committed at this critical moment.

On his decisions, on the line of conduct that he should pursue among the Catholic powers, was now principally to depend the progress or interruption of that universal restoration of Catholicism with which the world was occupied.†

From this side, therefore, Richelieu had nothing now to fear if he should determine to revive the opposition to Spain which had failed three years before. But he wished to proceed with perfect security; he was not in so much haste as the Pope and would not suffer himself to be disturbed in the siege of a place by which his ambition was fettered in its career. But he was all the more determined when once La Rochelle had fallen.*

Thereupon, that hostility to Spain and Austria which had so often displayed itself rose up with greater vehemence than ever. The jealousy of Italy once more called forth the ambition of France.* Thus the two leading powers of Catholic Christendom once more stood opposed to each other in arms. Richelieu again proceeded to bring his boldest plans to bear against the Spanish and Austrian power.

But if we compare the two periods, we perceive that he now held a far more substantial and tenable position than at the time of his enterprise in regard to the Grisons and the Palatinate. Then, the Huguenots had seized the moment for renewing the civil war. Nor were they completely subdued even now, but since they had lost La Rochelle they occasioned no further disquietude. Defeats and losses pursued them without intermission, so that they could no longer effect even a diversion. And perhaps it was of still more importance that Richelieu now had the Pope on his side. In his earlier undertaking the contest in which he was thereby involved with the policy of Rome was perilous even to his position in France. His present enterprise, on the contrary, had been suggested by Rome itself for the interests of the papal principality. Richelieu found it advisable on the whole to attach himself as closely as possible to the papacy. In the disputes between the Roman and Gallican doctrines, he now adhered to the Roman and abandoned the Gallican position.

How important the animosity of Urban VIII to the house of Austria had now become!

With the development of religious opinions, and the progress of Catholic restoration, were associated political changes, the principle of which continued to make itself more earnestly and deeply felt, and now placed itself in direct opposition even to that of the Church.

The Pope entered the lists against that very power by which the restoration and progress of Catholicism had been most zealously and most efficiently promoted.†

The Power Of The Emperor Ferdinand II
In The Year 1629

Meanwhile the Emperor proceeded on his way without regard to the displeasure of the Pope. He considered himself as the great champion of the Catholic Church.

He caused three armies to take the field at the same time.

The first went to the aid of the Poles against the Swedes and did, in fact, succeed in restoring the Polish fortunes to a certain extent. That was, however, not its only object. It was proposed by this campaign at the same time to restore Prussia to the empire and the Teutonic Order from which it had been wrested. Another body marched upon the Netherlands to support the Spaniards in that country. It swept across the open plains from Utrecht toward Amsterdam, and but for the accident of a surprise at Wesel, would without doubt have produced important results. A third force was meanwhile assembled at Memmingen and Lindau, for the purpose of proceeding into Italy.*

And now the secular rights of the empire, as opposed to those of the Papal See, were also brought to recollection.

Ferdinand II was desirous of being crowned, and required that the Pope should come as far as Bologna or Ferrara to meet him. The Pope dared neither to promise nor positively to refuse, and sought to help himself through the difficulty by a mental reservation (*reservatio mentalis*). The question was raised respecting the feudal rights of the empire over Urbino and Montefeltro. The papal nuncio was told with little ceremony that Wallenstein would obtain further information on the subject when he should descend into Italy. And this was in fact Wallenstein's intention. He had previously opposed the Italian war, but he now declared that seeing the Pope and his allies were seeking to destroy the power of Austria he considered that war necessary. He intimated that it was a hundred years since Rome was last plundered, and that she must now be much richer than she was then.

The house of Austria thus assumed a position from which it continued its efforts against the Protestants with the utmost boldness, while at the same time it kept a firm hand on the movements of the Catholic opposition and powerfully restrained even the Pope himself.

Negotiations With Sweden— Electoral Diet At Ratisbon

In earlier times whenever a contingency of this kind had been foreseen from afar, every power in Europe still retaining independence at once combined. It had now actually occurred. The Catholic opposition looked for aid and sought it—not now from mere jealousy, but for defense and as a help in its utmost need— beyond the limits of Catholicism. But to what quarter could it turn? England was fully occupied at home by the disputes between the King and his Parliament; she was besides already engaged in renewed negotiations with Spain. The Netherlands were themselves overwhelmed by the enemy; the German Protestants were either beaten or overawed by the imperial armies. The King of Denmark had been compelled to conclude a disadvantageous peace. There remained none but the King of Sweden. While the Protestants had been suffering defeat in all quarters, Gustavus Adolphus alone had achieved victories.* To this prince the French now turned.*

But could there be a reasonable hope that Gustavus Adolphus could alone overcome the force of the allied imperial armies and could conquer them single-handed in the field? Nobody thought it possible. It therefore seemed desirable above all things that a movement should be excited in Germany itself, which might co-operate with and aid him in his enterprise.

And here, without doubt, the Protestants might safely be counted on; whatever might be the policy adopted by individual princes from personal considerations or fear, yet their spirits were fully occupied by that ferment which penetrates to the ultimate depths of our social life and is the precursor of mighty tempests. I will but mention one idea of those prevalent at the time. When the Edict of Restitution had begun to be enforced in various places, and the Jesuits already signified their determination to pay no regard even to the Treaty of Augsburg, the Protestants gave it to be understood in their turn that before matters could proceed to that length, the German Empire and nations should be utterly over-turned—"rather should all laws and civilization be cast away, and Germany thrown back to the wild life of its ancient forests."

In aid of all this there came discontent and dissension, which now appeared on the Catholic side as well.

It would be difficult to describe the commotion that ensued among the clergy on perceiving that the Jesuits proposed to con-stitute themselves possessors of the recovered monastic property. The Society of Jesus was reported to have declared that there were no Benedictines now remaining, that all had departed from the rule of their founder and were no longer capable of resuming their lost possessions. The merits of the Jesuits themselves were then brought into question by the other side, which maintained that they had performed no conversions: what seemed conversion was merely the result of force. Thus, even before the restitution of ecclesiastical property had taken place, it had already excited discord and contention for the right to its possession between the orders, and for the right to the collation between the Emperor and the Pope.

But these ecclesiastical differences were accompanied by others of a secular character, and of far more extensive importance. The imperial troops were found to be an insupportable burden to the country; their passage through a district exhausted the land and its inhabitants. As the peasant and the burgher were maltreated by the soldier, so were the princes by the general. Wallenstein allowed himself the most arrogant language. The oldest allies of the Emperor, the chiefs of the League, and above all Maximilian of Bavaria, were dissatisfied with the present and anxious about the future.*

While affairs were in this position it happened that Ferdinand assembled the Catholic Electors at Ratisbon in the summer of 1630, for the purpose of procuring the election of his son as King of the Romans. It was not possible that such an occasion should pass away without the discussion of all other public affairs.

The Emperor clearly saw that he must concede something, and his intention was to do this in regard to some portion of the German affairs. He showed a disposition to suspend the edict for restoring church property, insofar as it affected the territories of Brandenburg and Electoral Saxony. He desired some definitive arrangement in respect to Mecklenburg and the Palatinate, wished to conciliate Sweden, negotiations for that purpose having been already commenced, and meanwhile to concentrate all his force upon Italy.*

Ferdinand probably thought that since he had to deal with German princes, he should effect more for his own purposes by concessions in German affairs than by any other means. But the position of things was not so simple.

The spirit of opposition, as embodied in the league of the French and Italians, had made its way among the Catholic electors and now sought to avail itself of the discontents existing in their minds for the furtherance of its own purposes.*

By the agency of intermediaries the French and Italian opposition soon made the German allies of the Emperor completely its own. For the reconciliation of the empire with Sweden, for the pacification of the Protestants, nothing was done, and never would the Pope have consented to the suspension of the Edict of Restitution. On the other hand, the electors pressed for the restoration of peace in Italy and demanded the dismissal of the imperial commander-in-chief, who was conducting himself in the fashion of an absolute dictator.

And so irrepressible was the influence exercised, so craftily was it brought to bear on all points, that the mighty Emperor, though at the zenith of his power, yielded to its force without resistance, and without conditions.*

At the moment when he might have mastered Italy, he suffered it to elude his grasp; at the moment when he was attacked in Germany by the most formidable of enemies, the most practiced of warriors, he dismissed the commander who alone was in a condition to defend him. Never have policy and negotiation produced more important results.

Swedish War—Situation Of The Pope

And now war broke out in earnest. Gustavus Adolphus commenced it, as must be admitted, under the most favorable auspices; for had not the imperial army been brought together in the name of Wallenstein, and was it not wholly devoted and bound to his person? The Emperor even disbanded a part of it and subjected the contributions levied by the generals, which had previously been regulated by their own discretion, to the control of the empire. It is not to be denied that the Emperor, when he dismissed his general, destroyed his army at the same time and deprived it of its moral force. Torquato Conti, an Italian who had formerly been in the papal service, had to offer resistance with troops in this state to an enemy high in courage and full of zeal. It was in the nature of things that this was a failure. The imperial army was no longer what it had been, nothing was seen but irresolution, weakness, panic, and defeat. Gustavus Adolphus drove it completely from the field, and established himself in firm possession of the lower Oder.

It was at first believed in Upper Germany that this was of little importance to the rest of the empire. Tilly continued his operations in the meantime with great composure along the Elbe. When he at length gained possession of Magdeburg, the Pope considered it a great victory and the brightest hopes were founded on this conquest. At the suggestion of Tilly, a commissar was appointed "for the purpose of arranging the affairs of the archbishopric in accordance with the laws of the Catholic Church."

But it was by this very measure that all the Protestant princes who had remained undecided were determined to attach themselves to Gustavus Adolphus; and when Tilly sought to prevent this, he did but further involve them in hostilities with the League, so that it was no longer possible to distinguish between Leaguers and Imperialists. The battle of Leipzig followed. Tilly was completely routed, and the Protestant forces poured alike over the territories of the Leaguers and the Imperialists. Würzburg and Bamberg fell into the hands of the King. The Protestants of the remote north were met on the Rhine by those ancient defenders of Roman Catholicism, the troops of Spain; and there, near Oppenheim, one can see their diverse skulls. Mayence was taken, all oppressed princes sided with the Swedish King, and the expelled Count-Palatine appeared in his camp.

Thus it followed as a necessary consequence that an enterprise originated or sanctioned by the Catholic opposition for political purposes resulted in the advantage of Protestantism. The party before overpowered and beaten down now saw itself once more victorious. It is true that the King extended his protection to the Catholics generally, as the terms of his treaty with the allies compelled him to do; but he declared expressly, at the same time, that he was come to rescue his brethren in faith from the oppressions they were suffering for conscience' sake. He received to his special protection the evangelical ministers living under Catholic governments—those of Erfurt, for example; in all quarters he caused the Augsburg Confession to be reinstated. The exiled pastors returned to the Palatinate, and the Lutheran worship made its way through the empire once more, together with the victorious army.*

Loud and bitter were the complaints of the Emperor. First, the Roman Court had prevailed on him to publish the Edict of Restitution, and then abandoned him in the war occasioned by it. The election of his son as King of the Romans had been impeded by the Pope, who had encouraged the Elector of Bavaria, both by word and deed, to pursue a separate line of policy and to ally himself with France. It was in vain to ask Urban for such assistance as earlier popes had so often afforded, either of money or troops; he even refused to utter a condemnation of the alliance of France with heretics or to declare the present war a war of religion. In the year 1632 we find the imperial ambassadors in Rome insisting on the last-mentioned point. They maintained that the declaration of his Holiness might still produce the most important effects, that it was not yet altogether impossible to drive back the King of Sweden, who had not more than 30,000 men.

The pontiff replied with cold pedantry, "With 30,000 men Alexander conquered the world."

He maintained that the war was not one of religion, that it related to matters of state only, and besides, that the papal treasury was exhausted, and he could do nothing.*

Urban VIII flattered himself for some time that the King of Sweden would form a treaty of neutrality with Bavaria and would reinstate the ecclesiastical princes who had fled their territories. But it soon became evident that all attempts to reconcile interests so directly at variance must of necessity be utterly vain. The Swedish arms pressed onward to Bavaria; Tilly fell, Munich was taken, and Duke Bernard advanced toward the Tyrol.

It was now no longer possible to be in doubt as to what the Pope and Catholicism had to expect from the Swedes. How completely was the state of things changed in a moment! The Catholics had been hoping to restore the Protestant endowments of North Germany to Catholicism, and now the King of Sweden was forming his plans for changing the South German bishoprics that had fallen into his hand into secular principalities. He was already speaking of his Duchy of Franconia and seemed intent on establishing his royal court at Augsburg. Two years before, the Pope had been dreading the arrival of the Austrians in Italy and had been threatened with an attack on Rome. Now the Swedes were appearing on the Italian borders, and with his title as King of the Swedes and Goths were associated recollections that were now revived in the minds of both parties.

Restoration Of A Balance
Between The Two Confessions

I will not enter into the details of that struggle which for sixteen more years extended over Germany. Let it suffice that we have made ourselves aware of the means by which the mighty advance of Catholicism, which was on the point of taking possession of our fatherland forever, was at once arrested in its course, was opposed, when preparing to annihilate the Protestant faith at its sources, by a victorious resistance. It may be remarked generally that Catholicism, considered as one body, was not able to support its own victories; the head of that Church himself believed it imperative to oppose, from political motives, those very powers by whom his spiritual authority was most effectually defended and enlarged. Catholics, acting in concert with the Pope, called forth the yet unsubdued powers of Protestantism and prepared the path for their progress.

Purposes as vast as those formed by Gustavus Adolphus when at the height of his success could not indeed be carried out after his early death, and for the obvious cause that the successes of Protestantism were by no means to be attributed to its own unaided power. But neither could Catholicism, even when its forces were more closely combined—when Bavaria had again made common cause with the Emperor, and when Urban VIII once more contributed subsidies—find the necessary strength to overpower the Protestants.

This conviction soon gained acceptance, at least in Germany, and was indeed the main cause of the Treaty of Prague (1635). The

Emperor suffered his Edict of Restitution to drop, while the Elector of Saxony and the Estates in alliance with him resigned all thought of restoring the Protestant faith in the hereditary dominions of Austria.*

Now Urban VIII, although in practice he had contributed so largely to the defeat of all the plans formed by Catholicism, yet in theory would not relinquish any portion of his claims; but all he effected was to place the papacy in a position removed from the living and effective interests of the world. This is rendered manifest by the instructions he gave to his legate Ginetti when the latter proceeded to Cologne at the first attempt to negotiate a general peace in the year 1636. The hands of the legate were tied precisely in regard to all those important points on which everything was absolutely depending.* Even the conclusion of peace with Protestant powers the Pope refused to sanction. The ambassador was commanded to withhold his support from any proposal for including the Dutch in the peace, and to oppose every cession to the Swedes (the question at that time was merely one relating to a seaport): "the divine mercy would certainly find means for removing that nation out of Germany."

The Roman See could no longer entertain a reasonable hope of overpowering the Protestants; yet it is a striking and important fact that its own pertinacity in adhering to claims which had now become utterly untenable was the true though involuntary cause of making their subjugation forever impossible, and moreover rendered itself incapable of exercising any efficient influence on the relations of its own adherents to those of the Protestant faith.*

A peace was concluded before the eyes of the papal legate such as the Pope had expressly condemned. The Elector-Palatine and all the exiled princes were restored. It was so far from being possible to think of the demands set forth by the Edict of Restitution that many Catholic endowments were absolutely secularized and given up to the Protestants. Spain resolved at length to acknowledge the independence of those rebels against Pope and King, the Hollanders. The Swedes retained a considerable portion of the empire. Even the peace which the Emperor concluded with France was such as the Curia could not approve, because it included stipulations relating to Metz, Toul, and Verdun, by which the rights of Rome were infringed. The papacy found itself under the melancholy necessity of protesting. The principles which it did not possess the power of making effectual, it was at least resolved to express. But this also had been foreseen. The articles relating to ecclesiastical affairs in the Peace of Westphalia were opened by a declaration that no regard should be paid to the opposition of any person, be he whom he might, and whether of temporal or spiritual condition.

By that peace the great conflict between Protestants and Catholics was at length brought to a decision, though to one very different from that proposed by the Edict of Restitution.

How entirely vain had it moreover now become even to think of such enterprises as had formerly been ventured on, and had even succeeded! The results of the contests in Germany reacted immediately on the neighboring countries.

Although the Emperor had succeeded in maintaining the Catholic faith supreme in his hereditary dominions, he was nevertheless compelled to make concessions to the Protestants of Hungary; in the year 1645, he saw himself constrained to restore to them a not inconsiderable number of churches.*

Even in France the Huguenots received favor from Richelieu, after they had been deprived of their political independence, and still more effectually did he support the principle of Protestantism by continuing to wage against the predominant Catholic power, the Spanish monarchy—a war for life or death, by which it was shaken even to its foundations. That dissension was the only one which the Pope could have adjusted altogether without scruple. But while all other discords were effectually composed, this remained unappeased and continued to convulse the bosom of the Catholic world.

Until the Peace of Westphalia, the Dutch had continually taken the most successful part in the war against Spain. This was the golden age of their power, as well as of their wealth; but when laboring to attain preponderance in the Orient, they came at once into violent contact with the progress of the Catholic missions.

It was only in England that Catholicism, or at least something analogous to that faith in its outward forms, seemed at times on the point of finding admission. Ambassadors from the English Court were at this time to be found in Rome, and papal agents in England. The Queen, to whom a sort of official recognition was accorded in Rome, possessed an influence over her husband which seemed likely to extend even to religion; many of the Church ceremonies began to reflect the usages of Catholicism.

But from all these things there resulted the very reverse of what might have been expected. It can scarcely be supposed that Charles I ever dissented in his heart from the tenets of Protestantism, but even those slight approaches which he permitted himself to make to the Catholic ritual led to his ruin. It seemed as if the violent excitement which had produced such long-continued, unremitting, and universal conflicts in the Protestant world at large had become concentrated in the English Puritans. Vainly did Ireland struggle to escape from their domination and to organize itself in the spirit of Catholicism; the subjection of the country was but rendered the more complete by these efforts. In the aristocracy and commons of England a secular power was formed and matured, the rise of which marked a revival of Protestantism throughout Europe.

By these events, limits were imposed at once and forever to the extension of Catholicism, which has now its appointed and definite bounds: that universal conquest formerly projected can never more be seriously contemplated.

Indeed, the spiritual development itself has taken a turn which makes this impossible.

The impulses endangering the higher principle of unity have become preponderant; the religious element is repressed—political views and motives rule the world.

For it was not by themselves that the Protestants were delivered. It was by a schism in the bosom of Catholicism that they were enabled to recover themselves. In the year 1631 we find the two great Catholic powers in league with the Protestants—France confessedly so, Spain at least covertly. It is certain that the

Spaniards had at that period formed friendly relations with the French Huguenots.

But the Protestants were not more perfectly united among themselves than the Catholics. Not only did the Lutherans and the Reformed, or Calvinists, fight with each other—that they had always done—but the different sects of Calvinists, although they had a common cause to battle for, yet proceeded to attack each other during this war. The naval power of the French Huguenots was broken solely by the support which their ancient allies and brethren in the faith had been induced to afford the crown of France.

Even the supreme chief of Catholicism, the Pope of Rome, who had hitherto directed the attacks on the Protestants, finally placed the higher interest of the spiritual authority in abeyance, and took part against those who had labored most zealously for the restoration of the Catholic faith. He proceeded in accordance with the interests of a secular sovereignty only, and returned to that line of policy which had been abandoned from the time of Paul III. It will be remembered that nothing furthered the cause of Protestantism in the first half of the sixteenth century so much as the political aspirations of the popes. It was to these, so far as human judgment can decide, that Protestantism now owed its deliverance and confirmed strength.

And this example could not fail to produce an effect on the remaining powers. Even German Austria, which had so long preserved herself immovable in her orthodoxy, at length adopted a similar policy. The position of that country after the Peace of Westphalia was based on her intimate connection with North Germany, England, and Holland.

If we now attempt to investigate the deeper causes of this phenomenon, we would be wrong to seek them in the banalization or decay of religious impulses. We must, I think, look elsewhere for the first cause and the significance of the events.

If the first place, the great spiritual contest had completed its effect on the minds of men.

Christianity in earlier times had been rather a matter of tradition, of simple acceptance, of faith undisturbed by doubt; it was now become an affair of conviction—of conscious and deliberate adoption. It was of great significance that men had to choose between the different confessions—that they could reject, abjure, or pass from one to the other. The individual man became the subject of direct appeal; his freedom of judgment was called into action. Thence it followed that Christian ideas became more closely intertwined with and penetrated more deeply into every portion of life and thought.

To this must be added another aspect.

It is perfectly true that the prevalence of internal dissension disturbs the unity of the collective faith; but if we do not deceive ourselves, it is another law of life that this circumstance prepared the way for a yet higher and greater development.

In the pressure of the universal strife, religion was adopted by the nations after the different modifications of its dogmatic forms. The system thus chosen had blended with and been fused into the feeling of nationality—had become, as it were, a possession of the community of the State or of the people. It had been won by force of arms, was maintained amidst a thousand perils, and had become flesh and blood.

This has meant that the states on both sides have formed themselves into great ecclesiastico-political bodies, whose individuality was characterized on the Catholic part by the measure of their devotion to the Roman See, and their tolerance or exclusion of non-Catholics; but still more decidedly on the Protestant side, where the departure from the symbolical books by which one swears, the mingling of the Lutheran and Calvinistic confessions, and the nearer or more remote approximation to the episcopal constitution, presented the foundation of so many clear and manifest distinctions. The first question in regard to every country is, what form of religion is predominant there? Christianity appears under manifold aspects. However striking the contrasts, no one party can dispute with another its possession of that which forms the basis to the faith of all. These various forms are, on the contrary, guaranteed by compacts and treaties of peace, in which all have part, and which form what may be called the fun-

damental laws of a universal republic. The idea of exalting one or
the other confession to supremacy of dominion can never more be
entertained. All must now depend on how each state, each people,
may best develop its energies, proceeding from its own religious
and political principles. On this depends the future of the world.

BOOK VIII

THE POPES ABOUT THE MIDDLE
OF THE SEVENTEENTH CENTURY——LATER PERIODS[27]

**Transition To The Later Periods
Of The Papacy**

It must ever be considered a remarkable fact, and one that affords
us an insight into the general course of human affairs, that the
papacy, at the moment of failure in the accomplishment of its plans
for the recovery of supreme dominion over all nations, also began
to exhibit symptoms of internal decline.

During the period of progress to which our attention has been
directed, the restoration was fully established. At that time the
tenets of the Church had been strengthened, ecclesiastical privileges more powerfully centralized, alliances had been formed
with temporal monarchs, the ancient orders had been revived

---

[27] The following sections have been omitted: "Lapse of Urbino";
"Increase of Debt in the States of the Church"; "Foundations of New
Families"; "The War of Castro"; "Innocent X"; "Alexander VII and
Clement IX"; "Elements of the Roman Population"; "Architectural
Labors of the Popes"; "Digression Concerning Queen Christina of
Sweden"; "Administration of the Roman States and Church"; "The
Jesuits in the Middle of the Seventeenth Century"; "The Jansenists";
"Position of the Roman Court with Regard to the Two Parties"; "Re-
lation of the Papal See to the Temporal Power" (pages 3–115).

and new ones founded, the political energies of the Papal States had been consolidated and converted into an instrument of ecclesiastical activity, the spirit and the purpose of the Curia had been reformed, and all was directed to the one purpose of restoring the papal power and the Catholic faith.

This, as we have seen, was not a new creation. It was a reanimation brought about by the force of new ideas, which, removing certain abuses, carried forward by its own fresh impulses the existing elements of life.

But it is obvious that a renovation of this kind is more liable to decline than a perfectly new and unworn creation.

The first impediment encountered by the Catholic restoration was presented by France. The papal authority could not assert itself by its new policy; it had to countenance the rise of a church, which, though Catholic, was not subjected to the rule that Rome was seeking to enforce, and was further compelled to accept a compromise with that church.

This then led to internal dissensions—controversies respecting the most essential points of doctrine and touching the relation of the spiritual to the temporal authority.

There was nevertheless one grand and general aim toward which the Papal See continued to press forward with extraordinary fortune. In favor of this supreme object, all conflicts were reconciled; disputes concerning single points of doctrine and questions of conflicting spiritual and temporal claims were silenced, the discords of sovereign powers were composed, the progress of common enterprises was sustained; the Curia was the guide and center of the whole Catholic world, and the work of conversion proceeded in the most imposing manner.

But we have seen how it happened that the end was yet not attained, but that, on the contrary, the aspiring papacy was thrown back upon itself by internal discords and by opposition from without.

Thenceforward all the relations of the State, as well as its social development, assumed a different aspect.

To the spirit of conquest and acquisition that would devote

itself to the attainment of a great object, there must be associated an earnest devotedness; it is incompatible with the narrowness of self-interest. But the desire for enjoyment—the love of gain—had invaded the Curia; that body had resolved itself into a company of pensioners, feeling entitled to the revenues of the State, and to all that could be extracted from the administration of the Church. This right they abused in a most ruinous manner, yet clung to it at the same time with a zeal and tenacity that could not have been exceeded had the whole existence of the faith been bound up with it.

But it was precisely on this account that an implacable opposition to the Curia arose, at one and the same time, from many different quarters.

A doctrine had been propounded, which, proceeding from new perceptions of the more profound truths of religion, was condemned and persecuted by the Roman Court, but was not to be suppressed by the utmost exertion of its power. The several States assumed a position of independence and freed themselves from all subservience to the papal policy; in their domestic affairs they claimed a right of self-government, by which the influence of the Curia was more and more closely restricted, even as regarded ecclesiastical matters.

It is on these two important points that the history of the papacy henceforth depends.

Periods then follow in which, far from evincing any spontaneous activity, the papacy was rather occupied with the sole thought of how it should best defend itself from the various antagonists that, now assailing it on the one side, and now on the other, employed its every moment and all its cares.

Our attention is usually attracted by activity, and events can only be understood from the side which moves them. It is not the purpose of this book to describe the more recent epochs of the papacy. The spectacle they present is nevertheless highly remarkable, and since we commenced with a review of the ages preceding those that form our immediate subject, so we cannot well close without making an attempt to sketch the later periods before the eyes of the reader.

Our consideration is first engaged by the attack from the side of the States. This is most immediately connected with the division of the Catholic world into two adverse parties, an Austrian and a French, which the Pope could neither overpower nor pacify. The political position of Rome even determined the degree of spiritual devotion accorded to her.

Louis XIV And Innocent XI

Louis XIV was without doubt much attached to the Catholic faith, yet he found it insufferable that the Roman See should pursue a policy not only independent of, but also frequently in direct opposition to, his own.*

He confiscated ecclesiastical property by acts of arbitrary power, was continually oppressing one or other of the monastic orders, and arrogated to himself the right of loading church benefices with military pensions.* He further inflicted the most severe injury on the holders of Roman pensions by subjecting all funds remitted to the Curia to a closely restrictive supervision.

This he continued to do under the pontificate of Innocent XI, who pursued on the whole a line of policy similar to that of his predecessor, but from that pontiff Louis encountered resistance.

Innocent XI, of the house of Odescalchi, of Como, had entered Rome in his twenty-fifth year, furnished only with his sword and pistols, for the purpose of employing himself in some secular office, or perhaps of devoting himself to the military service of Naples. On the advice of a cardinal, who looked more deeply into his character than he had himself been able to do, he was induced to change this purpose for the career of the Curia. He conducted himself with so earnest zeal, and gradually obtained so high a reputation for ability and righteousness, that the people shouted his name beneath the porticos of St. Peter during the sitting of the conclave, and the feeling of satisfaction was very general when he proceeded from that assembly adorned with the tiara on September 21, 1676.

The manners of this pontiff were remarkable for humility;

even when calling for his servants, he would do so under the condition that they were at leisure to attend on him, and his confessor declared that he had never discovered in him anything that
could estrange his soul from God. He was most gentle and sensitive in disposition, but that same conscientiousness by which
his private life was governed now impelled him to the fulfillment
of his official duties without any regard to mere expedience.*

And with firmness of resolution, the Pope now opposed the
attacks of Louis XIV.*

It has always been a maxim of the French court that the papal
power is to be restricted by means of the French clergy, and that
the clergy, on the other hand, are to be kept in due limits by means
of the papal power. But never did a prince hold his clergy in more
absolute command than Louis XIV. A spirit of submission without parallel is evinced in the addresses presented to him by that
body on solemn occasions. "We hardly dare venture," says one
of them, "to make requests, from the apprehension lest we
should set bounds to your Majesty's ecclesiastical zeal. The
melancholy privilege of stating our grievances is now changed
into a sweet necessity to express the praises of our benefactor."
The Prince of Condé declared that if it pleased the King to go
over to the Protestant church, the clergy would be the first to
follow him.

And certainly the clergy of France supported their King
without scruple against the Pope. The declarations they published were from year to year increasingly decisive in favor of the
royal authority. At length the convocation of 1682 was assembled.
"It was summoned and dissolved," remarks a Venetian ambassador, "at the convenience of the King's Ministers, and was guided
by their suggestions."*

But the Pope also still had a weapon. The members of this
assembly were promoted and preferred by the King before all other
candidates for episcopal offices, but Innocent refused to grant
them spiritual institution. They might enjoy the revenues of those
sees, but ordination they did not receive, nor could they venture to
exercise one spiritual act of the episcopate.

These complications were still further perplexed by the fact that Louis XIV at that moment resolved on that relentless extirpation of the Huguenots, but too well known, and to which he proceeded chiefly for the purpose of proving his own perfect orthodoxy.*

New points of contention continually arose. Matters finally reached a state where the French ambassador in Rome was excommunicated, the papal nuncio in France was detained by force, thirty-five French bishops were deprived of canonical institution; a territory of the Holy See was occupied by the King. It was in fact already an open schism, yet Pope Innocent refused to yield a single step.

If we ask to what he trusted for support on this occasion, we perceive that it was not to the effect of the ecclesiastical censures in France, nor to the influence of his apostolic dignity, but rather, and above all, to that universal resistance which had been aroused in Europe against those enterprises of Louis XIV that were menacing the existence of its liberties. To this general opposition the Pope now also attached himself.*

Even admitting that Innocent XI was not acquainted with the entire purpose in contemplation, it is yet undeniable that he allied himself with an opposition arising from Protestant impulses, and sustained for the most part by Protestant resources.*

The consequences of this war turned out nevertheless, as regarded France, to be exceedingly favorable for the papal principle. If the Pope had promoted the interests of Protestantism by his policy, the Protestants on their side, by maintaining the balance of Europe against the "exorbitant power," also contributed to compel the latter into compliance with the spiritual claims of the papacy.

It is true that Innocent XI did not live to see this result. The deportment of the King was altered; he restored Avignon and entered into negotiations.*

The negotiations continued for two years. Innocent XII, who had meanwhile succeeded Innocent XI's successor Alexander VIII, more than once rejected the formulas proposed to him by the clergy of France, and they were, in fact, compelled at length to declare that all measures discussed and resolved on in the Assembly of 1682 should be considered as not having been discussed or resolved on: "casting ourselves at the feet of your Holiness, we profess our unspeakable grief for what has been done." It was not until they had made this unreserved recantation that Innocent accorded them canonical institution.

Under these conditions only was peace restored. Louis XIV wrote to the Pope that he retracted his edict relating to the four articles. Thus we perceive that the Roman See once more maintained its prerogatives, even though opposed by the most powerful of monarchs.*

The Spanish Succession

The fact that the Spanish line of the house of Austria became extinct was also an event of the utmost importance to the papacy.

To the condition of rivalry constantly maintained between France and the Spanish monarchy, and by which the character of the European policy was chiefly determined, the papacy also was finally indebted for the security of its freedom and independence of action for a century and a half; the principles adopted by the Spaniards had preserved the Ecclesiastical States in peace. Whatever the outcome, there was always danger to be apprehended when an order of things to which all the usages of political existence were habitually referred should be reduced to a state of uncertainty.

But the peril became much more urgent from the fact that disputes arose with regard to the succession, which threatened to burst forth in a general war; a war, moreover, of which Italy must be the principal battleground. Even the Pope could hardly avoid the necessity of declaring for one of the parties, although he could not hope to contribute anything essential toward the success of that which he would espouse.*

At that time the Roman See was on good terms with Louis XIV. Therefore Clement XI brought himself to believe in the luck and the power of the great king. He did not doubt that Louis XIV would ultimately obtain the victory. The success of the French arms in the expedition undertaken against Vienna in the year 1703, which seemed likely to bring everything to a conclusion, occasioned the Pope so much satisfaction that the Venetian ambassador assures us he found it impossible to conceal his joy.

But at that very moment fortune took a sudden turn. The German and English antagonists of Louis, with whom Innocent XI had been allied but from whose party Clement XI had gradually estranged his interests, achieved unprecedented victories. We do not here propose to discuss all the bitter contentions in which Clement XI became involved.* Clement had previously congratulated Philip V; he now saw himself compelled to acknowledge his rival Charles III as Catholic King.

This event inflicted a severe blow, not only on the authority of the papacy as supreme arbiter, but also on the political freedom and independence of the Holy See; the latter was, indeed, virtually despoiled of all liberty and self-determination. The French ambassador left Rome, declaring that it was no longer the seat of the Church.*

By the Peace of Utrecht, countries which the pontiff regarded as his fiefs, such as Sicily and Sardinia, were consigned to new sovereigns without his advice or consent being even requested. In place of that infallible decision hitherto awaited from the supreme spiritual pastor, there now ruled the convenience and interests of the great powers.*

One of the most prominent objects of the Roman policy had ever been the exercise of influence over the remaining States of Italy. The Curia sought, indeed, to exercise an indirect sovereignty over them all whenever it was possible to do so.

But now, not only had German Austria established herself in Italy while in a state of almost open warfare with the Pope, but even the Duke of Savoy had attained to royal power and a large extension of territory in defiance of the papal opposition, and thus matters continued.*

The word by which the great contest was decided at the most critical moment had come from England. In open contradiction to the Papal See the Bourbons forced their way into Italy.* The secular authority of the Apostolic See was by this means annihilated even in its most immediate vicinity.

An important effect could not fail to be produced by these changes on the controversies touching the ecclesiastical rights of Rome, which were so closely connected with her political relations.

How severely had Clement XI already been made to feel this!

More than once was his nuncio sent out of Naples, and in Sicily, on one occasion, the whole of the clergy whose views were favorable to Rome were seized in a body and sent into the States of the Church. Throughout the Italian sovereignties an intention was made manifest to confine the gift of ecclesiastical dignities exclusively to natives of the several States.*

These dissensions became more and more serious, the differences extending from year to year. The Roman Court no longer possessed within itself that power and energy required for the preservation of union even among those holding its own creed.*

Anybody with eyes to see could have noticed in Rome that everything was at stake, that her existence depended on the immediate conclusion of peace.

The memory of Benedict XIV—Prospero Lambertini (from 1740–1758)—has been held in honor because he resolved on making the necessary concessions.*

There is no doubt that the most remarkable act of his pontificate was the concordat that he concluded with Spain in the year 1753.* In like manner Benedict XIV concluded with most of the other courts arrangements involving concessions.*

By these measures the Catholic courts were again reconciled to their ecclesiastical chief, and peace was once more restored.

But could one pretend that all contentions were thus brought to an end? Was it to be expected that the conflict between the State and the Church, which seems to be almost a matter of necessity in Catholicism, should be set at rest by such easy transactions? It was not possible that these should suffice to maintain peace beyond the moment for which they had been adopted. Already there were signs in the depths of other and far more perilous storms.

Changes In The General Position
Of The World, Internal Commotions, Suppression
Of The Jesuits

Important changes had been accomplished, not only in Italy and the south of Europe, but in the political condition of the world generally.

Where were now the times in which the papacy might entertain the hope, and not indeed without apparent grounds, of once more subjecting Europe and the world to its dominion?

Of the five great powers by which, even so early as the middle of the eighteenth century, the course of the world's destinies was determined, three had risen to influence who were not of the Catholic faith. We have alluded to the attempts made by the popes in earlier times to subdue Russia and Prussia by means of Poland, and to overcome England by the forces of France and Spain. These very powers were now taking prominent part in ruling the world; nay, we may even affirm, without fear of deceiving ourselves, that they had at that time obtained the preponderance over the Catholic portion of Europe.

It was not that one system of doctrine had vanquished the other—that the Protestant theology had prevailed over Catholicism; this was no longer the field of conflict. The change had been brought about by the action of national interests and developments, the principles which we noticed above. The non-Catholic states displayed a general superiority over the Catholic. The monarchical and concentrating spirit of the Russians had overpowered the disunited factions and aristocracy of Poland. The industry, practical sense, and nautical skill of the English had obtained the supremacy over the careless indolence of the Spaniards and the vacillating policy of the French, which was ever contingent on the accidents of their domestic affairs. The energetic organization and military discipline of Prussia had in like manner procured her the advantage over those principles of federative monarchy which were then predominant in Austria.

But although the superiority obtained by these powers was in nowise of an ecclesiastical character, yet it could not fail to exercise an immediate influence on ecclesiastical affairs.*

But more extensive causes were in action. As early as the second half of the seventeenth century, when England had attached herself to the policy of France, when Russia was in a position equivalent to separation from the rest of Europe, and the Prussian monarchy of the house of Brandenburg was but just rising to importance, the Catholic powers, France, Spain, Austria, and Poland, had governed the European world, even though divided among themselves. It appears to me that the consciousness of how greatly all this was changed must now have forced itself on the general conviction of the Catholic community. The proud self-confidence inspired by a politico-religious existence, unrestricted by any superior power, must now have been destroyed. The Pope was now first made aware of the fact that he no longer stood at the head of the powers by whom the world was ruled.

But finally, would not the question of whence this change arose present itself? When the conquered party does not utterly despair of his own fortunes, every defeat, every loss will necessarily occasion some internal revolution, some attempt at imitation of the antagonist who has evinced his superiority—an emulation of his efforts. Thus, the strictly monarchical, military, and commercial tendencies of the non-Catholic nations now pressed themselves upon the Catholic states; but since it could not be denied that the disadvantageous position into which the latter had fallen was connected with their ecclesiastical constitution, the first efforts of the movement were directed toward that point.†

It is a forever remarkable phenomenon what influence the religious impulses of Louis XIV exercised on not only the French but the European spirit in general. In his eager determination to root out the Protestant creed and to annihilate every dissenting opinion intruding within the pale of Catholicism, he had employed the utmost excesses of violence, had outraged the laws of God and man, directing his every effort to the production of complete and orthodox Catholic unity throughout his kingdom. Yet scarcely had he closed his eyes before all was utterly changed. The spirit so forcibly repressed broke forth in irresistible commotions. The disgust and horror awakened by the proceedings of Louis XIV led, without doubt, directly to the formation of opinions making open war on Catholicism, nay, on all other positive religion of whatever name. From year to year these opinions gained internal force and wider diffusion. The kingdoms of southern Europe were founded on the most intimate union of Church and State. Yet here was a manner of thinking by which aversion to the Church and religion was organized into a system affecting all ideas relating to God and his creation, every principle of political and social life, and all science. A literature of opposition arose which involuntarily attracted and fettered all minds.†

The Revolution

It is manifest that the event which dominates modern times, the French Revolution, was immeasurably promoted by the antagonism of two hostile parties on every question touching religion—by the incapacity of the dominant party to maintain itself on the field of opinion and literature, and by that general aversion which, not without having in some measure deserved it, this party had brought upon itself. The spirit of opposition, whose origin must be sought in the discords prevailing within the pale of Catholicism itself, had continually increased in force and had become ever more firmly consolidated. Step by step it pressed forward, and during the stormy period of the year 1789 it attained the power which saw its mission in the destruction of the old and the construction of a new world. In the general overthrow decreed for the "most Christian" realm, its ecclesiastical constitution was necessarily subjected to the most violent convulsions.

All things concurred in the production of one and the same result—financial embarrassment, individual interests, as those of municipalities, with indifference or hatred to the existing religion; finally, the proposal made by a member of the superior clergy itself for the acknowledgment of a right in the nation, that is, in the secular power, but more particularly of the National Assembly, to dispose of ecclesiastical property. Thus far that property had been regarded not as the special possession of the French church alone, but as belonging to the Church universal, and as requiring the assent of the sovereign pontiff for its alienation. But how remote were the times and the ideas from which convictions of that character had originated! Now after a short debate, the Assembly arrogated to itself the right of legislation concerning all Church lands—the power, that is, of absolute alienation—and with an authority more unconditional than had been contemplated by the original proposal. Neither was it possible that these measures should stop at the point thus attained. Since by the sequestration of Church property, which was carried into effect without delay, the continued existence of the established order was rendered impossible, it became necessary at once to proceed to new arrangements; and this was effected in the civil constitution of the clergy. The principle of the revolutionary state was extended to ecclesiastical affairs. Priests were no longer to be installed as by the decisions of the concordat, but to be chosen by popular election, and a salary from the government was substituted for the independence conferred by the possession of real estate. The disposition of all the dioceses was changed, the religious orders were suppressed, vows were dissolved, all connection with Rome was interrupted; even the reception of a brief was now regarded as one of the most criminal offences.*

The Roman Court still flattered itself for a moment that these commotions would be arrested by an internal reaction, and the Pope neglected nothing that might tend to the promotion of that event. But all these efforts were now in vain; the revolutionary tendencies maintained their ground. The civil war which had been kindled principally by the fervor of religious impulse resulted in the advantage of the innovators and their new arrangements. And well would it have been for the Pope had the matter rested there— had France torn from him nothing more than herself.

But that general war by which the whole aspect of European affairs was to be so entirely changed had meanwhile burst forth in all its violence.

With that irresistible fury, compounded of enthusiasm, rapacity, and terror, which had been displayed in the internal conflict, the torrent of revolutionary forces rushed beyond the French confines and poured itself over the neighboring countries.

All that came within its influence was now similarly changed.* The campaign of 1796 secured the mastery of the new form of things in Italy. Revolutionary states arose in all directions; the Pope was already threatened by them, not only in his territories, but in his capital also.*

The Directory found the rule of priests in Italy incompatible with its own. At the first pretext, afforded by a mere accidental commotion among the populace, Rome was invaded and the Vatican occupied by the French. Pius VI entreated his enemies to let him die where he had lived; he was already eighty years old. They replied that he could die anywhere. His chambers were plundered before his eyes—they deprived him of even the trifles required for his personal comfort and drew the ring he wore from his finger. Finally, they took him to France, where he died in August 1799.

It might, in fact, have now seemed that the papal power had been brought to a final close. That spirit of enmity to the Church which we perceived to take birth and have marked rising into vigor had now attained the degree of strength that might well embolden it to aim at securing such a result.

Times Of Napoleon

But succeeding events effectually prevented the realization of any such purpose.

One of the most immediate consequences of that hostility experienced by the Papal See from the revolutionary governments was that the remaining powers of Europe, whatever might be their general dispositions toward the papacy, now took it into their protection. The death of Pius VI occurred precisely at a time when the Coalition had again achieved victory. It was thus rendered possible for the cardinals to assemble in the church of San Giorgio at Venice, and proceed to the election of a pope (Pius VII, chosen March 13, 1800).

It is true that the revolutionary power was soon afterward again triumphant and obtained a decided preponderance even in Italy. But at this moment that power itself had undergone a material change. After so many metamorphoses, effected amid the storms of that momentous period, it assumed a direction toward monarchy. A ruler appeared representing the purpose of a new universal empire, and who, beholding the general destruction and ruin prevailing and profiting by his experience obtained in the East, had arrived at the conclusion, which is the principal matter for our present consideration, that to secure his end he required the unity of religion and hierarchical subordination.

Even on the very battlefield of Marengo, Napoleon deputed the Bishop of Vercelli to enter into negotiations with the Pope in regard to the reestablishment of the Catholic Church.

This was a proposal in which there was doubtless much to allure and tempt, but it also involved much that was dangerous. It was manifest that the restoration of the Catholic Church in France, and its connection with the Pope, could be purchased only by extraordinary concessions. To these Pius VII resolved to submit.*

There now followed what a short time before could by no means have been expected—the restoration of Catholicism in France and the renewed subjection of that country to ecclesiastical authority.*

But could it be reasonably concluded that by the Concordat of 1801, a close and cordial alliance was indeed and at once effected between the ancient spiritual power and the new revolutionary state?

Concessions were made on both sides, but in spite of these each party adhered firmly to its own principle.*

The restorer of the Catholic Church in France was the prime mover in the immediately following complete and final ruin of the stately edifice of the German church. The transfer of its possessions and sovereign powers to secular princes, indifferent whether Catholic or Protestant, was effected by his means.*

And meanwhile a concordat of similar spirit to that with France was also prepared for Italy. There, too, the pontiff was called on to sanction the sale of ecclesiastical property and resign the nomination to benefices to the temporal power; nay, there were so many new restrictive clauses, all for the advantage of one side, annexed to this agreement that Pius VII refused to publish it in the form proposed.*

The Constituent Assembly had labored to detach itself from the Pope; the Directory had desired to annihilate him. Bonaparte's idea was to preserve his existence, but at the same time to subjugate him completely to his purposes—to make him the mere instrument of his own unlimited power.*

What no previous Catholic prince had even ventured seriously to contemplate, the autocrat of the Revolution had now actually accomplished. The Pope agreed to be subject to the French Empire. His authority would for all time have become an instrument in the hands of the new dynasty. By this it would have been enabled to secure the obedience of its own territories, and to confirm in relations of dependence those Catholic states which it had not yet subdued. The papacy would, to this extent, have returned to the position which it held with regard to the German emperors, when those monarchs were in the plenitude of their power—more especially under Henry III—but it would have been subjected to much heavier bonds. In the power by which the Pope was now over-mastered, there was something that directly contradicted the essential principle of the Church. It was in effect no other than a metamorphosis of that spirit of opposition to ecclesiastical influences which had made itself manifest in the eighteenth century, and which involved so determined a disposition to positive infidelity. To this malignantly hostile power, the papacy would have been subjected and placed in a state of vassalage.

Yet on this occasion, as on others, affairs were not destined to proceed to such an extremity.

The Restoration

The empire, of which it was intended that the Pope should constitute the hierarchical center, was still engaged in doubtful warfare with unconquerable enemies.* When Prussia rose—immediately after the proclamation to arms of the King had appeared—Pius VII summoned courage to revoke the Concordat of Fontainebleau, concluded but months before. When the conference of Prague was assembled, he ventured to cast his eyes beyond the boundaries of the empire that held him captive, and to remind the Emperor of Austria of his rights. After the battle of Leipzig, he had regained confidence to such an extent that he rejected the proposals then made for the restoration of a part of his territories. And when the Allies had crossed the Rhine, he declared that he would negotiate no further until he should be completely reinstated in his dominions. Events then followed with the utmost rapidity. When the Allies took possession of Paris, the Pope had already reached the frontiers of the Ecclesiastical States, and on May 24, 1814, he made his entry into Rome. The world then commenced a new age, and a new era was also commenced for the Roman See.

The years since then have derived their character and tenor principally from the conflict between those revolutionary tendencies, still maintaining so powerful a hold on the minds of men, and the ideas to which the older states returned with redoubled earnestness after their victory. In this conflict, it is manifest that the supreme head of the Catholic Church could not fail to assume an important position.†

And now that the Pope had once more acquired a free and independent position among the sovereigns of Europe, he could devote his undisturbed attention to the renewal of spiritual obedience.† But the question really at issue was respecting the necessity of restoring to the clergy their practical influence on the state, the communes, families, public life, and public education. Not a word was now said of those liberties which the Gallican Church had either possessed or expressly attributed to itself. By the new concordat then projected, it would have been submitted to a degree of dependence on Rome more absolute than had been known at any former period.

But it was not in the nature of things that proceedings so decided should at once achieve the victory over that spirit of the

Romance nations, which had been developed amid views and tendencies so entirely opposite. The old antipathies to the hierarchy burst forth in France with loud cries of war against the new concordat. The legislative power of that country was constituted in such a manner as to render the execution of the plans formed in 1815 altogether impossible. A reaction no less violent was excited in Spain by the regressive government of Ferdinand: a revolution broke out, which, while immediately directed against the absolute power assumed by the King, who could offer it no resistance, evinced at the same time a decided tendency to oppose the claims of the clergy.* Commotions of a similar character instantly arose in Italy. They extended into the States of the Church, which were filled with analogous elements of discord; and at one time, the Carbonari had even fixed the day for a general insurrection throughout the ecclesiastical dominions.

But the restored sovereigns once more received support and assistance from the great powers by whom the late victories had been obtained—the revolutions were suppressed. It is true that on this occasion the non-Catholic states took no immediate part in the repression of the commotions, but it was not opposed by any, and by some it was approved.

And Catholicism had meanwhile received a new organization, even in the non-Catholic countries. The opinion that positive religion, of whatever confession or form, was the best support and guarantee of civil obedience universally prevailed. In all countries measures were carefully taken for the rearrangement of dioceses, the foundations of bishoprics and archbishoprics, and the establishment of Catholic seminaries and schools.*

There seems to be evidence that the conflict respecting creeds was altogether set at rest in the higher regions, while it was perceived to be continually losing its violence in civil life and gradually ceasing to exist. A recognition was now accorded by Protestant literature to ancient Catholic institutions, which would have been found utterly impossible in earlier times.

Wherever the more rigidly Catholic principle, however, which attaches itself to and is represented by Rome, came into conflict with the Protestant temporal authorities, it tended to prevail.

In one of these contentions it achieved a decided victory—in

England namely, in the year 1829.* And a still more brilliant and unexpected triumph was immediately thereafter achieved in Belgium.*[28]

The Roman Court did not, as far as we know, take an active part in either event, however advantageous the outcome was for its authority. In a third undertaking, in the disputes with Prussia, it participated directly.* In the violent storms which shook France at this time, Catholicism gained a decisive advantage.*

All these great successes promising even greater ones to follow thus redounded to the benefit of reviving Catholicism in all parts of the world. In view of the fact that they are related to the tendency to emancipate oneself from the established authorities, one cannot but expect that these would also emerge at the immediate base of the pontificate, in the Papal States. We now approach those events which are nearly more a part of politics than of history. If we are to understand the position of the papacy in the modern world, it is nevertheless unavoidable to bring them to mind at least in rough outline.

Church And Papal State Under Pius IX (1846–1878)

When the governments of southern Europe were restored, that of Rome was far from reverting to its former state. The leading statesman, Cardinal Consalvi, considered the French occupation a happy event enabling him to give the administration of the Papal State unity and uniformity without regard to the traditional privileges of the communes, the nobility, and the provinces; it has been said of him that he planted liberalism in the soil of superstition. Only in one point did he adhere to the ancient tradition of the Papal See: he entrusted the administration of the uniformly ordered state to the Ecclesiastical Corporation which had been excluded from it for some time.

Under the two following administrations, it seemed prefer-

---

[28] At this point our text departs from the Fowler translation which contains three more pages forming the previous conclusion which was omitted in the final edition prepared by Ranke.

able to revert to the system which preceded the revolutionary epoch, but the attempt which was made in this direction was ineffective, merely serving to arouse still further the antipathy of the populace toward the continuing rule of the clergy. As soon as the European order was shaken in 1830, tumult also arose in the Papal State. Gregory XVI, who had just then succeeded to the tiara, was happy that it did not turn against him, but only against the system which had been introduced. He was determined to preserve that system. After the tumult had been suppressed, the great European powers, as a consequence, expressed the desire that a greater part in the administration of the temporal affairs of the Papal State be entrusted to the laity. Some steps were thereafter taken in this direction, but with such restraint that it was more in the nature of a refusal than a concession. The demands became ever more general, more pressing, more embracing, but the repression was only all the more brutal. At the time of Gregory's death, there were close to 2000 exiles or political prisoners.

In the course of this conflict, the most diverse opinions were voiced by the cardinals. One of them, an active servant of the state, said he was well aware that a secularization of the administration was necessary; but could one expect it from the spiritual overlord? Yet another, a man in orders, to whom the people, hoping for relief, destined the tiara, told the masses: he would provide them with a livelihood, but simultaneously he would erect tribunals for their chastisement. A third point of view prevailed in the conclave. Pius IX was elected Pope. He was convinced of the divine right of the Pope over the state, but was yet of the opinion that he could accede to all just demands without compromising this right.

He opened the prisons and then proceeded to introduce some variations of the existing system, which were welcomed with universal joy even though they were not thoroughgoing; for it is not the deeds of themselves, but the tendencies they manifest which draw the applause of men. Gradually, he removed the men representing the Gregorian reaction. He nominated to the commissions which were to introduce the intended improvements members who were not ecclesiastics and who had the general reputation of particular insight and ability. Finally, a *consulta*, which he himself called a consultative representation, was established to support his government in legislation and administration. Under the direction of a secretary of state, this was in due course composed primarily of laymen. By these means, Pius IX intended to execute the advice of the powers.

But, already, times and opinions had changed. The Pope was driven much further by the incipient movement of the year 1848. He, too, was willing to listen to the cry for constitutional forms. The former liberties, as he put it, having once been abolished could not be restored; yet on account of them he was willing to establish a constitution composed of two chambers or, as they were called, councils. The first of these was appointed directly, the other, however, was based on a census and the election of the people. But this was not a constitution like others, and could hardly be so, for the authority which the Pope conceded was limited. Furthermore, every law which had passed both councils was first to be inspected and approved in secret session by the cardinals before the prince gave his sanction. The supreme authority remained in the hands of the clergy.

But the demands of the laity, as had often been manifested, tended to give temporal affairs exclusively into lay hands. Could one expect that they would accept restrictions which were not in accordance with the principle of the adopted system once a strong representation in parliament had been conceded to them?

This was an unavoidable conflict which immediately became interwoven with an even more comprehensive and possibly more urgent question.

Thus far the innovations were related to the February Revolution in Paris. The fact that in Vienna the government against which the national spirit had for four decades fought in vain was overthrown was even more directly influential on Italy and Italian conditions (1848). In Rome, this event was celebrated by the ringing of bells and the triumphal cry of "Italy." In response to the proclamation of Carlo Alberto of Piedmont, announcing his impending advance into Lombardy to drive the aliens from Italian soil, a company of volunteers was readied in Rome to assist in this undertaking. The Pope himself appeared to share these feelings. This, at least, was the interpretation given to his proclamation in which he called down the wrath of God upon those "who will not recognize the voice of God in the storm which demolished cedars and oaks," and exhorted the peoples of Italy to unity.

But this can hardly, in fact, have been his intention.

When the volunteers moved out, he refused to appear on the balcony to send them off. Those whom he himself called up, he instructed to do no more than defend his house. He had but shortly before seen out a dispute with Austria concerning the preservation of his rights in Ferrara; now his ambitions did not appear to go beyond the preservation of the integrity of the Papal State. When his constitutional ministers requested permission to have the regularly organized troops, which by then also had advanced to the borders, cross the River Po, he relented but on the condition that he would withdraw with them whenever he felt it opportune. He did not condone the suggestion but neither did he resist it emphatically.

Thereupon the papal general felt himself empowered by his instructions to take part openly in the war against Austria. He proclaimed universally that the servant of God, the great and just Pope, was favorably disposed. He had blessed the swords of the soldiers going to join with Carlo Alberto for the war against the enemies of God and of Italy. Just as men had identified, in a fairly confused manner, the Austrian domination of Italy with the empire of the Hohenstaufen, so now they thought they saw in Pius IX a new Alexander III, who would decide to place himself at the head of a Republican movement. The ministers of the Pope were themselves thus inclined. They called upon him to follow the movement of the time, to undertake the war with courage. Then he would dominate the present and secure the future.

The Pope felt himself most unfortunately implicated. Any republican sympathies were totally alien to him. He called upon the Italians to be obedient to their benevolent princes; he saw the unity of Italy in an alliance between the princes and with Austria as an Italian power; and his pontifical status was much more important to him than any consideration of Italy. In answer to his ministers' urgings, he spoke to a consistory of the cardinals (April 29) in which he asserted that he did not intend to wage war against Austria and that he embraced all nations in equal love in accordance with the duty of his supreme Apostolate.

But he thereby not only separated himself from the Italian communal spirit; he also came into redoubled conflict with the parliament which now was united in the surge of national spirit.

The most distinguished of the ministers of that time, Mamiani, was trying to implement the idea of removing the state entirely from the influence of the cardinals and concentrating the temporal power in the hands of the parliament and of responsible ministers, whom the Pope would then have to follow like any other constitutional prince. But how was this to be achieved in view of the stipulations of the Statute and the hierarchical consciousness of Pius IX? Pius IX could hardly ever come to an agreement with these ministers which could be officially made public.

Finally a man was found who undertook constitutional government of the state in accordance with the tenor of the Statute and the inclinations of the Pope. Pellegrino Rossi was one of the statesmen of the epoch who saw in constitutional forms the sole means of protecting the modern state at once against the reaction of absolutism and against the destructive tendencies of the republicans. He was honest in his opinions, in full command of the culture of the century, energetic, and fearless. He declared that the Statute was the cornerstone on which the edifice of liberty had to be erected. In negotiations concerning the alliance of the constitutional states of Italy, which was the primary concern of the moment, he rejected the all-embracing designs of the Piedmontese and maintained the preeminence of the papacy as "the only living greatness which Italy possesses." He intended to reestablish the shaken public order on this basis, but by now nobody was interested in a federation of the old style, in an alliance of the spiritual power with the constitutional system. The fact that Rossi appeared capable of implementing such an alliance, the stern manner and the success with which he exercised public authority, brought all passions to play against him. The system which had just been brought down by the February Revolution in France was not to come to the fore in Rome. As Rossi was mounting the steps of the *cancellaria* to open the new session of parliament (November 15, 1848), he was stabbed and died on the spot. In the Assembly not a murmur of sympathy for him was heard.

The Pope himself was implicated in the disaster of the minister. At the first resistance which he offered to the demands of the excited masses concerning the formation of a new ministry and the Italian question, he saw himself besieged in his palace. Bullets penetrated his antechamber. One of the prelates of his court was shot to death. In this tumult he conceded what was demanded of him without, however, pacifying the masses. When it was suggested to the deputies that they reaffirm their allegiance to the insulted Holy Father, the suggestion was, after some debate, refused. Thereupon, the Pope decided to save himself from further coercion by means of flight, and with the help of the foreign ambassadors who were present on November 24, he succeeded in escaping to Gaeta in Neapolitan territory where more than one pope before him had already found refuge. There a court of *émigrés* and diplomats soon gathered around him, showing him to be the head of the Catholic world. In Rome, on the other hand, constitutional government could not be continued after the flight of the Pope.

The junta, which had been elected by the deputies to take over the government, was itself aware that it had no legal basis and only accepted its office until such a time as a constitutional assembly had duly considered the political order. Because there was no princely authority within the land, the concept of national sovereignty was adopted. After a few days a National Assembly was called "so as to give the state a regular, firm, and comprehensive constitution in accordance with the wishes of the nation or its majority." It was to be chosen by universal suffrage and direct election. In spite of the ecclesiastical censures which the Pope imposed for participation in these elections, they still took place and even, as was proudly proclaimed, with a rare degree of order. On February 5, 1849, the first session of the National Assembly took place. One of the proposals was to leave the decision concerning the future constitution to a constitutional assembly of all Italy. But the Roman assembly had too high an opinion of its own rights and would not be sidetracked. On its sole authority, it decreed that the papacy had forfeited the government of the Roman state, both in law and in fact, and that this state was now to revive the glorious name of the Roman Republic, reestablishing a relationship with the rest of Italy in accordance with their common nationality. How abruptly the conflicts inherent in the ideas confronted one another! Seceding from the Pope, who derived his possession of the state from an explicit decree of God in favor of the freedom of the Church, the Assembly established the thesis that sovereignty was an eternal right of the people; the republican idea arose on the ruins of the spiritual rule. Even so there was no wish to exclude the Pope entirely from Rome. Already men had framed that formula, so often repeated since then, that he would receive all the necessary guarantees for the exercise of his spiritual powers.

Pius IX was not yet reduced to accepting the former subjects of the Church as its protectors; he still felt sufficient power and support around him to take up the fight anew. Just as he had abandoned the Italian idea to avoid conflict with his position at the head of the universal Church, so in this misfortune, which he had met with in consequence, he called on the Catholic powers for help. At that very moment, Austria was preparing for a new test of arms with Carlo Alberto, which was destined to end badly for the latter. So as not to allow Austria to become omnipotent in Italy, France took to arms against the Roman Republic which was allied with the King. The Austrians captured Bologna and Ancona; the French troops turned on Rome. On the very day that the Roman Republic proclaimed from the Capitol its new constitution, characterized by the principle of the sovereignty of the people, the French advanced over the Ponte Sisto "to return the capital of the Catholic world to the sovereignty of the head of the Church, in accordance with the fervent wish of all Catholics."

The republic was thus dissolved; the exercise of the civic function was transferred to a commission of cardinals appointed by the Pope. In the spring of 1850, Pius IX returned to Rome and then revived the institutions of his previous years—council of state, *consulta*, municipal and provincial colleges—in such a man-

ner that the laity was always assured of a not insignificant portion
of the administration; but the sum of all public power in every
branch, in internal and external affairs, jurisprudence, education,
and supervision of the press was again conferred upon the high
clergy which was restored to its privileges. This was a victory of
the clergy over the laity, of the monarchical tendencies over the
republican, above all of the sympathies of the zealous Catholics
with their Head over the national Italian impulses.

And immediately after this interruption, the ecclesiastical authority achieved new growth; the conflict itself brought unexpected success.

Let us record that as in earlier times, the Spanish government
took the initiative in bringing about an understanding between
the Catholics and contributed energetically to all decisions. In the
year 1851, there followed a concordat which completed the understanding, which had already been in preparation for a number of
years, between the papacy and the Spanish state. On the Iberian
peninsula, ecclesiastical property had also been put up for sale,
property which, as was remarked in a former allocution, the
Church had managed to retain under the rule of the infidel. These
sales had been restricted by preliminary agreements which had,
however, repeatedly been subject to question; the concordat contains the final arrangement in this matter. Approximately two-
thirds of this property remained to the Church; the Roman See
agreed to the loss of the rest. On the other hand, it could register
the great triumph that the Catholic religion once more was raised to
exclusive dominance in Spain and its colonies, and that education
was once again subjected to exclusively ecclesiastic supervision.

Let us mention in passing that in the former colonies, the
now-independent states of South America with which treaties were
concluded, the Catholic religion was recognized as the religion of
state, even where it was not the exclusive religion. The bishops
were entrusted with the supervision of the press and of education
insofar as these pertained to religion, and free communications
with the pope were guaranteed.

One might have expected a renewal of imperialistic intentions on the part of the revived imperial might in France, in

memory of the founder of the same. Some words fell in this sense, but no one chose to hear them; at first, matters tended in a different direction. The French clergy grasped the strong hand by which their newly won position was protected against the convulsive movement which a continuation of the republican constitution threatened to bring about. They held the Prince, who was yet a President, in high esteem because he had contributed importantly to the reestablishment of the Pope in Rome by his influence and by his weapons. The ecclesiastical Catholic attitude, which the new ruler showed on his travels, aroused universal satisfaction. He spoke, so they said, like a Constantine; in this spirit he was received by the clergy. The ecclesiastical party thought it had prepared the act of December 2 itself; it helped to legalize it by the unanimous vote of its adherents. The bishops attached themselves to the new empire, which considered their popular esteem and influence one of its supports and was therefore in turn indebted to the ecclesiastical interest. Cardinals sat in the senate of the empire; ecclesiastical needs down to those of the parish churches were taken into account in the budget. Nominations to the episcopal sees were never made without consultation with the Roman Court.

In Austria, the third great Catholic empire of Europe, the century witnessed a similar, even more conspicuous advance in favor of the papacy.

The very March Revolution in Vienna, which had overthrown the old much-feared power, gradually appeared to the high clergy at home as a liberation because the dispositions of emperor Joseph II still held sway, which imposed the strict tutelage of the state on the ecclesiastics, with respect to their internal discipline, their influence on education, their dotation, and their connections with Rome. In Austria it was also asked what the promised freedom was worth if the Church did not equally receive its freedom. The Austrian bishops appeared at the Diet of Kremsier with comprehensive demands. They themselves requested a concordat in order to put an end to unilateral legislation of the temporal power. But they found no hearing from the delegates to whom the ecclesiastical power appeared rather too strong than too weak. The Diet

which feared for the religious peace and the freedom of the individual rejected the petition [March 1, 1819] and retained the principles of the laws of Joseph II. What the Diet refused, the government which closed it a few days thereafter tendered willingly. In
the course of the negotiations in Gaeta the termination of the laws
which were so repulsive to the papacy was also discussed. The
return of the Pope to his state and the closer connection with the
Austrian episcopacy went hand in hand. It was believed that the
source of the popular storms which suddenly struck the empire,
so long apparently exceptionally protected against them, lay in a
lack of religious conviction which stemmed from those restraints
on the ecclesiastical influence. The empire thought it saw support
for its own authority in the unrestricted cooperation of the local
ecclesiastical authorities with the universal. The concordat which
was agreed upon some time thereafter [1855] was based on these
views. The state returned to the clergy the prerogatives which
were theirs "according to the divine order and the Catholic laws"
—unrestricted communication with Rome and, above all, comprehensive direction of education and religious instruction. Nobody
could fail to observe what opposition this must cause in the land,
but that was the very conflict toward which the internal political
antagonisms and the predominant opinion were driving. This
move apparently also offered a grandiose prospect for the position
of the Austrian empire in both Italy and Germany. The Roman
Curia and the Austrian episcopacy allied themselves most closely;
they united in the desire and the hope to execute perfectly the
rulings of the Council of Trent after a lapse of three centuries.

What was happening in Austria was of a different character
from the events in France and Spain. Here the advancement of
Catholic ideas was more popular and in keeping with the wishes
of the legislative assemblies. In France, even the opposition, insofar as one can speak of an opposition, adopted this approach. In
general all this reinforced itself: from the renewed understandings
with the three powers, the hierarchy attained firm support by
virtue of its increased self-assurance.

The idea of ecclesiastical unity based on the primacy of the
Roman bishop has, in consequence, hardly ever been expressed

more emphatically than by Pius IX: "Through him the apostle speaks on whom the Church was founded; he is the living authority which gives an infallible decision in all disputes; the unity of priests emanates from the See of St. Peter; around him all the faithful must gather."

How much the bishops were inclined to accede to these claims became evident in 1856 when a new dogma was promulgated. The doctrine concerning the Immaculate Conception of the Virgin Mary, and of her freedom from original sin, had arisen in times of hierarchical omnipotence, but even then had been rejected by the most renowned teachers whom the Church followed. Mighty popes of later times had approved of it but had held back. Pius IX undertook to give it the stamp of church dogma by virtue of his own authority. From all parts of the inhabited earth, the bishops came together. Nevertheless, they did not form a council; what the Pope proclaimed as revealed truth they recognized faithfully as such. Never had papal infallibility appeared in more absolute a form although it had not yet been dogmatically determined. The doctrine of the Immaculate Conception is the keystone of the cult of Mary; this was close to the heart of Pius IX— for this purpose he introduced a new service and a new mass.

The papacy is indeed the most monarchical, the best coordinated organization in the present world; and every day it extends further around the earth. At the side of the South American churches, in which the religious ideas of Philip II continued, there arose a new hierarchical edifice in democratic North America. Within a few years two new archbishoprics and twenty bishoprics were founded there. The ecclesiastical foundations followed the advance of traffic and of settlements to California, to the Australian Islands. At the same time, on the African Coast and in East India the establishments of an earlier epoch were being maintained in their old subordination. In the Near East six new bishoprics of the Armenian Catholic rite were founded. In all the world up to the Arctic Pole, apostolic prefectures and vicariates in large numbers were erected.

But, insofar as the Pope also claims to be the father and teacher of all Christians, the head of the whole Church, and while

it is true that there was no scarcity of individual conversions—
for the idea of community and infallibility corresponds to the
religious need of the human heart and the faithful are strong in
propagandistic zeal—his efforts failed in respect to the divergent
forms of the other great religious communities.

"Hear what I say," he called, "all you in the Orient who glory
in the name of Christians but have no communion with the Roman
Church." By the salvation of their soul he implored them to conform; but from the answers which he received from the Oriental
patriarchs, one noticed that they remembered rather the ancient
animosities than the old communion. They reproached the Roman
Church both with the arbitrary determinations of its medieval
doctors and with the impetuosity of its present propaganda.

Turning toward the West, the Pope arranged to organize
Catholics in traditionally Protestant countries (such as Holland
and England) in separate church provinces. For England, Pius IX,
"in the hope of resurrecting the Catholic cause in the flourishing
empire," established an archbishopric and twelve bishoprics without consulting the government. All of these took their titles from
English localities—the archbishopric from Westminster. The new
archbishop, simultaneously Cardinal of the Roman Church, was
proud of the fact that from now on the acts of Catholic England
would regularly revolve around the center of ecclesiastical unity.

But England had fought for centuries to exclude the papal authority from the country; having finally succeeded, it was steadfastly maintained that the country had not been separated from
the universal Church in the ideal and was still truly Catholic. The
constitution of the country is based on part of the spiritual power
having been reserved to the Crown. What an impression the Pope's
innovation made under these circumstances! The highest authorities in the country as well as the low classes of the people, clergy
and laymen, Anglicans and dissenters, raised their voices critically
against it. They saw in it an attack on the country by the Pope,
such as had often been attempted in earlier times but had long
since apparently been abandoned. Was it true that the animosity or
at least disregard which this procedure evidences actually, as has
been said, stems from the fact that England remained neutral in

the reestablishment of the Pope in Rome? At first the innovation created a significant perplexity for the English government which could not tolerate this but had to take care not to infringe the principle of religious freedom inherent in the constitution which it was defending. This consideration led to the restriction of countermeasures to the arena of temporal affairs; merely the arrogated titles were forbidden, just as any Catholic state could not have tolerated such an infringement. But this did not serve to nullify its effect. In spite of all tolerance, it turned out that a conversion of the proportions expected in Rome was inconceivable. Protestant convictions appeared as those of the nation: it did not let itself be mislead by individual apostasies. Furthermore, was not English policy soon thereafter influenced by these events? Did it not reflect the disaffection which had been aroused in the masses and their leaders by the papal aggression?

The Propaganda attached the greatest hopes to the dissensions existing between the German Protestants. How often have they been told that their church was on the point of dissolution, was close to ruin. As if Protestantism had ever existed without the internal disputes which are part of its very essence, insofar as they are based on a living acceptance of the religious ideas. A deep feeling of community and an effort to make it manifest opposes itself to the divergent tendencies and, in turn, has its successes. The derogatory expressions of its adversaries have contributed to making Protestantism conscious of its historical justification. The spirited prince who then occupied the Prussian throne conceived of Protestantism as a particular form of Christianity, equal to all others. However one may judge momentary conditions and opinions, the value of Protestant-German science cannot be exaggerated. It is not only so well founded in itself that every attack is repelled; rising above all petty animosities, it exercises a daily growing influence on the learning of Catholics, who feel closer to its methods and its results than to the Roman rules. Theological inquiry, however, without the surveillance of the ecclesiastical authority, contradicts the concept which has been established once and for all concerning the role of the cathedra of the prince of the apostles.

Thus contrasts, spiritual and temporal, national and universal, scientific and civic, relate to one another and fill the spirits with incessant agitation with respect to the papacy which still forms a great center. One no longer meets with the great faith of former times which created and destroyed. There is no such force in either attack or defense; it is an incessant meeting, advance and retreat, attack and defense, action and reaction. No situation is the same as another. Diverse elements unite and separate again; every exaggeration is followed by its opposite; the most disparate elements influence one another. It is characteristic of this contest that it is conducted under the incessant influence of the past as it has entered living memory. All the disputes which have ever moved the world on this subject are once again championed in the arena—the dispute between the council and the ancient heretics, between the medieval power of the popes and of the emperors, the ideas of the Reformation and of the Inquisition, Jansenism and the Jesuits, religion and philosophy. All this occurs in the ebb and flow of receptive and outward-looking character of our time, which presses forward in violent disunion to unknown goals, self-assured but forever unsatisfied.

In spite of the changeability of the opinions, one may well say that the hope of reconciliation which might for a time have seemed justified is losing rather than gaining ground.

Other events most disadvantageous to the Roman Court opposed themselves to the extension of the ecclesiastical organization.

In the north, in the countries bordering on the Greek faith, the Catholic Church suffered an irreparable loss such as it had not experienced since the years of the Reformation. Under the leadership of their bishops, two million Greeks returned to the Greek church of their forefathers. In response to the fact that the insurrections of the Poles assumed a religious character as even the clergy took to arms, the Russians confronted them with the religious impulse which permeates their national feeling; the suppression of the insurrection was accompanied not only by the limitation but even by the persecution of Catholicism so that it finally came to an open break with Rome (1866).

More important than all this is the fundamental dispute, both spiritual and temporal in character, into which the papacy was directly enmeshed in Italy.

As Pius IX was restoring the rule of the clergy in temporal matters as far as he could, Piedmont, where constitutional forms of government had persisted, was undertaking to destroy, or to confine within the most restricted possible bounds, the traditional influence of the clergy. First higher education was withdrawn from the surveillance of the bishops. Shortly thereafter, a doctrine entirely contrary to papal aspirations came to prevail at the University of Turin, denying ecclesiastical authority all justifications other than that which it had received by virtue of concessions from the power of the states, and these were considered capable of being rescinded. In accordance with this doctrine in 1850, the legislative power in Piedmont declared that episcopal tribunals, ecclesiastical privileges, church asylum, and the acquisitions in mortmain were illegal. The highest ecclesiastical dignitary of the country sought in vain to arouse religious antipathies against this measure; he paid for his resistance by being exiled. The tribute of the golden chalice was no longer offered. In spite of the many proclamations of the Roman See, civil marriage was introduced in the year 1852. Some time later there followed the decisive step of abolishing monasteries and spiritual associations.

The conscious intent was to introduce an ecclesiastical state of affairs in the Sardinian and Piedmont possessions by way of legislation such as had resulted from the storms of the Revolution in France. Just as Austria was giving up the legislation of Joseph II, Piedmont copied it.

The Roman Curia once again applied its ecclesiastical censures against these measures. It banned each and every one who had participated, or might yet participate, in the attack on the ecclesiastical properties as a member of the chambers or as a civil servant. But this condemnation was too extreme to be effective, and meanwhile the situation of the world had changed.

The government of Sardinia and Piedmont gained added support by joining the alliance of the powers against Russia in the entanglements of the Crimean War. At the Congress of Paris, which took place in the spring of 1856, it did not need to justify its innovations at length. On the contrary, it could take the initiative of a complaint against the papal administration in the forum of the powers. It pointed out that none of the promises made at the time the Pope was reinstated had been properly executed. In consequence popular feeling had been so aroused that it would never be possible to remove the Austrian troops which were still stationed in the Legations. And yet no Italian balance of power would be possible as long as they were present in the Papal State and in central Italy. Their presence was entirely in conflict with the spirit of the treaties in 1815. Piedmont suggested conceding administrative independence to the Legations and secularizing their governments in accordance with the example of Napoleon I.

In the spring of 1857, Pius IX undertook a trip to central Italy. It was noticed that he was received with enthusiasm in foreign territories where he appeared only as Pope, while he met with conspicuous restraint in his own possessions where the public orations by which he was welcomed also contained bitter complaints. None deceived himself about the fact that another revolt was imminent here at the first opportunity.

As yet, the total condition of the Papal State was based on the understanding between Austria and France. But how severely this could be shaken, as soon as disputes arose between these powers concerning the very affairs of Piedmont and Italy which finally led to war in the year 1859! As soon as the Austrians left the Papal State to save Lombardy after their first losses, the insurrection broke out, first in Bologna, where a junta was established in place of the papal administration, and then, following this example, in the neighboring provinces. A National Assembly based on universal suffrage was convened. Its first decree, dated September 1, 1859, corresponded to the decision with which the constituent assembly had taken up its work in Rome ten years before. Invoking the rights of the people, the temporal power of the Roman Pope was declared to have expired. This time, however, it did not proceed to adopt republican forms; the provinces indicated their desire to be united with Piedmont, which appeared as the bearer of a great idea which held sway over all spirits, the idea of the unity of Italy. In former centuries, the popes themselves had seemed destined to realize it. In the nineteenth, under Pius IX himself, the Papal See had been tempted to raise the banner of unity. Now, the mighty idea turned against Rome. Because Modena, Parma, and Tuscany also tore themselves from their dynasties of Austrian and Bourbon origin in favor of Piedmont, which also received Lombardy from the French who had conquered it, the Italian idea attained form and future in this power. The French temporal authorities, acquiescing in this development, required the Pope to recognize the autonomy of the insurrectionist provinces, although merely in the form of a Piedmontese vicariate, and to introduce simultaneously in the other provinces the reforms which had already been decided upon. In return, the Catholic powers would secure him in these and support him for this purpose with money and troops.

Pius IX refused all these demands. For to accept the guarantee of a part of his territory would imply the renunciation of the insurrectionist provinces, and to that he would never consent. He even thought that he could help himself by taking to arms.

But what an undertaking, in the midst of a populace inclined to desert him, without allies, in the face of a determined foe who championed the national principle and had the moral support of the principal powers of Europe! Events took a rapid turn as soon as they were given the chance. At the first opportunity, the separatist provinces proclaimed their union with Piedmont by a virtually unanimous plebiscite, and were accepted; by April 1860, parliament could open with the participation of central Italy. Thereupon the Marches and Umbria also deserted. In some places the feeling of municipal independence was aroused in favor of submitting to Italian unity. The troops which the Pope had assembled to preserve the ecclesiastical ideas could do nothing to prevent this development. The local regiments refused to serve as soon as they encountered the Piedmontese. Men raised the tricolor wherever this was possible, and wished to be annexed. The capital city itself was only secured by the French occupation forces. which, after this turn of events, were faced with another great danger. The King of Sardinia took the title of King of Italy, and his prime minister expressed the opinion that the new kingdom could only be considered founded when it had Rome as its capital. Thereafter, the consideration of this demand formed one of the most important elements of the politics of France and Italy, and not without being influenced by the changes wrought in European conditions in general; for by now Italy already represented a power which had to be considered in all political calculations. Unsatisfied with what was happening in the North, the French Emperor in 1864 thought it advisable to put his understanding with Italy on a firmer footing. His own suggestion, to make Florence the capital city of the Italian kingdom, implied a recognition of Italian unity. But this proposal did not settle the most important question, it merely postponed it. In the Treaty of September 1864, the French Emperor promised to remove his troops from Rome within two years, by which time the Pope could gather new and sufficient forces around him to maintain internal order. The Italians, in turn, undertook neither to attack the church-state in its present form, nor to allow it to be attacked. The policy of the French Emperor was based on the attempt to maintain a good relationship with Italy without thereby breaking with the Pope. The former was made necessary by his European position, and the latter by the influence of papal authority on the internal conditions of France. Louis Napoleon thought that a reconciliation between Rome and the new Italian kingdom was still possible, based on moderation of the principles to which the Pope had thus far adhered. This would have had the most salutary consequences for all of the Catholic world. The Pope would recognize the liberal ideas which were the foundations of most states, and would offer the faithful some proof of the ability of the Catholic religion to recognize and support the progress of mankind. Actually, this was asking too much of the Pope at a time when the ideas which he was supposed to sanction were endangering his very existence. How could he accept the sovereignty of the people which declared him deposed, or the unity of Italy which threatened to rob him of his temporal possessions?

In answer to all the suggestions in respect to the Papal States, the Pope continued to propound the idea of ecclesiastical unity and his pontifical duty: "For the rights of the Roman See cannot be abdicated like the rights of a temporal dynasty; they belong to all Catholics; their surrender would infringe upon the oath by which he was bound, and simultaneously give encouragement to principles which were bound to become dangerous to all princes." So he once wrote to the French Emperor. He did not hesitate to impose full excommunication on all the rebels and usurpers of the separated provinces of the Papal State in the fulsome words of the traditional formula, and with particular reference to the decrees of the Council of Trent. In the Breve which he issued for this purpose, he explained that in view of the diverse interests of the princes, it had been one of the wisest institutions of providence to grant to the Roman Pope temporal power such as conveyed political freedom; for the Catholic Church should not have to fear that the administration of its general affairs would be dependent on alien and temporal influence. In accordance with this purpose, the rule of the Roman Papal State must of necessity have an ecclesiastic character, its concern for the physical well being of its subjects notwithstanding.

From time to time, festivities took place in Rome which once more manifested the mystique of the ancient papacy, embracing heaven and earth. At Whitsun, 1862, a number of monks were canonized who had died for their missionary zeal three and a half centuries earlier in Japan, expressly because it was felt that in times of stress "the church needs new advocates before God." In the great assembly of bishops which convened for this purpose (240 were counted) more immediate concerns were also discussed. The bishops expressed joyous satisfaction that they could once again come freely to their free Pope and King, as well as the conviction that the Pope should be neither subject nor guest of another prince. His domicile had to be in his own domain, his own kingdom. As Pius had said that he would rather lose his life than to relent in this matter which was the affair of God, of justice, and of the Church, so they now expressed their willingness to share imprisonment and death with him for this purpose.

It became known that some bishops took exception to this, but the overwhelming majority agreed in refusing any negotiations concerning the Papal State; the Catholic episcopate supported the ecclesiastical policy of the Holy Father.

Among the lower clergy, however, other opinions were voiced. Renowned ecclesiastical authors of orthodox reputation came out against the temporal rule of the papacy, and the literature of the day was in general against it. But the agreement of September 1864 was yet far from restoring to the Pope the security on which the reputation of his predecessors had for many centuries been based. It had been concluded without his participating in the negotiations. After having consulted with the cardinals in this matter, he hesitated to make any statement concerning it. Privately he was preoccupied with designs by which he hoped once more to gain recognition for the traditional ecclesiastical principles. His advisors, and the Jesuit fathers in particular, reinforced him in this attitude. It was decided to counter the opinions of the time which were inimical to Church and doctrine with a comprehensive and authentic declaration. This was accomplished in an encyclical issued on December 8, 1864, which was accompanied by a list of the errors which had already been condemned earlier by the Pope himself. This part was directed primarily to the innovations of Piedmont. But the proclamation proceeds beyond these to the most comprehensive principles, directed against the omnipotence of the state in general. It speaks of those who claim that the state should be governed without regard to religion, and in consequence consider that the Catholic Church is worthy of protection only insofar as its infringement would disturb the public peace. Some would subject the acts of the head of the Church to promulgation by the temporal power and concede no effect to them without this. Some would abolish the spiritual associations and the Church holidays because the new economics so required. Some would remove the education of youth from the surveillance of the clergy, as if they were a hindrance to the progress of science and civilization, while thereby in reality preparing the way for pernicious opinions. To counter these opinions the bishops were encouraged to inculcate the teachings of the earliest Popes, namely that the empires are based on the foundation of the Catholic faith.

There had even been those who maintained that it was not within the rights of the Church to punish those who disregarded its rulings. The binding force of the decree of the Council of Trent concerning the Papal State was denied because it confused the spiritual and temporal order of affairs. The divine right of an independent ecclesiastical authority was denied in general. In condemning these opinions, Pius IX simultaneously preserved the tradition of his predecessors who had vindicated the Church's beneficial authority over nations and princes, and defended his own political position. In his typically theological didactic fashion, he then proceeded to search for the causes of the general aberration and found them in the exaltation of reason over revelation and in the opinion that the supreme law lies in the expressed will of the people. Some consider freedom of conscience and of religion the natural right of every person, and unrestricted freedom of the press the demand of a well-ordered state; some declare that Protestantism is a form of church in which one could live in a God-fearing manner. Pius, however, did not admit that there was any hope for the eternal salvation of those who were outside the Catholic Church. While maintaining the privilege of the See of St. Peter over general councils, he condemned even more forcibly the notion of bringing disputed questions to a decision by means of a national council. Once more he spoke out against the covenant societies, the truest product of the religious spirit of old England, as well as against civil marriage which is an exigency of modern legislation; and he defended celibacy.

One can well understand the sensation caused by this pronouncement. How often had the clergy expressed the wish that the Pope might accommodate himself to the liberal ideas! This expectation promoted the renewed sympathy which he found in France as it was expressed by the Emperor. But now the new encyclical proved this to have been a false hope! The Pope condemned, perhaps not in every exact detail but certainly in general, the system of modern convictions and doctrines which have become a part of the convictions of living mankind.

The papacy opposed itself to the approaching waves of politics and opinions in its established self-consciousness; whether

it would give way under their onslaught or offer resistance became one of the major questions of the century.

The Vatican Council

Pius IX himself was not about to undertake alone the fight for
which he now prepared. He intended to support his pronouncements by a universal authority which had, in former times, generally appeared in conflict with the papacy but which had already
once proved of greatest help. On December 6, 1864, in a session of
the Congregation of Rights, the Pope caused the current business
to be interrupted and had the civil servants who were present leave
the chamber so as to make a special announcement to the assembled cardinals. For some time, he told them, he had been considering an idea which pertained to the welfare of all the Church,
namely the calling of a universal council to care for the exceptional
needs of the Christian people by exceptional means. He requested
the cardinals to let him have their advisory vote in this matter.
After this announcement, the civil servants were recalled and the
current business resumed. This request was made not only to the
cardinals who were present at the Congregation but to all members of the College. In due course 21 opinions were received, the
overwhelming majority of which supported the intention of the
Pope. Only two were against it.

The dominant conviction was that the conflict of prevalent
opinions with the doctrines of the Papal See, and the straits of the
Church in general, necessitated the application of this extreme
measure. The point of view prevailed that condemnation of the
principal errors by the Pope alone would not achieve the desired
results. Just as the doctrines of Luther had once been condemned
by the Popes, and this condemnation had only become effective
when the Council of Trent had adopted and confirmed it, so it
now appeared necessary to erect a similar bastion against the
erroneous doctrines which had arisen. Once more the cardinals
mentioned Jansenism; but this could hardly have been the object of their worries in view of its insignificance at that time. Their

principal attention was directed to the philosophical doctrines which had arisen in the past century and which, supported by the temporal authority, stood in full contradiction to the doctrine of the Church: for the latter was based on revealed truth, the former were the figments of the human mind, left to its own devices and become arrogant. While on the one hand Pius was extending his concept of divine right and divine intervention so far as to declare possession of the Papal State by the Pope sanctified and unassailable, on the other hand the intention to wrest this possession from the Pope had just been based on the contradictory doctrines. On all sides religious, and in particular Catholic, opinions were being attacked by their adversaries. All the teachers of the Church, as well as the episcopacy, were implicated in these tendencies.

Pius IX received the supportive opinions of the cardinals with satisfaction, and he established a commission to direct the necessary preparations for the convocation of the Council. This commission met for the first time in March 1865. In November the nuncios in Paris, Munich, Vienna, Madrid, and Brussels were informed of the intention to call the Council. They were requested to nominate learned men who might be brought to Rome to prepare the work of the Council. The Pope intended to have materials destined to be deliberated in the Council considered in the preparatory congregation even before the publication of the summons to the Council. At its meeting of May 1866 it turned out, however, that the congregation was still far from its goal. We then find a long interval of consultations during which the situation of the world was transformed by major events which also directly involved the Pope. The war between Austria and Prussia had been fought; the Battle of Königgrätz had decided the fate not only of Germany but also of Italy; Venetia had fallen into the hands of the King of Italy, who, moreover, declared that his program was not yet fulfilled. He repeated what his ministers had already said long before, namely that the unity of Italy necessarily required the incorporation of Rome.

If we inquire what was the basis of the continued existence of the Papal State, in spite of this avowed intent, we will see that it was the September Treaty alone, which the French still emphatically adhered to. In December 1866, they left the capital, but before a year had passed they found it necessary to return. For the Italian government could barely restrain the national movements for the conquest of Rome. It had not provoked the popular aggression of the followers of Garibaldi, but it appeared willing to turn this to its own ends and to cross the borders of the Papal State. To prevent this from happening, the Emperor of the French had Civitavecchia occupied. Garibaldi and his followers were repulsed by French arms, and once more the Pope was protected in his possession of the Papal State. In view of the consideration which the Emperor owed Italy and the vicissitudes that his policy was subject to, this was hardly a support on which reliance could be placed.

At this time it once more became apparent how important the possession of the State was for the Church. Pius IX had invited the bishops from all over the world to celebrate the eighteen-hundredth anniversary of the feast of the Apostles Peter and Paul. In the eyes of the Church this celebration had to take place in a territory which was subject to no other rule than that of the supreme pontiff or, as the bishops expressed it, that the legitimate authority of the Pope be maintained. The Pope, so they said, must retain the freedom of his power and the power of his freedom. He must keep the means for exercising his high office which everybody needed. Their very assembly was directed toward the support of his territorial authority which was under attack on all sides, and to proving that it was indispensable in ruling the Church. In view of the danger on all sides, and supported alone by the spirit of community among the bishops, the Pope considered that the time had come to announce the convocation of the universal council. One would not do him justice if one were to see the preservation of the temporal principality as its sole purpose. Although it is true that the dispute was essentially an Italian one between the unifying tendencies of the new kingdom and the independent existence of an ecclesiastical state, it derived a universal character from the circumstance that the Italian king expressed and accepted the modern ideas in all their consequence. The papacy, on the other hand, in-

tended to renew and to sanction in their totality the Church doctrines which were opposed to these ideas. Now that the bishops
had taken the side of the Pope-King in the particular question, one
could expect this support all the more in the general, which concerned them personally. There is something grandiose in the fact
that Pius IX, just when the temporal power and the pressure of
inimical and unecclesiastical opinions threatened to wrest the remains of his State from him, decided to have a general assembly
of the Church sanction anew those doctrines on which the papacy
in general and its temporal possessions in particular were always
based. Particularly, as these doctrines as they had now developed
were positively contrary to the state of the temporal power. The
intention was to counter them with a strong opposition from the
side of the Church, not only to the kingdom of Italy, or to European politics which had by then virtually deserted the cause of
the Papal State, but to the system of modern ideas which had
themselves transformed the states. The sovereignty of the people,
for which the most eminent spokesmen of the papacy had once
showed sympathy, now aroused the opposition of the Church
since the prince against whom it was being applied was vested
with the highest spiritual dignity. A general council having been
convened, its purpose was to protect in the name of the Church
the doctrines and interests of the papacy, and to condemn those
doctrines which were opposed to the papacy however prevalent
they may be. It was an act both of isolation and of antagonism.
The doctrine on which the modern state, more or less involved by
the revolution, was based, was to be questioned so that the state
might lose its doctrinal foundation, at least in the eyes of the faithful. Nobody was to speak of the impotence of the Roman See. Its
power is infinite insofar as it has the body of the Church, which
comprises hundreds of millions of living and thinking people, on
its side.

The deliberations of the preparatory congregation which resumed its sessions on July 28, 1867, are characteristic. They took
place at the very moment that the Italian Parliament once more
declared itself in favor of the principle of nonintervention, that is
of no support for the Pope by France. One of the first preliminary

questions was to what extent the princes were to be invited to participate in the Council in accordance with established practice. This had still been the practice at the Council of Trent; and it is known that that assembly of the Church owed its successful conclusion only to the agreement of a former Pius, the fourth of this name, with the most prominent among the temporal princes, above all with the German Emperor of the time and with the King of Spain. In the first session of the commission, the suggestion was again made that the princes should be invited to participate in the Council through their legates. It is, however, obvious what difficulties this might raise. For even the King of Italy, with whom the Pope was in direct and irreconcilable conflict, would have had to be invited. The commission did not reach any decision in this matter and left it to the Pope who saw himself compelled to reject the suggestion, and not only for the reason indicated. It was his general intention to have an exclusively ecclesiastical assembly. He did not in any way wish to further the notion that the state stood above the Church. When the final bull of convocation was drawn up, the favor of the princes for the assembly of the Council was requested, but no mention was made of their personal participation, either individually or through legates.

Yet another deviation from former usage arose in composing the bull of convocation. Paul III had caused his to be read in the Consistory of Cardinals. They had given their consent and their signatures. Pius IX seemed content to have the bull examined by the preparatory commission, composed of his most trusted cardinals. The cardinals were only asked as to the suitability of the planned time of convocation and gave their consent.

What then were to be the mutual relationships between the Pope and the Church dignitaries who were being assembled?

Nothing had aroused greater resentment at the reopening of the Council in Trent under Pius IV than the claim that the propositions should emanate from the papal legates. The bishops of Spain particularly had opposed this from the outset, in accordance with the stipulations of the Catholic king who exercised his influence on the Council through those very bishops who

were devoted to him. A similar reaction was now to be expected
if not of the same vehemence. This was to be avoided under all
circumstances.

By convening the Council himself, the Pope remained true to
his concept of primacy which excluded any independent consultation. In the preparatory discussions of the executive commission,
this point of view had been given particular emphasis. From the
concept of primacy which had been bestowed upon the Roman See
by divine institution it was deduced that only the Pope as the
visible head of the mystical body of the Church could have the
right of proposition. The successor of the Holy Apostle Peter was
entrusted with the pastoral care of the entire Christian flock. In
convening the bishops at his See in time of danger, particularly of
the proliferation of dangerous errors, it was up to him to inform
them of the purpose which he had in mind through the proposition
of the affairs to be discussed.

The bishops were not entirely denied any right of proposition, but they were to inform the Pope, or rather the congregation
which had been instituted for this purpose, in advance. The objection that by this procedure good suggestions might be disregarded
was countered with the observation that everyone should be
satisfied with having done his duty and should otherwise trust
Divine Providence.

Formerly there had also been congregations attached to the
Lateran councils for the purpose of studying the suggestions which
were submitted, but these had been formed by way of election
from the assembly itself. This time the Pope took the nomination
of its members in hand on account of his difficult duty of providing leadership for the deliberations of the Council.

We see how the Pope understood the idea of the Council. He
would allow no temporal influence on it, either of the princes
themselves or of their legates. He even reduced the influence of
the Roman Curia as constituted by the cardinals. For he was far
from soliciting an independent opinion, and in convening the
bishops he had no intention of conceding them any independence.
In his relationship with them he steadfastly maintained his concept of primacy, of the supreme pastoral office. He did not so much

request their advice as their consent. He intended to fix and to perfect alike the ecclesiastical authority of the popes in this consultative form.

The feast of Peter and Paul in the year 1868 was celebrated by setting the definite convocation of the universal council for another feast which Pius IX held in particular esteem, the feast of the Immaculate Conception, December 8, 1869. The final wording reflects quite clearly the spirit which had manifested itself in all previous deliberations. The idea of the papacy was therein linked with the most sublime mysteries of faith and advanced with absolute autonomy, isolated but well prepared and carefully considered in all directions.

Was Pius now to have full scope for its development, was he going to be allowed, while in danger of being destroyed in his temporal rule, to effect the most comprehensive claim in the realm of ecclesiastical affairs?

Upon publication of the decree it was immediately noticed that contrary to previous usage the temporal powers had been excluded. France considered forthwith whether it should not demand participation in the negotiations of the Council, but the advantage of the papacy after the Revolution was that this was hardly possible because the civil authorities had renounced their Catholic character in accordance with the constitution. They professed the principle of religious indifference. The revolutions had for the greater part originated in an antagonism against the intimate union of Church and State which they had then dissolved. There had been times when popes and emperors disputed over the right to convene a council, but then Church and State had in a sense been identical. The emperors had on occasion been more ecclesiastical than the popes. But now this temporal power had in a sense itself been secularized by its acts of secularization. This secularized power manifested itself in several great powers which confronted one another, most often in a hostile manner. What form might be devised to allow the state as such to be represented at the Council? Such a device was briefly sought, but this attempt was quickly given up. Nonetheless nobody had any intention of leaving the assembly of the Church to the influence and discretion of the Pope.

Opposition arose as well in the bosom of the clerical community. Those former councils which had established themselves at the side of the papacy, of independence, occasionally even in sharpest opposition, remained in particularly vivid memory. No one expected a similar opposition from the new conciliar assembly, but a deliberation of all open questions in the most independent manner of consultation was anticipated. In Germany men felt justified in expecting the establishment of a harmonious movement of the two powers under which man passes his life, of the State and of the Church. There was a need to determine the relationship of the clergy and of the faithful in general to universal culture and science and the extent of lay participation in the ecclesiastical institutions. Someone suggested that the general council revive the national, provincial, and diocesan synods which had proved their value over centuries. Even the majority of the high clergy shared this view. In France people demanded a more precise definition of the relationship of the Pope to the bishop, of the bishop to the priest, and improved composition of the College of Cardinals and of the Roman Congregations, which were to be composed of delegates of various nations.

How conflicting were the intentions of the Pope and a number of bishops as well as of the spiritually influenced laity: the Pope was intent on the justification and reinforcement of the highest authority in the traditional sense, while they looked to a transformation of the spiritual authority in a sense more consonant with the century. The Pope intended to reinforce and to centralize the authority of his predecessors, but a not insignificant number of bishops was more intent on decentralization. They wished to see a renewal of the characteristic ecclesiastical life of the various provinces and states. There was no question of differences in matters of faith. The Pope intended not only to exclude the popular principles which had attained general validity but even to combat them. Among the bishops many were inclined to an accommodation with the modern doctrine. They considered the Council a welcome opportunity to introduce their tendencies.

On December 8, 1869, the Council was opened in the basilica of St. Peter. The assembly comprised seven hundred and sixty-four members from all parts of the world, but more than a third of them were Italians. In the directory they appeared as a single great corporation ordered according to the ecclesiastical rank which they occupied and in every rank according to the time of their elevation.

This was an assembly which certainly merits the title of an ecumenic one. It reminds us of the council which had once (in 1215) assembled around Pope Innocent III from orient and occident; but it was infinitely more comprehensive than that, for the Far East and Africa as well as the new world beyond the ocean had delegated their prelates. Quite another difference, however, became evident in comparing the Rome of those times with the present. Under Innocent III the papacy had been in the process of developing its universal dominance. The temporal rulers had appeared in large numbers, zealously intent on being considered living members of the Catholic Church. Now they were missing altogether, or at least they had been excluded on purpose. The assembled bishops could testify how far the anti-ecclesiastical spirit had progressed in their dioceses. Even though many of them, as has been said, were of the opinion that the ecclesiastical principles could only be saved if one were, so to speak, to conclude a treaty with the spirit of the times, which without leading to an open breach, would yet not concede it dominance. In the course of the elections to the deputations of the Council which were immediately held it soon turned out how difficult they would find merely voicing their intentions. The Pope and his congregation were supported by a powerful majority of 550 votes, and they held so closely together that the candidates of the minority, which was the weaker by more than half, were virtually disregarded.

Nevertheless a strong and vital opposition made itself felt in the discussion of the first proposition, which intended a dogmatization of syllabus. The expressions were so energetic and made so great an impression that it did not seem advisable to proceed in this form. We have already mentioned the restrictions which the rules of procedure imposed on the assembly concerning propositions, but freedom of debate such as was now attempted also contradicted the Pope's conception of the prerogatives of his primacy. Pius IX thought it necessary to curtail it.

By means of an amendment to the rules of procedure it was decided that all objections against a proposition before the Council were to be put in writing and accompanied by a suggestion for improvement. The commissions were to inspect the comments and thereupon report back to the Council. A debate would take place only after this form of screening, and could be interrupted by the president. It might be closed by a majority vote upon petition of ten members.

Undeniably any thorough and effective discussion was made impossible by these means. The Council was told even more precisely what role it was destined to play. It appears more in the light of a synod on a grand scale than of an assembly in the style of the old councils. There was no scope for free debate and objection.

At this stage the major question concerning the infallibility of the Pope, which was already on everybody's mind, was earnestly raised. Originally this doctrine was conceived in its relationship to Gallican opinions. For how could the old questions concerning the superiority of the councils over the Pope and the relationship of the conciliar to the papal authority in general have failed to come to mind in connection with the convocation of the Council? Any legal opposition within the Catholic Church was essentially based on this conflict. The main difference between the Catholic and Protestant conception is the fact that the latter rejected not only papal but also conciliar authority. The Catholic Church, however, maintained both. But the conflict between them had never been resolved in the Catholic world. The prince who rendered perhaps the greatest services to the old Church in the last few centuries, Louis XIV, when at the height of his power once again supported the claims of the Council. Pius IX, however, would never have convened a council with such pretensions. He adhered to the superiority of the papal authority, which necessarily developed into infallibility once all contradiction had been removed. The aspirations of the old councils were alien to the Vatican Council which he convened—it was to end them forever. The infallibility of the Roman See was to be defined by a conciliar pronouncement, so that no opposition of the national churches against it need be feared. In the preliminary commissions, this point was raised without particular emphasis.

The authentic communications do not show that the Pope, as had been claimed, convened the Council for the express purpose of this declaration, but it cannot be doubted that he was considering it in view of his attitude in general. The claim to infallibility now created an even greater impression, however, because it was considered without immediate reference to those Gallican doctrines, solely in the light of the opinion that the Pope was incapable of erring with respect to morals and dogma.

For a moment the notion of achieving recognition of papal infallibility by acclamation had prevailed. The tenor of the assembly made this impossible. But the majority produced an address to the Council itself in which it called upon this body to declare that the papal authority was free from all error.

This address originated among the Italian and Spanish bishops whose ecclesiastical schools still adhered to medieval traditions. They were opposed above all by the German bishops whose training had an entirely different basis. They maintained on the one hand that the Council could not be considered a representation of the Church without the Pope, on the other hand that decisions in matters of the faith depended on the apostolic tradition and the consensus of the Church. They warned against establishing the infallibility of the Pope as a dogma in their dioceses, for this would serve as a pretext to allow the civil authorities to restrict the rights of the Church still further.

The French bishops also supported this argument. They repeated it practically word for word, omitting only a few lines in which the Germans had recognized an independent authority of the Roman See in the very earliest times before the first councils. They avoided anything which might be in direct conflict with the Gallican constitution. Independently of them, the Oriental bishops pointed out to the Pope the difficulties and dangers to which they would be exposed by accepting the suggested decree. In England, the Catholics had been required to reject precisely this doctrine when they had been emancipated. The Puseyites who were close to Catholicism sent a warning note that unification of the Anglicans to the Roman Church would forever be made impossible by such a ruling.

If the draft of the declaration of infallibility caused serious demonstrations within the bosom of the clergy itself, how much more must it arouse to contradiction those who were observing the conciliar events from the outside. The schema concerning the ecclesiastical authority which was to be put before the Council had quickly reached the public, whether by accident or design. It was well suited to arouse the conflict of the temporal governments with the claims of the hierarchy concerning the general affairs of the countries. During the second half of February, the French government, which had not yet renounced the Gallican traditions, took this occasion to protest against the hierarchical tendencies of the Council in general. Originally the projected schema had only spoken of the infallibility of the Church. It covered not only the doctrines of the faith, but also the means by which to maintain the possession of the same, not only revelation, but also everything which was considered necessary for its explanation and defense. The French minister of external affairs observed that this was a means of expressing the superiority of the spiritual authority over the temporal wherever they met. Thus the power of the Church would come to appear absolute, independent of the temporal power of respect to the legislature and the courts. The authority of the Church would therefore embrace the constitutive principles of society, the rights and duties of the governments and the governed alike, the right to vote, the families themselves. Should the infallibility of the Church, as had been suggested and intended, be conferred on the Pope, each and every authority would be dependent on him. How could one expect the princes to restrict their authority before the attributes of the Roman See which had been determined without their participation? The minister demanded interim information concerning the questions to be deliberated as well as the admission of a French plenipotentiary to the Council.

His intentions were most comprehensive. What he proposed would lead to an arrangement between the strictly ecclesiastical doctrines and the constitutional system which had arisen out of the movements of the century, an arrangement between the supreme authority of the Church and the necessities of the diverse countries.

In the French press, particularly in the periodicals which were close to the government, analogous but even more far-reaching theories could be observed. It was maintained that the Council was no longer free. A minority, which was in fact the majority if one considered the size of the dioceses, was being tyrannized by a majority which could only be considered a minority under this point of view and which was totally committed to the ultramontane leaders. And the very concept of a conciliar assembly would seem to imply the independence of its deliberations. The convocation by the Pope was necessary but it must choose for itself the subjects of discussion as well as the form of debate. All that the Council was supposed to do was to search for some means of mediating between ecclesiastical doctrines and the exigencies of public life and to bring both into agreement. It should reject and void the syllabus which the Pope had convened it to reinforce. There was even talk of appealing from an unfree council to a free and authentic one which would be conducted by the Holy Spirit, and that meanwhile the present one must be prorogated. Nevertheless the Council existed. No one had protested against its convocation. It moved down the predetermined track to the predetermined goal. All that the adherents of the Pope saw in the objections which were now raised was a threat based on the ideas of 1789 which had been the origin of all destruction and which now had vigorously to be opposed. Even assuming that ambassadors were received by the Council to bring to bear the ideas of one of the governments, it was not to be expected that they would make an impression on the majority of the assembly. The Council was not only a European but also an ecumenical one. How could one ask prelates convened from all parts of the earth to accept suggestions which conformed only to the momentary interests of a French or an Austrian ministry? The very intention was to give the ecclesiastical ideas themselves more scope. All of the objections that were raised and protestations that were made, all the complaints which were introduced, had quite the opposite effect.

In the first days of March 1870, the Pope decreed that a section concerning the infallibility of the Roman pontiffs be included in the schema on the Church. This schema explicitly ratified the primacy of the Roman Church once more, in the sense that the Pope was to be considered the true vicar of Christ, head of the entire Church, the father, teacher, and supreme judge of all Christians. The opinion that one might appeal from the Pope to a council possessing superiority over the Pope was expressly rejected. The following paragraphs justified the necessity of a distinct temporal principality for the Roman Pope with the argument that to exercise his divine office in full freedom he should not be the subject of any prince. This line of reasoning connected the most extensive ecclesiastical authority with the possession of temporal dominion which was essential to Pius IX. To reinforce this doctrine a special declaration of infallibility, which was implied in the concept of primacy as Pius IX understood it, would not have been necessary. Nevertheless the manifold divergent opinions which had been voiced in the bosom of the Council itself and which received emphatic support, as we have seen, from the governments outside, made such a declaration appear very desirable. The section which was now inserted stipulated that the Roman bishop, whose duty it was not only to maintain the truth of the faith but also to decide disputes concerning the same, could not err when determining what the entire Church should believe concerning matters of faith and morals. This section was thereafter to be considered an article of faith. At the same time the Roman government attempted to refute the objections of the French minister and to allay his fears by assuring him that the proposals contained nothing which might jeopardize the independence of the temporal powers. The ecclesiastical authority was merely asserting its ecclesiastical point of view which happened to pertain not only to the eternal but also to the temporal. No direct influence was being postulated. No state could exist without moral principles underlying its institutions. The nature of these principles alone was the concern of the Church. The purpose of the new proposition was given out to be merely an effort to remind the modern world of what was just, and thereby to promote peace and well being. The infallibility of the Pope was claimed to be as old as the Church itself. Far from restricting the bishops, this doctrine could contribute to adding support to their prestige; and not only to that of the bishops, but also to that of the governments. For the peace of the states was said to depend on the understanding of the two powers. In giving this interpretation the secretary of state was careful not to discuss the radical conflict between the doctrines of the Church and the principles on which the modern state is based. All he claimed was a form of moral supervision by the Church which a Catholic regent could not well deny.

This did not yet, however, satisfy the French minister who put his opinion in the form of a memorandum which the Pope was then requested to communicate to the Council. The Pope accepted the document. However, he refused emphatically to communicate it to the Council.

It now became a political and ecclesiastical question of major importance whether the French government would insist on its dissent. The other governments had also discussed the dangers which the theocratic decision of the Council implied. There was talk of an ambassadors' conference side by side with the Council to provide protection against the encroachments of the ecclesiastical authority, and some effect might well be expected from such a measure as long as an opposition still maintained itself with some vigor within the bosom of the Council itself. This opposition emphasized the necessity of free deliberation which was inseparable from the concept of a council. The adopted procedure in general, and the new rules in particular, were contrary to ecclesiastical liberty. The rule established in all councils from Nicaea to Trent had been that decisions concerning dogma did not depend on the majority but on a moral unanimity of the assembly. In the course of the debate concerning the preamble of the schema *de fide* which was first brought before the Council, the Bishop of Syrmia and Bosnia caused considerable offense by not only rejecting the attacks against Protestantism which were included therein but particularly by attacking the rules of procedure in their decisive point. He said the Council could not reach decisions and promulgate rules by numerical majority but only by moral unanimity as long as these were to be binding in the temporal world and eternity. The present procedure would cause the freedom and truth of this Council to be denied. These views created a tumult in the assembly which hindered the bishop in continuing his speech. The presidium undertook nothing against this interference. The following day the bishop complained about the treatment he had received and emphatically demanded a definite decision about the questions he had raised: otherwise he would not know whether he could remain at a council in which the freedom of the bishops was so utterly disregarded. This protest was supported by a significant number of other bishops so that a community of interests and ideas between some of the bishops and the opposing governments became apparent. This promised to have further ramifications. Now as in earlier times it was in the interests of the governments to indicate a certain independence from the Roman Curia for the bishops with whom they were in daily communication. The unconditional authority of the Pope was repulsive to both. In trying to assess this question from a historical perspective one should remember that a state of affairs such as had existed for three and a half centuries in Germany, and on which the entire development of the German nation is based, would have been impossible had the bishops been as entirely dependent on the papacy as was now projected, for the popes never did and never could accept the Religious Peace. However, the bishops of the Empire, the German hierarchy, had recognized the Peace even in conflict with the papacy. The Religious Peace has always been considered legal and the popes have never dared to proceed forcefully against it. Under the Peace the high clergy in Germany were assigned a position which was of incalculable historical importance and most salutary for the nation as a whole. Even though this relationship had been ended by the dissolution of the ecclesiastical Estate, no law subjected the spiritual authorities of the Empire to that of the Pope. It would have been in accordance with established custom if a new relationship had been established, taking into account the changed times and allowing the governments and the national bishops an autonomous union in urgent cases. To achieve success in this direction it would have been necessary for the governments to maintain a firm unity and for the bishops to assert their position with vigor. The French government possessed means of coercion: its troops had occupied Civitavecchia. It has been said that the Council could have convened only under their protection. By virtue of this relationship the political developments of the time were interwoven with the questions of the Council. In spring 1870, it seemed hardly likely that understanding and concerted action might be achieved between the legates of the most important powers, Prussia, Austria, and France. The popular and military action of the French nation, which considered the preponderance which Prussia had achieved over Austria in the last war unbearable, made everyone apprehend the beginning of a new European conflict in which even Austria might become embroiled. The position of the French government was not such that it could afford to alienate one or the other of conflicting parties in Italy.

We have been told that at this moment it was suggested within the French government that it might be possible to force the Pope to a more earnest consideration of French views by the withdrawal of troops from Civitavecchia: for one could not allow a deliberation to proceed which would lead to a condemnation of the civil and political constitution of France. Even from a broadly ecclesiastical viewpoint, one had to do everything to restrain the Church from a course which estranged it forever from the modern ideas. But the other considerations which we have just mentioned held sway in the Tuileries. Gallicanism had been a means to the political ends of Louis XIV; Napoleon III needed the devotion of a clergy obedient to the Pope, and of the Pope himself. Moreover the troops had not been sent to Civitavecchia to protect the Council but to protect the Papal State against Italian invasions. Nobody was about to advocate giving up the Papal State for the sake of a conciliar question. Since the other governments did not raise serious objections—they considered themselves strong enough to resist the execution of unacceptable decisions after the fact—Pius IX retained his freedom of action in this direction. His idea of excluding the temporal powers from any participation in the spiritual deliberations was in fact accepted by these themselves. The state of European affairs could not have been more advantageous for the Pope, and even the opposition within Catholicism was proving weaker from day to day.

After some concessions had been made, this test of the temper of the Council concluded and the Pope was advised to present the articles concerning infallibility. Originally these had been designed, as we have mentioned, to be inserted into the schema concerning the Church. The deliberations on this schema would have detained the Council longer than was desirable. It seemed preferable to present the question of infallibility separately. On May 10, Pius IX had a draft of a constitution distributed which, under a general heading, contained primarily the dogma concerning papal infallibility. It again condemned the doctrine concerning the superiority of the council over the pope and the appeal from papal authority to that of a council. It particularly emphasized that the decisions of the Roman See do not need confirmation by a temporal power to be valid. It set great store by the principles which had formerly been brought to bear on the disputes between the Latin and the Greek churches. How curious that this document of the second half of the nineteenth century repeats words which a patriarch of Constantinople had written more than thirteen centuries earlier to the Roman Pope in response to the latter's demand— words which contain the most solemn recognition possible of the preeminence of the Roman See and its infallibility.

The disputed interpretations of the decisions of the Second Council of Loudun and of the Council of Florence were here maintained as being beyond doubt. The tendency was rather to extend and complete the scope of papal infallibility than to retreat.

All these determinations formed a continuous chain of demands and aspirations which the Pope hoped to bring to universal recognition such as they had never before received.

The general debate began on May 14.

Once more objections were raised which were based on the temper of the various nations and the reaction which the decree would provoke. It was said that it would favor the radicals in Switzerland, that the Protestants in England themselves were hoping for this, that the Catholics of Ireland were not decidedly in its favor. Nobody could doubt that German scholarship was in conflict with it. The Americans pointed out that only the most free Church could hope to progress in the United States where it was generally thought that just as the king ruled for the sake of his subjects, so the Pope was appointed for the sake of the Church, to benefit it and not to dominate it. The Bishop of Syrmia observed that this decree would complicate the relationship of the 8,000,000 Catholic Croats with their compatriots of different creeds, and they themselves would be shaken in their faith. The Archbishop of Prague intimated that in Bohemia the decree would have the effect of making the populace first schismatic and finally Protestant. Darboy, Archbishop of Paris, made the most comprehensive claim. He explained that the declaration of infallibility would neither revive oriental Christianity nor promote the conversion of the heathens nor contribute to returning the Protestants to the fold of the Catholic Church. And more important still: it would have a detrimental effect within the Catholic states. Everywhere legislation and the administration of the state were of a decidedly temporal character. Even the family itself was implicated in the law of marriage. Now it was proposed to force a new dogma on those who were trying to shake off the burden of old doctrines; and at that through an assembly whose freedom was questioned by many. The world was not willing to have truth forced on it by command. The syllabus had become known all over Europe. What had its effect been even where it had been accepted as an infallible oracle? In two overwhelmingly Catholic empires, Spain and Austria, it had created a commotion detrimental to religion. The Archbishop intimated that the decree would cause the separation of Church and State in France, and that this example would be followed elsewhere in Europe. In view of the force of these objections and the impression they created, the self-awareness of the minority was revived. When the general debate was suddenly terminated, there was some talk among the minority of abstaining from any further active participation in the Council or at least of proceeding through formal protestations. But there was an internal fetter which made all serious opposition impossible: the respect for the Pope who had convened the assembly and the general ecclesiastical intention which was shared by all.

In the course of the detailed debate which began on June 6 and by June 15 had already reached the fourth and decisive chapter concerning infallibility, yet another doctrinal point of view became apparent. A negative voice was raised by the Dominican Order which had never been on very friendly terms with the Jesuits.

A cardinal belonging to this order, together with fifteen other Dominican bishops, maintained that the infallibility of the Pope did not stem from some form of personal inspiration, but that it only obtained when the Pope expressed the opinion of the bishops and of the universal Church. He suggested a canon according to which the pope would not promulgate definitions by his own free will but on the advice of the bishops who represent the tradition of the Church. He referred to St. Thomas, whom he interpreted in this sense. This was an objection which nobody had expected and which now aroused the particular indignation of the Pope: "I am the tradition of the Church," he was reported to have said. He accused the cardinal of supporting the liberal Catholics, the Revolution, and the Court at Florence. In the following congregation the cardinal was instructed that the bishops were secondary, for their authority derived from the Pope; only the assistance of the Holy Spirit was important. But this pronouncement did not yet resolve the dispute. The belief in the unerring judgment of the Church is essential to Catholicism. In this context special emphasis was traditionally placed on the pronouncements of the bishops and doctors, particularly when gathered in a council. Peculiar rights were attributed to them, derived from their own inherent authority. The most renowned authorities of modern times have derived the infallibility of the Church from the fact that the Savior continues to live in His Church, the Divine in the human. The question was through whom it expressed itself. Many reproached the Council with not being capable of determining the collective consciousness of the Church. In the eyes of the Pope this objection was immaterial. Even while insisting on the legal force of the decisions of the assembly of the Church which he had convened and on the value of episcopal consent, he still did not consider himself bound by these.

The revised schema which came to a vote on July 13 entirely denies any participation of episcopal authority in the infallibility. It emphasizes the following. It had often happened that the bishops either singly or together turned to the Papal See with difficult questions concerning the faith so as to seek a solution to the problems where faith was never lacking. On occasion the Apostolic See had considered it desirable to formulate a definition of that which it had recognized by the aid of God as being consonant with the revelations and the apostolic traditions through universal councils or even in particular synods. For the Roman popes had been assured of the assistance of the Holy Spirit so that they might preserve and explain the faith as it was transmitted by the apostles. The successors of St. Peter had been granted the grace of never failing faith so that the Church might be maintained in its unity without running the danger of schism. Previous drafts had said that the infallibility was to be made an article of faith. Now it was declared with even greater emphasis to be a dogma revealed by God that when the Roman Pope speaks *ex cathedra*, that is, when he defines doctrines concerning faith and morals for all of Christianity by virtue of his apostolic authority, he is endowed with the infallibility which Christ had promised His Church. For Pius IX it was immaterial whether the assembled bishops were capable of representing and expressing the consciousness of the Church. He did not need them because he claimed for the See of St. Peter the infallibility which was promised the Church. It had already been said that the Pope promulgates immutable definitions of faith through himself alone. So as to leave no room for doubt, the phrase "not on account of the consent of the Church" was appended to the words "through himself."

In this form the draft was brought to a final vote on July 18, 1870, when Pius IX appeared on his throne in full papal robes. The entrances to the chamber were thrown wide open. Although the draft opposed the preconditions of an independent episcopal authority, there was practically no dissent. It is true that a significant number of bishops absented themselves for one reason or another. The dogma was adopted virtually unanimously by those who were present—535 were counted: only 2 answered with *non placet*. Amidst general jubilation the result of the vote was announced. In breathless silence the Pope then pronounced his definitive decision, rising from his chair and confirming with apostolic authority the articles as they had been presented, to which the holy Council now gave its consent. This act occurred amidst the thunder and lightning of a storm which had gathered over the Vatican. Zealous supporters of the Pope did not hesitate to refer to the announcement of the Law of Moses on Mount Sinai.

The Council was not yet at an end. It was merely adjourned. But the decree which had been adopted and sanctioned in all formality is of itself of substantial importance.

The dispute concerning the relationship of episcopal authority to the supreme pastoral authority, of the conciliar to the papal authority—a question that had led to raucous disputes over a long series of centuries—was thereby resolved in favor of the absolute authority of the Roman See. The national impulses of the Church, represented by its bishops, which had once appeared about to triumph, were put to an end. What some people considered most important was the recognition of a living authority based on divine intervention in a world racked by disputes whose origin was the unwillingness to recognize any authority. It was a personification of the idea of the Church. This had always been the goal of Pius IX; now he had attained it. The now infallible Pope having pronounced against all the innovations of modern life, this dogma represented a reinforcement of his attitude sanctioned by the assembled body of the Church.

No bishop could dare contradict the dogma which had now been announced without endangering his existence and coming into conflict with the authority on which his own was for the most part based. In the course of time the declaration of infallibility was unquestionably destined to exercise the greatest influence on the Catholic states. Of course those reactions of which the Pope had been warned and which he had not deigned to consider must also be expected to occur in one form or another. But this was no longer the most important eventuality which was to be expected.

In the very days in which the Pope had his infallibility proclaimed and confirmed, war broke out between France and Prussia. I cannot definitely find that religious motives played a role in the French aggression. But who might say what would have been the results if the luck of arms had been with the Catholic nation?

What new predominance might thereby have accrued to the papacy even in the attitude which it now took?

The opposite was the result. A state prevailed which had risen in antagonism to the exclusive rule of the papacy, and which now also became the champion of the German cause. It attained a position which guaranteed an important part in the universal political and religious movements of the world. A convinced Protestant would say this was the divine decision against the pretensions of the Pope who claimed that he was the sole interpreter of the faith and of the divine mysteries on earth.

The eruption of hostilities was already disastrous for the existence of the Papal State, not only because France was forced to withdraw her troops but also because she had to concentrate on maintaining the neutrality of Italy. It has been said that to pacify this power one would have to draw the thorn which the protection of the temporal power of the Pope represents. The Italians saw in the Papal State, even as it then was, a focus of reaction which they would not tolerate, or even the danger of a republican revolution which they could not permit. The French empire having been overcome by Prussian arms, they were at liberty to do as they pleased. The defense of Rome against a great Italian army by the volunteers who stood by the side of the Pope was inconceivable. The Pope gave way with dignity. He did not sign any agreement, but he allowed the annexation to take place without real resistance. He himself ordered the white flag to be raised over the Castello Sant'Angelo when he saw that this was unavoidable. As they left, he gave his blessing to the troops who had assembled to defend him. He restricted himself to his spiritual authority, the unhindered exercise of which the Italians had guaranteed in face of all other powers.

To what extent this would be possible under the changed circumstances will be of fundamental importance for the present and for the future.

Index